4-16-70

MIND, SCIENCE, AND HISTORY

CONTEMPORARY PHILOSOPHIC THOUGHT

The International Philosophy Year Conferences At Brockport

MIND, SCIENCE, AND HISTORY

Edited by Howard E. Kiefer and Milton K. Munitz

STATE UNIVERSITY OF NEW YORK PRESS

ALBANY

PUBLISHED BY STATE UNIVERSITY OF NEW YORK PRESS
THURLOW TERRACE, ALBANY, NEW YORK 12201

© 1970 BY STATE UNIVERSITY OF NEW YORK,
ALBANY, NEW YORK. ALL RIGHTS RESERVED

LIBRARY OF CONGRESS CATALOG CARD NUMBER 69-14642
STANDARD BOOK NUMBER 87395-052-6
MANUFACTURED IN THE UNITED STATES OF AMERICA

DESIGNER: RHODA C. CURLEY

1571492

CONTENTS

PHILOSOPHY OF HISTORY

INTRODUCTION

The three groups of essays in this volume,—on The Philosophy of Mind, The Philosophy of Science, and The Philosophy of History,—illustrate one of the major interests and functions of Philosophy. This consists, in one direction, in examining the basic *concepts* at work in a particular area of experience or domain of inquiry with a view to clarifying their ramifications and involvements, how they are different from or similar to basic concepts in the same, adjacent, or wholly disparate areas. A related but distinct concern is to make explicit and assess the *methods* employed in achieving knowledge of some particular subject matter. These twin concerns—with concepts and methods—is sometimes described as an interest in the "logic" of various domains of human experience or discourse, what they share and wherein they are different. Such an interest does not consist in making or examining claims of a factual sort that would add to the existing store of information and knowledge. The philosopher's role is not to do the job, for example, of the psychologist, physicist, biologist, or historian. It is rather to reflect —at second remove from the subject matter itself—upon the conceptual resources, tools, and methods that might be brought to bear in reaching factual information and understanding about mind, for example, or about the past, or about the world of empirical phenomena in general.

The field of philosophical inquiry commonly designated as "The Philosophy of Mind" (or, alternatively, "Philosophical Psychology") has been intensively cultivated in recent decades. In part, this is due to the special attention this receives in the writings of Wittgenstein and Ryle, and the fertile suggestions those writings contain for dealing with what have been a number of perennial issues. In part, this is due to the ferment in the science of psychology itself and the numerous occasions that science provides for examining its foundations in the light of the strong rivalries among its different "schools". In part, this is due to the need to be clear about the connections between our views about mind and consciousness, and other areas of philosophic concern. For example, how does our view of the "body–mind problem" stand with respect to the free–will problem? Or, again, how does our analysis of the powers of the human mind relate to our views in epistemology, for example the roles of perception, memory, and language, in the expression of belief and knowledge? Or, finally, what shall we say of the status of the person as seen in the context of biological phenomena, or against the background of the historical and cultural dimensions of human experience?

What goes by the name of "Philosophy of Mind", accordingly, covers a number of different types of inquires, and some of these are illustrated in the essays that follow. While some issues are broad and generic, others are more narrowly focused and restricted in scope. Thus some general issues center around the question of how to characterize "mind", "personality", "consciousness". It is to this theme that the essays by Brand Blanshard and William P. Alston belong. Blanshard, in challenging various species of behaviorist views, argues for the irreducible uniqueness of consciousness. Richard Taylor, in his response to Blanshard examines the role of causal and teleological types of explanation as these function in the domain of human behavior. Alston, departing from the usual preoccupation of philosophers of mind with various cognitive functions and powers, explores the nature of personality. He offers a suggestive classificatory scheme for dealing with the kinds of concepts typically employed by the psychologist as it bears on this topic. Gilbert Ryle's essay illustrates another kind of concern to be found in the philosophy of mind: the need to be clear about individual powers, faculties, and capacities of the mind. His subtle and illuminating discussion addresses itself to the difficult question as to what it is that *thinking* consists in. Stuart Hampshire's response to Ryle's essay raises some interesting questions about "pondering" as one of the chief forms that thinking takes. In the concluding group of essays in this section, those by Kenneth Stern, and John Catan's reply, still another dimension of the philosophy of mind is illustrated: in this case the problem of "other minds"—how or whether we can ever know what's going on in another person's mind. This problem is examined with special reference to the notion of belief.

The papers on The Philosophy of Science fall into two broad groups: those dealing with fundamental issues in the *logic* of science and those dealing with *epistemological* questions. The papers by Ernest

Nagel and Mario Bunge (including Peter Caws' response to Bunge) belong to the first group; the papers by Richard Schlegel (including Nagel's response to Schlegel) and by Bentley Glass belong to the second. Nagel's paper on "The Logic of Reductive Explanations" raises the general question of what it means to say that the statements of one science can be "reduced" to those of another. To what extent can one claim that certain explanations are more fundamental than others? For example in what sense are those of electromagnetic theory more fundamental as compared to those of physical optics, or, those of physics generally, to those in biology? After sketching his own views on this subject, Nagel critically examines those of others, with especial reference to those of Paul Feyerabend. Bunge directs his attention to another central topic in the logic of science: what is involved in submitting a scientific theory to the test of experience. His disentangling of the various subtle ramifications and ways in which this is accomplished is intended to overcome a too–simplistic account that, in his judgment, often dominates much of the writing in contemporary philosophy of science. Peter Caws raises some doubts about what precisely is the target of Bunge's negative criticisms.

Questions of an essentially epistemological sort posed by science differ from those we may properly call "logical". Whereas those of a logical character examine the "internal" structure and interrelations of the various strands and components of science, the epistemological approach raises questions as to the powers and possible limitations of science in giving us knowledge of the structure of the world in which we live. Schlegel explores this question, and seeks to place science in what he calls an "epistemological continuum". He discriminates the type of experience we call mystical, from the scientific; he points out the essential differences *within* science between the role played by sensory experiences from that performed by the symbolic, highly abstract constructions of theory and mathematics. His views on this subject are subjected to searching critique in Nagel's response. In a parallel treatment, Glass explores the extent to which, contrary to the usual claims made in behalf of "the objectivity" of science, there are in fact elements of inherent subjectivity in the procedures and conclusions of the sciences. He relates this theme to the evolutionary development of the human species, and explores the way in which human cognitive processes must be viewed in the light of this development.

The first two papers in the section on the Philosophy of History— those by P. H. Nowell-Smith and Alan Donagan—treat of a theme that has received much recent attention, the nature of historical explanation. The theory that historical explanation is essentially of the same type as explanations given in the physical sciences, and that these typically involve the use of causal laws has come to be known as "the covering–law theory". Karl Popper and Carl Hempel have been among the leading proponents of this view. Both Nowell-Smith and Donagan critically assess this model and point out various difficulties connected with its use. In another paper, that by W. H. Dray (who himself has been a leading critic of the covering–law theory) another aspect of historical explanatory narrative is explored. Dray addresses himself to the central question of what it is that guides the historian in his selection of facts to be reported. What principle determines their selection? He identifies what he calls the "causal fertility principle" and shows how it may be used as a criterion for specifying what is causally important. He further shows how it would be possible to trace among the various consequences of an historical act the way in which some chains of consequences break down and become intransitive. David Braybrook turns his attention to still another theme in the Philosophy of History, viz., to what extent one can discover a "dialectical" pattern in the succession of cultures. He reexamines the classical Marx–Engles thesis that the chief sources of cultural change are due to internal contradictions that result from changes of a technological nature. Braybrook appeals to the recently developed techniques of the logic of norms as developed by Von Wright as a way of re–stating with precision the character of the dialectic of historical change. In a related, though more traditionally oriented inquiry, Mihailo Marković raises the general question as to what it is that differentiates the social from the natural sciences with respect to the concept of causal determination. In this connection he explores the question of the relation between social determinism and individual freedom of action. The final paper, by Henry Steele Commager, in taking The Philosophy of History as an enterprise in which the philosopher draws "moral lessons" from the past, argues that most practicing historians are impatient with philosophy of history in this sense. He maintains that any such analysis is inherently subjective and can exist only in the "historian's mind".

M. K. M.

PHILOSOPHY OF MIND

PHILOSOPHY OF MIND

THE LIMITS OF NATURALISM

Brand Blanshard

I

The Issue

The purpose of this paper is to consider whether science, as currently conceived, is adequate to the study of the mind.

The claim of natural science to cover the whole field of knowledge has been stated often and confidently. Bertrand Russell has remarked that what is knowledge is science, and what is not science is not knowledge. This is a very large claim, but even doubters are commonly reluctant, in view of the imposing success of science, to suggest any limits to its advance. Its standing in the eyes of learned and laymen alike has never been higher. In physics, in biology, in astronomy, in medicine, it has achieved one impressive breakthrough after another, with resulting advances in technology that have transformed our way of life. Since I am presently going to venture some questions about its adequacy, let me say at once that I think these achievements should be met with unqualified gratitude and admiration. If one compares the progress made in the past century in natural science with that made in other intellectual disciplines—in humanistic scholarship, for example, or history, or theology—the achievement of science seems unique. It is the most impressive intellectual force of our age.

Nevertheless, thoughtful humanists have begun to raise questions about the current pretensions of science. Is it truly justified in claiming all knowledge as its province? Is it really qualified to take over the domain of the historian, the moralist and the critic? Jacques Barzun (*Science the Glorious Entertainment*) and Joseph Wood Krutch (*The Measure of Man*), Douglas Bush (*Engaged and Disengaged*) and Floyd Matson (*The Broken Image*) have offered sharp strictures on these claims. They have protested that to employ the methods of physical science in the

3

study of man and his works is to beg some very important questions about human nature. These men—all humanists—hold that science as now conceived is, in principle, unqualified to deal with the set of activities with which humanists are concerned, and that any attempt to deal with them in a purely scientific way is bound either to by-pass or to distort them. In this not very popular view I think the humanists are right, and I shall devote this paper to the attempt to say why I think so.

If the issue is to be argued profitably, we must know at the outset what "the humanities" and "scientific method" are to mean.

By a humanistic study I shall mean an attempt to understand or appraise any conscious and purposeful human activity. History and biography are obvious examples of such study. So is the study of literature in all forms—fiction, drama, poetry, etc.; indeed it is doubly so, for it involves studying not only the creative activities of the writer, but also the activities of the creatures of his imagination. Studies of the religions and cultures of mankind would also be humanities, though not in so far as they are mere transcriptions of fact, for a mere transcription of fact is not an attempt either to understand or to appraise. Studies of art, morality, humor, music, and sport are likewise humanities. Philosophy and science hold ambiguous positions: Both are purposive activities of the human spirit, and the study of them as such would therefore rank among the humanities; but these activities themselves, insofar as they are concerned with the structure of the physical world, would not be humanistic, for while they are attempts to understand, they are not attempts to understand human activity.

Next, when it is claimed that science can provide us with such understanding, what is meant by "science"? No one would claim that science has already achieved such understanding. But many would say that if it has not, this is a failure in fact rather than in principle; there is nothing in human conduct that falls beyond the scope of scientific method, ideally employed. It is important, then, to see what such ideal employment requires. I shall call here upon the words of some respected exponents of scientific method. In a list of "criteria of the scientific method," Herbert Feigl puts in first place "intersubjective testability," remarking: "This is only a more adequate formulation of what is generally meant by the 'objectivity' of science." It is "the requirement that the knowledge claims of science be in principle capable of test (confirmation or disconfirmation, at least indirectly and to some degree) on the part of any person equipped with intelligence and the technical devices of observation and experimentation. The term *intersubjective* stresses the social nature of the scientific enterprise." [1] This requirement is further explained by Gustav Bergmann and Kenneth Spence as follows: Such terms as "sensation," "consciousness," and "image" are not necessarily meaningless, but "it is the methodological ideal of the sciences of behavior to use such mentalistic terms only after they have been introduced by (*operational*) *definitions from a physicalistic meaning basis*." These terms are properly used only when "every statement which contains such terms can be tested by the *scientist's* observations (unquantified) and measurements (quantified) of physical objects." All such terms, when used by scientists, "should be behavioristically defined." [2]

This preliminary comment on terms sharpens the issue. The question before us now is whether conscious and purposive human activity can be dealt with by a scientific method in which mind is conceived in terms of physical behavior and whose statements are tested by the common observation of such behavior. There are naturalists, indeed, who would not accept this "reductionist" view of scientific method, who would hold that mental activity is distinct from physical, even though all control of behavior is exerted from the bodily side. We shall deal with this softer naturalism in the concluding part of this paper, but first let us consider the more extreme form.

I shall begin on a note that is perhaps querulous. It is distressingly difficult to get from the harder naturalists a simple, straightforward statement of what they mean. Take the statements we have just been quoting. We are told that "it is the methodological ideal of the sciences of behavior to use such mentalistic terms only after they have been introduced by (operational) definitions from a physicalistic meaning basis." What does this ponderous pronouncement mean? If a "definition from a physicalistic meaning basis" is a statement that consciousness is physical, why not say so? On the other hand, if consciousness is not physical, not capable of being publicly observed, then to define it, in the interest of scientific convenience, as really being so, is to begin with a manifest untruth which will vitiate everything that is later said about the conscious realm. It is as if these philosophers had an obscure sense that if their theory were put quite simply it would lack plausibility, and were trying to shield it by a cover of thick magisterial prose.

Philosophers of science who are also humanists often write as if for them there were really no problem here at all. Thus Mr. Feigl, who is a distinguished example of both types, writes an article contending that every kind of knowledge that a reasonable humanist can ask for is provided by science. At the same time he says that if knowledge is to be scientific, it must be "intersubjectively testable" through observation or experiment. But take this at face value and the science he is offering the humanist is one from which the entire range of humanistic experience is excluded at the outset. Suppose Professor Lowes wants to study what went on in Coleridge's mind in writing *Kubla Khan,* or what goes on in your mind when you read it. Mr. Feigl would agree, I think, that one cannot observe with the naked eye or with any conceivable instrument either Coleridge's consciousness or yours, and it follows that the study of this sort of object is off bounds for science. Mr. Feigl lists twelve of the most important criticisms of science offered by the humanist, but for some reason this fundamental objection is not discussed. And surely it *is* fundamental. The scientist says to the humanist, "You have nothing whatever to fear from me; every legitimate field of study is still left open to you by science as I conceive it," and then adds by implication: "Of course the world of feelings and purposes and memories and imagination and reflection in which you live is for science nonexistent or inaccessible"—to which my reply would be: science cannot have it both ways. If what the scientist here says *is* so, then the humanist world *is* off limits. If he is to include that world in his study, then his science cannot be confined to observable behavior; its province and its methods must be radically reconceived.

Scientists have naturally been uneasy about such wholesale exclusions from their domain. They are sure that if mental facts are facts at all, science can deal with them. But if it is to deal with them, they must be intersubjectively observable and confirmable, and that means that they must be movements in space. This is the conviction that lies behind the long series of behaviorisms of the past half-century. Three of them seem to me particularly characteristic of scientific struggle and frustration in dealing with mental facts.

II

The Earlier Behaviorism

Of these my favorite is the first. There was nothing mealy-mouthed about John Watson. He hesitated for a time over whether his behaviorism should be merely a method of study, with the existence of mental facts left doubtful, or whether he should deny them altogether. But he came to see that for a behaviorist to admit such facts was to admit the incompetence of his science in its own special field, and he therefore decided "either to give up psychology or else make it a natural science." [3] If the behaviorist disregarded consciousness, he held, it was for the same reason that the chemist disregarded alchemy and the astronomer astrology, namely that he wished no longer to deal in fictions. "If behaviorism is ever to stand for anything (even a distinct method) it must make a clean break with the whole concept of consciousness." For this concept, like that of the soul, is a relic of mediaeval superstition. "The behaviorist cannot find consciousness in the test tube of his science. He finds no evidence anywhere for a stream of consciousness, not even for one so convincing as that described by William James." [4] Science has moved beyond it. It must be dismissed like the other myths that survive from the childhood of the race.

Did this mean that Watson waved aside the whole humanist range of experience? Would he deny that there was any such thing as what Shakespeare meant by "imagination" when he said that "imagination bodies forth the forms of things unknown"? Would he deny what Hood meant by memory when he said, "I remember, I remember the house where I was born"? Would he exclude what the Prayer-Book means when it speaks of "envy, hatred, and malice, and all uncharitableness"? Would he say that Carlyle was using words without meaning when he remarked that "literature is the thought of thinking souls"? The answer to all these questions is Yes. Of course, nothing is clearer than that the persons who said these things were talking about conscious experiences, and it is hard to believe that Watson, when out of his white coat and his laboratory, would find any difficulty in following them. Yet his view of science required him to say that these words meant nothing. If such terms are to be retained by science, they must be equipped with a new set of meanings. Thus "memory" will mean "the resumption of a habit after a period of no practice;" "emotion" will refer to certain massive responses in the autonomic nervous system; and the philosopher will at last realize that "thinking is merely talking, but talking with concealed musculature." Images remained a puzzle to Watson; he did not know what in the nervous system to reduce them to, and being deficient in imagery, he hardly knew what he had to reduce. He was thus able, as some critic has noted, to elevate a personal defect into an ontological unreality.

I do not intend to enter here upon an appraisal of Watson's behaviorism. I did that in some detail and with no effect some thirty years ago.[5] Two remarks must suffice. First, it is obvious that no humanist could be a Watsonian behaviorist, or such a behaviorist a humanist, except by virtue of a gargantuan muddle. What goes on in the mind of anyone who thinks he is both, it is hard to say; he is probably misreading behaviorism as meaning only that brain and consciousness are intimately connected causally. But this is not at all what the theory means; indeed it is a denial of behaviorism, for it holds that cause and effect are distinct, and the distinctness of consciousness from the physical is just what Watson will not accept. Secondly, though many psychologists still call themselves behaviorists, few would admit that they are Watsonians. Even when they are reductionists, their reduction is more elaborate and sophisticated, less naive, and less interesting. With Watson you knew

where you were. For courageous, dogmatic, forthright, Philistine obtuse-
ness, he stands out like a monument on a plain.

III

Physicalism

Our second type of behaviorism is the physicalism of the logical
empiricists. Their motives were in part similar to Watson's. They
wanted to make psychology a natural science, and this could not be
done so long as the entities which were given entrance were neither observable nor measurable by the methods of the other sciences. But the
logical empiricists had a wider ambition than Watson. They had a program for the unification of all the sciences and for the relegation of all
other ways of knowing—philosophy for example—to the position of
handmaids of science. The instrument by which both ends were to be
effected was a new theory of meaning, formulated by Moritz Schlick,
who contended that the meaning of any factual statement was its mode
of verification. Make any statement of fact you wish, for example that it
is snowing. Then ask yourself what would serve to assure you of its
truth. You would presumably answer in this case, "Going to the window and seeing snowflakes falling," or "Going out and feeling them on
head and hands." Very well, Schlick would say, the meaning of your
statement, "it is snowing," is that if you went to the window or out-
doors you would perceive falling snow. The statement has a meaning because it is verifiable, and the way of verifying supplies that meaning. But
suppose there is no way of verifying it? Then there is no meaning in it
either. Kant said that an unknowable exists which is not in time. Is
there any observation by which you could assure yourself that this statement is true? None. Then it is neither true nor false; it is meaningless;
it says nothing. According to the logical empiricists, most of the statements of traditional metaphysics were of this kind, and the verifiability
theory of meaning was the tool on which they relied for exposing such
pseudo-knowledge.

Many persons who had been frustrated and repelled in their attempts to penetrate Teutonic metaphysics greeted this demand for clar-
ity with acclaim. At first sight it seemed remarkably simple and compel-
ling. But soon doubts developed. What about statements regarding the
remote past or future? We cannot verify them; are they therefore meaningless? What about statements regarding photons and electrons which
are unobservable, or regarding tables and chairs at times when nobody
observes them? Above all, what about other minds? Historians and biographers are largely concerned with what goes on in other minds, but
they obviously cannot observe these as they can the movements of other

bodies. No statements they make about other people's thoughts or feelings are verifiable in their own perception, and therefore if the test is rigorously applied, they must all be set down as meaningless.

Note that the physicalists did not deny that these thoughts and feelings existed, for to deny their existence would be as meaningless as to affirm it. What they did was to introduce the notion of multiple languages, and then raise the question whether a sentence in the mental language was translatable into a sentence of the physical language; this was accepted as a meaningful question. It was the physical language that was fundamental, not that of psychology or the social sciences, for if "mental" terms were introduced, they could always be translated into the physical language while the reverse process was not generally possible. If a man is said to be "angry" or "in pain," for example, there will always be some statement about the occurrence of a process in his body that will also be true. In accordance with the logic accepted by these theorists, two propositions will be technically equivalent to each other if both are always true or false together. By an inference of a very curious kind they seem to have passed from the plausible assertion that the mental and physical sentences are in this technical sense equivalent to the totally different and quite implausible assertion that the mental sentence can be translated into the physical one without change of content —in short, that they say the same thing. If that is so, when I use the sentence "You are in pain," my sentence can be translated without loss of meaning into "You are now holding your head and grimacing." Indeed this is the only sort of meaning that a scientist may entertain. As Professor Feigl put it, "to ascribe to our fellow men consciousness *in addition* to overt behavior with discoverable physiological processes implies a transcendence, an introduction of unverifiable elements;" [6] and such transcendence must be avoided if one is to avert the ultimate ignominy of talking metaphysics. Professor Ayer, writing about the same time, said that "each of us must define the experience of others in terms of what he can at least in principle observe. "I must define other people in terms of their empirical manifestations—that is, in terms of the behavior of their bodies, and ultimately in terms of sense contents." [7]

It is curious how little awareness these positivists betrayed of what their doctrine implied for the humanities. Almost all of them had come into philosophy from science; they were evangelists of science; if their doctrine was destructive of speculative philosophy they took that as good riddance; and in the implications of the doctrine for the study of literature and history they took little or no interest. These implications, however, were essentially the same as those of Watson's behaviorism. What, for example, would a physicalist make of Boswell? The biographer could indeed observe his subject's puffing and blowing, his sitting at his desk and his walking abroad, his avoidance of cracks in the sidewalks and his collecting of orange peel; and these of course have their interest. But the instant Boswell went beyond these bodily acts into Johnson's ideas and arguments, his feelings about Scots and Whigs, his fear of death, his affection for his Tetty, his wit and humor, his rages and his depressions, he was literally talking nonsense. But take all this away and what is left of Boswell's account? Virtually nothing at all, since then even Johnson's bodily oddities would have lost most of their significance for us. It is interesting to reflect that at the very time the physicalists were propounding their doctrine, Collingwood was writing a famous essay to show that the subject matter of history was self-conscious and purposive activity.[8] On positivist premises any attempt to discuss activity of this kind must be meaningless, and hence, so far as Collingwood is right, the historian is disinherited of his kingdom. To venture again at random, what would a physicalist make of James's *Varieties of Religious Experience?* Two generations of readers have found in it vivid descriptions of mystics, of divided selves and their unification, of conversion, of religious morbidity and healthy-mindedness. About these things James, as a scientific psychologist, presumably had no right to speak at all, and he was indulging in something like metaphysics when he did so.

We may be reminded that it is one thing to deny that someone else is conscious and another to deny the meaningfulness of saying that he is. But in a question of such practical importance as this, the distinction is a quibble. Presumably one's action should accord with one's belief, and if one's belief is that to ascribe pain to a man with a broken leg is nonsense, one should act accordingly. There is clearly no reason to relieve a pain that one does not believe to exist. It may be said, again, that the implications we have just noted, even if all are accepted and put together, do not constitute a logical refutation of physicalism. This is true. It remains a logical possibility that one's friends are all automata, bodies to which no thought or feeling is to be ascribed, which have no memory or recognition of the person who greets them, and are as free from fear or pain as an IBM computer. This view was accepted by some of the 17th century Cartesians regarding dogs and cats and led to irresponsible treatment of these animals. But that theory rested on a mediaeval theology which held that in the creation of animals, immortal souls had been denied them. This the positivists would rightly decry as mythology. At the same time they accepted a theory which made it illegitimate not only to ascribe pain to animals, but also to ascribe it to their fellow human beings. I am not, of course, attacking anyone's character. Many of these writers I knew, and found them invariably kindly, thoughtful and sensitive persons who would not wish to hurt an earthworm. They would not dream of practising their theory, and those of them who are still living have all, I think, given it up. But physicalism remains an instructive episode in human thought. It shows that when one tries to make a philosophy out of the logic and method of natural science, without taking due heed of the rest of human experience, one is likely to wind up in absurdity. The positivists no doubt regarded such philosophers as the Cairds, A. E. Taylor, and Bosanquet as victims of metaphysical superstition, but can one imagine any of these humane and civilized minds committing himself to anything as incoherent with general human experience and as barbaric in its larger implications, as physicalism was?

IV

The Behaviorism of Skinner

It may be well to look at one other attempt to deal with human experience in accordance with the demands of physical science, and one which, unlike the other two, is flourishing today. Professor B. F. Skinner, like Watson, denies the distinct existence of sensation and thought, feeling and purpose. His chief difference from Watson is this: that whereas Watson was much concerned to identify the processes in the nervous system in terms of which sensation, thought, and emotion are now to be defined, Skinner by-passes this endeavor as being, at the present stage of science, unprofitable. We know comparatively little about the chemistry and physics of brain cells and of the conduction of nervous impulses through them, and the growth of such recondite knowledge is likely to be slow. But the study of behavior, which is the proper business of psychology, need not wait upon such knowledge, for we may study the connection of stimulus and response independently of it. We can vary indefinitely the situations in which the organism is placed and note how the response varies with each change. We may expose a pigeon to a black, a white, and a red disc, while it can get food only by pecking the white one, and observe how many mis-pecks it makes before learning to peck at the white disc only. Here we are studying the connection between observable stimuli and observable responses without any regard to the changes that may go on in the pigeon's nervous system. That is the way we should study human behavior.

Suppose one replies to Skinner: Surely it is what happens between the stimulus and the response, the part you are leaving out, that is psychologically of most interest to us. Present those discs to a man and he may do any one of a hundred things because he has the power, which the pigeon has not, of thinking. He can consider, deliberate, entertain purposes, plan, and hence respond, in a way you cannot foresee. Skinner's reply would make three points. First, if you mean by such terms as "deliberating" and "planning" a set of conscious processes distinct from what goes on in the body, they are fictions; there are no such events.[9] Secondly, since they are fictions, they cannot affect the responses that actually occur, and hence are of no value in explaining those responses. Thirdly, though they do not exist, the physical changes that we ought to mean by these names do exist and do make a difference, but it is a difference that it is needless at present to take into account.

Suppose you have a series of events A, B, C, and that A is the sufficient cause of B, and B of C. Then if you know that A occurs, you know that C will occur, and you can connect A and C by a perfectly reliable causal law in which B does not figure at all. B here stands for events internal to the organism, the "intervening variables" as the psychologists call them, between the observable stimuli and the observable responses. We have no doubt that Cs, forms of behavior exhibited by the organism, issue from Bs, changes within the organism, and we have no doubt that the Bs are all ultimately due to changes occurring outside the organism. The two extremes are physical events that are within the present range of our observation. Most of the intervening variables are not. What is proposed is that, without denying the existence of these variables, we proceed to establish connections directly between the several forms of A—A^1, A^2, A^3—and the several forms of C—C^1, C^2, C^3. We shall then have a set of causal laws whose components are as truly observable as anything in physics.

There is no objection to seeking such linkages, and the method has been applied with success, particularly to lower animals. But certain comments should be made about what is distinctive in it.

(1) It denies the existence of consciousness as flatly as Watson did. The classical works on psychology are full of discussions of sensation, imagery, emotion, the association of ideas, the processes of thought. Professor Skinner tries to eliminate such misleading terms from his writing. The result is that for a humanist it makes curiously difficult reading. It is as if someone had taken a chapter of Proust or Henry James and attempted to rewrite it entirely in terms of the movements of muscle and limb on the part of the characters, with no mention of anything that went on in their minds. That thoughts and emotions do commonly express themselves in such motions seems clear enough, but an account of them exclusively in terms of these motions gives the impression of elaborate indirection or evasion, a continuous, gratuitous missing of the point.

(2) The fact that one can directly link the stimulus and the response, without mention of the intermediate links, does not imply that those links are absent. They are there and performing their function, whether we take note of them or not. Would Professor Skinner agree? Yes, if by these intermediate links we mean changes in the nervous system; No, if they mean thoughts, choices or purposes. When we say, for example that what a man says is "disorganized because his *ideas* are confused," or that he pauses because he is trying to make up his mind, "it is obvious that the mind and the ideas, together with their special characteristics, are being invented on the spot to provide spurious explanations." [10] If Professor Skinner omits talk about intervening mental variables, it is because they never do intervene. His "purpose" to sit down at his desk and write makes no difference to what he does; he never "chooses" to write one sentence rather than another because its "meaning" is relevant to his "end"; indeed, he never chooses to do anything if that means that his "choice" appoints what he does. You can never explain an action, even in part, by saying that the man who did it "intended" or "preferred" or "decided" or "wished" or "thought he ought" to do it.

What are we to say of these programs to make of psychology a science like physics or chemistry? We must be clear on what they are proposing to us. Sometimes this is represented, not as a denial of conciousness, but as a study of its physical aspects and connections. If mind is stimulated into action by physical events, expresses itself in physical events, and is intimately and manifoldly connected with events in the nervous system, is it not possible to confine oneself to the study of these events? The strict answer is No. How is one to choose, for example, which events in the nervous system to study, except by noting which are correlated with mental events? And then one is *not* confining oneself to physical events only. Behaviorists have frequently stated their position as if they were not concerned with ontology but only with method. Professor Skinner writes: "The objection to inner states is not that they do not exist, but that they are not relevant to a functional analysis." [11] This sounds as if desires and purposes in the traditional sense were admitted to exist, but were being ignored because they fell outside the scientific province. But such language is misleading. If these psychologists were asked whether science, as they conceive it, is adequate to the study of the mind, they would undoubtedly say Yes, and add that science is the best means we have of dealing with any facts. If mental events are ignored, then, it is not for methodological reasons only. Science ignores mental facts, because these "facts" are not genuine facts. The words that seem to refer to them refer to physical facts or else to nothing. To talk about a nonphysical purpose or intention is, to Watson, like talking about astrology; to the physicalists, it is talking metaphysics; to Skinner it is a surrender to the "fictional;" and to Ryle it is the superstition of a "ghost in the machine."

V

The Failure of Behaviorism

There seems to me something grotesque in a solemn argument about whether consciousness, and what we commonly mean by pains and pleasures, fears and desires, exist. If a person insists that all he means by a toothache, for example, is a movement of some kind in his nervous system, he must no doubt be allowed the last word, for he is in a privileged position to know. But then so are the rest of us about our own meanings. I remember vividly an evening at Swarthmore when G. E. Moore was holding a conference hour for undergraduates. Only one student turned up that night, and he was a student in physics. The conversation began with his remarking that by his sensation of blue he meant a physical change in his optic nerve. Moore explained that he could understand this if what was meant was that such a change occasioned the sensation, but "surely you don't mean, [he went on,] that the movement of particles in the nerves *is* your sensation of blue?" Yes, the student insisted, that was exactly what he did mean, and he held to it despite Moore's expostulation. The veins began to stand out on Moore's forehead. He must have been through this countless times, and he apparently felt that a man who could believe that sort of thing, could believe anything. The weariness and futility of the discussion overcame him, and he fell obstinately silent. After a time I led him away.

Argument about the point is not, however, necessarily futile. It did, after all, persuade the physicalists to change their view. But the arguments that are likely to be effective here are not technical; it is indeed the technical people, who approach the problem from an ideal language or from a preconceived notion of what is required by science, who seem most confused, and who most need to be brought back to common sense again. It is curiously easy to be mistaken about one's own meaning, and one can only think that behaviorists are the victims of this kind of confusion. There are many ways of showing this, though nearly all of them are variations of the general argument that behaviorists cannot conform their intellectual practice to their reported meaning, that is, they cannot hold to this meaning consistently.

(1) Consider the behaviorist who has a headache and takes aspirin. What he means by his "headache" is, if he belongs to one school, a set of motions among the molecules that form the cells in his brain, or if

he belongs to another, the grimaces or claspings of the head that an observer might behold. Since these *are* the headache, it must be these that he finds objectionable. But it is absurd to say that a set of motions in his head, which he could not distinguish from a thousand others, are in themselves objectionable; it would never occur to him to find them so except as they are associated with the conscious pain. In denying the pain, therefore, he is denying the only feature that makes the situation objectionable. Suppose, again, that he identifies the pain with the grimaces and outward movements. Then all he would have to do to banish the pain would be to stop these movements and behave in normal fashion. But he knows perfectly well that this is not enough; that is why he falls back on aspirin. In short, his action implies a disbelief in his own theory.

(2) The characters he assigns to physical events are different from and incompatible with those he assigns to mental events. Physical changes are ultimately motions, and it is commonly assumed that what moves has mass, is governed by gravitational law, and moves in a certain direction with a certain velocity. But it would be nonsense to say that a pain or a memory has mass, gravity, direction or velocity. Again, we speak of a pain as sharp or dull, intense, or mild, excruciating or easy to bear, and such terms are meaningless as applied to motions. Professor Skinner, when confronted with this consideration, agrees that "a *motion* is not likely to be dull or excruciating. But *things* are. Indeed these two adjectives are applied to pain just because they apply to the things which cause pain. A dull pain is the sort of pain caused by a dull object, as a sharp pain is caused by a sharp object. The term 'excruciating' is taken from the practice of crucifixion." [12] But (a) Dull toothaches or headaches are not normally caused by dull objects, or sharp ones by sharp objects. (b) Even when the term "sharp" is used both of a physical thing and of a pain, it is used in wholly different senses. The sharpness or dullness of a thing is a matter of its shape; a pain has no shape. (c) When Professor Skinner says that we call a pain sharp because the physical thing that causes it is sharp, he seems to admit the difference between the conscious process and its physical cause. He may say that he means here the cause outside the body, and that the sensation is a change within the body and presumably in the brain. But then he arrives at the same paradox as before, since a molecular thing or movement can no more be identified with a sensation than a molar thing or movement.

(3) The implausibility of identifying the conscious event with a change in the brain may be seen in another way. When we refer to a conscious experience, we may be perfectly clear as to what we mean,

though if asked what brain change we were referring to, we should not have the faintest notion how to answer. Plato could discuss with precision the varieties of pleasure, and Aristotle the varieties of inference, without knowing that these psychical processes were connected with the brain at all. Even when we do learn that these processes are causally correlated with changes in the brain, we may not know which brain changes are involved. We made a distinction a moment ago between the sharpness of a tool and the sharpness of a pain; the making of that distinction was a mental act which we can now recall. What exactly is the brain process that in our new way of thought we are supposed to be recalling? Not even Adrian or Penfield would attempt to specify the correlate of that act in the brain. If we can clearly specify the mental act that we mean and yet are unable to specify the physical change we are supposed to mean, to say that the two meanings reduce to one is most implausible.[13]

(4) Even when we do know approximately what physical change is correlated with a given psychical change, there may be an extreme qualitative difference on one side which, so far as we know, corresponds to nothing on the other side. We know that when an impulse from the eye reaches a point in the back of the brain, a sensation of color normally arises, and that when an impulse from the ear reaches a point at the side of the brain a sensation of sound normally arises. No two experiences differ from each other more completely than one of sound and one of color. But the nervous impulses that are the correlates of these sensations seem to be the same in structure and movement. As Lord Adrian says, "the surprising thing is that a disturbance of this kind in one part of a sheet of nerve cells (the cortex) should make us see a light, and that the same kind of disturbance in another part should make us hear a sound." [14] If the sensations are entirely different while the nervous changes are, so far as we know, entirely alike, what we mean by the sensations must be distinct from what we mean by the physical changes.

(5) The attempt at identification cannot get under way without the implicit admission of its untruth. You want to know, for example, what brain change is now to be identified with "a sensation of color" and what with "a sensation of sound." The test of whether you have found the cerebral equivalent of a sensation of color is whether, when you alter or remove that cerebral process, the sensation is affected. On that ground you eliminate everything in the brain but a small area in the occipital lobe as the basis of the color sensation, and everything but a small area in the temporal lobe as the basis of the sound sensation. But the assumption of this procedure is that you have definite knowl-

edge of the color and sound sensations *before* you know what their physical correlates are. It is only because you have definite antecedent knowledge of these sensations that you can hunt for their correlates, or check your hypotheses as to what these are. If all you meant by sensation was its physical correlate, the search could not begin, for you would have no means of recognizing which of a million physical processes filled the bill. It is only if sensation and physical process are distinct that you ever reach the terminus of the search, a terminus which, once reached, is then incoherently identified with the starting point.

(6) The language used by behaviorists, despite their efforts to avoid compromising terms, continually betrays their position. Psychologists used to say that a response was confirmed or "stamped in" if it was pleasurable, and inhibited or discouraged if it was disagreeable. But "pleasurable" and "disagreeable" clearly refer to qualities of conscious experience, and Professor Skinner reminds us that science therefore does not use such terms or any equivalents for them.[15] What we should say instead, for example, is that the response of eating is "reinforced" by one sort of food and "extinguished" by another; these words are innocent of mentalist connotations. But he finds it impracticable to keep to this rule. He writes: ". . . though we have been reinforced with an excellent meal in a new restaurant, a bad meal may reduce our patronage to zero, [and again, on the next page, that in extinguishing a response,] "the currently preferred technique is punishment." [16] When, however, we refer to an "excellent" meal, is there no connotation of pleasantness? When we refer to a "bad" meal or to punishment, is there no connotation of disagreeableness? Would an "excellent" meal reinforce our tendency to repeat it if it were *not* pleasant? Would punishment be punishment if it were *not* disagreeable? It seems clear here that Professor Skinner, despite his gallant efforts to free his usage from the mentalistic blight, is not only reintroducing it but relying on it to make reinforcement and extinction intelligible.

However desperately the behaviorist tries to exclude these connotations of consciousness, they keep pouring in through the cracks in every wall he builds to keep them out. Strictly speaking, we should never say of Jones that he ran because he was afraid or because he wanted to catch a train, for these words attribute to him unobservable states with which science has nothing to do. But suppose Jones *says*, "I am scared half to death" or "I am frantic to catch that train." It is perfectly legitimate to take such an "observation report" into account because it is itself an observable part of Jones's behavior. But is it? No doubt an external observer can hear a succession of sounds emitted by Jones's body, but is the emission of these sounds all we mean by Jones's *saying* something? Clearly not. The point has been made by Professor E. M. Adams in an article in which a large variety of these unnoticed but illicit usages by behaviorists are catalogued and analyzed. "In what sense, [he asks,] is 'said' a pure observation term? Is it meaningful to ask, Does what he *said* make sense? Is what he *said* consistent? Can you put what he *said* differently? Can you translate what he *said* into French? Does he literally mean what he *said?* Is what he *said* supported by evidence? Was he justified in saying what he did? Is what he *said* true?" [17] These questions are clearly in order if "say" is used as we all do in fact use it. But they are both irrelevant and unanswerable if the term is used strictly as an "observation term." A mere series of heard sounds could not be "justified" or "supported by evidence" or "said differently" or "translated into French;" such expressions assume that the speaker was using the sounds to convey conscious meanings and that the hearer can apprehend those meanings. They must be used in this way by the behaviorist also if they are to do the work he asks of them. But he cannot use them so with consistency, since, for him, to apprehend the meanings of another mind would be to leap out of the physical world into forbidden territory. In short, he finds it impracticable to conform to his own requirements even in the use of so simple a word as "say."

(7) These requirements he believes to be imposed on him by science, and in the interest of science, as he conceives it, he is quite ready to part company with common sense. But in other places he clings to common sense in a manner that places him in clear conflict with science. When Professor Skinner talks about stimuli he does not ordinarily mean the impact of microwaves on nerve ends; he means observable things or changes such as colored discs or the sounds of a voice or the impact of a hard object. Since these are observable, they are assumed to be physical. But would a physicist of sophistication take them to be physical, just as presented? Would he accept the color of a disc as something spread out in physical space over the surface of the disc? Would he take the sounds that are heard, as distinct from waves in air, to be physical existents? Having explained to us that a football consists of millions of micro-particles in motion, would he add that this aggregate is *hard?* Most philosophers since Locke have held that the "secondary qualities" belong in consciousness, not in the physical world, and reflective physicists have thought likewise. There is no doubt that we experience them, and they must, therefore, have lodgement in some recognized realm of being. But Professor Skinner has no room for them in any realm of being. If he puts them in physical space, as he seems inclined to do, he loses the much coveted support of natural science. He cannot put them in consciousness, for there is no consciousness to put

them in. Nor would he identify them, as Watson tried to do, with nervous changes in the body. He would consider it absurd to hunt for a sound in the nervous system. In our conscious experience of nature these qualities are almost everywhere, but in the world of the behaviorist they are without a home.

(8) Consider but one more paradox, which, if possible, is more striking still. In the round terms of traditional philosophy, the intrinsic values of life were often said to be truth, beauty and goodness. Whether we accept this thesis or not, the old terms are still of importance and in constant use. What meaning can the behaviorist attach to them? Take first the meaning of "truth." What is true is a proposition, a belief or an assertion, but these are not observable entities unless identified with movements of the lips or with other bodily movements. But it is meaningless to say that *movements* are true or false. There is nothing more true or false about any one movement in the universe than about any other. And since there are no events in the behaviorist universe except the motions of matter, it has no room for truth either.

Again, what would the term "beauty" stand for in such a world? Is it a scientifically observable property? Hume imagines a geometer gloating over the beauty of one of his figures, say a five pointed star. He proceeds to indicate its properties to an observer—the uniform structure of its five triangles, the equal length of their sides and of their bases, and so on. His companion then asks him to point out the quality of beauty that he has been speaking of. Could he do it? Hume rightly answers that it would be impossible, that beauty is not something that can be observed like a line or a shape. Still less is it something that could belong in a wholly physical world. Strictly speaking there is no beauty apart from the enjoyment of it, and the enjoyment of it is a form of consciousness. In a behaviorist world, a necessary condition of beauty would thus be lacking.

What about moral goodness? Moralists have commonly held that this depends either on the motive of an act or on the intrinsic values of its consequences. Skeptics regarding these positions have argued that "good" and all other value terms are the expressions of emotions or attitudes in the minds of those who use them. No one of these theories of goodness could be restated in behaviorist terms without eviscerating them of their meaning. In short, the world of the behaviorist is one in which neither truth, beauty nor goodness, as traditionally understood, can consistently be given a place.

I have argued the case at wearisome length because behaviorism is not a historic curiosity merely, as by this time it ought to be, but is very much alive. Indeed, with the help of the Ford Foundation, the Carnegie Corporation and the federal government, Professor Skinner has recently produced a book on *The Technology of Teaching* that offers a program for making education entirely a matter of physical conditioning. Such a work, with such support, lends some color to Count Keyserling's acid comment that behaviorism is the natural psychology of a people without inner life. Furthermore, the movement has received encouragement, strange enough, from that traditional seat of the humanities, Oxford, in Professor Ryle's brilliant and wayward book, *The Concept of Mind.* I have not dealt with that book, partly because its account of the mind is not, like our three American behaviorisms, an attempt from within the circle of science to draw psychology back into the fold, partly because it has been so effectively dealt with in its own country. I have in mind particularly Professor C. A. Campbell's essay, *Ryle on the Intellect,* in which the difficulty, even for a skillful dialectician, of holding consistently to the behaviorist thesis, is convincingly shown.[18]

VI

The Identity Hypothesis

But materialism dies a lingering death. In recent years a number of philosophers have been exploring whether the identity of mind and matter cannot be rehabilitated, and to that end they have been examining anew the notion of identity. The word "is," they point out, is ambiguous. There is the "is" of definition and the "is" of composition. The "is" of definition means a logical identity, as when we say that a square is an equilateral rectangle. Here the identity is such that neither side would be conceivable in the absence of the other. We also use an "is" of composition, as when we say that a cloud is a mass of droplets in suspension, or that lightning is a motion of electric charges.[19]

Here there is no identity of concept between subject and predicate, for either could be conceived without the other. Most holders of the identity hypothesis are reluctant to say that consciousness and bodily change are the same in the logical sense. They have given up the view, which never was plausible, that the distinction between mind and matter is a merely linguistic affair, and that when a man says he has a toothache he is referring in a different language to precisely what he means when he speaks of an injury to his dental nerve, or to grimaces and gestures that would be observable from without. It is only too obvious that the one language is not translatable into the other. If the identity hypothesis does claim identity in the extreme or logical sense, then the arguments already adduced against behaviorism are in order again.

But in spite of the sophistication of the identity philosophers, some of them are advancing a theory that is hard to distinguish in principle from extreme behaviorist reductionism, apparently denying, for example, that there is any such thing as sensation, as distinct from bodily response. Thus Professor J. J. C. Smart imagines a group of congenitally blind men in the company of normal men who are sorting wools of different colors into piles. These piles are arranged in a series in which each pile can barely be differentiated from its neighbors. The blind man knows that a tomato is called red, and lemons yellow, and he knows that when wool from a certain pile is dropped into a bowl of tomatoes, the sighted people around him find it especially hard to pick it out, and when the wool from a certain other pile is dropped into a bowl of lemons, it too becomes hard to pick out. The blind man thus coordinates the color words for the various piles with the color words used for objects he knows otherwise, such as tomatoes, lemons, and lettuce. Would the blind man use color words in the same way that we do? Professor Smart replies that he would, and that "the objective criteria for the redness of an object are exactly the same with him as with us. These objective criteria are the discriminatory responses of normal percipients. As against the common view that colour words are meaningless to the congenitally blind I would rather say, therefore, that the congenitally blind can understand the meaning of colour words every bit as well as sighted people can. [And he concludes,] The idea that a congenitally blind man cannot understand colour words is connected, I suspect, with a pre-Wittgensteinian view of meaning not as 'use' but as a mental experience which evokes and is evoked by a word." [20]

Here I am hopelessly pre-Wittgensteinian. To say that a blind man who learned to imitate the physical and verbal responses of normal men "can understand the meanings of colour words every bit as well as sighted people can" implies that there is nothing in the color discrimination of even normal men beyond their physical responses. The example surely gains such plausibility as it has through confusing two quite different kinds of discrimination. When the normal man discriminates red from yellow, he is distinguishing the content of two conscious sensory experiences. When the blind man responds "correctly" with "red" to one pile of wool in a series and "yellow" to another, these vocal responses are not discriminations between colors at all. To say that they are is to return to Watson and Skinner with their attempt at literal conceptual identification of two things—a conscious experience and a physical response, which are as different in kind as any two things in the world. Does the normal man have no advantage over the blind man? Obviously he has. In what does it here consist? In this: that he can see or experience or be aware of colors, that he can imagine them, and distinguish them consciously. The blind man, having never experienced them, has not the slightest idea what these phrases mean to the man with sight.

Most defenders of the identity theory, however, are not reductionists of this type. They would prefer the other kind of identity, that of composition. The best analogy of the sense in which consciousness is brain process, is to be found, in the opinion of Mr. Place, in the statement that lightning is the motion of electric charges. The meaning of "a flash of lightning is occurring" is clearly different from "a motion of electric charges is occurring," as is evidenced by their being verified in totally different ways. Yet layman and scientist alike are content to say that the lightning *is* the motion of electric charges. Why? Because the motions observed by the scientist "provide an immediate explanation of the observations made by the man in the street. Thus we conclude that lightning is nothing more than a motion of electric charges, because we know that a motion of electric charges through the atmosphere, such as occurs when lightning is reported, gives rise to the sort of visual stimulation which would lead an observer to report a flash of lightning." [21] If it is permissible to use "is" in this case, there is no reason why we should not use it also in the case of consciousness and brain process. When a scientist feels an acute pain, he is no more thinking of the motions in his nervous system than, when seeing a flash of lightning he is thinking about the movements of electric charges. He can, however, perfectly well say, in the same sense of "is," that the pain *is* the motion of particles in his brain.

I may have missed some link in the argument, but I must confess that I can see nothing in it that tends to show even the second type of identity, let alone the first. The seen flash, which is a conscious event, does not *consist* of the motion of charges in the atmosphere; the two are entirely different and temporally distinct events. If we follow the analogy through, we shall have to deny that the conscious pain either *is* or *consists of* the change in the nerve; the most we can say is that the two events are connected. What sort of connection is it? Mr. Place has suggested the answer when in discussing the lightning case he says that the motion of electric charges "provides the immediate explanation" of the visible flash. And what does "explanation" mean? It means what scientific explanation generally means—explanation through causal law. But such explanation, far from supporting the identity hypothesis, is incompatible with it. For if the nervous events and the pain are connected as cause and effect, their identity is out of the question. They are *two* events, not one.

VII

Soft Materialism

The attempt to establish identity appears to end, then, with a notion of consciousness, not as identical with events in the nervous system, but as their result or effect. We are thus carried on to epiphenomenalism. This, I suspect, is the position really implicit in the thought of most physiologists and psychophysicists of the day, whether they are familiar with the terminology or not. Certainly they would not swallow the notion that consciousness does not exist, nor would they be prepared to equate it with physical motions, which amounts to the same thing. If they were to set out their position, it would probably run as follows: Sensations, emotions, recollections, judgments, acts of reasoning, desires, purposes, choices, are mental events, to which physical attributes like volume, mass and motion plainly do not belong. But there are the best of reasons to believe that, though not physical events themselves, they are always causally dependent on physical events, whose location in the cortex we are able to specify more and more definitely.

Does causation run in the opposite direction also—from mind to brain? If causation means only correlation, we should be justified in saying Yes; we could say, as common sense does unhesitatingly, that if the dentist's injuring the nerve-end causes the pain, it is also true that the patient's resolution to bear the pain stoically makes him sit still and restrain his outcry. But I do not think that most physiologists or psychologists really accept the correlation theory. Though they would say without hesitation that the injury to the nerve produces the pain, they would hesitate long, and probably in the end decline, to say that the resolution caused anything to happen in the body. As at least would-be natural scientists, they would say that physical events must have physical causes. Speaking strictly, therefore, a mental resolution or decision can never so much as divert the course of a nervous impulse as it passes across a synapse. What really produces the bodily change is not the mental event but the physical counterpart of that mental event, which is of course always present and available as the true cause. In this way we confine causal agency to events in the natural order and resist unwanted intrusions from a supernatural order, whether psychical or superstitious.

And if we deny causal efficacy to the psychical events, we may as well take the further step of denying them agency even in their own realm. Suppose we find our thoughts to have been following a line of "free association" and passing idly from the blue sky to the blue Danube and thence to the St. Louis Blues. Has one associate given rise to another? In appearance, Yes, in reality No. What has actually occurred is that the cortical basis of the first thought has given rise to the cortical basis of the second, and that of the second to that of the third. The succession of ideas is thus explained without yielding the claim of the physical order to be the exclusive source of all events, mental as well as physical. The theory is sometimes diagrammed as follows:

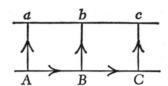

There is a series of cortical events, A, B, C, with a series of corresponding psychical events, a, b, c. The order of executive causality runs horizontally from A to B to C, and also upward from A to a, from B to b, and from C to c. But it does not run horizontally from a to b to c, nor downward from these to anything in the physical succession.

Stated thus in the abstract, the theory is neat and plausible, and as defended by such persuasive writers as T. H. Huxley and Santayana, is more plausible still. C. D. Broad has said of it: "Unless there be reason to believe that minds can survive the death of their bodies, I should consider that some form of epiphenomenalism was the most reasonable view to take of the nature of mind and its relation to the body." [22] It is not strictly a naturalist theory if, as such, it would have to remain within the limits of physical science, since it admits that consciousness is not physical in character or structure. But it is naturalistic in the sense that matter is regarded as the only agency in nature, the sole determinant of events, and the basis of all causal explanation. It seems to be the most plausible of those theories that by any stretch of the term can be called naturalistic. I suspect that many men of science accept it for this reason without giving much thought to its implications regarding human nature and practice. We shall do well, therefore, before commenting on its validity, to draw out some of these implications, so that if we are inclined to accept it we shall at least know to what we are committing ourselves.

The view implies that no volitions, purposes or desires ever influence behavior. When one sits down at a desk in order to write a letter, one's intention makes no difference to one's sitting down or writing. No decision made by Eisenhower in Europe, or MacArthur in Korea, or Westmoreland in Viet Nam made the slightest difference in the conduct of their various wars. The purpose of Albert Schweitzer to serve the African needy had nothing causally to do with his going to Africa, any more than the purpose of Hitler to liquidate the Jews had any effects in the way of death or misery. Schweitzer did not do right, nor Hitler wrong; nor has anyone ever done anything good or bad, if that means that what he did issued out of his choice. The desire of a youth for an education never leads him to go to college, or his desire for a girl to propose to her, or his desire to win a race to enter a contest or to run faster. Again, our *thoughts* make no difference to what we do or say. There is nothing in Russell's fifty volumes that was written because he had one conviction rather than another. When a debater argues a case, his interest in proving that case never makes any difference to the words or sentences he uses. No student sitting for an examination will ever write a better paper because he thinks more clearly or recalls more completely the relevant facts. Shakespeare's conception of Lear or Cordelia had no influence on what he wrote in the play, nor did Coleridge's imagination make him set down or delete anything in *The Ancient Mariner*. Euclid's seeing that the angles of a triangle must equal two right angles, Aristotle's seeing that a Barbara syllogism is valid, had no effect on what they taught. Again, feeling and sensation are without influence on conduct. The pain of getting burnt has no part in leading the child to avoid the fire. No one ever stops his car at a crossroad because he sees a red light rather than a green one. No one ever swears because he is angry, or sends a valentine out of affection, or pays a debt from a sense of duty, or bundles up from fear of a cold. Again, no thought or purpose ever accounts for any mental event that comes after it. No one ever accepts a conclusion because he sees that the evidence demands it, or, for that matter, because he wants to believe it; rationalization in the Freudian sense is as impossible as it is to be rational, if that means being guided by what one takes to be the demands of reason. Nor does any idea ever give rise to another through resemblance or relevance or association. Beethoven never added one bar to another because of what aesthetic requirements demanded or seemed to demand. Consciousness, in short, is an impotent observer from the sidelines in the conduct of life.

What then is the real executive agent in biography and history? It is the body. It was Russell's durable and efficient body that wrote that row of volumes, with never an assist from his thought. The body is the only saint or sinner, for motives have nothing to do with what it does. There once was a body that, unprompted by its mind, made the set of marks on paper called King Lear, and another that rose to its feet and gave Churchillian speeches, while the consciousness of each of these bodies, like the fly that rode the elephant, no doubt took a pathetic satisfaction in its own performance. Of course the brain of a man is an unimaginably complex apparatus, composed of billions of cells, each of which has countless components. Still the components are all physical, and the natural scientist believes that the laws governing their behavior are in the end exclusively those of physics and chemistry.

VIII

The Failure of Epiphenomenalism

Does our budget of paradoxes disprove the theory? No, I think not. It involves a prodigious change in our view of human nature, and, I think, a high degree of improbability, but not a decisive disproof. It is hard to set clear limits to what an apparatus as complex as the human body can do without purposive guidance. Fortunately we do not have to rely on probability only. There are other considerations that seem to me to defeat the theory decisively.

First there is a consideration drawn from the nature of inference. I have several times made this point in print, and have been fortified by finding that the fire it drew seemed to leave it intact. Epiphenomenalists commonly hold that the laws of science are empirical laws, and therefore without logical necessity. In explaining why brain state *B* should follow brain state *A*, one cannot resort to any necessity linking the character or the content of these states. Nor can one resort to such necessity in explaining why the conscious state *b* follows the conscious state *a*, since in the realm of consciousness nothing exerts causal constraint on anything else. I think this is false and that its falsity can be demonstrated. Take any case of valid inference: "Either the death of President Kennedy was the work of a group, or Oswald was the assassin. But no group was involved. Therefore Oswald was the assassin." The inference here is a psychological succession, ending with the thought of the conclusion. Why did this terminal thought pop into mind instead of any one of a thousand others? The natural answer is that a moment before we had laid hold in thought of the premises, and that we went on to the thought of the conclusion because it was entailed by these premises. I think that this natural answer is correct, though it is not the whole of the answer. And it is quite inconsistent with epiphenomenalism, since it implies that one conscious event determines through its content or character (or more precisely through the logical relation of its content to another content) the emergence of a later event.

Let us move cautiously here. Implication and inference are, of course, not to be confused; implication is a timeless relation between characters; inference is a succession of events in time. What I am maintaining is that the timeless relation of implication which links the con-

tents of the successive events, plays a part in explaining why the inference took the course it did. Again, I am not maintaining that this
relation of implication is the sole condition of the conscious passage, for
there are many other conditions, such as an interest in knowing, being
in normal health, perhaps having had a cup of coffee and not being dis-
tracted at the moment. But if one asks oneself why, with these premises
in mind, one leaped to this conclusion rather than to the thought of
cherry trees in May, one surely cannot disregard the fact that it is the
conclusion required by the premises we just had in mind.

Indeed we must note that the kind of explanation we are offering is
doubly inconsistent with the epiphenomenalist account. That account
holds, first, that the character of event *a* makes no difference to the occurrence of event *b*. But we can see in retrospect that unless an event
having the character of *a*, that is, of being an apprehension of these
premises, had occurred, there is no reason whatever to believe that the
event *b* would have occurred. We can only believe, therefore, that the
character of *a* did make a difference. Secondly, our explanation involves
a *type of causation* of which epiphenomenalism knows nothing. We ordinarily think of the cause as preceding the effect. The entailment of
the conclusion by the premises is neither before nor after the conclusion, because it is timeless. But since it does clearly contribute to the
course of the inference, we must concede that causal influence is not
confined to antecedents in time. Some critics, thinking this incredible,
have insisted that the emergence in thought of the conclusion is due,
rather, to a particular psychological event, the event of seeing that the
premises entail the conclusion. This is both inconsistent with epiphenomenalism and logically unsound. For what we have to explain is the
emergence of the conclusion in the thinker's consciousness, and when
he has seen that the conclusion is entailed, that conclusion is of course
already before him. The critic is thus explaining the emergence by assuming that it has already occurred. What we must say, strange as it
seems from the naturalist point of view, is that it is not the thought of
the entailment that contributes to the emergence of the conclusion, but
the actual entailment itself. A. E. Taylor once wrote, in language alien
to present ways of speech, of "the initiative of the eternal." That, to be
sure, is metaphysics. It is none the worse for that. Indeed I am arguing
that when empirical and natural science reaches the level of human
thinking it must either incorporate metaphysics or go bankrupt.

A theory that allows no influence of thought on behavior has another consequence, which to some will be more disturbing. It is self-contradictory, in the sense in which it is self-contradictory to deny the
Cartesian *cogito;* the thesis is inconsistent with its own enunciation and

defense. When one states the thesis, it is with the intention of reporting one's belief to others; we assume that this intention will affect what we say, and without that assumption we should not have been so foolish as to entertain the intention at all. Again, we assume that it is possible, when considering whether a thesis is true, to order our thought about it with reference to our purpose, inhibiting ourselves from wandering off into irrelevance, dwelling specially on matters of greater importance, and moving on to a conclusion appointed by the weight of the evidence. If this process were not possible, there would be no point in thinking at all. Eminent present-day philosophers of science, following Santayana, whether knowingly or not, describe what happens in a course of thinking as follows. "The dark engine of nature," as Santayana calls the process in the brain, grinds along a track of purely physical causality. There is presumed to be no such thing as purpose or relevance or evidence or necessity among the neurones of the cortex. Nevertheless, these churnings of the dark engine have a surprising way of pushing up into consciousness at the end conclusions that have every appearance of having been reached by the consideration of, and constraint by, relevant evidence. Since the working of the machine has been unguided by the purpose of the thinker, this happy ending is, relatively to that purpose, a piece of pure luck. Surely if our naturalistic psychologists really believed this about their own thinking, they would lack the heart to launch themselves on the process. If this process takes its course unaffected by considerations of relevance, and if the seen weight of evidence can make no difference to one's acceptance of a thesis, why think? Similarly, if the argument, transmitted to another mind, can make no difference to his conclusions, why try to communicate? The constant conduct of the naturalist in presenting and defending his theory is inconsistent with the truth of that theory.

Consider, thirdly, the moral aspect of this sort of naturalism. A moral choice commonly involves the contemplation of two or more courses of action and the election of one as the right one. There is much difference of opinion as to what makes a course right, but we do not need at the moment to raise that thorny question. Most of us would probably agree that there is some course of action that would be the right one to take, and that we should find it and follow it if we can. We should probably agree further, that if we believe a course to be right, we ought to take it, and that in taking it because we believe it to be right lies the highest form of moral goodness, even if not the only one, as Kant supposed. Now the interesting thing is that for the kind of naturalism before us, there is no such thing as a good action in this sense. No one ever chooses anything because he sees that he ought to, for one psychical event never causes another. No choosing or deciding to act in a certain way ever causes us to behave in that way, since that would be an action of the mental on the physical. Moral goodness in this sense ceases to be.

Indeed the ethical consequences go far beyond this. With this theory, how could we even be egoists? The egoist is the man who habitually chooses his own good in preference to that of others. But to act with reference to one's own good once more assumes the possibility of the mental controlling the physical. Again, there can be no moral responsibility, since if nothing one's body does springs out of one's own volition, how could one be held accountable for it? Rewards and punishments would be pointless. They could not be justified retributively for the reason just given; they could not be justified as encouragement or deterrence, since that assumes that the anticipation of results may affect behavior.

It seems fair to say that if no one ever acts as he does because he sees, or thinks he sees, one action to be better than another, ethics is being ruled off the board. It is true, however, that this type of naturalism has one advantage over behaviorism. It can recognize intrinsic values, even though it has no place for the pursuit of them. Pleasure and affection, knowledge and the experience of beauty, lie in consciousness, and for this sort of naturalism consciousness at least exists. On the other hand, for a consistent behaviorist there are no values, since there is no place for them in his universe. When Mr. Rogers objected to Mr. Skinner that science could decide questions of means but not of ends, Mr. Skinner replied: "Whether we like it or not, survival is the ultimate criterion." [23] This reduction of value to fact, reminiscent of Herbert Spencer, is the inevitable behaviorist reply. It is perhaps enough to say regarding it (1) that in some cases (extreme agony and helplessness, for example) survival is an evil not a good, and (2) that survival may have various forms, in which some are obviously better than others. In neither case could survival be the ultimate test.

There is one other consideration that should be mentioned if we are to see in perspective the attempt of natural scientists to deal with the mind. It is the extraordinary oscillation in their thought as to the meaning of "physical." In the usage of Professor Skinner, the term seems to mean what it does for common sense: physical objects are such things as tables, chairs and one's body, which are all on a common footing in public space; and their shapes and sizes, weights and colors, belong to them in their own right. This thought of the body as a solid independent thing has also been standard among epiphenomenalists. Huxley, who invented the name, took this view for granted until he read Hume. From then on he was in trouble. Hume's thesis about the sensible order seemed irrefutable, namely that everything we immediately experience belongs in the realm of consciousness. But if you combine this with the commonsense view of the body, as Huxley tried to do, you end in a never-never land in which the universe has all but vanished. First you hold that the body, the solid observable thing, has a mind connected with it which is a useless by-product or shadow. You then find that this body, which is basic to mind, is itself a set of characters and relations all of which belong within consciousness. Hence the body, the basic reality for Huxley the biologist, becomes for Huxley the philosopher the fragment of a shadow.

Now it is notorious, natural, and probably right that scientists should not concern themselves much with philosophy. In the commonsense view of the body they feel themselves, as Professor Skinner does, to be secure and with their feet on the ground. But this commonsense body is of course very far from that of the physicist, whose views of matter are taken by other scientists, at least in their professional moments, as authoritative. And if these others did think of the body as the physicist does, the mind-body problem would be transformed for them. It is instructive to see what has happened in the thought of that wonderful old man, Lord Russell. In his youth he was the leader of the extreme realists, holding that every quality of physical things, including one's own body, existed independently of its being experienced. In his last important work, *Human Knowledge: Its Scope and Limits*, he comes round to the view that everything we immediately experience lies in the realm of consciousness. The body is not now a solid object among others in public space, but a boiling mass of unobserved and unobservable particles in a space of their own. And the mind is not a set of shadowy processes, but the whole "choir of heaven and furniture of earth" that forms one's experienced world.

Russell the ancient sage is nearer the truth, I think, than Russell the bright young man. And if so, the place of consciousness in the scientific scheme of things is transformed. For consciousness is then no longer a tenuous shadow whose very existence is doubtful, but our base and starting point, the region of greatest certainty, while the realm of the physical becomes a twilight zone of inference, of hypotheses about the invisible and impalpable, of flights of metaphysical speculation. Matter has become, says Russell with a dash of his pleasant hyperbole, "a wave of probability undulating in nothingness." No one knows much about it; Bohr's model of the atom was outdated a decade or two later. Meanwhile both the values and the certainties of life, which lie in the sphere of consciousness, are much the same as they were thousands of years ago.

It is time scientists ceased to downgrade consciousness, without which they would have no starting point and no verification for their theories, and of course no theories either. Is there not something grotesque in the sight of psychologists, literally the scientists of the mind, denying that they have any distinct subject matter, and insisting that even in this denial they are only talking? Why do they sacrifice their own discipline in this manner? Primarily because of a misplaced notion of rigor. Because thoughts and feelings are not public and measurable, they are not quite respectable as objects of study. If the inner life were accepted on its own terms as permeated by purpose, oriented toward values and striving to realize them, the purity of a strictly natural science would be contaminated. True research and the hope for significant advance lie in turning away from teleology toward purpose-free physical science. And all this in spite of the fact that the one first-rate contribution to psychology in this century, that of Freud, sprang from a precisely opposite assumption.

If we may hope for the time when physical scientists will no longer downgrade the mind, we may perhaps also hope for a day when psychologists cease to apologize for their minds. When they write an article or an argument, they are surely aware that their purpose has determined the course of their thought, and this knowledge is more certain than any theory that would make their thought the mirror or by-product of a hypothetical and purposeless process in their brains. When they find themselves acting for the good or the hurt of another, they may be more certain that they are acting for some purpose—even if they may be mistaken as to what it is—than they are of any theory of the conservation of energy or matter (assuming these still to be distinct) that would veto this kind of action. In holding to the existence and efficacy of consciousness they are not being naive or rash; the rashness pertains rather to those who would deny the obvious in the interest of a speculative theory. A generation ago G. E. Moore, in his "Defense of Common Sense," brought the metaphysicians up short by asking them whether they were more certain that time and space were unreal than that they were writing a sentence on paper spread out in space before them and taking a minute or two to do it. Have we not a similar right to ask the metaphysicians of science whether they are really more certain that the energy in the physical universe remains in exact balance than that they have sometimes decided successfully to stand up or sit down. Such questions tend to put our "certainties" in a better order of priority.

I am not, of course, opposing metaphysics; far from it. But I follow Hume in thinking that human nature is the best launching pad for metaphysics, and that we should not, in the interest of ulterior conclusions, distort the facts about it at the outset. And those facts are not what scientific naturalism would have us think they are. In human nature as we know it at first hand, our thinking, feeling and acting are suffused with purpose; our reasoning at its best is under controls of which empirical science knows nothing; our processes of creation in art and literature are, so to speak, Aristotelian processes, not Newtonian, in which that which is coming to be somehow determines the course of its own fulfillment; actions may be genuinely obligatory and our sense of this may bring them about. These processes cannot be understood, or even properly studied, by a science whose model is physics.

In short, as was suggested at the beginning, science is at a crossroad. Either it should reconceive its program so that it can deal with the facts of mind, or, admitting that these facts fall beyond its province, it should cheer the birth of a more humane and sensitive discipline that can deal with them as they are.

NOTES

1. *Readings in the Philosophy of Science*, Herbert Feigl and May Brodbeck, ed. (New York, Appleton-Century-Crofts, 1936), p. 11.
2. *Ibid.*, pp. 104–105; italics in text.
3. John B. Watson, *Behaviorism* (Chicago, the University of Chicago Press, 1958), p. 6.
4. John B. Watson and W. McDougall, *The Battle of Behaviorism* (New York and London, 1928), p. 26.
5. Brand Blanshard, *The Nature of Thought*, (New York, Humanities Press, Inc.), V. I, ch. 9.
6. *Philosophy of Science*, V. I (1936), p. 4.
7. Alfred J. Ayer, *Language, Truth and Logic* (Gloucester, Peter Smith, Publisher), pp. 203, 202.
8. R. G. Collingwood, *The Idea of History* (ed. T. M. Knox) (Oxford, Clarendon Press, 1946), pp. 308ff.
9. B. F. Skinner, *Science and Human Behavior* (New York, The Macmillan Co.), p. 30.
10. *Ibid.*, p. 30.
11. *Ibid.*, p. 35.
12. B. Blanshard and B. F. Skinner, "The Problem of Consciousness: A Debate," *Philosophy and Phenomenological Research*, Vol. XXVII, No. 3 (March, 1967), p. 329.
13. Cf the following from Lord Brain: ". . . as regards the physical events occurring in the nervous system we have at present only the most elementary knowledge of them at comparatively simple levels of organization, and none at all of the ultimate physical basis of thinking, willing, and remembering." J. R. Smythies (ed.), *Brain and Mind*, 54.
14. Lord Adrian in *Body, Mind, and Death*, A. Flew ed., (New York, The Macmillan Co., 1964) p. 234.
15. *Science and Human Behavior*, p. 81.
16. *Ibid.*, pp. 70, 71.

17. E. M. Adams, "Mind and the Language of Psychology," *Ratio*, Vol. IX, No. 2 (December, 1967), p. 127.

18. *Cf* his *In Defense of Freedom*, pp. 243–275.

19. U. T. Place, "Consciousness is Just Brain Processes," in *Body, Mind, and Death*, p. 278.

20. J. J. C. Smart, "Colours," *Philosophy*, Vol. XXXVI, No. 137 (April–July, 1961), p. 141. I have abbreviated the illustration in a way that I hope does not obscure the principle.

21. Smart, *op. cit.*, p. 283.

22. C. D. Broad, *Mind and Its Place in Nature* (New York, Humanities Press, Inc.), p. 476.

23. B. F. Skinner, *Cumulative Record*, (New York, Appleton-Century-Crofts, 1959), p. 34.

CAN THERE BE A SCIENCE OF HUMAN BEHAVIOR?

(A RESPONSE)

Richard Taylor

I should like to defend Professor Blanshard in one claim—his central one—but wish to reject another claim that underlies all of his remarks. I believe he is correct in maintaining that there can be no scientific knowledge of man in terms of those criteria of scientific knowledge prevailing in the physical sciences and in experimental psychology. If, on the other hand, the expression "scientific knowledge" is a redundancy, that is to say, if by science we simply mean knowledge, as we should, then quite obviously there can be a scientific knowledge of man because there is.

For example, if the historian asserts that the German command halted the attack of the German army on the British expeditionary forces and thus inadvertently enabled them to escape across the channel from Dunkirk, and that the German command did this in order to provide greater participation for the German air force, and if what the historian says is true, then the historian has explained a complicated specimen of human behavior. But in a clear sense it is not a scientific explanation. It is an explanation in terms of purpose. Again, if I explain the behavior of protestors by saying they are trying to influence administrative decisions, and if my statement is true, I have explained this behavior up to a point. But it is not a scientific explanation in the way in which these explanations are now conceived. It is an explanation in terms of the purposes of the protestors. Or, to take the simplest example of all, if one explains why a given man raises his hand on given occasions, and the explanation is that he did this in order to attract the speaker's attention, he has given an explanation of the man's behavior but, again, it is an explanation in terms of purpose. These are not, to be sure, complete explanations in the sense that nothing more could be added, but explanations seldom are. That is, even the simplest explanations in terms of causation rather than purpose are seldom complete in that sense. If a fire is explained in terms of the ignition of a match, it is explained, though of course not completely.

The examples I've cited are all explanations in terms of agents' purposes, that is, in terms of what Aristotle calls final causes. They are not scientific in the narrow sense described by Professor Blanshard. They are not the kind ever admitted into physics at all or into experimental psychology. But in the proper sense of science, which is simply knowledge, they are explanations, because they are things that are sometimes known and they are explanatory. I shall return to that point later.

What I reject in Professor Blanshard's account is the supposition made throughout that such explanations as these refute materialism. In other words, that they show that men have minds; that human behavior is sometimes explained by a causal influence of men's minds on their bodies; that nonmaterial events or processes in men's minds or souls provide causal explanations of human behavior. The issue here is not between materialism and psychophysical dualism, it is not a conflict between two ontologies. What is at issue is not, as Professor Blanshard appears to assume, whether men have minds as well as bodies, whether there are such things as thoughts, purposes, ideas, etc. It is rather a conflict between two rival types of explanation, roughly, explanations in terms of causes on the one hand and reasons on the other, or in older terminology between efficient and final causes. This issue can be discussed with complete neutrality as regards materialism versus psychophysical dualism and similar theories. Thus I shall maintain that we can assume materialism to be true, so far as anything pointed out by Professor Blanshard is concerned. That is, none of his data or arguments really cast doubt upon materialism, meaning by this, in this context, that a man, or a person if you like, is a physical being and nothing else. I shall maintain, first, that a man is not a mind, not a composite of mind and body, and that a man does not in any literal sense have a mind. And I wish, secondly, to maintain that Professor Blanshard is nevertheless dead right in maintaining that behaviorism, epiphenomenalism, and the other theories of human nature associated with contemporary experimental psychology are fundamentally and drastically wrong. The error consists, not in affirming materialism, but in assuming that the only kind of explanation of human behavior that is allowable or scientific is the kind of explanation appropriate in the physical sciences; that the explanation, to be scientific, must be scientific in the narrow sense that he describes: or, that the only acceptable explanations are causal explanations.

It seems to me that even Professor Blanshard falls into what I regard as an error here, when he appears to suppose that it is an explanation of a man's behavior to say that behavior is *caused* by events and processes transpiring in his mind. Actually, the type of explanation he repeatedly cites is not explanation in terms of causes at all, but in terms of reasons, of final causes, ends, or purposes. Thus, he gave a page or two of what he calls a budget of paradoxes, citing what he took to be absurd implications of the theories he criticized. He said, for example, that Albert Schweitzer's purpose in serving the African needy had nothing causally to do with his going to Africa, any more than Hitler's purpose in liquidating the Jews had any effects in the way of death and misery; the desire of a youth for education never leads him to go to college; nor his desire for a girl, to propose to her; nor his desire to win a race, to enter a contest, or to run faster. These remarks Professor Blanshard regards as absurd. I regard them as false, but I would like to suggest that they should not be construed as causal explanations in the first place. Every one of them is an explanation in terms of reasons or purposes. It was Albert Schweitzer's *purposes* that led him to behave as he did; likewise, for the youth, Hitler, and so forth.

Now I should like to show by means of a simple illustration what I think is the difference between explanation by causes and explanation by reasons. I have used the example before. It is the example of a little old lady who is part of an assembly line in a factory, and her job is to thread needles as they go by her. She is quite skilled at this, getting the thread through the needle about nine times out of ten. But then let us suppose that due to a disagreement with her employer or to her desire to frustrate his purposes and perhaps get higher wages, she begins missing *on purpose*. Now she gets the needle through only four times out of ten on the average, let's say, and she does this on purpose. She is dissimulating, pretending to put the thread through the needle but missing on purpose. Now we have, in the description I gave, an explanation of her behavior, of why she is missing; she is trying to, she is doing it on purpose. She has a purpose, an ulterior motive, which she serves by this deliberate behavior. It seems to me the example is quite clear.

Let us now suppose that the lady is replaced by a machine which is to thread the needles as they go by, and it, too, works quite efficiently. It gets the thread through nine times out of ten. But then let us suppose that the machine starts missing. Like the old lady, it now gets the thread through the needle about four times out of ten. Can any sense be made of the suggestion that the machine is missing on purpose? Obviously not. If the machine misses it is because of mechanical defects in the machine. Two machines could not be built which would behave in exactly the same way, i.e., which would miss six times out of ten, one doing so on purpose and the other simply because it needs adjustment. I can think of no description which would distinguish one such machine from another. No matter how differently they were constructed, nothing would ever emerge to suggest which one was the one that was missing on purpose. There *is* a difference between a human agent who merely misses and one who misses on purpose, in terms of my example. This difference cannot be expressed, so far as I can see, in the terminology of physical science, it cannot be described in the language of causality. But there is no difference between (a) a machine which misses and (b) one which misses on purpose. The latter expression has no meaning that I can discover in terms of mechanics.

Note, however, that explanation in terms of purposes or reasons is perfectly consistent with the denial that human agents have minds. That is to say, the difference between the machine and the lady is not that the lady has a certain something that the machine lacks, namely a mind. Giving the machine a mind would not convert it to a purposeful object; it would still be a machine. What is at issue is not whether men do or do not have minds, but rather what kind of explanation is explanatory of human behavior. Professor Blanshard is right in maintaining that human behavior cannot be explained within the framework of mechanics, nor within the framework of science, if we must presuppose that purposeful explanations are nonscientific ones, (which we need not presuppose if science means simply knowledge). I do not believe he is justified in concluding, on the basis of this terribly important point, that materialism is false, that is, that men have minds. This I think is not even a significant issue.

I shall now address myself independently to the issue of materialism. Let us assume for the sake of discussion that materialism is true; that is, that a human being, a man, or a person, is a visible, palpable being, a physical object—though we must *not* add here, "just like any other physical object." Now my question is, In the light of that assumption, do any of the obviously true observations by Professor Blanshard concerning consciousness, thoughts, purposes, ideas, images, sensations, pains, etc., cast doubt upon the assumption? I think they do not, for they are correct observations concerning the states and capacities of men. Such men can still be assumed to be visible, palpable beings, that is to say, physical objects.

I shall give some examples. Instead of saying, for instance, that a given man has an image of something, and that "imagining" means that he possesses or is aware of a nonmaterial thing called a mental image, say, instead, that he imagines something, and let him be a material object, namely a man. It seems to me that that is exactly what the

first sentence says, and that the second one does not imply his possession of a nonmaterial thing called "an image." It implies an act or a
state, namely that of imagining something. Again, instead of saying A's
raising his hand is caused by his purpose of getting the speaker's attention—a type of locution which Professor Blanshard sometimes uses
when he speaks of purposes as causing men to do things—I suggest we
say instead, A raised his hand in order to get the speaker's attention. In
that locution we can suppose A to be a material object, that is, a man,
who is a visible, palpable being. Then, instead of saying, A is possessed
of consciousness—and understanding consciousness to be a nonphysical
mental process in A's mind—I suggest we can say instead, A is a conscious being, and let A again be a visible palpable being, that is to say, a
man. Being conscious will then be a state of that corporeal man and in
this sense a physical state. That is, it will be the state of a physical object, but not a physical state "just like any other," as one might sometimes be tempted to add. This last type of expression, in which I substitute "A is a conscious being" for the expression "A is possessed of consciousness," can be treated, I suggest, in exactly the same way as "A is
possessed of life." Such a statement was once understood in philosophy
to mean that A (whether A be a man or, let us say, an insect) is a physical being possessed of something nonphysical which quickens it or
makes it living. Plato and Aristotle often spoke that way. But of course,
as everyone now recognizes, to say that A is possessed of life is simply
equivalent to saying that A is a living being, and A can be a material object such as an insect or, we can suppose, a man. Being living or being
alive can thus be understood as being in a certain state. And since this
can be understood as a state of a visible, palpable object, such as a fly or
a beetle, then, in that sense, it is a physical state. But we must *not* add,
"just like any other physical state."

SOME PROBLEMS ABOUT THINKING

Gilbert Ryle

I want to try to thrash out some questions about thinking. But let me say from the start, I am not concerned directly with questions about belief or the having of opinions. To say that someone thinks that so and so is the case is nearly equivalent to saying that he believes it or is of that opinion; but to say this is not at all like saying of him that he is now thinking, e.g., now pondering, calculating, meditating, or weighing the *pros* and *cons*. Some languages, like French, Italian, German, and Latin, are conveniently equipped with quite different verbs for the two sorts of things. We have some verbs with which we can repel ambiguity. Pondering is cogitating, not being convinced. Rodin's statue is of *le Penseur*, i.e., of a pondering or pensive man, not of a credulous man or a man who has made up his mind about something. I shall be partly concerned with what pondering or being pensive consists in, what is going on when a person is occupied in thinking or, if you like, what he is doing that the telephone-bell interrupts, when he is sitting on a rock, perhaps with knitted brows and chin in hand and, according to the cinematograph camera, doing nothing at all. *What* is *le Penseur* busy over or absorbed in?

There is one sweeping answer that is constantly given to this question; it was given by Plato, in his *Sophist*, and it is often given now. It is said that the pensive man is saying things to himself, silently perhaps, or under his breath, or even aloud. Nowadays this answer is sometimes put by saying that Thought is Language. But this is a very bad way of putting it. What the pensive man is engaged in cannot be the English language or the French language. It might be that what he is engaged in is saying things to himself in English words, phrases, and sentences. Similarly when I was telephoning this morning my telephoning was not the English language; I was telephoning things *in* a few bits of the Eng-

lish language. But even this amended equation is almost totally false. A
person who is not thinking may be saying things in his head or *sotto
voce* or aloud; two persons whose thoughts are very different may be saying things to themselves in the same English words and sentences; and
we may be thinking while not saying anything at all to ourselves in English or in any other tongue. Saying things to oneself is neither a sufficient nor even a necessary condition of thinking; nor, if we do know
what someone has been saying to himself, does this knowledge by itself
suffice for us to know what thinking he has been doing, if any. I shall,
in a moment, substantiate this threefold negative point. But I do hold
that there are levels or dimensions or kinds of thinking where one cannot be operating without working with bits of a language, or of something analogous to language. In the severest sense of the word 'Reason',
at least some exercises of Reason, since they embody argumentation, do
require talking or writing or something analogous to them. Indeed one
of my objectives is to make this special connection intelligible. But I
cannot do this until I have disposed of the overly fashionable practice of
equating thinking with saying things to oneself. So let me now
substantiate my assertion that saying things to oneself is neither a
sufficient nor a necessary condition of thinking.

(1) The delirious man babbles strings of, say, English words and
phrases, but, being delirious, he is not thinking what he is saying. He
is saying things without attention, intention, or control. He is not selecting his words and phrases, amending them, recapitulating them, mar-
shalling them, organizing them into answers to questions, rebuttals of
objections, contributions to a conversation, etc. His utterances are not in
aid of anything. He is not thinking any more than I would be if I had a
jingle or a catch-phrase running through my head while I was, in fact,
completely occupied with other things. The child who, knowing no
French, sings herself to sleep with "Sur le pont d'Avignon" is not thinking thoughts answering to what her words would convey to a French lis-
tener. Nor, surely, does the hawker perpend his commercial offer the
thousandth time he cries "Who'll buy my sweet lavender?" Must the
actor, on the thousandth night, be considering whether it is better to be
or not to be? Things merely babbled, echoed, or uttered by rote are, in a
thin sense, "said"; but their utterers are not thinking what they are saying, and so they are either not thinking at all, or are thinking thoughts
that have nothing to do with what their words do or might convey.

(2) Half a dozen people might have said to themselves "Thirteen
squared is one hundred and seventy nine." Primus was formulating the
result of a piece of miscalculation. Secundus, on oath in the witness box,
was garbling the last words of the murdered man. Tertius was mistrans-

lating a German sentence. Quartus, a Frenchman, was trying, unsuccessfully, to pronounce these eight English words. Quintus, an actor, was idly rehearsing some of his words, yet still needed prompting on the opening night. Sextus, a schoolmaster, was sarcastically denouncing Primus' miscalculation, but was taken by the class to be giving the right answer. All were thinking what they were saying; all of them made mistakes which they regretted afterwards. But their mistakes were entirely different mistakes, and only one of them was an arithmetical mistake. They were all trying, with attention and intention, to accomplish tasks; but they were six different tasks and their subsequent self-reproaches were for completely different lapses and failures.

(3) The composer at the piano is in a brown study; after long or short pauses he tentatively taps out short sequences of notes on the keys; some of these he rejects altogether and does not repeat; others he repeats once or twice with modifications. He is trying to solve his composer's problem; he considers alternatives; he selects and rejects candidate-sequences, and does so for reasons; he retains and recapitulates and later strings together the successful candidates and then carefully practises these strings. Surely he is thinking. He is experimenting with full concentration, trying out, comparing, discarding, selecting, collecting, organizing, reorganizing, rehearsing and so on. If called to the telephone, he can non-metaphorically complain that his thinking has been interrupted. But must he have been saying anything to himself? What is there that he must have been saying? How could music be composed in English or in Latin? When baffled, was it for the right word or sentence that he was vainly searching? When successful, had he hit on a desired epigram, epithet, alliteration, metaphor, or enthymeme? Do we appraise his completed concerto by phonetic, literary, rhetorical, or logical standards? I may be more fluent and precise in English prose than he is, but I cannot compose music or evaluate what he composes.

Consider the child with a jigsaw puzzle. He has five pieces unplaced, and he is trying to fill a particular vacancy. He rejects pieces A and B at sight, since A is obviously much too big and B much too small. He looks twice at C, but its outlines are curvilinear, while those of the gap are nearly rectilinear. He tentatively picks up D, and rotates it over the vacancy, but it won't go. He then quite untentatively picks up piece E, turns it around and inserts it into its niche.

What *must* he have said to himself? He knows no geometry, but if he did Euclid provides no names for these irregular shapes. He has no measuring appliances, but if he had he could not determine in square millimetres the exact surface areas of the jagged or blobby pieces and vacancies. While he is still baffled, could we grown-ups help him in any degree by supplying him with geometrical dictions or dimensions? Would we ourselves use these dictions while we were trying to solve the jigsaw puzzle? Notice that even we cannot continue trying to solve the puzzle when the light goes out. Yet this darkness does not impair our ability to say to ourselves whatever we want to say, but only our ability to scan the pieces, pick them up, and compare them visually with the vacancy. On behalf of my composer some sentimental and over-philosophical aestheticians will probably say, quite falsely, that music is a language, though not, of course, one in which we can ask what day of the week it is or into which we can translate Gibbon's *Decline and Fall of the Roman Empire*. But even they would not be so hardy as to say that jigsaw puzzle pieces are bits of a language, any more than are the tiles that the builder is trying to fit into my bathroom floor.

A young chess player is deliberating what move to make. If this deliberating reduces to saying things to himself, why does he keep his eyes on the board and make alternative hypothetical moves first with his Bishop and then with his Queen between his fingers and thumb? Is he only fidgeting with them? Then why can he not decide what move to make if forbidden to fidget? He himself, if asked by his opponent whether he is making his move, will reply, with his fingers still round his Bishop, "No, not yet—I am still thinking what move to make."

You have tied a clove-hitch. Wanting to learn how to tie a clove-hitch, I cautiously undo yours, step by step, repeatedly restoring each turn or twist that I undo so that at the end I may assemble, in due sequence, all the turns and twists that culminate in a clove-hitch. Surely I am thinking. I am not fiddling absent-mindedly and I am not attending to anything else. The telephone bell is a vexatious distraction, which requires me to start again from the beginning. To me knots are difficult things to think out. But there is nothing for me to say to myself that is of any use. Indeed, even when I have mastered the knot, I am still flummoxed by your challenge to describe it, and while I was still trying to master it, I could have learned a lot from just watching your slow-motion demonstration of the requisite finger-movements, but nothing or next to nothing from your verbal description of it.

I need give no further illustrations. Once we begin, we can all go on and think of dozens, hundreds of occupations for which the agent certainly qualifies as thinking, pondering, wondering, puzzling, experimenting, inventing, checking, avoiding, eliminating, selecting, comparing, and so on, though he need not be, and often cannot be, saying anything to himself, or at least anything that is of any use.

So let us dismiss the sweeping equation of Thought with Language, or, better put, of all thinking with saying things to oneself.

·　　·　　·　　·

I want now to make a new start. You understood me when I said that the delirious man is not thinking what he is saying, nor is the actor nor the English child singing the French song. This use of the verb "to think" goes just as well with doings as with sayings. The absent-minded professor crossing the street is not thinking what he is doing. He is walking athwart two traffic-streams, but he is not attending to the traffic. He is not trying to avoid it. If he crosses unscathed it is by luck and not by his good management. He is perhaps totally absorbed in the implications of Gödel's Theorem. In tying my shoelaces each morning I am not thinking what I am doing. I don't have to be now, though I did once. I can tie them automatically now, while chatting to some-one else about the Test Match. But I have to think even now when my fingers are sticky or numb and then I stop chatting about the Test Match. The committee-member who doodles on the blotting paper is not thinking what he is doing with his pencil. He is surprised to find what is on the blotting paper when the meeting ends. He had not meant or decided to depict a giraffe on the top of a pyramid, nor consid-ered how best to depict this unlikely scene. I daresay that the newspaper cartoonist who has drawn a hundred cartoons of de Gaulle hardly thinks what he is doing with his pencil while churning out another de Gaulle nose. But you and I usually do think what we are doing when we cross busy roads or try to draw cartoons of de Gaulle. Even my after-dinner speeches have not become mechanical by constant repetition, and your contributions to ordinary conversations are not, with a few exceptions, totally predictable, even if they are not, with a few exceptions, especially surprising.

Well then, what is the difference between doing or saying some-thing, thinking what one is doing or saying, and doing or saying it ab-sent-mindedly, mechanically, frantically, or deliriously? The absent-minded professor is not, but I usually am, paying attention in crossing a busy street; and the cartoonist, with an unhackneyed subject, is, while the doodler is not, trying his best, or at least trying a bit to produce a recognizable picture of someone in particular—the Prime Minister per-haps. Let us stick to the cartoonist. He is attending to what he is doing with his pencil, and is therefore not attending, or not attending much to anything else. He wants his drawing to capture features which the Prime Minister has and de Gaulle and Nasser and you and I have not. So he either avoids inscribing lines and dots which won't do, or having inscribed them, he rubs them out and puts in new ones. All the time he, unlike the doodler, is fending off possible, and correcting actual faults and failures. There is something quite specific to get right, and so there are countless quite specific defects to avoid or repair. In a word, he has to draw with some degree of care—not just feeling some vague anxiety, but taking quite specific precautions against quite specific mistakes and inadequacies.

Trying to get things right as opposed to wrong, adequate as opposed to inadequate, that is, trying to avoid or repair mistakes and deficiencies is nowadays sometimes classified as being "rule-governed"—a rule being nothing more or less than what a fault, mistake, or inadequacy is a breach of or lapse from. The phrase "rule-governed" is rather a stuffy one and suggests a lot of inappropriate things, so I shall avoid it. But there is one important thing that the phrase is properly meant to cover, namely, that for a person to avoid or correct a particular kind of fault or lapse he must already have learned and not forgotten what it is to get that sort of thing right. The unschooled Red Indian cannot avoid or correct mistakes of multiplication or spelling, for he has not learned how to multiply or spell. He can neither solve nor mis-solve problems in multiplication or in spelling. He cannot even be baffled by them. Similarly, I cannot keep or therefore even break any of the rules of Chinese grammar or pronunciation, for I cannot even try to say anything in Chinese. If I happen to make a noise which sounds to a Chinaman like a Chinese word, I have not succeeded in bringing this off, any more than the casual stone-thrower has succeeded in hitting the flying wasp which his stone does actually hit. He was not aiming at it, so there was no question of his aim being good or bad. He was just chucking.

In brief, for a person to try to so and so, he must have learned in some measure, however small, the *how* of so and so-ing, and he must, therefore, have learned in some measure what not to do and what, if done, to cancel or to repair. Trying to so and so involves taking at least a little care, and taking care involves knowingly avoiding faults, risks, and inadequacies. To be here and now trying to ø involves here and now applying already learned lessons in the how of ø-ing and therefore in the major how-not-to's of ø-ing. It is to exercise just a bit of expertness.

But this is not the whole story about trying to so and so, though contemporary philosophers sometimes speak as if the notion of rule-observance does contain the whole story. For I may have learned and not forgotten some bits of French grammar, and for weeks and weeks I make no grammatical mistakes; but I have kept my record clean by the indolent expedient of never embarking on a French remark. I have indeed made no mistakes, but I have not got anything right either. My knowledge of French grammar has been kept in the refrigerator. I use or exercise my knowledge of French grammar only if I say or write something in French. That is, I must both initiate a bit of French talk and control its construction, pronunciation, etc. For an acquired expertness to be exercised and not merely possessed, it must be *exercised*. Similarly, a shipowner might ensure that his ship never struck a rock by not letting his ship set sail. It then never sails into trouble, but also it never sails anywhere. If his ship is to sail for a destination, it must both set sail and be steered. It must both have actual wind in its sails and have a rudder that is being actually employed and a chart that is being actually read and followed.

So the notion of trying to so and so involves the two distinguishable, but not separable features of (1) essaying, undertaking, launching, initiating, or making a positive move; and of (2) care, circumspection, control, steering, or trouble-avoidance. To be actually playing chess I must both make positive moves and make them in accordance with the already learned rules of the game.

I suggest, therefore, that, unlike the absent-minded professor or the delirious man, a person qualifies as thinking what he is doing or saying just insofar as he is trying to so and so, e.g., trying to cross the busy road unscathed, or trying to take his proper part in the conversation. If he has both embarked on doing or saying something, and is doing or saying it with some degree of attention, intention, and care, then he is thinking what he is doing or saying; he is giving his partly trained mind to his task. His little ship has both set sail for a destination and is being steered clear of at least some already charted hazards. To think what one is doing is both to do something, and to do it with at least minimal circumspection.

Next, though to describe someone as doing X with care is to say more than just that he is doing X, it is not to say that he is doing more things, e.g., that he is doing X and also doing Y. Certainly, if I drive with a song, I am doing two things, either of which I could stop doing while continuing the other. But if I drive with care, this is not so. My driving-care cannot be exercised after I have stopped driving or before I have started. As the word "carefully" is an adverb, so taking care is, so to speak, adverbial upon some positive activity like driving or climbing or drawing. The order "Take care" cannot be obeyed or disobeyed by itself, any more than the orders "Persevere," "Obey" and "Concentrate."

There are many notions commonly conveyed by active verbs which in the same generic way, though in very different specific ways, are, so to speak, adverbial notions. You cannot hurry, start, hesitate, stop, shirk, attempt, or obey unless there is some non-adverbial action that is done hurriedly or obediently or some non-adverbial action that you start, continue or stop, hesitate over, attempt, shirk or stick to. Unless some non-adverbial action, like running, knitting, or reading is implicitly given, you cannot obey or disobey an order like "hurry," "slow down," "begin" or "stop," for such an imperative does not by itself convey an order to do something or not to do something in particular. To say "For 10 minutes he was just concentrating" or "just shirking" is nonsense. We can do things reluctantly, vigilantly or obstinately, but there are no autonomous, non-adverbial actions of reluctating, vigilating, or obstinating. So, although crossing the road thinking what one is doing is very different from crossing it absent-mindedly, it is still not doing two separate things, as the man who drives with a song is doing two separately do-able or autonomous things. Walking circumspectly is not doing a bit of walking and also doing a bit of circumspecting, any more than sloping arms obediently is doing a bit of rifle-drill and also doing a separately do-able bit of obeying. Your obeying *is* your sloping arms when ordered by the right N.C.O., on parade, and so on. You obey by sloping arms.

So, though you really are thinking what you are doing, on the road, the tennis court, or at the tea party, you are not, on that account, sandwiching some separately do-able bits of thinking between some bits of steering, volleying, or chatting. You are moving or talking purposively, alertly, pertinently, etc., but you are not, on that account, doing any bits, however fleeting, of what, by contrast, *Le Penseur* really is engaged in. You do not even momentarily look pensive, for you are not even momentarily being pensive. Indeed, you will complain when interrupted, not that your thinking had been interrupted, but that your driving, tennis-playing, or conversing had been interrupted. Or, if asked what you were doing when the clock struck, you would not say, as *le Penseur* would, that you had been thinking, or meditating, but rather that you had been making a remark or changing gear or returning a volley. Of course you would not mind adding, if asked, that you had changed gear on purpose, at the right moment and for a reason, or that you had not made your remark or your return absent-mindedly or mechanically. You had had your wits about you, but you had not exercised your wits in pondering, but, say, in changing gear. You had judged or perhaps misjudged things, but you had not come out with any considered or ill-considered judgments. You had only made, say, some well- or ill-timed strokes.

So now we need to confront head on the contrast between this adverbial notion of thinking what one is doing and the non-adverbial or autonomous notion of thinking or pondering which we employ when we say that what *le Penseur* is engaged in is thinking or pondering. For the sake of brevity I am often going to use the verbs "to reflect" and "to meditate" for what *le Penseur* is doing and what the tennis-player, say, need not be doing and most of the time had better not be doing, since in doing so he would be switching his attention from the tennis juncture to something else. I shall, rather artificially, use these verbs, 'to reflect' and 'to meditate', for all such things as pondering, wondering, weighing pros and cons, musing, calculating, deliberating, etc., i.e., for all varieties of pensiveness.

We need to bear in mind that there are many varieties of pensiveness. For all we can tell from his appearance *le Penseur* may be trying to compose a poem or a piece of music; he may be trying to prove a theorem, solve an anagram, or work out a multiplication sum; he may be going over the events of his distant schooldays; he may be dreaming up new ways to live if he should come into a fortune; he may be trying to run through the Greek alphabet backwards from Omega to Alpha; he may just be brooding over an insult; he may be debating implications of Gödel's Theorem; and so on. If the telephone rings during any one of these occupations, he will say that his thoughts have been interrupted, unless he has been, as he might have been, too much absorbed in his thoughts to notice the bell. Here the reflecting or meditating does seem to be a non-adverbial, autonomous activity. The schoolmaster can tell his pupil to think, e.g., to worry the problem out, as he cannot tell him just to pay heed or just to persevere or just to concentrate or just to obey or just to hurry.

Very often, though not quite always, a person engaged in reflecting is trying to solve a problem or accomplish a task. His reflecting can be successful or unsuccessful, and if unsuccessful, he may arrive at the wrong answer or he may not find an answer at all; he may remain baffled. Indeed Rodin's *le Penseur* does look as if he is at least for the moment baffled, unable to make any headway.

For some sorts of reflecting, such as computing and anagram-solving, there exist procedures a thorough drilling in which enables us to make sure of solving a problem if we only work patiently enough. For other sorts of reflecting, such as those of a detective, a judge, or a composer, while no drill suffices, there is training, including self-training. The young barrister cannot yet think like an Appeal Court Judge; but he will quite likely be able to do so in twenty years time.

That is to say, to reflect, no less than to play tennis, at least often involves trying, i.e., attention, intention, and the exploitation of learned hows. The delirious or the absent-minded man cannot now be computing, composing, or deliberating between rival policies any more than he can now be playing chess or tennis or translating from Latin into English. *Le Penseur* in reflecting, no less than the tennis-player in playing, must be in some measure, however small, operating with initiative, care, patience, pertinacity, and interest. *Le Penseur* must also be thinking what he is doing. He cannot reflect without exercising his somewhat trained wits. He cannot be an absolute beginner. Reflecting is also an exercise of an expertness or of several expertnesses. But—and this seems to me a real crux-question—*what* is he doing, such that if he were doing it deliriously, absent-mindedly, or merely by rote, he would no more qualify as reflecting than his counterpart on the tennis court would qualify as playing tennis, or his counterpart at the piano would qualify as trying to compose a rhapsody? On the tennis court a maniac or a sleepwalker might make a move or stroke as like as you please to a tactically shrewd move or stroke made by an alert tennis player on the defensive at a critical stage of his game. But what moves or strokes are made purposively, shrewdly, and warily by *le Penseur*, which, if concussed or crazy, he might have made without any attention, intention, or wariness? *What* is he doing experimentally and self-censoriously which, if he had been drugged or exhausted, he might have done vacantly, unexperimentally, and uncensoriously?

Well, if *le Penseur* were a composer, he might be whistling or humming some notes, aloud or under his breath, and, by chance, just such notes might have been whistled or hummed by him when concussed, and therefore when not trying to complete a near-finished rhapsody.

The dummy-moves that the deliberating chess-player makes, Bishop in hand, when considering the *pros* and *cons* of alternative ways of meeting the threat of his opponent's Queen, could, by chance, all have been made by a fidgeting boy who does not know the game at all. Or the very words uttered aloud or spoken silently to himself by Euclid while trying to prove a theorem might be uttered tomorrow by his parrot or his tape-recorder, neither of which is doing geometry.

Consider now the town-planning architect sitting on a hill above the town-section that he is to reshape. Can he weigh the *pros* and *cons* of alternative arrangements like the chess-player or the jigsaw puzzle player by physically picking up the warehouse, the canal, or the cattle-pens and experimentally making dummy-transfers of them? Can he, with fingers and thumb, experimentally transplant meadows and shopping-centers? Obviously not. They are too big and unwieldy for him to pick up and manipulate. But give him some little plastic toys and a small board, and now he can do his planning, since he can pick these up and shift them around, try ideas out, and reject or accept them, coordinate them, and so on. Now too he can exhibit to the dim-witted Mayor and Corporation his two or three alternative plans without having to find nursery topographical dictions simple and graphic enough for them to follow.

Or give to the lad, who can cope well with ordinary jigsaw puzzles, a jigsaw puzzle the size of a football field with pieces which are as big as carpets and too heavy to lift. Why can he not begin to solve this Goliath-like jigsaw puzzle? Obviously because the pieces are not all under his nose, and are not manipulable by his unaided fingers. He cannot toy with them, i.e., make tentative moves with them. Or consider the plight of the would-be composer who owing to bronchitis cannot hum or whistle and has no piano. All he has is a regimental brass band a hundred yards away, which is ready and anxious to produce whatever notes he wants to try out, reject, rearrange, etc., if only he will send it written messages saying what he wants. Or consider, lastly, the artist, who while in prison is trying to design a complex mural pattern. Lacking paper, palette, blackboard, etc., he draws his tentative lines in the mist that he breathes on the window pane. But these lines evaporate almost as soon as they are made. Why is it that he can excogitate his design by drawing, erasing, and redrawing pencil lines on paper, but not by drawing, erasing, and redrawing evanescent lines on the ephemerally misted glass? Obviously because what he has put down does not stay put. His lines are not there a second later to be reconsidered, corrected, or linked to other lines.

Some reflecting, then, requires that the thinker be producing and experimentally toying with things which are under his control or at his absolute beck and call. They are there when he wants them, they will go just where he wants them to go and just when he wants them to go there, and they will stay where he wants them to stay. His moves are hardly at all conditioned by recalcitrant externalities, as the tennis-player's moves are conditioned by what someone else has done or is about to do, as well as by the wind, the puddles on the court, the net, the side-lines, etc. Unlike the tennis-player or the automobile driver, *le Penseur* produces for himself and controls the situations with which he is to cope. While the tennis-player and the driver are not, he is pretty well detached from what is going on outside his private field of action; pretty well detached, but not always completely detached. My composer at the piano is hindered a bit and perhaps totally obstructed if several of the piano keys stick or if his fingers are numbed or if the children are playing hide-and-seek in the music-room. But usually he can prevent such interferences occurring; usually he is not at the mercy of external circumstance, but is in full control of a working piano and working fingers and so has at his absolute beck and call the notes that he wants to produce, try out, cancel, modify, and coordinate.

It may be that *le Penseur* is engaged in composing not music but a poem, an after-dinner speech, or a letter. If so, then unlike the composer of music he is trying to find and arrange sequences of English or

French words and phrases. If the language of his composition is his own language, then he probably needs no such external aids as dictionaries. The words and phrases that he summons up, discards, selects, arranges, recapitulates, and rearranges come to him without much or any difficulty. Unless he is suffering from aphasia, he is in complete control of, so to speak, the "pieces" that he is mobilizing, testing, rejecting, and organizing. He need not even voice his candidate-words aloud or *sotto voce*. He can say them silently to himself, that is to say, he can merely imagine himself saying them aloud. If his memory is good he may not even need to write his words down on paper. So, too, the composer may manage without a piano and without even humming his notes aloud or under his breath. He may be just imagining himself playing or humming them. Similarly, the chess-player and the town-planning architect may be able to think up and compare their tentative projects by just visualizing in their minds' eyes the possible placings of their pieces or their buildings. These operations with merely visualized or imagined things are obviously 100% disengaged from recalcitrant external circumstances. Roughly, it does not matter to *le Penseur*, as it does to the tennis player or the driver, what is going on around him; it does not even matter whether his fingers are numb or his chest is bronchitic.

These varieties of reflecting are conditioned by no engagement with unaccommodating circumstance. Here *le Penseur* is doing specific things, like mobilizing and combining words or notes, though only in his head, and just these words or notes might have bobbed up randomly in his head without his trying to compose a poem or a speech, that is, in the absence of attention, intention, or control. Indeed they are apt so to bob up in the moments just before we fall asleep, when we are not trying to construct anything. For pretty much as the committee-member's fingers produce pictures or patterns on the blotting paper, so we often doodle—so to speak—when we say or hum things to ourselves, and a moment later have no idea what we have "done". For there was nothing that we had been trying to accomplish. Just as doodling, being unpurposed and uncontrolled, is not drawing, but, so to speak, a hangover from drawing; so merely saying things in our heads is not reflecting, but, so to speak, only a hangover from reflecting. The same thing can be true of the man at the piano who is fingering the keys while absorbed in the Test Match commentary on the radio. He is not composing; he is not even playing the piano, since there is nothing that he is trying to do on the piano, even though notes are being produced by his fingers. He too is just doodling or just fidgeting and not thinking what he is doing.

This, I suggest, answers my crux-question about reflecting or being pensive: *What* is *le Penseur* doing such that if he were doing it without attention, intention, or control, e.g., absent-mindedly, it would not amount to reflecting? He is, in a thin sense of the word, doing some such things as fingering the keys, humming notes aloud, under his breath, or in his head, producing words and word-strings aloud or *sotto voce* or in his head, plucking at a piece of knotted string, or inscribing lines and dots on the blotting paper. . . . All such "doings" are nearly or quite circumstance-disengaged, and all of them do rank as reflecting, planning, designing, composing etc., but only if the doing of them is attentive, intentional, and controlled by the already acquired knowledge of quite specific hows and how-not-to's, i.e., if *le Penseur* is thinking what he is doing, and not doing it absent-mindedly or by rote or frantically, etc.

But—and I am now drawing towards the end—you will feel inclined to grumble that so far as I have got there does not seem to be any great difference in principle between a non-verbal thing like composing music and a verbal thing like composing an after-dinner speech; between tackling a non-verbal jigsaw puzzle and tackling a verbal puzzle like an anagram; between deliberating between alternative chess moves, and deliberating between alternative English phrases. Yet surely people like Newton, Aristotle, and Euclid are entitled Thinkers for something more than thinking up rhymes or epigrams or pointed phrases. Granting that a Herrick, say, and a Kipling must be thinking and thinking well in order to compose their poems or their stories, still neither qualifies as a Thinker of Thoughts just for this. Surely the exercises of Reason, at least at its professional zenith, issue in Thoughts, in the sense in which the Thoughts of Herrick, if he had any, are not to be distilled out of his admirable poems; and the Thoughts of Kipling were few and poor ones, though his literary excellences were great and numerous. Rodin's *le Penseur* may indeed, for all that we can tell from his looks, be only trying to think up a poem, a speech, or a piece of music, but we rather hope that he is doing something different, namely, trying to think up a new theory or a new theorem. If successful, his success will, we hope, be a new truth, an addition to the corpus of human knowledge. Certainly this success, if it occurs, will require him usually, but only in an ancillary way, to formulate his new findings in, maybe, English words and sentences. But what he will have discovered will not itself be a literary felicity. Kant was a first-rate thinker, though he did not write very well; Hazlitt was a first-rate writer, but was not a great thinker. Thinking Thoughts does not reduce to, though it may require, thinking how to word things. The Thinker's achievements differ in kind or level from those of the writer. But the same man can be both; and the Thinker cannot be absolutely nothing of a writer.

Very brusquely I put the contrast in this way. The "pieces," so to speak, with which the writer of the oration experimentally and censoriously operates, are words and phrases. The pieces with which the Thinker of Thoughts experimentally and censoriously operates are full statements. He tries out, mobilizes, maneuvres, discards, and combines stated or statable truth-candidates or propositions. His proprietary acid tests are inconsistencies, non-sequiturs, contradictions, and irrelevances, and not just such things as dissonances, clichés, repetitiveness, and mixed metaphors. For what concerns us, the Thinker of Thoughts may be an astronomer, a historian, a mathematician, an economist, a philosopher, even, if you like, a theologian. What he presents to his colleagues, his critics, and to the world, whatever its literary or rhetorical excellences, is in their eyes a bad piece of work in so far as it does not capture or hold logical water.

This does not mean that Gibbon's pages are or should be like Euclid's pages, i.e., occupied largely or entirely by demonstrations and deductions; or that they are or should be like, say, Aristotle's or G. E. Moore's pages, occupied largely or entirely by *pro* and *contra* argumentation of the sort or sorts that are proprietary to philosophers. But it does mean that Gibbon's statements, to qualify as historical, need to be proof against historians' objections—aganst objections not to their literary defects, if any, but to their defects as items in a would-be true explanatory narrative. To show that it is unevidenced, under-evidenced, contrary to the evidence, irrelevant, in conflict with other parts of the narrative, and so on is to show that it is a historian's blunder, even if it is, at the same time, a writer's *tour de force*. To use a cant-phrase that I have so far avoided, however well "verbalized" Gibbon's thinking was, it was not a good historian's thinking unless it had merits of a different order as well, i.e., unless it was the thinking of a scrupulous and self-moving historical researcher. That his results should be well, rather than badly or drably stated is something; but that they should be the right and not the wrong things to state is cardinal. It is, I suggest, the ability to work according to success- *versus* failure-conditions of this latter sort that constitutes Reason, in its severest sense. If you say that this is platitudinous, I ask for no more encouraging epithet.

A PECULIAR KIND OF THINKING
(A RESPONSE)

Stuart Hampshire

I have one preliminary difficulty in replying to Professor Ryle's paper: that I agree with most, though not quite all of it, which is a disabling position to be in. But I have another difficulty as well: that I am not altogether clear about the problem which he has put as "what is going on when a person is thinking in the sense of pondering or meditating. What does pondering consist in?" I want to talk principally about this problem because I suspect that such differences as we have are over this notion.

What is *le Penseur*, he asks, absorbed in or busy over? Professor Ryle has no great difficulty in persuading me by examples that there will, in varying circumstances, be a bewildering variety of admissible answers to this very general question and that no simple and equally general answer could be adequate. In fact he persuades me of much more than this: that the question itself is not only too general but also wrongly put. The "what is going on when" formula suggests that the words "pondering" or "meditating" are verbs of performance, and so one looks for what are, as he puts it, the moves in this performance which are meditating and pondering. This is, I think, the wrong way to elucidate the notion, because these verbs do not stand for performances. And this is the point at which I think there is difference between us. I think that the formula "what is going on when," was introduced into the literature, or thought to be helpful, when people were concerned with an epistemological question; that is, with the question "how can we be in a position to know that someone is pondering and meditating": and more difficult, "how can we be in a position to know what he is pondering or meditating about?" It was in this context that we got stuck with the formula "what is going on when." It seemed useful to ask this question because the answer to it might reveal some signs, symptoms, or perceptual evidence that we use when we guess—as we

53

certainly do—or infer, or come to know, that someone is meditating, pondering or reflecting, and even when we guess or know what he is meditating about when he hasn't told us.

I am therefore going to approach the question of pondering and meditating in a different way, keeping the original "how can we know" question in mind. For I think that the philosophical problem about thinking, at any rate about this kind of thinking, is principally, though not only, an epistemological one. I want to say, and to say dogmatically —because time doesn't permit me to say it any other way—that pondering and meditating and reflecting are processes that are not open to the common view and that they are what we would ordinarily call inner processes. Given certain assumptions about knowledge, there is indeed a problem about how we can know what the direction and content of a man's meditations are: for example, can he, the meditator, *le Penseur*, make a mistake about the contents or substance of his own meditations, and if so, what kind or kinds of mistake? And if he can make a mistake, how is an observer to know that he has done so? Is there any way of finding out that a person has misreported the direction or content or substance of his meditation? Looking then at the real man who is the model of Rodin's *le Penseur*, we infer that, circumstances being what they are, he must be meditating or reflecting. Circumstances may even enable us to tell with some competence what he is meditating or reflecting upon. He may have a chess-board, or a piano, or various other things, as Professor Ryle suggests. If, says Professor Ryle, he is meditating or reflecting at all, he is exercising an expertise. I think he says this, but am not quite sure if he means to say that whenever he is reflecting, he is exercising an expertise. Professor Ryle suggests that his activity must be controlled by some learned know-how, and he must at least be taking precautions against error. This does not seem to me to be true— or if true, trivially true and uninformative; if, taken in an interesting sense, it seems to me not to be true.

There is certainly a sense in which a man engaged in any activity, even the activity of doodling, has to take precautions if he is not to deviate from the activity on which he is embarked. If he starts to draw the man sitting opposite him, he will no longer be doodling. That is, there is a sense in which, if I am to stick to some particular course of action, I have to see that my activity does indeed fall under that heading—that I am sticking to it. But there are many things that one does which one would not call exercising expertise—for example, chucking a stone. If one is just chucking a stone, which is another example given, or just doodling, one isn't referring one's activity to any specific standard of correctness, or trying particularly to get something right. It seems to me very important that there are types of meditating and reflecting which are not cases of trying to get something right in a specific way. That, as a matter of fact, is why I think rather highly of doodling as an activity; because I think that it could merge into, or become, something which is neither drawing a portrait of the person opposite, nor just doodling, but something in between, namely, that process that a man goes through when he is operating with a pencil and a piano or thinking (but not with a predetermined standard of correctness or a given problem before him).

Professor Ryle, I think, tends to suppose that meditating generally occurs in problem solving situations; hence the examples he takes are examples from the applied arts, such as an architect who has a predetermined problem and therefore a predetermined criterion of correctness. It seems to me that some so-called thinking, and some meditating which just isn't day-dreaming, may be very like doodling and not be the exercise of an expertise, or a learned know-how, while, of course some may be very like drawing or an exercise of an expertise. Meditating and pondering are still very general words. Perhaps they exclude mere free association, which is a very difficult thing to do.

They do exclude the kind of play of imagery which a man may experience when he is half awake, as Professor Ryle mentions. They do not exclude the activity in which I indulge when in the railway train or airplane: I put down my book and look out of the window reflecting and meditating upon a whole number of topics that come to mind in what may seem to be a random order, some of real concern, some apparently trivial; I would say if I were asked that I've been thinking of a variety of different things, but some of this meditation might seem to me to have been in outcome effective and useful, even though it wasn't governed by a preexisting standard of correctness or aimed at a solution to a particular problem. In other words, it might be that I have hit upon answers to questions that I have previously wanted to answer. But I might have done this in no orderly and directed way, though of course, when I recognize an answer and evaluate it, I am indeed applying standards. But that is not to say that this was the point of the activity or its purpose. I might just have had an idea or seen something in a new way—just as I might be looking outside at the landscape, just looking at it, and from time to time I might observe something of interest. It wouldn't be true to say that my looking was the exercise of an expertise, unless this simply meant that I wouldn't have noticed the thing unless I had previously had a certain training, which is indeed true of any activity whatever. So my meditation taking the three quarters of an hour of my journey as a whole was aimless, at least in the sense that I had no single aim or even that I had no easily summarized set of aims; but of course I did follow various trains of thought—long ones and short ones —just as my wandering gaze did, for a time, fix on various features of the landscape.

This kind of meditation-reflection isn't just free association, and it may sometimes have a very important part to play in discovery. I am suggesting that the model of reflection as always being both the conscious exercise of expertise, and goal-directed in problem solving, is misleading. Even though the relevant expertise is stored in the mind and comes from past learning and so on, even though this is a necessary condition, it is not what I am conscious of. This can be illustrated by asking at what age a child, past infancy, becomes capable of meditating, and above all of reflecting; reflecting for example on his perceptions and feelings. When can one reasonably ask a person—I mean at what age—as he sits or walks pensively, What are you thinking about, reflecting or pondering on? He needn't have much expertise when, at the age, I would guess, of four or five, he tells us of his fantasies and perhaps of his very realistic reflections on what has happened around him. The important thing is that he and he alone is in a position to say—without need of inference or testimony, and immediately—what his reflections are about and what the substance of them was. Everyone else has to wait for him or to guess.

Reflecting is, so to speak, ordinarily contrasted with acting as in the phrase "stop and think," which means stop what you are doing and think. In general we contrast reflecting and thinking in this sense with acting; reflecting is a typical activity of the inner life, as moving about is moving one's limbs; I suppose, moving things around one is a typical activity of the outer or observable life. Of course the pensive child or adult may misreport by misnaming the topic of his meditation, and the confusion which would appear in the report would no doubt also appear as a confusion in thought in most cases; if his thought is evaluated as having arrived at true or false statements, right or wrong solutions. But his reflections need not be or are not always so evaluated; nor evaluated in any other way so as to arrive at something good or bad.

Meditations, therefore, need not be controlled by respect for reality or for solutions to problems; they may be imaginative and they may be wishful in the transposition of reality thought, and still a person can tell you what his thoughts were. So this suggests to me the question, Must a person always know the answer to "what were your thoughts?" It may, sometimes, be difficult to answer, and if there is difficulty, there should be the possibility of going wrong. It is a peculiar kind of difficulty, not that of finding a correct description of my thoughts, my meditations, my ponderings, because I don't describe them when I tell you what they are, as I describe, say, sensations—I, present them to you, as it were, express them, utter them, or, typically, put them into words. In expressing them and putting them into words, I might make the mistake of making them more respectable, more organized and coherent, and cast them more into a statement form than they originally were; because language, so to speak, leaves me not much option but to tighten up my ponderings and, as I report them, to prune them and to leave out the less respectable transitions. My thoughts, in the sense of my meditations, may have ungrammatical features, but these I will prune away ordinarily in reporting them.

Even if errors are possible in reporting, I entirely agree with Professor Ryle's polemic against thought being always, or even typically, internal speech. Indeed, the mere phrase that we put our meditations into words suggests that this must be wrong: even when the meditations do terminate in beliefs, supposals, commands, etc. But they needn't terminate in these linguistically closed entities and often don't. And this doesn't mean that they are valueless to us or that they have no useful application. I don't think anyone can be much deceived about the passage of his thoughts. This doesn't seem to be a possibility. A man may not know what he believes, wants—but we're not talking about that. Can he suspect that while he is apparently following one train of thought and meditating on one topic, he is really following another, as if the train of thought, the succession of reflections that pass through his mind were a mask for another train? I think not. I can't see what the contrast of the apparent to the real here could be. So those who have reasons to speak of preconscious and unconscious thought are using thought, I think, in a more usual, less restricted sense. I unconsciously think of something else without knowing that I do; but they don't want to say, that, so to speak, I have conscious thoughts, meditations which follow a train or succession and that these mask some other ones.

In fact, reflections, meditations, ponderings are what is typically going on in the minds of persons who are not fully employed in some specific task or performance. Reflection and meditating may be just the things that we do contrast with performing. It seems to me very strange to think of my meditations, or of what goes on when I stare out of the window of an airplane, as any kind of *doing*, if this carries a strong sense of performance which I evaluate as a performance. So it seemed to me that somehow Professor Ryle demands too much here; he has a prejudice in favor of a verb of activity. And this is connected with the original question, What is going on when? The important philosophical point, it seems to me, is that we all recognize this kind or, if you like, sense of the word "thinking," the reflecting, pondering, meditating one, which typically has no immedate consequences in behavior, no generally invariable effects of a behavioral kind. And it also and most interestingly, has no immediate natural expression, physiognomic or otherwise. After all, Rodin largely invented that particular image. And many others have been and could be invented to be the picture of the thinker.

Insofar as we can speak of a visible natural expression of pensiveness, of the meditating mood, so to speak, it is a very general one, namely, inactivity. For it is natural to think of meditation stopping when activity begins and vice-versa. It seems almost impossible that I could meditate or ponder in the middle of a football scrimmage. I'm bound to take the railway train as a natural setting, so it looks as if the inner life takes over when the outer life of activity or performance falls away. Well, I don't know why I think these facts are philosophically interesting very clearly—I think because they are overlooked by those with an interest in a particular theory of knowledge, who try to expound verbs of thinking, and indeed psychological verbs generally, wholly in terms of witnessed activities and performances. I think that I seize on the case of meditating as a clear case where this exposition is not convincing.

TOWARD A LOGICAL GEOGRAPHY OF PERSONALITY: TRAITS AND DEEPER LYING PERSONALITY CHARACTERISTICS*

William P. Alston

The conceptual topography of personality description is still largely virgin territory. Recent analytical philosophy of mind, preoccupied with the philosophical tradition, has primarily concerned itself with such topics as one's knowledge of one's own mental states and those of others, the "mind-body relationship," and the motivational explanation of action. Little has been done to distinguish and interrelate the concepts we employ in specifying the relatively stable and long-lasting psychological respects in which one person differs from another. There has been talk about "pro-attitudes" by philosophers concerned with meta-ethics (C. L. Stevenson, P. Nowell-Smith) and with the explanation of action (D. Davidson), but quite disparate items have been included in this category, and little has been done to trace its boundaries. Psychologists have, of course, a professional concern with personality characteristics, but the conceptual sophistication with which they handle this area is not outstanding. With a few notable exceptions (D. C. McClelland, H. A. Murray), they have placed a great variety of items, including desires, traits, attitudes, interests, likes, and abilities, under some single heading, usually "trait," and have, implicitly or explicitly, supposed that a single schema of definition is applicable to all.

In this paper I shall seek to make a beginning at a logical geography

* An earlier version of this paper was written while the author was a Fellow of the Center for Advanced Study in the Behavioral Sciences, Stanford, California. I wish to express my appreciation to the Center for providing ideal conditions for scholarly work, as well as financial support. I should also like to express appreciation to those who have contributed much to my thinking about personality characteristics, notably Donald Campbell of the Department of Psychology, Northwestern University, John Holland of the American College Testing Program, Daniel Miller of the Department of Psychology, University of Michigan, my colleague, Richard Brandt of the Department of Philosophy, University of Michigan, and, not least, the students in my seminars on the subject.

of personality description. More specifically, I shall try to isolate a category of personality characteristics that are naturally called "traits" (T's), in contrast to other "deeper-lying" characteristics (D's), which include relatively long-lasting desires, beliefs, attitudes, needs, interests, and likes. I would hope that the results of this investigation would be useful to psychologists working in the fields of personality assessment and personality theory, as well as to philosophers seeking to understand the nature of persons.

In order to give an initial rough idea of what I mean by "trait," I offer the following as examples of trait terms.

acquisitive	ebullient	opinionated
affected	energetic	optimistic
affectionate	enthusiastic	painstaking
amorous	exhibitionistic	patient
analytical	excitable	pedantic
anxious (anxiety prone)	expansive	persistent
appreciative	formal	phlegmatic
argumentative	frank	poised
arrogant	friendly	polite
austere	generous	pugnacious
benevolent	gentle	reliable
boastful	gluttonous	reserved
cautious	helpful	responsive
cheerful	honest	sadistic
clumsy	imitative	sensitive
conscientious	impulsive	shy
conventional	introspective	slow
cooperative	irritable	sympathetic
credulous	lethargic	suggestible
critical	methodical	tactful
domineering	obedient	talkative

temperate   thoughtful   vindictive

tense   trustful   vivacious

The emphasis in this paper will be on T's rather than on D's. The latter will be treated only as far as is necessary to throw into sharper relief the conceptual features I will be attributing to T's.[1] Indeed, I shall restrict explicit consideration to only one kind of D, viz., desires. I shall assume that the main outlines of what I have to say about desires will also apply to attitudes, needs, likes, interests, etc., although changes would undoubtedly have to be made in the details of the treatment.

I shall proceed by first pointing out and elaborating two salient features of T's that are not shared by D's. Next, on the basis of these features, I shall develop a schema of analysis for T-concepts, and suggest a different kind of schema for D's (or at least for desires). Finally, on the basis of these analysis schemata, further contrasts will be drawn between T's and D's, including their roles in personality description and the prediction and explanation of behavior. The contrast that will be at the core of our treatment can be roughly stated thus: T's are surface regularities, while D's are components of the psychological structure underlying such regularities.

I

Our first contrast is the following:

I. For each T but for no D, there is a manifestation type, M, such that "P is T" entails that P has done or undergone some M's.

The M's for some of the T's we have listed would be:

Talkative—talking
Argumentative—arguing
Obedient—obeying orders
Imitative—imitating others
Persistent—continuing an activity in the face of difficulties
Exhibitionstic—seeking to display what one takes to be one's
        attractive aspects
Domineering—seeking to control the activities of others
Polite—acting in accordance with accepted rules of polite intercourse
Conventional—conforming to social conventions
Friendly—acting in a friendly manner toward others

Appreciative—showing appreciation for benefits received from
                others
Energetic—doing things vigorously
Methodical—organizing one's activities in a rationally planned
                manner
Introspective—paying attention to, dwelling on, one's own
                thoughts, feelings, and other conscious states
Analytical—thinking about problems in an analytical way

Thus, for T's, I implies that, e.g., unless P has obeyed some orders, it cannot be correct to call him obedient, unless P has actually shown appreciation he could not be termed appreciative, unless he has conformed to social conventions, he is not conventional. A person who has never obeyed any orders might be correctly called "potentially obedient," "an obedient type," or "a person who would be obedient if he had the chance"; but we could not be justified in terming him "obedient" *tout court*. The occurrence of some instances of the correlated manifestation category is a necessary, though not sufficient, condition for the application of the trait term.

With D's, on the other hand, no such claim is justified. The manifestations of a particular desire, e.g., the desire to be liked by others, consist of such things as (a) doing something in order to get other people to like one, (b) feeling disappointed, depressed, or desolated if one comes to believe that one or more other people do not like one, and (c) feeling jubilant, relieved, or secure if one comes to believe that one or more other people do like one. But there is no one manifestation-type such that the occurrence of instances is a necessary condition for the possession of that desire. As for (a), one could have even a strong desire to be liked, and yet never actually do anything in order to get other people to like one, because such attempts are always inhibited by a stronger fear of overt rejection or by the conviction that such attempts are more likely to have the opposite effect. Such extreme cases (of no attempts) may not *in fact* occur, for it seems unlikely that one would have such strong fears or convictions without having tried a few times to get others to like one and noting the results. However, it seems quite unjustified to suppose that it is part of what we mean by "wants X" that attempts to get X have actually been carried out. Of course a still more obvious counter-example can be constructed if we allow ourselves to envisage a desire that has *always* been *repressed*, say a desire for homosexual intercourse.

The other manifestation types listed are even weaker candidates for necessary conditions. Having the desire in question, I may never feel jubilant at coming to believe that someone likes me or downcast at coming to believe that someone does not like me. This may be because I never come to have beliefs of one or the other kind; the whole subject may be so painful to me that I just shut out any awareness of relevant indications. Or it may be because my delight in other people liking me is smothered by negative reactions to other aspects of the situation, so that my overall reaction in each case is one of discomfort or guilt, rather than delight.

The manifestation of a desire for S that would seem to be least often totally lacking is S's seeming attractive or desirable to one. Here it seems that it is only the existence (or possibility) of repressed desires that shows us the possibility of having a desire for S without ever having a conscious sense of the attractiveness of S. In fact, that may be the best way to bring out what being repressed amounts to in the case of desires. To say that a desire is repressed is to say that the object of the desire, when before the mind, does not seem desirable.

II

This first difference between T's and D's can be thrown into sharper relief if we make explicit the concept of a *manifestation* that is being employed. The precise notion we want is that of a manifestation of the fact that a certain thing (for our purposes this can be restricted to persons) has a certain characteristic.

> M is a manifestation of $\underline{P\ is\ C} =_{df}$. M is a directly empirically accessible occurrence, and the existence of M in a suitable relation to P (perhaps given certain further conditions) counts toward (is some evidence for, contributes to having a reason for supposing) [2] P's having C.

Several points are to be noted about this definition.

First, a manifestation is an occurrence, something that happens at a time, that is "datable." [3] This is not a precise concept; e.g., there is no answer to the question, How much duration can an occurrence occupy? Nevertheless, an action, an emotional upset, and a train of thought are clear cases of occurrences; whereas desires, attitudes, and traits are clear cases of non-occurrences. Of course, the acquisition or loss of a desire and the becoming conscious of a desire, may be occurrences too. The restriction of manifestations to occurrences prevents a desire from being a manifestation of itself; otherwise I would certainly hold true for desires.

Second, the restriction to "directly empirically accessible" occurrences reflects a concern with the empirical basis for personality description. The reason for not using the more idiomatic term "directly observable" is that I wish to include items like thoughts and feelings, the occurrence of which are capable of being known directly by their possessor, though not by others. Since the notion that one normally observes one's own thoughts and feelings by "introspection," "inner sense," or whatever, has been effectively criticized by Ryle, Wittgenstein, and others, I want to avoid extending the term "directly observable" to what is immediately knowable (not through sense perception) by one and only one person. But since this immediate self-knowledge comes in some sense from one's conscious experience, in contrast to one's knowledge of logical truths, I feel justified in grouping it with perceptual knowledge under the heading "empirical." The concept of "directly empirically accessible" is also by no means a precise one, as is evidenced by the difficulty philosophers of science have in drawing a distinction between observation statements and non-observation statements. Nevertheless, I take it that most actions, demeanors, and bearings are directly observable, and that most thoughts, feelings, images, moods, intentions . . . are immediately knowable by their possessors; whereas desire (attitude, trait) acquisitions, and losses are not directly empirically accessible. We can, of course, come to know about them through our experience, but only through experiencing other things and getting to know about the former through our experience of the latter.

Third, there are various ways of specifying a manifestation type, and the necessity for further conditions to be satisfied before the occurrence of an instance of the type counts toward the attribution of the characteristic, will vary with different modes of specification. For example, P's refusing a drink could count toward P's being temperate, but only on condition that he had already partaken in such quantity that taking more would be excessive. We can avoid dependence on an extra condition by absorbing it into an enriched manifestation-type, *refraining from drinking to excess*. Similarly, we could take as a manifestation type for the trait of obedience, *doing something*. For P's doing X, whatever X is, will count toward P's being obedient, provided the additional condition is satisfied that P has been ordered to do X by someone who has authority over him. Again we can absorb the condition into an enriched manifestation-type, *obeying an order*. A similar point can be made about desires. We can regard *doing* X as a manifestation-type for wanting to play in the World Series, with the stipulation that an instance of this type counts toward the possession of that desire only on the further condition that the agent did X in order to contribute to his chances of getting to play in the World Series. Or we can specify the richer manifestation-type, *doing X in order to increase one's chances of playing in the World Series*.

Now if we were to leave the specification of manifestation-types as open as it is left by our definition, I would be trivially true of T's and D's alike. For as the above paragraph indicates, given any trait, it is generally possible to designate a manifestation type as broad as "do X." And the claim that a necessary condition of P's being obedient is that P has performed at least one action in his life, is hardly an exciting one. Again, if *doing* X is a manifestation-type for a desire for S, one could hardly have that desire in the absence of any instances of that type. Hence I shall lay it down that I, and our discussion generally, is to be restricted to manifestation-types that are distinctive of the personality characteristic under discussion. This will block off the possibility of shoving all the distinctive content into the additional conditions.

This restriction does not yield a unique way of specifying a manifestation-type for each trait, as is indicated by the above example of *temperate*. Here is another example. A natural way of specifying a manifestation-type for *talkative* is "talking"; a talkative person is one who talks a lot. Nevertheless, as Mr. J. O. Urmson once pointed out to me, a person who does a lot of talking just because his job is to man an information booth, but does not talk much off the job, is not termed "talkative." It is not talking under any and all conditions that counts toward being talkative. Thus if our manifestation category for *talkative* is simply "talking," we shall have to say that instances of this type count toward being talkative only under the condition that the social situation does not require it. Or, alternatively we can absorb this condition into the manifestation type, in which case it will come out as *spontaneous talking* or *talking on one's own initiative*.

III

In view of the widespread impression among both psychologists and philosophers that traits are "behavioral dispositions," or regularities or consistencies in "behavior," [4] it is worth pointing out that if we consider the full range of trait concepts in ordinary discourse and/or in the systematic study of personality by psychologists, trait manifestations are by no means restricted to overt, publicly observable behavior.

There are traits, the manifestations of which are emotional states—*irritable, excitable, anxiety-prone;* or trains of thought—*introspective, analytical*. Of course a person who is irritated or excited may, and ordinarily will, act irritated or excited. But P's getting irritated over something will count as a manifestation of irritability, even if in that instance P succeeds in inhibiting all overt manifestations of his being irritated. This may not be a practically important point for emotional liability traits just because we relatively rarely have emotional states of any considerable intensity that are not "shown" to others in some way. But the situation is different with "cognitive conduct" traits like being introspective or analytical. It is certainly possible for a person to pay a lot of attention to his thoughts and feelings, or to think about matters in a highly analytical way, without exhibiting this in his speech or other overt behavior.

To get a clearer picture of the situation it will be useful to make certain distinctions within the category of manifestations. First note that the original definition embraces both analytic and contingent manifestations, where M is an analytic manifestation of "P is T" *iff* it is an analytic truth that the occurrence of an M in a suitable relation to P (perhaps together with the satisfaction of further conditions) counts toward P's being T. Where it is only a contingent truth that M's count in favor of P's being T, we will speak of M as a contingent manifestation of T. So far we have been concerned with analytic manifestations; all the examples listed on pages 61–62 have this status. It is clearly part of what we mean by "obedient" that obeying orders counts as evidence that one is obedient; it is clearly part of what we mean by "persistent" that continuing activities in the face of difficulties counts as evidence that one is persistent. Clearly wherever any manifestation-type is such that possesssion of the characteristic entails the occurrence of some manifestations, as with the examples on pages 61–62, we are dealing with analytic manifestations. However the converse does not hold; we can have analytic manifestations, occurrences of which are not necessary conditions of the possession of the trait. I would argue that this possibility is realized by the desire-manifestations considered above. It seems that it is part of what we mean by "X has a desire for S" that X's doing something in order to get an S counts as evidence (not conclusive evidence) for his having a desire for S. Nevertheless, as we have argued, it is possible for a person to have a desire without any such actions occurring.

There are also contingent manifestations of T's and D's. If it is an empirical fact that people who often make attempts to dominate others often get upset when they are not invited to a party given by a friend, then it will be a contingent fact that P's getting upset in such a case counts toward his being domineering. And so a manifestation of *domineering* will be that a domineering person often gets upset when not invited to a party given by a friend even though this is not part of what we mean by "domineering".

Now let us consider a distinction that crosscuts the distinction between analytic and contingent manifestations. We will call a manifestation-type primary (for C) if and only if its being a manifestation-type (for C) is not dependent on its relation to any other manifestation-type (for C); otherwise it is secondary. Attempting to dominate others is a primary manifestation-type for being domineering. P's attempts to dominate others count toward his being a domineering person, regardless of what other sorts of occurrences accompany them, give rise to them, result from them, manifest them, etc. Such occurrences stem "directly" from the trait. It seems clear that all contingent manifestations are secondary. If it is not an analytic truth that M's count toward the attribution of T, then they can so count only through being in fact regularly connected with some other manifestation, as in the example above.

Analytic manifestations may be primary or secondary. Suppose, e.g., that we construe an emotional state, like being irritated at X, as having at its core a state of autonomic arousal of a certain pattern, brought on by certain kinds of cognition (in this case, taking it that S has done something which one disapproves of). Let us further suppose that, in a given case of such arousal, it is logically possible for any one, or even all, of the typical overt manifestations of irritation to be absent. Finally, let us suppose that it is an analytic, and not merely contingent truth, that certain overt manifestations (frowning, abruptly withdrawing, etc.) typically issue from the state; so that it is analytically true that such occurrences in the right kind of circumstances, constitute evidence (nonconclusive) that the person is irritated at Y. In this case I would want to say that X's frowning at Y is an analytic manifestation of X's being irritable but not a primary manifestation. Its status as a manifestation stems from its relation to a primary manifestation—being irritated. It is not a manifestation of irritability on its own, so to say, but is mediated through its being one of the typical manifestations of the state of being irritated. But since both connections—irritability-being irritated and being irritated-frowning—are analytic, the connection between the outside terms is also.

In terms of these distinctions, we can say that for any trait for which there are intersubjectively usable empirical tests (and this presumably includes all the trait terms in actual use) there must be publicly observable manifestations. For if it is possible for me to get empirical evidence for another person, P's, having or not having T, there must be things I can observe that count as evidence for P's having T. But it does not follow, without further argumentation along the lines of Wittgenstein's private language argument (if then), that every trait has publicly observable *analytic* manifestations. And this line of argument, even if successful, would not show that every trait has *primary* publicly observable manifestations. To return, then, to the emotional and cognitive traits mentioned above, even if we grant that there are reliable ways in which one person can tell what emotional state another is in and what the other is thinking, it will still remain true that the primary manifestations of these traits are not publicly observable and do not consist in instances of overt behavior. The observations I make to determine whether another person, P, is introspective, analytical, or excitable, are efficacious, if they are, only because they constitute reliable indications of particular instances of P's consciously noting and thinking about his mental states, of P's thinking about problems in an analytical fashion, or of P's being excited. These primary manifestations are not themselves publicly observable.

Furthermore, even where primary manifestation categories contain publicly observable items, they may also contain private items. One can obey by thinking about something as well as by overtly doing something; it depends on what has been ordered. Making plans and mapping strategy in one's mind is as much a part of "trying to dominate others" as overt interaction with people, and so it manifests being domineering as directly as the appropriate overt behavior. Again, traits with primary overt manifestations will often have private manifestations that are either secondary or constitute a coordinate category of primary manifestations. Being sympathetic can be manifested by feeling distressed when hearing of the misfortune of others, as well as by seeking to aid and comfort another. Being affectionate can be manifested by feeling a warm glow when around close friends, and by often thinking of them in positive terms, as well as by "acting friendly."

IV

Once we get a firm grip on the notion of a trait-manifestation, we are in a position to develop an illuminating classification of trait concepts in terms of the types of manifestation categories involved. I shall briefly describe such a classification here, reserving a more detailed presentation for another occasion.

Let us call the traits (at least some of) the primary manifestations of which are publicly observable actions or aspects thereof, "behavioral traits." Whereas those traits that have only privately accessible occurrences for their primary manifestations we shall call "phenomenal traits."

Each manifestation category could be thought of as containing a "principle of unity" that makes indefinitely many occurrences all have the status of manifestations of a certain trait. The subclassifications of behavioral and phenomenal traits that we will now suggest are in terms of the kinds of principles of unity involved.

In the (intuitively) simplest case, what binds the manifestations together is *what* the person is doing, the *kind* of action he is performing

—talking, criticizing, eating, boasting, complaining, etc. What makes something a manifestation of *talkative* is that it is an instance of talking. What makes something a manifestation of *critical* is that it is an instance of criticizing. Let us call such traits "action-consistent."

Most behavioral traits are not action-consistent. For example, there is not just one kind of action that counts as a manifestation of obedience. Given an appropriate situation, one can obey by eating, walking, saying something, standing on one's head, driving a car, or doing any one of the innumerable other things that can be commanded. Not all traits which do not fall in the first group are so wide open in the possibilities of behavioral manifestation as obedience. With respect to friendliness, one could hardly imagine the circumstances in which scowling, speaking contemptuously, or walking away in the middle of another's sentence could count toward his being a friendly person. Nevertheless the range is still wide. A man's friendliness may be manifested by offering to give directions to someone who is lost, responding in a warm manner to an invitation, giving reassuring smiles to one who is ill at ease, etc.

Behavioral traits whose manifestations are not bound together by being performances of the same kind of action, themselves differ as to their principle of unity. In some cases it is the relation of the action to antecedent conditions. Thus, what makes an action a manifestation of obedience is that it is the carrying out of an order by a duly constituted authority. What makes an abstention a manifestation of patience is that it is an abstention from an expression of annoyance or hostility which would naturally have been evoked by another person's activity or lack thereof. What makes an action a manifestation of conscientiousness is that it is a carrying out of a task or obligation which there is some reason to think a person might neglect. Since in these cases the manifestations are constituted as such by their relation to an antecedent condition, we may call these traits "response consistent."

With another group the unifying principle is the goal to which the actions are directed. Again, if we consider *acquisitive, domineering,* or *helpful,* what a person does in manifesting these traits can vary enormously. Among the things that might count toward my being acquisitive (given in each case the proper setting, inner as well as outer), are engaging a certain person in conversation, reading the want ads in the newspaper, and going to a certain store. There is nothing about these kinds of action as such which makes them manifestations of acquisitiveness. What gives them that status is the fact that they are all performed in order to contribute to the agent's possession of goods. What they have in common is the goal to which they are directed. If I can show that P did not engage Mr. B in conversation in order to get him to sell some property at a low price, or in order to produce any other result which he believed would enlarge his possessions, but simply because he happened to be standing next to him at the party and with no thought in mind other than passing the time in an appropriate manner, then I have shown that his doing so does not count toward his being acquisitive. Similarly a person can manifest his domineering nature by doing a variety of things, depending on context: talking continuously, hatching plots, acting sullen until he gets his way, and so on. What makes them all manifestations of this trait is the fact that they are all directed to the goal of controlling the behavior of others. Such traits we may call "goal-consistent."

Next consider politeness. In different cultures and subcultures, and even in different situations in the same culture, what counts as polite behavior varies widely. What binds them all together is their relation to a certain kind of socially recognized norm. A manifestation of politeness is an action (or abstention) which is in accordance with a norm or rule of polite behavior for the group or subgroup in which one is acting. We may term such traits "norm-consistent" traits.

What about being an affectionate, friendly, or appreciative person? We have already had occasion to note that friendliness can be manifested in a large, though not unlimited, variety of ways. One can build a high affectionateness score by caresses (directed toward appropriate persons), by smiles (properly timed), by regularly inquiring after the health of someone close to one (if done in the proper manner), and so on. What makes all the members of a certain class of occurrences, manifestations of friendliness or affectionateness? Here we bring in the notion of a "disposition" or "attitude" expressed by the manifestations. What binds friendliness-manifestations into a unity is that they are all exhibitions or "expressions" of friendliness. What binds affectionateness-manifestations into a unity is that they are all displays of affection. Thus the principle of unity here is a relation of the manifestations to a kind of attitude.[5] We may call these "attitude-consistent" traits.

For the kinds of traits so far considered, other than action-consistent traits, the action-manifestations are not limited to one kind of action. Nevertheless there are definite limitations which stem from the trait concept. Given appropriate contextual features there are severe restrictions on the type of action that can count as a T-manifestation. Thus, given a person's preferences, his beliefs as to what sort of goods he is most likely to achieve next, and what lines of action are most likely to lead to this, we can say just what actions will count toward his being acquisitive. Having specified the rules of etiquette governing behavior in a given setting, we can say what actions in that setting will count toward the agent's being polite. Thus:

1. For action-consistent traits, we can specify in general, without dependence on additional information, what actions will count toward possession of the trait.

2. For response-consistent, goal-consistent, attitude-consistent, and norm-consistent traits, we can furnish information, for a given person and a given situation, which will severely limit the class of actions which, in that situation, will count toward possession of the trait.

Now let us consider such traits as *energetic, lethargic, expansive, clumsy, gentle,* and *methodical*—traits which have received considerable attention from psychologists under the heading of "stylistic" or "expressive." It is noteworthy that for these traits even the weaker condition 2 does not hold. That is, whatever the situation, whatever the person's beliefs and desires, there is no limitation on what actions will count toward his being energetic or clumsy, so long as it is an action which can be performed more or less energetically or more or less clumsily. Here what makes an action a manifestation is something about the *way* in which it is performed rather than what action it is. We shall call these traits "manner-consistent."

Turning now to phenomenal traits, an obvious distinction is between those traits with "cognitive" manifestations, like *credulous, introspective,* and *analytical,* and those whose manifestations are "affective," such as *irritable, excitable,* and *anxiety-prone.* These classes can undoubtedly be futher subdivided. Thus, the principles of unity for some of the "cognitive" traits like *credulous* are analogous to the principles of unity for behavioral response-consistent traits, in that what binds the manifestations together is a certain kind of reaction to an antecedent occurrence outside the person, in this case an assertion made by someone else. Whereas *introspective* is a cognitive content-consistent trait, in that its manifestations are such, by virtue of having intentional objects of a certain kind—the person's own psychological states. And *analytical* is a cognitive manner-consistent trait, in that the manifestations are such by virtue of being carried out in a certain way, regardless of the content and the circumstances in which they occur. Undoubtedly subclassification could be carried further, but this should suffice for an indication of the possibilities along this line.

We may sum up the classification at which we have arrived, thus far, as follows:

I. Behavioral traits

A. Action-consistent (argumentative, boastful, critical, generous, gluttonous, pugnacious, talkative)

B. Response-consistent (cautious, cooperative, imitative, obedient, patient, persistent, reliable, reserved, responsive)

C. Goal-consistent (acquisitive, benevolent, domineering, exhibitionistic, sadistic)

D. Norm-consistent (conventional, honest, polite, tactful, temperate)

E. Attitude-consistent (affectionate, appreciative, enthusiastic, friendly, sympathetic, vindictive)

F. Manner-consistent (affected, arrogant, ebullient, energetic, formal, impulsive, methodical, poised, slow, tense, vivacious)

II. Phenomenal traits

A. Affective (anxious, cheerful, excitable, irritable, phlegmatic, sensitive)

B. Cognitive
   1. Content-consistent (introspective, optimistic, superstitious, trustful)
   2. Response-consistent (credulous, opinionated, suggestible)
   3. Manner-consistent (analytical, thoughtful)

This classification brings out several different ways in which trait concepts fail to conform to a hard-boiled behaviorist restriction to direct public observables. The most obvious point is the one already noted, viz., that for some trait concepts, those we have dubbed "phenomenal," the primary manifestations are not cases of overt behavior at all and are only directly accessible privately. But our classification reveals another equally important point. It is easy to suppose that at least what we have termed "behavioral traits" can be defined in behavioristic terms. But once we bring out what makes a certain instance of overt behavior a manifestation of a certain trait, we see that many behavioral trait concepts involve concepts of attitudes, desires, and norms. Since what binds together all the manifestations of acquisitiveness is that they are all performed as a result of a desire for goods, we cannot understand the trait of acquisitiveness without being able to understand and identify desires. Since what binds together all the manifestations of friendliness is that they are all expressions of a friendly attitude, we cannot understand the trait of friendliness without being able to understand and identify attitudes. We cannot spell out what it is to be acquisitive or friendly without utilizing desire and attitude concepts. Hence these trait-concepts are not analyzable in behavioristic terms unless desires and attitudes are also.

To be sure, one might set out to describe personality in terms of a host of lower level S-R regularities formulated in the observation language, a program put forward by the "specificists." [6] But we should be clear that such people are proposing to replace the trait concepts employed by common sense, and by practically all psychologists who do detailed work on personality description, with a quite different conceptual framework. This involves cutting ourselves loose from the matrix of common sense ways of describing personality and starting with a clean slate, an endeavor on which no psychologist in the area of personality has really embarked. We must rid ourselves of the comforting (to a behaviorist) thought that the trait concepts actually in use could, in principle, be analyzed along such lines.

V

Our second major contrast between T's and D's is the following:

> II. For each T, but for no D, there is a manifestation type, M, such that the intensity or degree with which P has T is a function of the frequency with which P does or undergoes M's.

T's and D's could be contrasted in this way even if we were mistaken in supposing that I holds for T's but not for D's.

The basic idea behind II is a simple one. A very talkative person is a person that talks *a lot*; a very polite person is a person who *often* acts politely; a very methodical or energetic person is a person that does *many* things methodically or energetically; a very excitable person is a person who *frequently* gets excited. On the other hand, a person may have a very strong desire to be liked by others even though he does not frequently try to get others to like him, feel pleasure in being liked, etc. These manifestations may often be inhibited by fears and other contrary factors mentioned in connection with I, even if such factors do not inhibit all manifestations of the desire. However to give an acceptable general statement of this contrast is a complex task.

First, we should try to be more explicit about the term "frequently." How often is "frequent"? There can be no single answer (like "three times a week") to this question for all manifestation-types. "Frequent" will have to be interpreted in a context-sensitive way like "large" and "lots." A volume or weight that, if possessed by a rat would make it a very large rat would, if possessed by a dog, make it a very small dog. There is no general answer to "How much is large?" Similarly, the minimum yearly number of attempts to hurt others for no further reason that would count as frequent (and hence would support an attribution of "very sadistic"), might be much smaller than the minimum yearly number of energetic behavings that would count as "frequently behaving energetically." So far as I can see, the only general statement that can be made is that for each trait attributions are made against the background of a standard (usually rough and implicit) for estimating frequency, with a live possibility that this standard will vary somewhat from one judge to another. Often this standard is, or is derived from, an evaluative standard, with the result that the trait term, as ordinarily employed, carries evaluative implications. A boastful person, for example, is one who boasts more than he should, or so much as to be tedious.

A thornier problem is this. However standards of frequency may differ for different traits, it is clear that II, as stated, implies that for a given trait, T, there is some M-category such that, if P_1 does or undergoes significantly more M's than P_2, then P_1 has T to a higher degree than P_2. The trouble with this is that there seem to be sources of variation in the frequency of M's that do not reflect differences in the degree of T. Consider two people, one of whom spends a good part of his waking hours in social groups of varying sorts and sizes, while the second is a recluse and only rarely in contact with others. It seems clear that the first might act in a polite manner much more frequently than the second, even though the latter is more polite, just because the former has many more opportunities to act either politely or impolitely. His raw score may be much higher but his relative frequency (relative to opportunities) much lower. This suggests that we should revise II as follows:

> IIA. For each T, but for no D, there is a manifestation type, M, such that the intensity or degree with which P has T, is a function of the frequency, relative to oppotunities, with which P does or undergoes M's.

Let us remember that I implies that opportunities are a necessary condition of trait possession. If P_1 has had no opportunities to act politely, then he has not failed in any of his opportunities, but this does not mean that he has the trait of politeness to the highest possible degree, for according to I he has failed to meet the necessary condition of possession of the trait to any degree, viz., the existence of some manifestations. But given some opportunities and some exploitiation of them, he may be judged *very* polite even though the absolute frequency is not great.

In making trait attributions, both in ordinary discourse and in self-conscious "personality assessment," we often ignore this complexity. The best way to rationalize such a procedure is to say that we are assuming the opportunities to be approximately equal. Such an assumption will often be justified and often unjustified. It is worthy of note that there are some traits, particularly manner-consistent traits, where it is always, or almost always justified. No special setting is needed for one to do whatever he is doing energetically, slowly, methodically, or impulsively. Manifestations of goal-consistent traits also are more independent of external conditions than the other traits we have been considering. I can do something designed to contribute to my domination of others in almost any situation, especially if we count planning such behavior as a manifestation. But for traits of the other sorts more of a stage setting is required.

VI

The situation is more complex still. It is not just a matter of the sheer number of opportunities and responses. Opportunities and responses can vary in respects which are relevant to the degree of trait possession. To set this out systematically, let us note that according to IIA, if two persons have had the same number of opportunities and the same number of M's, we are justified in attributing T to them in the same degree. However, there are various possible differences between the two cases, each of which would force a modification of that conclusion. Consider, then, P_1 and P_2 who have had an equal (and considerable) number of opportunities to be sympathetic to someone, and have acted sympathetically an equal number of times. If any of the following differences in their sets of opportunities and responses is present to a significant extent, we would still not be justified in attributing the trait *sympathetic* to them in equal degree.

First, the variety of situations in which sympathy has been displayed may be quite different. P_1 has shown sympathy only to those undergoing physical pain, while P_2 has also shown sympathy to those who have failed in some endeavor, been betrayed by friends, or lost money. We suppose a man to have a trait to a higher degree if he manifests it in a wider variety of situations. A man is more enthusiastic, not only as he shows enthusiasm more often, but as he gets enthusiastic about a greater number of things.

Second, the magnitudes, in relevant respects, of the situations evoking sympathy might be different for the two sets of opportunities. P_1 might have shown sympathy only when the suffering or adversity of the other person had reached very large proportions, while P_2 might sometimes or often have shown sympathy when the other person was suffering only a little, had only partially failed, or had lost a small proportion of his worldy goods.

Third, the responses in the two subsets may differ in the extent to which they are carried on in the absence of environmental support. It is harder to be sympathetic with some people than with others. Some people resist or repel expressions of sympathy, act offended by them or stiff about them; while other people encourage them and seem appreciative. We take it that one who shows sympathy with people of the first sort as well as with people of the second sort is thereby a more sympathetic person, *ceteris paribus,* than one who shows sympathy only to persons of the second sort. By the same token one who will talk only when other encourage him to do so is thereby a less talkative person, *ceteris paribus,* than one who will talk in the absence of encouragement.[7]

Fourth, the manifestations themselves may vary in magnitude along relevant dimensions. P_1 and P_2 may differ in that the former simply "goes through the motions" or does the minimum by way of showing concern; whereas P_2 overwhelms his target with expressions of sympathy and goes to a great deal of trouble to try to help. The manifestations of other traits can vary in magnitude in a variety of ways. One can obey with greater or lesser alacrity, one can try more or less hard to dominate others, one can act with more or less energy, one can become more or less irritated, and so on.

These considerations provide abundant testimony to the fact that the degree of trait possession is not a simple function of frequency of manifestations relative to number of opportunities. However, they do not necessarily show that frequency does not play a central role. A modified frequency formulation that takes account of these complexities would be this:

> IIB. For each T, but for no D, there is a manifestation type, M, such that the intensity or degree with which P has T is a function of the frequency and strength with which P would do or undergo M's in a properly constituted set of situations.

Consideration 4 is reflected in the fact that strength as well as frequency of manifestations is taken to affect degree of trait possession. Considerations 1—3 are reflected in the switch from an actual frequency in whatever set of situations is actually obtained, to the frequency that would be obtained in a "properly constituted" set of situations. A properly constituted set of situations would be a rather large set that is widely varied in relevant respects. It is best to leave open to a certain extent just what respects are relevant. Of course if we had no idea how to go about such a determination the principle would be useless. But, as the above discussion shows, we are not in that position. Among the features that are important for propriety of constitution are the type of situation, magnitude of eliciting features, and support for the relevant response. I would tentatively venture the further claim that these constitute all the most important respects in which a set of cases may be more or less well chosen for trait attribution. Of course we cannot apply these criteria with respect to a given trait unless we know what constitutes relevant variations in situations, what constitutes eliciting features of situations, etc., for that trait. But in general we do have such knowledge, and we can use this knowledge in determining the extent to which a frequency in a given sample is a reliable indication of the frequency that would be found in an ideally constituted sample. This is the kind of problem that faces us whenever we generalize from a limited sample.

IIB is reflected in our actual practice of trait attribution. Quite often we just assume that the range of situations is, for all practical purposes, sufficiently large and equivalent in extent and variety in relevant respects for all the persons being considered. We can then distinguish different degrees of trait possession in terms of the raw number of manifestations. This would seem to constitute such rationale as can be provided for self-report questionnaire techniques of personality assessment, where the questionnaire is designed to get a rough estimate of frequency of manifestations in a variety of situations. If, in a more subtle procedure, we do take into account possible differences in the range of cases for different persons, and if we do have reason to think that these differences are significant, we try to modify inferences from sheer frequency, though of course there are no precise rules for doing so. "Yes, he's almost always very cooperative and helpful, but that's just because he always gets a lot of appreciation for being this way. You put him over in J.B.'s office where no one gets any thanks for anything and I'll bet you won't find him so cooperative." "You get the impression he's very friendly, but of course he's only around people of his sort. Move him over into the ghetto, and we'll see how friendly he is there."

Having complicated II to this extent, the contrast between T's and D's will inevitably be less sharp. Presumably there will be some ways of choosing samples such that the degree of D-possession will be a function of frequency within such a sample. However there will still be a fundamental difference in what it takes to make up such a sample for T's and D's. The above discussion suggests that a set of situations for a T-assessment can be evaluated purely in terms of features of the situation external to the subject of the attribution, so long as they are recognized by him to be such. So long as the situations are properly varied in kind and magnitude, the degree of the trait-possession will be a function of frequency (and strength) of manifestations, regardless of what else is true of the agent—what other traits, needs, desires, attitudes, etc. he has. If P_1 acts politely much more frequently than P_2 in large sets of cases that are equivalent in number and equally and markedly varied in relevant respects, then it follows without more ado that P_1 is more polite than P_2, whatever be the psychological constitution of these persons otherwise, except for the requirement that each of them recognizes the situations to possess the relevant characteristics.

But this does not hold for desires. Two persons may engage in an equal number of attempts to get others to like them, in sets of situations equalized in all relevant external respects (and where both parties realize in each case that the situation has these features), and yet one may have a much stronger desire to be liked than the other. Then why doesn't P_1 engage in more attempts to get others to like him than P_2? Because his tendencies to make such attempts are frequently inhibited by even stronger aversions to possible failures, or because he has strong fears that such attempts will make him a laughing stock, or . . . Conversely, P_1 and P_2 may have desires for recognition of equal strength and yet, in externally equivalent ranges of cases, P_1 may engage in many more attempts to get recognition than P_2, because P_2 but not P_1 has strong fears of the consequences of such behavior, or because P_2 but not P_1 disapproves of trying to get recognition, or . . . To represent the strength of a desire as a strict function of the frequency and strength of manifestations in a certain set of situations, we should have to define the set (at least in part) in terms of the other D's (other desires, fears, attitudes, etc.) possessed by the agent. As the above considerations show, strength of desire is not a function of frequency and strength in a set of situations specified purely in terms of features external to the agent (even where we add the stipulation that the agent realize that these features are present). This is just because, as we have seen before, the occurrence or nonoccurrence of any particular D-manifestation is a function, not just of that D, but of a total psychological field in which that D interacts with other D's.

Thus we can make II strictly accurate, in its application to D's, by making explicit the method of specifying sets of situations for T-attributions.

> IIC. For each T, but for no D, there is a manifestation type, M, such that the intensity or degree with which P has T is a function of the frequency and strength with which P would do or undergo M's in a properly constituted set of situations, specified in terms of features external to (and recognized by) P.

VII

Having drawn these contrasts, let us see what general pattern of analysis for trait concepts will embody and reflect these points. I will find it most useful to concentrate on the "absolute" rather than the degree form of the concepts. That is, we shall be analyzing statements of the form, "X is methodical," rather than "X is methodical to degree————." It will do no harm to think of the "absolute" concept as a high position on the dimension involved in the degree concept; i.e., "X is methodical" = "X is very methodical." I am concentrating on the absolute form, even though the degree concepts are undoubtedly more fundamental in principle, partly because the points I wish to make can be made more simply, and partly because the metrical concepts are not sufficiently developed to furnish any considerable subject matter for analysis, over and above the absolute concepts.

I shall be seeking to develop the simplest pattern of analysis that will jibe with all relevant considerations. In developing thesis IIC we have already blocked a very simple interpretation (one that has actually been proposed) according to which the possession of a trait is to be identified with an actual frequency of manifestations. In getting thesis II. into acceptable shape we have been forced to recognize that one might have frequently acted politely up to now without being very polite, if one's circumstances up to now have been severely restricted and if it is the case that one would not act politely very often in a variety of other circumstances. And, contrariwise, one might be very polite, and yet fall short of the relevant standard in actual frequency up to this time, because most of the time up to now one has been in situations where it is unusually difficult to be polite. Since we are debarred from identifying a trait with any *de facto* frequency, the question of whether a trait attribution is simply a "record" or "summary" of past frequencies, or whether, on the contrary, it is a prediction of future frequencies, cannot arise. However we shall find that an analogous problem of temporal location does arise in the view we shall adopt.

The simplest interpretation of trait-concepts that will reflect what has been brought out thus far is the following:

A. "P is T" $=_{df.}$ There is a manifestation-type, M, such that

(1) P is so constituted that in a properly constituted set of situations P would do or undergo M's frequently.

(2) P has done or undergone M's significantly often up to now.

(1) of course reflects IIC, and (2), I. The reason for the "so constituted" clause is as follows. In asserting (1) of P we are not saying that a certain regularity or frequency holds as a matter of fact; we are asserting a dependable, "law like" connection between a certain kind of situation, and the frequency of occurrences of a certain kind. We are asserting a subjunctive conditional of P: if P were in a set of situations of the appropriate sort then P would do or undergo M's frequently. If it were a matter of M's actually happening frequently in a given set of actual situations, that might just be a result of biased sampling; it might not reflect any distinctive characteristics of P. But where a subjunctive conditional is true of P, it must be because of some features of P's structure or constitution; and if the conditional does not formulate an ultimate disposition (and presumably no psychological dispositions are ultimate), it must be possible to specify these features in other terms. Of course, in atrributing the trait to P we are not saying what these features are; we are merely committing ourselves to the existence of some feature(s) that yield this result.

We still have a temporal location problem, analogous to the one that arises on the *de facto* frequency interpretation as to whether a trait attribution is a summary of past manifestations or a prediction of future manifestations or both. There is no such problem for clause (2), for that unequivocally requires the actual existence of manifestations "up to now," i.e., prior to the time of attribution. But for clause (1) we have to decide on the period for which we are asserting the conditional to be true of P; if we are asserting that this is so only at the moment of attribution, then the truth of "P is T" is compatible with P's never producing a large number of M's, even if a properly constituted set of situations does eventuate. For such a set will take considerable time to actualize, and if P has the appropriate structural features only at the moment of attribution, he will have lost them long before they have had a chance to issue in the specified frequency. Moreover, our assertion will be compatible with its being the case that the past manifestations required by (2) stemmed from something other than the disposition required by (1). We certainly don't want that. If P's past record of polite acts stemmed from extreme social pressure or constraint, and he has just now acquired a disposition to act politely in a variety of situations (and may lose this disposition shortly), we would not be justified in calling him a (very) polite person.

The second point can be handled just by requiring that the past M's have (in general) stemmed from the disposition specified in (1). The future presents a more delicate problem. On the one hand, it is undeniable that personality does change; we do not want to restrict trait terms to inalterable features of persons. On the other hand we do not want trait attributions to be completely neutral with respect to the chances of M's occurring (given appropriate situations) in the future. I believe that we will secure the most accurate reflection of the force of actual trait concepts if we build into the analysis the presumption that (when dealing with adults, at any rate) [8] trait-dispositions are quite stable and generally change gradually, if at all; leaving open the possibility of change, and even the (more remote) possibility of sudden change, in any particular case. This move will give trait attributions some definite implications for the future, while making any given attribution logically compatible with the infrequency of M's in appropriate situations in the future. This is, of course, all rather indeterminate, and we could replace it with something more precise, e.g., that the disposition is retained for at least six months beyond the time of attribution. But then we would fail to embody in our analysis the indeterminacy present in our (including psychologists') actual use of trait-concepts. Moreover, in the present stage of development, we are not in a position to make effective use of concepts that are more precise in this respect.

With these emendations the analysis will read:

B. "P is T" $=_{df.}$ There is a manifestation-type, M, such that:

(1) P now has a relatively stable structural feature, S, such that in a properly chosen set of situations P would do or undergo M's frequently.

(2) As a result of having S, P has done or undergone a significant number of M's up to now.

Thus a trait attribution carries a straight-forward implication of a significant number of past M's, and a strong presumption of a relative frequency of M's in the future, provided there is a good spread of cases.

These are hybrid concepts; the division of the analysans into (1) and (2) is designed to highlight that fact. It seems clear that in principle we could have concepts that embodied (1) without (2), in which case T's would differ to a lesser degree from D's.

VIII

What sort of analysis of desires would conform to I and IIC and be acceptable on other grounds as well? Let us recall that in arguing for I and IIC, as applied to desires, we cited the fact that typical manifestations of a desire may fail to come off, either always or often, because of some inhibiting force, such as a stronger desire for something incompatible or a fear of the consequences. This suggests that a desire is the sort of thing that will issue in certain typical manifestations unless one or more appropriate interferences are present. This could be expressed by saying that a desire involves *tendencies* to its typical manifestations; where in saying that P has a tendency to M, we are saying that P *will* do or undergo M, unless P has a stronger tendency to do or undergo something incompatible with M (including as a special case a stronger tendency to avoid doing or undergoing M). That is, a tendency is the sort of thing that exists in a field or system of other entities of the same type, such that actual occurrences (of the kinds the tendencies are tendencies to) are determined not by any one tendency, but by the resultant properties of the system, which in turn is determined by the interrelations of the component tendencies, including both the compatibility or incompatibility of their realizations, and their comparative strength. The conception of a desire suggested by all this is that of a set of dispositions to certain tendencies.

> C. To say that P has a desire for states of affairs of kind, S, is to assert a conjunction of conditionals like the following:[9]
>
> (1) If P believes that doing A has some considerable chance of contributing to the realization of an S, P will have a tendency to do A.
>
> (2) If P realizes that an S has occurred, P will have a tendency to be pleased.
>
> (3) If P had been expecting an S and P realizes that it did not occur, P will have a tendency to be disappointed.

(4) If there are objects related to S in P's environment, P will tend to notice them.

If we are to make use of tendency notions, and terms defined by means of tendency notions, we shall have to have some idea of what can give rise to tendencies that will oppose or reinforce a given tendency. More specifically, if we are to tell whether a person has a given desire, interpreted as above, we will have to determine whether certain tendencies (e.g., to do A) are aroused under certain conditions. But any given tendency may or may not issue in a manifestation. Therefore, in order to tell whether a tendency to do A was aroused, in a case where no M was forthcoming, we have to know what other psychological factors could have overborne the tendency if they were present. As our discussions of I and IIC (as applied to desires) indicated, we do have such knowledge. One of the things that can interfere with a tendency to do A is a stronger fear of the consequences, and one of the things that can interfere with a tendency to be pleased at S is a sense of guilt for having brought S about. Our knowledge of such interrelations is inadequate both in completeness and in precision, but it is sufficient to enable us to make actual use of tendency notions.

Given this analysis, I holds for desires for two reasons. First, a set of conditional statements can be true of someone, even if none of the antecedent conditions are ever satisfied (and hence the consequents never result from the satisfaction of the antecedent conditions). I can be disposed to be pleased if I realize an S occurs, even though I never realize that an S occurs and so never have a chance to be pleased at the occurrence of an S.[10] However this is only a bare possibility, since for most desires, antecedent conditions of the sort specified in the analysis are going to occur a fair number of times. With respect to most states of affairs for which human beings have desires, e.g., getting a job, there will, at times, be some things one believes to have a fair chance of bringing about the state of affairs, there are going to be cases in which one expects a state of affairs of this type to come off, and so on. The second reason is the more important, and the one reflected in our initial arguments for principle I, viz., that in any case in which a given tendency is aroused, the manifestation may or may not actually occur, depending on the other tendencies present in the person's psychological field of the moment. This means that, for a given desire, it can happen that in no case where relevant tendencies are aroused are the manifestations actually forthcoming.

This analysis also shows us why IIC is true of desires. On C, the strength of a desire will be a function of the strengths of the constituent dispositions. And the strength of each constituent disposition will be a function of the (average) strength of the tendencies that are or would be given rise to by the satisfaction of antecedent conditions. A strong desire for S is one which is such that a recognized occurrence of an S will (generally) give rise to a strong tendency to be pleased, a belief that doing A will have some considerable chance of leading to an S will (generally) give rise to a strong tendency to do A, and so on. But even strong tendencies can be often, or even always, overborne by stronger incompatible tendencies, in which case there will not be a high frequency of manifestations, even though the desire is strong. The crucial point is that the frequency of manifestations is not a function of the absolute strength of the tendencies to those manifestations, but rather a function of the strength of the tendencies *relative* to the strengths of competing tendencies in the psychological field.

Comparing the analysis schemata for T's and D's, we note the following salient differences.

III. Whereas a D is simply a bundle of dispositions, T's involve an actual record of manifestations as well as the existence of an appropriate disposition.

IV. For a given T, but not for a given D, there is a single manifestation category. That is, insofar as a T is dispositional it is a single disposition with a single kind of actualization; whereas a D consists of a group of different dispositions with different kinds of actualizations, not reducible to a common rubric (other than the trivially unified rubric "actualization of that D"). D's, but not T's, are, in Ryle's terminology, essentially "multi-track dispositions."

V. The dispositions that make up a D have as their actualizations tendencies to manifestations, rather than the manifestations themselves; while the disposition involved in a T has as its actualization a relative frequency of manifestations. Thus even with respect to the dispositional part of T's (apart from the requirement of the actual past occurrence of manifestations) a T is related more directly to its manifestations than is a D.

Before drawing further implications of these T-D differences, let us just note that the picture is complicated by the existence of "higher level" trait concepts that have the same structure as those we have been discussing, the difference being that the manifestations are not directly empirically accessible occurrences. Examples are *fickle, independent,* and *easily influenced.* Here the manifestations are acquisitions and losses of D's. A fickle person is one who changes his likes and attachments frequently, an independent person is one who does not frequently adopt or drop beliefs or attitudes just because others around him do so or because there is external pressure to do so. These D-acquisition and loss processes do not have the degree of empirical accessibility possessed by actions, thoughts, and feelings. Our discussion in this paper is restricted to trait concepts with directly empirically accessible manifestations. A complete treatment of the subject would have to take into account the fact that trait-type concepts can be formed with "manifestation" categories of any level of conceptual complexity and any degree of distance from the observable.[11]

IX

We can now go on to contrast T's and D's, with respect to their roles in description, prediction, explanation, and theorizing, though our presentation will perforce be sketchy.

> VI. A particular T has much more predictive value by itself than a particular D.

It follows from the above that in attributing a given T to P we are committing ourselves to a frequency of manifestations of a particular category in a wide spread of cases. Therefore if all we know about a person is that he has a given trait, that alone will put us into a position to make some reliable predictions (and retrodictions) about his behavior, thought, and/or feeling. If all we know about him is that he is boastful, that will justify us in predicting that he will boast a lot if he is exposed to a number of typical social situations. But in attributing a given D to P we are making no such commitment; no one piece of knowledge puts us in any such position. If all I know about a person is that he wants very much to be recognized by others, that alone will not enable me to predict what he will do, feel, or think. In order even to know what tendencies spring from this desire, I would have to have other information, such as what lines of action he believes will give him the best chance of satisfying this desire, on what occasions he expects to be recognized by others, etc. And even after determining what tendencies will emerge I cannot know which of these will actually issue in manifestations, without knowing something about the contrary tendencies with which they will be in competition. A single D is "too far" from the surface of events to permit any such inferences.

VII. A given D, but not a given T, has a built-in capacity for entering into systematic relations with other factors to produce resultant tendencies to a great variety of manifestations.

The concept of a desire is, as we have seen, the concept of a set of dispositions to tendencies to various actions, feelings, etc., given other D's, such as beliefs and expectations. That is, according to our pattern of analysis the concept of a desire explicitly contains principles as to how a desire combines with other factors to produce tendencies. And further modes of interaction are implicitly presupposed. As we have also seen, we can make use of the notion of a given tendency only insofar as we have some ideas as to what factors can give rise to opposing or reinforcing tendencies. Thus in the background of our concept of a given desire lies a rich, though imprecise and largely inexplicit, system of principles as to how compatible and incompatible tendencies are generated by various combinations of particular desires, aversions, fears, beliefs, etc. One might say that D-concepts have built-in plugs and sockets for making such connections. By way of compensation for its lack of predictive force in isolation, a D-concept has a capacity for entering into D-systems that are almost unlimitedly fertile in yielding the determinants of a great variety of manifestations. Just because the relation of any particular D to any particular manifestation is mediated by other D's, it is possible to describe systems of D's that determine (or at least influence) a large variety of manifestations.

With T-concepts, by contrast, the predictive force of a particular attribution is bought at the price of isolation. Just because a particular T reflects so directly a particular kind of manifestation, it is not necessarily connected with other factors in a system. In saying that P is argumentative, we are committing ourselves to a lot of arguings (given an appropriate set of circumstances) and *that's all*. Add to this a lot of other knowledge about P's traits, desires, etc., and we are not *thereby* put in a position to use the fact that P is argumentative, in conjunction with the other knowledge, to trace out tendencies to a variety of actions, thoughts, and feelings.[12]

VIII. D's explain their manifestations in a much stronger way than do T's.

We can explain a particular polite act, like opening a door for a lady, by saying that the agent is a polite person. The force of this is to make it explicit that the act does count as acting politely, and that the agent is someone who can be relied on to act politely most of the time in most situations. This can throw light on the matter. But the provision of this explanation still leaves room for another kind of explanation of the same act (not an explanation of the possession of the trait) in terms of the agent's desires, needs, fears, etc. We may still want to know *why* the agent acted politely in this instance, and in other instances. Is it because he enjoys being polite? Is it because he fears being rejected if he doesn't? Or is it because he has a need to conform or to see himself as not "different"? We are inclined to say that the fact that he is a polite person doesn't *really* explain *why* he acts politely in any particular case. It just tells us that he usually does, and that there is some reason(s) for this regularity, but without telling us what that reason is. If, however, we explain his opening the door for Mrs. A by saying that he wants to ingratiate himself with her, we feel that this (if correct) really explains this act; it makes explicit *why* he did it. Of course we can go on to ask why he has this desire, but that would be a request for an explanation of another fact. There wouldn't be any job left over in the way of explaining the act. In particular, no further light could be thrown on this act by pointing out that P has some trait, e.g., politeness, of which this act is a manifestation; though this would give us further infomation about the person.

It would, no doubt, be a complicated job to bring out fully what lies behind these tendencies, but the previous principle (VII) gives us a start. I suggest that the superior explanatory efficacy of a D-concept comes from its essential entanglement in a system of D-concepts that conforms to what we may call the "motivational" model for the explanation of action. Our sense that desires "really" explain actions, whereas traits do not, reflects an attachment to a motivational model.[13] If we were to give up this model in favor of, say, a habit (or S-R bond) model as the fundamental model for explaining human action, we would, I take it, no longer have the sense that desires really explain, whereas traits do not. Though it would still be the case that existing trait concepts provide for only rough habit-type explanations.

IX. T's are explainable in terms of D's in a way in which D's are not explainable in terms of T's.

First let us note and set aside the kind of explanation in which there is a kind of symmetry. It is conceivable that T's should enter into explanations of the acquisition of D's, as well as vice versa. If the frequent performance of acts of a certain type, e.g., arguing (for some extrinsic reason) led to the acquisition of a desire, or liking, or disliking for arguing, then the fact that P has the trait of argumentativeness (and hence frequently performed acts of that type) could enter into the explanation of his acquiring a certain D. Conversely the fact that P likes arguing may explain his arguing frequently and hence explain his acquiring the trait of argumentativeness.

The asymmetry asserted in IX comes, once more, from features of the concepts. The concept of a T makes provision for the explanation of a T-possession in terms of D's, while the concept of a D makes no converse provision. It will be remembered that the concept of a T is (largely) the concept of a relatively stable basis (otherwise unspecified) for a hypothetical frequency of M's. It is clear that the very constitution of this concept guarantees that we can explain P's possession of T by making explicit what the basis of the hypothetical frequency is in his case; the concept contains a slot such that whatever fills that slot (correctly) is conceptually guaranteed to constitute an explanation of P's having the T. Furthermore if we accept a motivational model for the explanation of action, we commit ourselves to the possibility of filling in such slots with D's (or systems of D's). For if, as we saw in connection with VIII any particular action is explained most fundamentally by D's, then it follows that the actions, frequencies of which are involved in the possession of a given T, are explained most fundamentally by D's. But if particular instances of boasting or acting politely are explained by D's, then the fact that there are or would be frequent boastings or polite actions in a certain set of situations, is itself explained by D's. If each of a polite person's polite acts is explained by his wanting to be liked by others, and believing that acting politely will contribute to this, then this want-belief combination is likewise the explanation of the fact that polite acts occur (or would occur) relatively frequently in a certain set of situations. The frequency does not require explanation over and above the explanation of the particular acts. Hence if each of a person's polite acts are explained by this want-belief combination, it is this want-belief combination that constitutes the relatively stable basis of the trait. Of course, this is the simplest possible case. We cannot expect that all the manifestations of a given T will generally be explainable in terms of the same D-system. Another possible case is that in which some of the polite acts of a polite person are explainable as above, some are explainable in terms of a fear of being rejected, and some in terms of a desire to think of oneself as a polite person. In such a case the relatively stable basis of the frequency would be some set of D-systems, rather than a single D-system. But that does not affect the basic point.

Thus we see that our analysis of T-concepts, plus the principle that actions are most fundamentally explained in terms of a motivational model (by means of D's), implies that T-possessions can be explained in terms of D's. To put it another way: it is implied that D's are, in a way, constitutive of T's, and hence stand in a peculiarly intimate explanatory relationship. By contrast, there is no such conceptual linkage in the opposite direction. There is nothing in the analysis of D-concepts to *require* an explanation of D-possession in terms of T's. There are no "slots" in the analysis that must be (or even may be) filled in with T's. In our conceptual scheme, D's "underly" T's; they belong to a more fundamental stratum of explanation, and hence, in a very important sense, to a deeper stratum of the personality.

One important application of IX is that in two different cases the same T, involving exactly the same pattern of manifestations, can stem from quite different underlying D-systems. One person may act methodically on various occasions just because he gets satisfaction out of doing so, another because he is afraid that if he doesn't keep things in order some terrible, nameless doom will overtake him, another because he is seeking approval from orderly persons. P_1 may be unsociable just because he is more interested in things other than social interaction, P_2 because a strong fear of rejection inhibits him from approaching people, P_3 because he dreads becoming dependent on others. Wide differences in the underlying motivational structure may be covered up by identical surface patterns of manifestations.

It follows from the foregoing that:

X. T's are specially useful for fragmentary, *ad hoc* descriptions of persons, entered into for limited practical purposes. D's are more suited to the construction of a fundamental theoretical system for the explanation of human behavior.

For limited practical purposes, such as selecting an employee for a particular job, it may be more useful (because it is more specifically relevant to our particular interests) to have a description in terms of traits. If we are interested, e.g., in the likelihood of P's carrying out assignments conscientiously or being friendly with clients, a trait description will tell us just what we want to know in the concisest possible form. Even if an adequate account of P's D-system would put us in a much better position to specify the conditions under which P would or would not carry out tasks conscientiously, still we may not have time to go into all that, even if our present resources sufficed, as they do not, for arriving at such an account and applying it to a particular case. But the aim of developing an adequate science of personality is something else again. If we want to arrive at a manageable scheme of concepts, such that in terms of nomological principles involving those concepts we can obtain the maximum yield in the way of systematic prediction and explanation of human action, thought, and feeling, then D-concepts are more suitable, just because of the points brought out above (particularly VII and VIII). Since D-concepts embody (or presuppose in the background) a model for such a system, a model for which there does not seem to be any alternative that is nearly as promising, they are fitted for this role in a way in which T-concepts are not. Moreover the T-D contrast is something like the contrast in chemistry between observable, surface properties of substances (color, texture, hardness, etc.), and the unobservable molecular structures that underly and explain the surface properties.[14] It seems to be a fundamental lesson of science that we get a much more powerful explanatory and predictive system by utilizing relatively few underlying hypothesized factors, rather than by trying to construct our basic system out of the almost illimitable wealth of observable surface features. I see no reason to suppose that psychology is any exception to this principle.

X

Each of the contrasts we have enumerated brings out one or another aspect or consequence of the basic insight enunciated at the outset: T's embody relatively superficial aspects of personality, while D's represent underlying factors that are responsible for those surface aspects. I would urge that a firm grasp of the differences between these two sets of concepts is essential for any further advance, conceptual or empirical, in the understanding of personality.

NOTES

1. The rule that I have in the back of my mind for assigning items to the D-category is that D's are factors that are involved in motivational explanations (those that can be expressed in an "in order to" form). This involvement may be of two kinds. When a D is used in the explanation of an action, either this explanation is itself a motivational one or it presupposes that a certain kind of motivational explanation of the action can be given. Thus when one explains X's going to the kitchen by saying that he *wants* a bottle of beer, a close equivalent of this would be "He went to the kitchen *in order to* get a bottle of beer." And if we explain X's voting for Johnson in 1964 by saying that X was *opposed to* escalating the Vietnam war, this presupposes the possibility of giving some explanation like "X voted for Johnson *in order to* contribute to a lessening of the chances for the escalation of the Vietnam war," although this latter explanation is not even roughly equivalent to the original. Thus my background notion of D's reflects a distinction between motivational and other types of explanations of actions. However there will not be time for an elaboration of the general concept of D's in this paper.

2. I want to underline the point that in order for M to be a manifestation it is not required that it be conclusive evidence or even evidence of any considerable strength by itself. The minimum requirement might be expressed as follows: if all we knew about P is that he has done or undergone M, that would be some reason for attributing C to him.

3. I am not restricting the term "occurrence" to entities that involve internal change. A short-lived haughty look would count as an occurrence, even though it is not changing while it lasts.

4. e.g., "A trait is a tendency to react in a defined way in response to a defined class of stimuli." L. J. Cronbach, *Essentials of Psychological Testing*, 2nd ed. (New York, Harper & Row, 1960), p. 499.

5. Roughly speaking, an attitude, in the sense in which I am employing the term, is a complex of dispositions to act and to feel in certain ways toward a certain object or kind of object, where at least some of these ways can be characterized as being pro or con the object.

6. For a review and critique see Gordon W. Allport, *Personality* (New York, Henry Holt, 1937) Ch. X.

7. Note that in all these cases we can form a more restricted T-concept such that we would be justified in supposing P_1 to possess this trait to at least as great an extent as P_2. Thus for the first point, we could consider the trait, *sympathetic with those in pain*; for the second point, *sympathetic with those having a great deal of trouble*, etc. Of course, no matter how restricted our T-concept, a set of opportunities can still be more or less varied. For *sympathetic with those in pain*, a set restricted to people who have been injured would be less adequate than one that also includes persons suffering from a disease. However, as the T-concept becomes more specific, differences in the constitution of the set become less important. That is, we are on safer ground in inferring from repeated displays of sympathy when confronted with injuries to a high probability of sympathy when confronted with someone suffering pain from a disease, than we are in making a similar inference from sympathy with physical pain to sympathy with professional frustrations.

8. In effect our whole discussion is restricted to the attributing of traits to persons who have a fairly definitely formed personality. Prior to this, T-concepts do not have such a clear application.

9. C is to be interpreted as an indication of the type of analysis that is suitable for desire-concepts, rather than an actually worked out schema of analysis for such concepts. This is primarily because the particular list of conditionals given is intended to be illustrative rather than definitive. Indeed, the "open-textured" character of the concept of desire may well make it impossible to give a list that is precisely correct. For elaborations of this approach to desire-concepts the reader is referred to Richard B. Brandt and Jaegwon Kim, "Wants as Explanations of Actions, *Journal of Philosophy*, Vol. LX (1963), pp. 425–435; and to the present author's article, "Motives and Motivation," in Paul Edwards, ed., *Encyclopedia of Philosophy*, (New York, Crowell-Collier, 1967).

10. We could have desires without manifestations for this reason, even if a desire were construed as a set of dispositions to the manifestations, rather than in the more complicated way we have adopted, as dispositions to *tendencies* to manifestations.

11. We should also have to consider various kinds of T-D combinations. There are portmanteau characteristics that include an assortment of T's and D's— *masculine, mature, square*. A masculine person (according to some uses of this term) is one who has certain kinds of interests and desires, as well as having certain traits, such as *domineering*, and lacking others, such as *sensitive*.

12. This is not to deny that various traits might be empirically discovered to enter into nomological relations with other factors in the determination of a variety of manifestations. Thus it might be discovered that argumentative people generally do not feel very disappointed when they fail to get something they had wanted

and expected to get. The point being made here is that D-concepts already contain the outlines of such connections, whereas T-concepts do not. One might say that each general principle connecting traits with other factors is itself an isolated fact. It is purely empirical. Moreover, and this is a separate point, I suspect that the prospects are not good for integrating trait concepts in this way into complex systems of factors.

13. Roughly, the motivational model, as I interpret it, represents each (full-blooded) action as stemming from the strongest tendency in a contemporary field of tendencies, each tendency being itself the outgrowth of a belief as to how some desire or aversion might be satisfied.

14. Only "something like". Physical science does not seem to make any important use of concepts that are between observation-concepts and theoretical-concepts in just the way trait-concepts are.

BELIEF IN OTHER MINDS[1]

Kenneth Stern

Is there a problem of other minds? In what follows I shall maintain that there is such a problem, connected with, but different from the problem as traditionally formulated. What I shall do is to try to reformulate it in such a way as to immunize it against the various dissolutions of it which have been offered in contemporary philosophy, and then argue for a modified skepticism in that modified formulation of the problem. But we must approach slowly.

What seems to me central to the traditional skeptic's denial that we can know what sensations another has, is his contention that although on the one hand statements that ascribe sensations and feelings to others are "empirical" statements, and so, in this respect, are in the same class with statements that ascribe physical properties to people and things, such as "the book is gray" or "Jonathan has gained weight"— that is, they are established or disestablished by the "evidence of the senses"; on the other hand, the skeptic will hold that the sense-evidence which may be adequate for ascribing physical properties to people with certainty, will not be adequate for ascribing sensations or feelings to people with certainty, for, he will hold, there will be some bit of information which the subject of the sensation-ascription will have, which is inaccessible to anyone else, namely the sensation itself. For this reason, the skeptic holds that I cannot be as certain of someone else's sensations as I can be of any other (empirical) fact about him. There is, of course, a long philosophical tradition which argues for skepticism concerning ordinary empirical statements ascribing physical properties to people or to things, but the point, it seems to me, of what the skeptic contends concerning the sensations of others, is that even if the traditional "Cartesian" doubts concerning statements ascribing physical properties to things and to people were allayed, his problem would remain untouched. The skeptic concerning the sensations of others need not (although he may) be a skeptic concerning other empirical statements. He may, for instance, concede that another man is shouting, or that he is hitting the table with his fist, or that his face is flushed; indeed, in order to pose his problem, he must concede at least for the sake of the argument, that we can be certain about such matters; for after all, the skeptic wishes to argue that we can be certain about these matters and still not be certain that such a man is angry, for, he will say, we can be certain concerning such things without knowing the essential thing, namely what the man's inner state is. It is well, I think, to notice too that the grounds the traditional skeptic presents for his skepticism concerning other minds, differ quite considerably from those he gives for skepticism for other empirical statements. For the latter, the grounds given would consist of such arguments as that from illusion and hallucination, from dreaming, from the relativity of perception, and so on. But such grounds are not what the skeptic concerning other minds offers. There arises no possibility of having an illusion that another is angry, although one may concede the possibility of illusion concerning the outward behavior and circumstances surrounding that behavior which is supposed to be the grounds for the inference that another is angry. In other words, although the grounds upon which the inference is made to the mental states of others are traditionally considered subject to "Cartesian" doubts, the skeptical doubt concerning the ability of someone to know what the mental states of another are, is based on quite other considerations, and is furthermore logically independent of the former sort of doubts. Therefore, although skepticism concerning other minds is a skepticism concerning a (proper) subclass of empirical statements, the grounds for such skepticism are very different from those traditionally produced as the grounds for skepticism concerning the ascription of physical properties to people or things, and, indeed, the former skepticism is logically independent of the latter; it begins, as it were, where the other leaves off, and at least for the sake of the argument, regards the former sort as having been resolved.

The traditional reply to skepticism concerning other minds, which has gained the most support among philosophers since the time of Mill and which has been regarded by them as offering a satisfactory solution to the problem until Wittgenstein and Malcolm and others have recently posed powerful strictures on it, has been "the argument by analogy." As I understand it, this argument runs something like this: We can inductively support the conclusion that others have particular inner states if we are allowed to have as grounds for our conclusion the following kinds of premises:

(1) statements that describe the outward behavior of others, and the circumstances in which such behavior occurs;

(2) statements which describe inner states of ourselves and which we take (in Chisholm's phrase) to be "directly evident";

(3) statements which describe our behavior and the circumstances in which it occurs;

(4) statements which assert some contingent connection between the inner states described in the statements in group 2 above, and the behavior in the circumstances described in group 3 above, i.e. a connection between our behavior and our own inner states.

If we are allowed the above sorts of statements as premises, and if we are also allowed a familiar kind of inductive inference, we can then establish, with inductive certainty the conclusion that another is angry or has a pain. Proponents of this way of answering the skeptic, allowed, of course, that the conclusion would be only inductively certain as the conclusion of an inductive argument, and, if inductive certainty was invidiously compared with deductive certainty, then only probability was claimed for the conclusion. But even so, this merely meant that I could be as certain of someone else's sensation as of any other (empirical) fact, neither more, nor less.

I read Wittgenstein and Malcolm and others who follow them in their objections to the argument by analogy as making the following two strictures of it.[2] First, they deny that there exist such statements as those cited in group 2 above, i.e., those ascribing inner states to ourselves. Such sentences do not really express statements which can be said to be known or doubted. It makes no sense to talk of knowing that we are angry or in pain. Second, they deny the propriety of the reasoning used here to go from the premises to the conclusion, not on the grounds that analogical reasoning gives only inductive certainty, but on the more radical grounds that in reality what looks like analogical reasoning here is only a parody of it. No inductive inference is really being made here for it is essential to all inductive reasoning that its conclusion be in principle checkable, for otherwise the connection implied by the reasoning could not have been established in the first place. What is wrong with the analogical argument, as used here, is that the conclusion is not, even in principle, checkable. It should be added, for the sake of completeness, that both of these strictures are supported with arguments based on certain theories concerning the nature of language and that I have nothing to add to the numerous objections which have been raised in recent literature against the foundations of the Wittgenstein objections. What I wish to do now is to discuss the conclusion Wittgenstein and his followers have reached as a consequence of their objections to the argument by analogy. They have not, of course, held as a consequence of these objections that the skeptic is correct, but rather that we can, with certainty, ascribe mental states such as sensations and feelings to others non-inferentially solely on the basis of the behavior and the circumstances in which the behavior occurs. There is no need of any inference here, for such behavior and circumstances, when present, constitute the "criteria" that "settle" (in Malcolm's word) the question of whether another has a particular sensation or feeling. We have (indeed must have, according to Malcolm) such criteria for ascriptions of inner states to others just as we have for ascriptions of physical states to them. In the case of the former, just as in the case of the latter, there may be some question as to whether the criteria are *present*, but there can be no question that there *are* criteria, and it is just this last that the skeptic wants to assert. There is, so the argument against the skeptic goes, no essential bit of information which the subject of the inner state has, and which is in principle inaccessible to anyone else but him, and so there can be no real question as to whether we can be certain concerning the mental states of others. We can be, and very often are. And so, according to Wittgenstein: "I can be as *certain* of someone else's sensations as of any fact." [3] In passing, I might mention here that there is some question in my mind as to just how Wittgenstein is using the word "certain" here. Firth, in a recent article,[4] has pointed out that there are two uses of "certain," one in which to say that someone was certain when he made a particular statement is to entail that that statement was true (Firth calls this the "truth-evaluating use"), and another in which to say that someone was certain when he made a statement is not to entail that the statement was true (Firth calls this the "warrant-evaluating use"), but to say only that the person who made the statement had for that statement, grounds which would be required by any rational man who claimed to be certain of the truth of that statement. It seems to me probable that Wittgenstein in the above quoted passage was using "certain" in this latter "warrant-evaluating" sense which does not entail truth. What is interesting for my present purpose are Wittgenstein's remarks which follow immediately upon the above quoted passage. He continues, after telling us that we can be as certain of someone else's sensations as of any other fact:

But this does not make the propositions "He is much depressed," "25 × 25 = 625," and "I am sixty years old" into similar instruments. The explanation suggests itself that the certainty is of a different *kind*.—This seems to point to a psychological difference. But the difference is logical.[5]

I find a good deal that is puzzling in the above passage. Why, for instance, does Wittgenstein compare a third person statement ascribing a mental state, to an arithmetical statement which, although a "fact," is certainly not an empirical fact? Again, why does he compare these to an empirical fact in the first person? It is clear enough that Wittgenstein wants to maintain that despite the differences among them, we can, in circumstances that are conceivable, be certain of all the above statements,[6] but he nevertheless also wants to hold that there are "logical" differences among them (in some broad sense of "logical" made popular by Wittgenstein).[7] One such "logical" difference, would, I think, be a difference in the ways in which the different sorts of statements—of the kind Wittgenstein cites above—would be established. And, insofar as Wittgenstein not only contrasts empirical statements with nonempirical statements, ($25 \times 25 = 625$), but with *other* empirical statements, it would appear that even in the broad class of empirical statements there are "logical" differences among different members of that class. If the foregoing is right, then, although it may be quite correct to say that statements ascribing sensations to others are empirical statements, it may still be true that such statements do present problems special to themselves; that is, their "logic" may be very different from those ascribing physical predicates to persons. If that is so, then any attempt to assimilate them to statements of the latter sort, would be an error. I should not want to say that Wittgenstein, Malcolm, and others, like Ryle, have not pointed out differences between statements ascribing sensations to others and those ascribing physical properties to others; however, I shall try to argue that there is a crucial difference between the two classes of statements which is different from any which has been noted before. It does seem to me that although philosophers following Wittgenstein have distinguished between the two classes of statements mentioned, they have nevertheless tended to deny that at the bottom there is any more involved in ascertaining that another has a sensation, than in ascertaining that he has a physical property or that the former problem presents difficulties of anything more than greater complexity, rather than of any differences in kind. It is for this reason that contemporary philosophers have, after noting various differences between the two classes of statements, ended up by concluding that there is no special problem of other minds which can be formulated—no special problem, that is, over and above those "Cartesian" ills to which all empirical statements are heir. I intend to argue for a different position, namely one that falls in between the skeptic's position that statements concerning the sensations of others present is a problem utterly different from statements concerning the physical properties of others, so that for lack of what is logically inaccessible, certainty is unattainable in the first class of statements, and the contemporary position that such statements present no special difficulty other than one of greater complexity. I want to argue that although the skeptic's position is not right, there is something right in it, for the reason that there is something quite special that we have to know in order to be certain of statements ascribing sensations to others, and that moreover, what we have to know here plays a unique role in the range of evidence for such statements, inasmuch as no other bit of evidence plays such a role in the case of statements of the other sort, i.e., statements ascribing physical properties to individuals.

The point I wish to make can be rather simply put: A person's belief concerning his sensations "weighs" in the range of evidence another has concerning that person's sensations in a way which is quite different from the way in which a person's belief concerning any physical state he has "weighs" in the range of evidence another may have concerning that person's physical state. Suppose, to give an example, I assert or believe that another person has gained weight. Suppose too that I discover that he believes he has not gained weight, that my assertion or belief that he has is false, then it is clear, I take it, that his belief can be overridden by other evidence. *That* he believes that he has not gained weight may, no doubt, figure in the range of evidence which I have for whether he has gained weight, and, depending on the circumstances, it may figure strongly or weakly, but I do not think it will be denied that if I were to place him on a scale, and the scale clearly indicated that he had gained weight, then his belief that he had not would be overriden. I should be quite certain that he had gained weight in the face of his belief that he had not done so. Suppose now, to use the example from Wittgenstein, I believe or assert that another person is depressed. Suppose too that I discover that this other person believes that he is not depressed. Then, what I want to say is that the situation now is very different with regard to any belief I may have about the other's mental state. For another's belief that he is not depressed is not overridable by other evidence in the way another's belief that he has not gained weight is overridable. It seems to me that in such a situation, I cannot be certain that he is depressed in the face of his belief that he is not. In this sort of situation where a person's belief that he is not depressed is in conflict with other evidence I may have that he is depressed, I cannot be certain that he is depressed. Neither, of course, can I be certain that he is not depressed. The truth is, I think, that in such a situation, I cannot be certain. The fact (if it is one) that another's belief that he does not have a particular mental state plays the unique role I claim it has—such that it is sufficient to prevent another from being certain that he does have that particular mental state, despite any other evidence he may have that that other has that mental state—seems to me to distinguish quite decisively, between (empirical) statements ascribing sensations and feelings to others, and (empirical) statements ascribing physical states to others. It seems to me to make a "logical" difference of the sort Wittgenstein might have had in mind. And it seems also to have this further consequence, that there are situations in which I cannot be certain that another has a particular sensation or feeling, because a particular bit of evidence is missing—and this bit of evidence is unique in that no other evidence can either replace it or override it. In short, there seems to me to be truth in a suitably modified version of the skeptical position concerning other minds. I shall revert to this point presently, but first I wish to state more formally what it is that I wish to maintain so as to present you with a stationary target: I will then try to distinguish my position from another which may understandably be confounded with it.

I want to hold that:

(1) "A is certain that N has sensation s" entails "A is certain that it is false that N believes N does not have s" (Where A and N are different individuals).

The following corollary of 1.[8]

(2) "A is certain that N believes N does not have s" entails "A is not certain that N has s" (no matter what evidence A has that N has s).

The following proposition is also a corollary of 1.[9]

(3) "A is not certain that N believes N does not have s" and "A is not certain that it is false that N believes N does not have s" entails "A is not certain that N has s."

The point of 3 above is obviously to account for those cases in which A has no information concerning N's belief as to whether he (N) does have s or not. The possibility then remains open that N believes he does not have s. Since this condition might obtain for all A knows, A still cannot be certain that N has s.

I next want to point out that the position I hold may be with some justification called an epistemological counterpart of what is sometimes called the "incorrigibility thesis." There is one version of the incorrigibility thesis which my position, although quite compatible with, is logically independent of, in that the falsity of the incorrigibility thesis in no way entails the falsity of what I want to maintain. This version of it I take to be the assertion of one of the two propositions immediately below, or the joint assertion of both of them.

(4) "N has sensation s" entails "N believes that he (N) has s."

(5) "N believes he has sensations s" entails "N has s."

Both of the above propositions (or some version of them) have had busy careers in philosophy. The former has been beset with the difficulties which arise out of cases of "unnoticed sensations," i.e., those cases in which we have some inclination to hold that a man may have a sensation and at the same time he may be unaware of the sensation, i.e., some inclination to hold that he believes he does not have that sensation. For instance, a man who has been injured but is also in such a state of excitement, that he talks and acts as if he feels no pain. It is clear that there are such cases, both actual and conceivable, and although there is no space here to discuss them, it seems clear that they, at least prima facie, are counter-examples to 4. I am not saying that such cases are decisive against 4, only that such cases have to be explained (away) by anyone who wishes to maintain 4. Number 5 above suffers from similar well-known objections stemming from cases of hypochondria, hypnosis, and the like. Here too, as in the case of 4 above, I do not want to maintain that these objections are decisive against 5, only that they have to be dealt with and constitute prima facie evidence against 5. It seems to me an advantage of my epistemological counterpart to the incorrigibility thesis, that my theory is independent of the truth or falsity of 4 and 5. It is, furthermore, an advantage to sever the problem of other minds from the incorrigibility thesis, as I think I have done.

There is, however, a version of the incorrigibility thesis that is quite evidently incompatible with my theory. What this version holds is that the concept of belief is inapplicable to sensations. One neither believes nor disbelieves that one has a sensation, one simply has sensations. Clearly, inasmuch as my theory holds that it is possible for someone to disbelieve he has a sensation, my theory cannot be true, if the above version of the incorrigibility thesis is true. But is this version of that thesis true? It does not seem to me that it is as long as it is admitted that one can lie about having a particular sensation. If lying entails intending to deceive, then if intending to deceive entails saying something is true and at the same time believing that that thing is false, then certainly one can believe one does not have a particular sensation given that one can lie about one's sensations,[10] i.e., belief is applicable to sensations.

At this point, the following objection might be made to my contentions, 1, 2, and 3: Is not any evidence someone might have that some-one believes he does not have a sensation, just the same evidence that one would take as showing that that someone does not have that sensa-tion? There is no doubt that my evidence that someone had gained weight is quite independent of my evidence that he believed he had not gained weight. In the one case I have the reading on the scales, con-trasted with what the man says and how he behaves. But what is my ev-idence that a man believes he does not have a particular sensation, other than my evidence that he does not have that sensation? The above objection ought to be distinguished from another similar one, namely, Is not my evidence that you believe you do not have a particular sensa-tion simply *part* of any evidence that I may have that you do not have that sensation? If this latter objection really comes down to saying that N's belief that he does not have a particular sensation is *decisive* evi-dence that he does not have that sensation, then this latter objection seems to be a version of one of the conjuncts of the incorrigibility the-sis, in fact it is the contra-positive of 4. If anything weaker is intended by the phrase, "part of the evidence," then the objector becomes one of my supporters, *except* for the very important qualification that it is part of my contention that a person's belief that he does *not* have a particu-lar sensation, is not only evidence that he does not have that sensation, but that it plays a peculiar epistemological role, in that although it does not provide decisive evidence that the person does not have that sensa-tion, it provides a decisive reason for holding that one cannot be certain that the person does have that sensation, regardless of what *other* evi-dence one may have that the person does have that sensation.

As for the first objection, it does seem to me that if one is willing to contrast a person's behavior with what he says, then one can have evi-dence that he has a particular sensation (his behavior), and at the same time have evidence that he believes he does not have that sensation (e.g., his stating that he does not have that sensation). Now it seems to me that what the first objection is really getting at is this: Isn't it true that if we find that all the evidence supports "N has sensation s," and N says, "I do not have s" or "I believe I do not have s," we should simply take it that N was lying? That is to say, could there ever be a case in which it was allowed that there was *good* independent evidence that N believed he did not have s, in the face of good evidence that he did have s? Should we not always, in such a case, choose to disregard any ev-idence we had that N believed he did not have s? What the objection seems to come to then is not that there might be evidence for "N does not have s" that is not evidence for "N believes he does not have s" and vice versa, but the rather more subtle objection that one cannot both hold that the evidence that one could have for "N believes he does not have s" is sufficient evidence for that proposition's truth, and, at the same time, hold that one had sufficient evidence for the truth of the proposition, "N has s," even if one did hold that the evidence for "N believes he does not have s" is independent of "N does not have s." I suppose that to that objection, my reply must be that one can indeed have sufficient evidence for "N believes he does not have s" despite any evidence that one may have that "N has s" provided that one could also be said to have good additional evidence that when N says "I do not have s" or "I do not believe I have s," he is not lying. One could, it seems to me have such additional evidence which was independent of what N said. For instance knowledge about N's truth-telling tendencies, or inferences from the circumstances or tone of N's voice. But, there is an additional point here. I have perhaps been giving too much to the objector, for in the foregoing it was tacitly assumed that any evidence that I might have for "N believes he does not have s" was confined to what N said, and the circumstances surrounding his statement, and it was also tacitly assumed that the only evidence I could have for "N has s" would be N's behavior in certain circumstances. But I might easily have *physiological* evidence that N had s, e.g., a bad wound, or records of brain impulses, and N's *behavior* might be evidence for his believing he did not have s. That is, N might not only say he did not have s, but *behave* as if he did not believe he had s. Once the possibility of physiological evidence is brought into consideration, we see that behavioral evidence might support the proposition "N believes he does not have s." Naturally, if all the physiological *and* behavioral evidence went to support the proposition, "N has s" and nonetheless N continued to insist that he did not have s, we should have to decide, on my theory, whether N was lying, and so did in fact believe that he had s, or was telling the truth and so in fact believed that he did not have s. If we decided that the second was true, then on my theory we should simply have to say we could not be certain whether or not N was in pain. But whether we should decide that N was lying, or whether N believed he was not in pain should in the last analysis depend on the case. And in some cases it might be difficult to make a decision. But what my theory requires is not that there be no difficulty in any situation in making a decision as to whether N is lying, but rather that such a decision be in principle possible in some cases. I see no reason to think that such a decision is not in principle possible in some cases.

According to me then, another's belief that he does not have a particular sensation, s, has a peculiar status in the range of evidence that I may have for the strength of my belief that he has s. This status is as follows: any evidence that I may have for the statement that another has s will be outweighed by his belief that he does not have s. What I mean by "outweighed" is this: If the evidence I have that N has s would, in conjunction with the truth of "N believes he has s" make me certain that N has, then, if I am certain that it is true that N believes he does not have s, or if I do not know whether or not N believes he does not have s, then I am certain that N has s. It is clear that the above is not true for any substitution of a physical property for s. For any physical property N may have, I may be certain N has that physical property in the face of either my ignorance of whether he believes he has that property, or believes he does not have that property, and in the face of my certainty that he believes he does not have that property.

Next, I want to point out that I am by no means holding that I can never be certain that another person, N, has s, but rather that under a particular condition, namely when I am certain that N believes he does not have s, or I do not know whether or not he believes that, then, I cannot be certain that N has s. If I am right about this, then it is easier to understand the persistent notion in philosophy that the knowledge of other minds presents a peculiarly intractable epistemological problem. It explains as well why it has been held that it is impossible to know that another has a sensation, for, although this last is certainly false as it stands, for we can surely be certain that another has a sensation when our evidence for that is accompanied by another's belief that he has that sensation, it can always happen that another's belief may conflict with any evidence I might have that he has that sensation, or, it can happen that I may be ignorant of whether or not he believes he does not have that sensation. If all this is so, then although Wittgenstein is right when he tells us that we can be as certain of someone else's sensations as of any other fact, it is necessary to add that it will sometimes be impossible for us to be certain of someone else's sensation, on account of a bit of information, peculiar to such certainty, which bit of information has a peculiar evidential status in that it cannot be outweighed by other evidence. It is this last point which, in my view, makes our certainty regarding the sensations of others crucially different from our certainty concerning such a fact as physical properties of others. For, although it is surely true that in the absence of a particular bit of evidence, I cannot be certain that another person has a particular physical property, it is not true that there is any *one* particular bit of evidence the absence of which rules out certainty in the case of physical properties and the absence of which, in such a case, will outweigh, in the way I have sought to explain, all the evidence that could be conceivably arrayed against it. It is important to notice *both* that it is always, I maintain, the *same* bit of information, viz. whether N believes he does not have *s*, while in the case of physical properties ascribed to others, this is not true, *and also* that this bit of information is such that for its lack, certainty is ruled out. Unless what I have just said is emphasized, it might easily be held that nothing much of importance is being advanced as true, even if it is true, since, it might be objected, for any empirical statement, it might be true that for the want of some bit of information, certainty is ruled out. So what makes what I maintain important, if it is true, is that for the lack of a special bit of evidence, namely that concerning another's belief, no other evidence is sufficient for my certainty that he has a particular sensation, and in the presence of a particular bit of evidence, namely that another believes he does not have a particular sensation, no amount of countervailing evidence is sufficient for certainty. So, at the risk of embittering you, let me repeat that I maintain: (1) that it is always the same bit of evidence which is at issue, and (2) that this bit of evidence is special epistemologically. It is the combination of these two points which, it seems to me, does create a problem of other minds over and in addition to the question of certainty concerning empirical statements about the physical properties of others.

Let me conclude by pointing out that my reformulation of the problem of other minds raises a problem which must have occurred to many of you as you were listening to me. If what I have said is true, then the problem of other minds would then center on the special problem of certainty concerning the beliefs of others, for, in my opinion, it is there where the heart of the problem lies. I have already touched on this matter in a different way earlier in my paper, but let me point out that if it were maintained that even if all I have said is true, still, if it turned out that beliefs themselves were inveterately private then all I have said is undermined in a very fundamental way, in that a wholesale skeptical position could then be reestablished. For, consider, I have argued that my certainty concerning another's sensations has, as a necessary condition, my certainty concerning another's beliefs. But if I cannot achieve such certainty because beliefs are private, then skepticism in the old thoroughgoing sense remains. Worse, a new spectre is raised, for suppose beliefs are exactly like sensations, in that if I hold that I cannot be certain that another has a particular sensation if he believes he does not have that sensation, then perhaps I cannot be certain that that person believes he does not have that sensation, unless I can be certain that it is false that he believes he does not believe he has that sensation. But if something like the foregoing is true it turns out that the spectre which was raised was that most horrible ghost of all, the Ghost of Infinite Regress. Now, a ghost need only be to have been laid if it exists, and, as everyone knows, ghosts do not exist. I am myself unwilling to believe that beliefs *are* like sensations, i.e., that they have the special logical property I have argued sensations have. I have not any special argument to show this, and, in order to discuss the question, I should have to keep you even longer. However, let me simply say this: There is after all, no special reason to think that what is true of sensations must also be true of beliefs, and the possibility that it must be so seems to come from the consideration that both beliefs and sensations are, in some sense of that word, "mental." But Professor Ryle, among others, has taught us to hold that word in grave suspicion. "Mental" is a nebulous term, and there is really no special reason to think that what is true of one mental entity *need* be true of another. I admit there might be a problem, I do not admit that there need be one, and perhaps my admission will do at present.

NOTES

1. I am grateful for the enormous assistance I have received from Herbert Heidelberger in writing this paper. I am also indebted to Murray Kiteley, Alice Lazerowitz, and Malcolm Smith.
2. There is also sometimes included a third stricture having to do with the alleged connection between the inner state and its bodily manifestations.
3. *Philosophical Investigations*, IIxi, p. 224.
4. "The Anatomy of Certainty," *The Philosophical Review*, January, 1967.
5. *Loc. Cit.*
6. Strictly speaking, of course, we should be speaking of sentences and statements made by them in particular circumstances.
7. It seems clear from the context that Wittgenstein is here denying that the difference in certainty is *psychological*, say some degree of conviction. By "logical" difference, he means something like "epistemological" rather than psychological.
8. 2 follows from 1 with the assumption of the apparently unexceptionable epistemological principle, if a proposition is certain, then its negation is not certain. Thus: letting Cs stand for "It is certain that N has sensation s" and Cbs stand for "It is certain that N believes he has sensation s," etc. and letting $-$ be the negation sign:
(i) $Cs \rightarrow C-(b-s)$ formulation of 1 above.
(ii) $C(b-s) \rightarrow -C-(b-s)$ application of principle above.
(iii) $-C-(b-s) \rightarrow -Cs$ by contraposition of i.
(iv) $C(b-s) \rightarrow -Cs$ hypothetical syllogism from ii & iii.
$\qquad\qquad$ iv is 2 above in text.
9. 3 above is $-C(b-s)$ & $-C-(b-s) \rightarrow -Cs$, which is clearly logically equivalent to, $Cs \rightarrow C(b-s)$ v $C-(b-s)$ by De Morgan's Law and contraposition, and which is implied by 1. above, $CS \rightarrow C-(b-s)$.
10. I must confess that I am not at all sure that anyone does hold this version

of the incorrigibility thesis. There is the well-known thesis held by Wittgenstein and by Malcolm that one cannot *know* that one has a sensation. The grounds for this (at least in part) seem to be that in order for "I know that *p*" to make sense, it must also make sense to doubt that *p*, or to find out that *p*, or be mistaken that *p*, and since these latter expressions do not make sense, "I know that *p*" makes no sense. Quite apart from any cogency this argument might be thought to have, my question is whether the same argument is supposed to hold for the application of the notion of belief to sensations. My argument against the idea that belief is inapplicable to sensations, above, is like the one Ayer gives against the inapplicability of knowing to sensations, in *The Concept of a Person*, p. 59. Malcolm, in a foot-note to his recent paper, "The Privacy of Experience," in *Epistemology*, ed. Avrum Stroll, p. 157, writes:

> Ayer gives the following 'proof' that if we are in pain we know it, namely that one can tell lies about one's sensations. For 'to tell a lie is not just to make a false statement; it is to make a statement that one knows to be false; and this implies denying what one knows to be true.' I should take this as proof that telling a lie is not, in all cases, stating what one knows to be false. The word 'lying,' like the word 'game,' is applied over a broad range of di-verse cases.

I wish I could be enlightened as to why what Malcolm says concerning Ayer's argument is not a textbook example of begging the question. In fact, of course, Ayer's argument is unsound because it contains a false premise. It is not a neces-sary condition for telling a lie that one make a statement that one *knows* to be false. Else I could not tell a lie, and to my discomfiture discover that what I had said, *believing* it to be false, was actually true, or vice versa. What *is* a necessary condition for lying, is that the liar *believe* that the statement he made is false. The statement's turning out to be true makes him no less a liar. Malcolm might here attempt the same rejoinder concerning belief as he does against knowledge, but as I have already said, for him to say that the fact that we use belief in con-nection with sensations in the analysis of lying about sensation is a "proof" in that case, "lying" has a different use, without any independent argument for holding that "belief" is being differently used in such a context, can be no more than beg-ging the question.

THE MALIGN GENIE REVISITED

(A RESPONSE)

John Catan

Mr. Stern tells us that his position is somewhere between the Cartesian sceptic's postion that statements about the sensations of others present an utterly different problem from statements about the physical properties of others, and the contemporary position that there is no distinction between the two kinds of statements except one of greater complexity.

His position agrees with the sceptic that the two kinds of statements are different, but he disagrees on the grounds for the difference. He holds that in order to be certain of statements of belief ascribing sensations to others, that there is a bit of evidence that has unique epistemic privilege, namely, the other individual's belief assertion about his belief. He finds in this fact the grounds for reformulating the problem of other minds.

I think that a fundamental confusion has been generated by Mr. Stern's use of a narrative mode in the presentation of the examples that he uses to support his distinctions and conclusions. The difficulty results from the absence of quotation marks around the expressions in question. In contemporary logic, the rule is generally recognized that when we write down an expression for the purpose of talking about that very expression, we must show what we are doing by enclosing that expression within quotes; if this rule is not strictly observed, fallacies are likely to occur of the kind that I believe Mr. Stern has committed. In order to exhibit the difficulty let us take the examples that Mr. Stern believes support his analysis and put them in direct discourse.

The scene is set in a philosophical parlor: Stage directions—A enters and B is seated in the room. B says, "I believe that you've gained weight." A replies, sucking in his abdomen and inflating his chest, "I don't believe so." B in an aside with a stage whisper: "By George, then, my belief and/or my belief-assertion, 'that he has gained weight,' is false."

Let us interject Mr. Stern's portion of the narrative at this point. It then becomes clear what I meant by the charge that confusion results from the absence of quotes around expressions. Mr. Stern says, "Then it is clear, I take it, that his belief can be overridden by other evidence." The key terms are 'belief' and 'evidence.' Let us take them one at a time.

Our little scenario has only been a presentation of beliefs, although trivially it may be said to include belief-assertions. My first question then is what are we talking about—'beliefs' or 'belief-assertions.' If we consult Mr. Stern's manuscript he seems to be ambiguous although from the tenor of the argument, it is fairly clear that he wants to talk about belief-assertions. When he states his point simply, he writes 'beliefs,' whereas in his example he begins with 'I assert or believe that P' and the other person is reported as saying 'he believes that not-P'. Finally, Mr. Stern adds parenthetically, 'my assertion or belief that P' is false.' "

I think the point is obvious and need not be labored. It may be true in some important sense to speak of the truth or falsity of belief-assertions and even of their evidence as Professor Gerald Myers illustrates in his recent *Journal of Philosophy* article, "Justifying Belief-Assertions."

But what are we to make of 'beliefs'? Are beliefs believed or known? Are they true or false? Are they based on evidence? It seems obvious that we need some terminological precisions.

'I believe that P' is a belief-assertion. I shall call it a BA. Its elements are: 'I believe', which refers to a belief as a psychological disposition and this entails a believer, i.e., a person who holds or has a belief. I shall call the disposition D and the believer B. 'That P' is more difficult because of multiple reference; in the first place, it may refer to proposition, or generally, that which is believed—this I shall call P; it may also refer to the state of affairs presented by the proposition—this I shall call R.

One area of difficulty is negation: A belief-assertion may be denied, which means the proposition is negated thus 'not-P'; another possibility is a denial of belief in the form 'I do not believe that P'—this is a denial of belief as a disposition. The locution 'I disbelieve' is a denial of P not a denial of D, belief as a disposition.

Another difficulty is involved in 'belief' D when it concerns another D or BA especially when this D is asserted BA. For example: "I believe that he believes that such and such is the case."

It is a truism, and an important one, to say that truth or falsity belong to propositions. But since having a belief D does not logically entail making a belief-assertion BA, I do not see any reason to claim that Ds entail truth or falsity, unless the existence of Ds are denied. BAs of course, entail truth or falsity, but in two ways; one way becomes clear in the situation in which the P of a BA is challenged. At this point we may speak of evidence usually in terms of conclusiveness or inconclusiveness for the P of a BA, and in this sense the P is true or false. The other way also involves challenge: i.e., when someone challenges someone's BA in terms of whether it exists or not, i.e., whether or not he truly *believes*. Here the reiteration of the BA as Professor Myers has shown, if done sincerely, repeats the BA in such a way that the reiteration tends to justify the original BA. But the reiterated BA is only trivially a BA, i.e., it has the lingusitic form but not the logic of a BA. It is a linguistic performance, or, in Austin's terms a performative utterance.

Thus to say that a BA is true or false in my sense would mean either that we have conclusive or inclusive evidence for the P of the BA or that we do or do not have a belief D. In both cases some BA has been challenged. But notice that it is the BA in either case which is true or false and that its T or F is based on different elements, i.e., the D or the P.

To get back to Professor Stern's paper—there is an obvious ambiguity in starting with "I assert or believe" since I may assert without belief or I may make a belief-assertion. In the case of making a BA which is what Mr. Stern is concerned with, we ought to distinguish between D and BA and P and R, since they are different in important ways as I have shown.

Suppose we allow a contrariety to exist between the Ps of two BAs —the important question then becomes one of evidence. That there is evidence is not the problem, the problem is, what are the criteria.

What is the basis for admission as evidence with respect to the 'D' i.e. the belief of one of the individuals? Beliefs as dispositions may of themselves be different (it depends on how Cartesian one desires to be) but they can hardly be said to be contrary or opposed. The Ps of BAs may be contrary or opposed, but not the Ds. Again, beliefs Ds do not involve evidence, but only challenged BAs do, that is, their Ps involve evidence. A BA of itself does not necessarily involve evidence either. For example, as performative utterances in ritual situations. But once challenged either by oneself or by another then the P of a BA is being understood as based on evidence, or else the challenge would be otiose.

Mr. Stern's choice of example is unfortunate in that whether or not an individual has gained weight or not is a different kind of question than whether or not an individual is depressed or not. And different in precisely the way that confuses. The question about weight-gain points to a suitable method of verification that makes clear what answer, on what evidence would be pertinent and acceptable. Whereas, whatever one's position on so-called inner-states or private experience, the question of whether or not someone is depressed is not clear in precisely the way that weight-gain is clear. And the issue is evidence.

Putting the empirical question about weight-gain into a belief-assertion form, clouds the distinction between knowledge and belief and their relation to evidence, which I think is the important issue. Knowledge and belief are both related to evidence but in different and important ways. Evidence for the objective referent R of a belief-assertion is evidence for the conclusiveness or inconclusiveness of that belief-assertion, but one can have a belief without evidence or without asserting that belief. The evidence for the objective referent of a knowledge-assertion is concerned with the existence of that referent; if there is no evidence I cannot claim that I know. If the proposition P, for example, is false, then the claim to know 'that P' is unfounded—i.e., I simply do not know. In the same case with respect to the objective referent of a belief-assertion, I may believe 'that P' but then my belief-assertion is false, i.e., based on inconclusive evidence. I may, however, continue to believe 'that P', although I ought not to.

I think what has led Mr. Stern astray is something that Professor Ryle has pointed out in the *Concept of Mind;* "that belief and knowledge (when it is knowledge *that*) operate, to put it crudely, in the same field. The sorts of things that can be described as known or unknown can also be described as believed or disbelieved, somewhat as the sorts of things that can be manufactured are also the sorts of things that can be exported."

In essence, what I am claiming, is that Mr. Stern has been deceived by the presentation of his examples in indirect discourse into confusing belief with belief-assertions, and further to misconstrue the relation of evidence to belief-statements. Beliefs do not entail truth or falsity; belief-statements may entail truth or falsity; but this characteristic of a belief-statement is an accidental feature of its logical form.

I am afraid that Mr. Stern is leading us from an assimilation of belief-statements about physical states to belief-statements about sensations, but not in what is for the present purposes a trivial sense, namely, that they are both empirical statements, but rather in terms of the important relation they both have to evidence. And it is this relation that I believe he has misrepresented. How else can we explain his notion of evidence that includes such peculiar entries as a person's belief-assertions about his physical state? There is at least *prima facie* correctness to the notion that belief-assertions of one person could play the role of evidence in the denial of certitude to another's belief-assertion about that person's inner state. But it would be a strange pair that would allow in the range of evidence for a 'belief-assertion' that is challenged about a physical state, the belief-assertions of either. They are simply irrelevant. The criterion or criteria for the admission of evidence ought to be reasonable, not arbitrary. The only justification I can see is that Mr. Stern has reduced the status of belief-assertions of an empirical nature, i.e., of physical states, to those concerned with inner states. If this is so, then his analysis which is central to his thesis merely uncovers what he has put there, namely, a unique epistemic privilege for belief-assertions as destructive of certitude when they are evidence for the denial of another's affirmation about those inner states.

Thus, I do not find Mr. Stern to be situated midway nor at the sceptical extreme of Cartesian origin, but at the contemporary view, which is, I suspect, where he started. It would be interesting to see what would happen to his thesis if he were to consider belief-assertions about physical states and their relation to evidence that are not disguised (at least in their form) belief-assertions about inner states.

The point of the epistemic privilege of belief-assertion about another's inner state would be further trivialized if an example of a belief-assertion about another's physical state could be constructed that would deny certainty because of that person's contrary belief-assertion about his physical state. Perhaps some form of the phantom leg example would do, but I am not sure. The point is that one cannot be certain about any BA whose P concerns any objective referent R although the subjective referent D may be certain.

In conclusion, I submit that Mr. Stern has not shown that there is an unique epistemic status for evidence about belief-assertions of another's inner states such that that person's belief-assertion denies certainty to another person's denials or affirmations of the P of the other's BAs. First, because a belief (as a disposition) in no case figures as evidence for anything, unless identified with behavior. Secondly, the error that Mr. Stern made, if error it be, is the use of a narrative mode in his presentation which hid the difference between belief and belief-assertions. This concludes my attempts at internal criticism. I should like to essay a few words on external criticism.

Professor Stern has a particularly succinct and clear formulation of his position which I should like to quote for the purposes of justifying the title of my response which is the "Malign Genie Revisited." You will recall the famous First Meditation in which Descartes has applied his methodic doubt and has reluctantly seen classes of certitudes wither away. The next to last redoubt of certitude is mathematical knowledge and against this fortress of certitude the most incredible and awesome ground for doubt is unleashed—the Malign Genie. The Malign Genie is a metaphysical demon capable of systematically misleading the mind in its assertion of mathematical as well as other truths. My interest in the Malign Genie is in its role as the ultimate source of doubt, and thus as that which denies certitude to all consciousness of something, but which does not touch the last and final redoubt of certitude—the *Cogito*. The *Cogito*, the primeval certitude, has a strange character, it is consciousness qua consciousness. But enough of *ancient* history; let us do some *contemporary* history.

Mr. Stern says ". . . a person's belief that he does *not* have a particular sensation is not only evidence that he does not have that sensation . . . but that it plays a peculiar epistemological role in that although it does not provide *decisive evidence* [my italics] that the person does not have that sensation, it provides a *decisive reason* [my italics] for holding that one cannot be certain that the person does have that sensation regardless of what *other* evidences one may have that the person does have that sensation."

It is clear that we are dealing with a ground for doubt, one that is destructive of certitude. Thus the Malign Genie appears in Professor Stern's statement, ". . . my theory holds that it is possible for someone to disbelieve he has a sensation. . . ."

One possible way of attack is the classical strategy of showing that not everything possible is actual, or as the scholastics would say, "ad esse ab posse non valet illatio," (from possibility to actuality is not a valid inference) which is still a sound maxim. This strategy would lean heavily on counter examples. This attack, however, would not be fundamental. It would end by saying—"My theory holds that it is not impossible for someone to believe he has a sensation. Further, that a person's belief that he has a particular sensation is not only evidence that he has that sensation . . . but that it plays a peculiar epistemological role in that although it does not provide decisive evidence that the person has that sensation, it provides a decisive reason for holding that one can be certain that the person does have that sensation regardless of what other evidence one may have that the person does have that sensation."

Descartes tells us in the Third Meditation [Of God that He Exists] that in order to remove the Malign Genie I must find out whether there is a God and whether He be a deceiver. To translate: Professor Stern would need a believer who is sincere, and *knows* that he believes and can assert what he believes—a human God-like believer. But this is the incorrigibility thesis which he rejects.

All this reduces to the claim that a person's belief in whether he does not have a sensation is a decisive reason for the lack of certitude that another has about that sensation. Translated into Cartesian terms, belief and/or sincere belief assertions are the Malign Genie with regard to any claims for certitude about another's sensation. The only Cartesian exit from this difficulty is to talk about belief as a disposition so that in making a belief-assertion, the P is always open to doubt whereas the D is not. In doing so, one abandons the field of belief in *other* minds to the machinations of the Malign Genie, although the field of one's own mind is clear but empty, and *pace* Wittgenstein unsayable. Thus one ends paradoxically in saying *ad mentem* Descartes, I am certain that you believe, but I can never be certain that what you believe is *what* you believe.

This is, in my estimation, all nonsense, although it makes Cartesian sense. Mr. Stern's paper helps us to see the nonsense more clearly. If one accepts the disjunction of belief D from belief-assertions BA then Descartes and eventually Mr. Stern are correct. If one does not, as I do not, then we have another argument, but that would mean a response to another paper (not Professor Stern's) and I have, I hope, responded to Professor Stern.

PHILOSOPHY OF SCIENCE

PHILOSOPHY OF SCIENCE

ISSUES IN THE LOGIC OF
REDUCTIVE EXPLANATIONS

Ernest Nagel

A recurrent theme in the long history of philosophical reflection on science, is the contrast—voiced in many ways by poets and scientists as well as philosophers—between the characteristics commonly attributed to things on the basis of everyday encounters with them, and the accounts of those things given by scientific theories that formulate some ostensibly pervasive executive order of nature. This was voiced as early as Democritus, when he declared that while things are customarily said to be sweet or bitter, warm or cold, of one color rather than another, in truth there are only the atoms and the void. The same contrast was implicit in Galileo's distinction, widely accepted by subsequent thinkers, between the primary and secondary qualities of bodies. It was dramatically stated by Sir Arthur Eddington in terms of currently held ideas in physics, when he asked which of the two tables at which he was seated was "really there"—the solid, substantial table of familiar experience, or the insubstantial scientific table which is composed of speeding electric charges and is therefore mostly "emptiness."

Formulations of the contrast vary, and have different overtones. In some cases, as in the examples I have cited, the contrast is associated with a distinction between what is allegedly only "appearance" and what is "reality;" and there have been thinkers who have denied that so-called "common-sense" deals with ultimate reality, just as there have been thinkers who have denied that the statements of theoretical science do so. However a wholesale distinction between appearance and reality has never been clearly drawn, especially since these terms have been so frequently used to single out matters that happen to be regarded as important or valuable; nor have the historical controversies over what is to count as real and what as appearance thrown much light on how scientific theories are related to the familiar materials that are usually the points of departure for scientific inquiry. In any case, the contrast between the more familiar and manifest traits of things and those which scientific theory attributes to them, need not be, and often is not, associated with the distinction between the real and the apparent; and in point of fact, most current philosophies of science, which in one way or another occupy themselves with this contrast, make little if any use of that distinction in their analyses.

But despite important differences in the ways in which the contrast has been fomulated, I believe they share a common feature and can be construed as being addressed to a common problem. They express the recognition that certain relations of dependence between one set of distinctive traits of a given subject matter are allegedly explained by, and in some sense "reduced" to, assumptions concerning more inclusive relations of dependence between traits or processes not distinctive of (or unique to) that subject matter. They implicitly raise the question of what, in fact, is the logical structure of such reductive explanations— whether they differ from other sorts of scientific explanation, what is achieved by reductions, and under what conditions they are feasible. These questions are important for the understanding of modern science, for its development is marked by strong reductive tendencies, some of whose outstanding achievements are often counted as examples of reduction. For example, as a consequence of this reductive process, the theory of heat is commonly said to be but a branch of Newtonian mechanics, physical optics of electromagnetic theory, and chemical laws of quantum mechanics. Moreover, many biological processes have been given physicochemical explanations, and there is a continuing debate as to the possibility of giving such explanations for the entire domain of biological phenomena. There have been repeated though still unsuccessful attempts to exhibit various patterns of men's social behavior as examples of psychological laws.

It is with some of the issues that have emerged in proposed analyses of reductive explanations that this paper is concerned. I will first set out in broad outlines what I believe is the general structure of such explanations; then examine some difficulties that have recently been raised against this account; and finally discuss some recent arguments that have been advanced for the view that a physicochemical explanation of all biological phenomena is, in principle, impossible.

I

Although the term "reduction" has come to be widely used in philosophical discussions of science, it has no standard definition. It is therefore not surprising that the term encompasses several sorts of things which need to be distinguished. But before I do this, a brief terminological excursion is desirable. Scientists and philosophers often talk of deducing or inferring one phenomenon from another (e.g., of deducing a planet's orbital motion), of explaining events or their concatenations (e.g., of explaining the occurrence of rainbows), and of reducing certain processes, things, or their properties to others (e.g., of reducing the process of heat conduction to molecular motions). However, these locutions are elliptical, and sometimes lead to misconceptions and confusions. For strictly speaking, it is not phenomena which are deduced from other phenomena, but rather *statements* about phenomena from other statements. This is obvious if we remind ourselves that a given phenemenon can be subsumed under a variety of distinct descriptions, and that phenomena make no assertions or claims. Consequently, until the traits or relations of a phenomenon which are to be discussed are indicated, and predications about them are formulated, it is literally impossible to make any deductions from them. The same holds true for the locutions of explaining or reducing phenomena. I will therefore avoid these elliptic modes of speech hereafter, and talk instead of deducing, explaining, or reducing statements about some subject matter.

Whatever else may be said about reductions in science, it is safe to say that they are commonly taken to be explanations, and I will so regard them. In consequence, I will assume, that like scientific explanations in general, every reduction can be construed as a series of statements, one of which is the conclusion (or statement which is being reduced), while the others are the premises or reducing statements. Accordingly, reductions can be conveniently classified into two major types: homogeneous reductions, in which all of the "descriptive" or specific subject matter terms in the conclusion are either present in the premises also or can be explicitly defined by terms that are present; and inhomogeneous reductions, in which at least one descriptive term in the conclusion neither occurs in the premises nor is definable by those that do occur in them. I will now characterize in a general way what I believe to be the main components and the logical structure of these two types of reduction, but will also state and comment upon some of the issues that have been raised by this account of reduction.

A frequently cited example of homogeneous reduction is the explanation, by Newtonian mechanics and gravitational theory, of various special laws concerning the motions of bodies, including Galileo's law for freely falling bodies near the earth's surface and the Keplerian laws of planetary motion. The explanation is homogeneous, because on the face of it at any rate, the terms occurring in these laws (e.g., distance, time, and acceleration) are also found in the Newtonian theory. Moreover, the explanation is commonly felt to be a reduction of those laws, in part because these laws deal with the motions of bodies in restricted regions of space which had traditionally been regarded as essentially dissimilar (e.g., terrestrial as contrasted with celestial motions), while Newtonian theory ignores this traditional classification of spatial regions and incorporates the laws into a unified system. In any event, the reduced statements in this and other standard examples of homogeneous reduction are commonly held to be deduced logically from the reducting premises. In consequence, if the examples can be taken as typical, the formal structure of homogenous reductions is, in general, that of deductive explanations. Accordingly, if reductions of this type are indeed deductions from theories whose range of application is far more comprehensive and diversified than that of the conclusions derived from them, homogenous reductions appear to be entirely unproblematic, and to be simply dramatic illustrations of the well understood procedure of deriving theorems from assumed axioms.

However, the assumption that homogeneous reductions are deductive explanations has been recently challenged by a number of thinkers, on the ground that even in the stock illustrations of such reductions the reduced statements do not in general follow from the explanatory premises. For example, while Galileo's law asserts that the acceleration of a freely falling body near the earth's surface is constant, Newtonian theory entails that the acceleration is not constant, but varies with the distance of the falling body from the earth's center of mass. Accordingly, even though the Newtonian conclusion may be "experimentally indistinguishable" from Galileo's law, the latter is in fact "inconsistent" with Newtonian theory. Since it is this theory rather than Galileo's law that was accepted as sound, Galileo's law was therefore *replaced* by a different law for freely falling bodies, namely the law derived from the Newtonian assumptions. A similar outcome holds for Kepler's third planetary law. The general thesis has therefore been advanced that homogeneous reductions do not consist in the deduction or explanation of laws, but in the total *replacement* of incorrect assumptions by radically new ones which are believed to be more correct and precise than those they replace. This thesis raises far-reaching issues, and I will examine some of them presently. But for the moment I will confine my comments on it to questions bearing directly on homogeneous reductions.

i) It is undoubtedly the case that the laws derivable from Newtonian theory do not coincide exactly with some of the previously entertained hypotheses about the motions of bodies, though in other cases there may be such coincidence. This is to be expected. For it is a widely recognized function of comprehensive theories (such as the Newtonian one) to specify the conditions under which antecedently established regularities hold, and to indicate, in the light of those conditions, the modifications that may have to be made in the initial hypotheses, especially if the range of application of the hypotheses is enlarged. Nevertheless, the initial hypotheses may be reasonably close approximations to the consequences entailed by the comprehensive theory, as is indeed the case with Galileo's law as well as with Kepler's third law. (Incidentally, when Newtonian theory is applied to the motions of just two bodies, the first and second Keplerian laws agree fully with the Newtonian conclusions). But if this is so, it is correct to say that in homogeneous reductions the reduced laws are either derivable from the explanatory premises, or are good approximations to the laws derivable from the latter.

    ii) Moreover, it is pertinent to note that in actual scientific practice, the derivation of laws from theories usually involves simplifications and approximations of various kinds, so that even the laws which are allegedly entailed by a theory are in general only approximations to what is strictly entailed by it. For example, in deriving the law for the period of a simple pendulum, the following approximative assumptions are made: the weight of the pendulum is taken to be concentrated in the suspended bob; the gravitational force acting on the bob is assumed to be constant, despite variations in the distance of the bob from the earth's center during the pendulum's oscillation; and since the angle through which the pendulum many oscillate is stipulated to be small, the magnitude of the angle is equated to the sine of the angle. The familiar law that the period of a pendulum is proportional to the square root of its length divided by the constant of acceleration is therefore derivable from Newtonian theory only if these various approximations are taken for granted. More generally, though no statistical data are available to support the claim, there are relatively few deductions from the mathematically formulated theories of modern physics in which analogous approximations are not made, so that many if not all the laws commonly said by scientists to be deducible from some theory are not strictly entailed by it. It would nevertheless be an exaggeration to assert that in consequence scientists are fundamentally mistaken in claiming to have made such deductions. It is obviously important to note the assumptions, including the approximate ones, under which the deduction of a law is made. But it does not follow that given those assumptions a purported law cannot count as a consequence of some theory. Nor does it follow that if in a proposed homogeneous reduction of a purported law to some theory, the law is only an approximation to what is entailed by the theory when *no* approximative assumptions are made in the deduction, the purported law is being replaced by a totally different one.

iii) Something must also be said about those cases of homogenous reduction in which the law derived from the reducing theory and "corresponding" to the initial hypothesis for which a reduction is attempted, makes use of concepts not employed in the latter. Thus, while according to Kepler's third (or harmonic) law, the squares of the periods of the planets are to each other as the cubes of their mean distances from the sun, the Newtonian conclusion is that this ratio is not constant for all the planets but varies with their *masses*. But the notion of mass was introduced into mechanics by Newton, and does not appear in the Keplerian law; and although the masses of the planets are small in comparison with the mass of the sun, and the Keplerian harmonic law is therefore a close approximation to the Newtonian one, the two cannot be equated. Nevertheless, while the two are not equivalent, neither are they radically disparate in content or meaning. For the Newtonian law can be construed as identifying a factor determinative of the motions of the planets which was unknown to Kepler.

II

I must now turn to the second major type of reductive explanations. Inhomogeneous reductions, perhaps more frequently than homogenous ones, have occasioned vigorous controversy among scientists as well as philosophers concerning the cognitive status, interpretation, and function of scientific theories; the relations between the various theoretical entities postulated by these theories, and the familiar things of common experience; and the valid scope of different modes of scientific analysis. These issues are interconnected, and impinge in one way or another upon questions about the general structure of inhomogenous reductions. Since none of the proposed answers to these issues has gained universal assent, the nature of such reductions is still under continuing debate.

Although there are many examples of inhomogeneous reductions in the history of science, they vary in the degree of completeness with which the reduction has been effected. In some instances, all the assumed laws in one branch of inquiry are apparently explained in terms of a theory initially developed for a different class of phenomena; in others, the reduction has been only partial, though the hope of completely reducing the totality of laws in a given area of inquiry to some allegedly "basic" theory may continue to inspire research. Among the most frequently cited illustrations of such relatively complete inhomogenous reductions are the explanation of thermal laws by the kinetic theory of matter, the reduction of physical optics to electromagnetic theory, and the explanation (at least in principle) of chemical laws in terms of quantum theory. On the other hand, while some processes occurring in living organisms can now be understood in terms of physicochemical theory, the reducibility of all biological laws in a similar manner is still a much disputed question.

In any case, the logical structure of inhomogeneous reductive explanations is far less clear and is more difficult to analyze than is the case with homogeneous reductions. The difficulty stems largely from the circumstance that in the former there are (by definition) terms or concepts in the reduced laws (e.g., the notion of heat in thermodynamics, the term "light-wave" in optics, or the concept of valence in chemistry) which are absent from the reducing theories. Accordingly, if the overall structure of the explanation of laws is taken to be that of a deductive argument, it seems impossible to construe inhomogeneous reductions as involving essentially little more than the logical derivation of the reduced laws (even when qualifications about the approximative character of the latter are made) from their explanatory premises. If inhomogeneous reductions are to be subsumed under the general pattern of scientific explanations, it is clear that additional assumptions must be introduced as to how the concepts characteristically employed in the reduced laws, but not present in the reducing theory, are connected with the concepts that do occur in the latter.

Three broad types of proposals for the structure of inhomogeneous reductions can be found in the recent literature of the philosophy of science. The first, which for convenience will be called the "instrumentalist" analysis, is usually advocated by thinkers who deny a cognitive status to scientific laws or theories, regarding them as neither true nor false but as rules (or "inference tickets") for inferring so-called "observation statements" (statements about particular events or occurrences capable of being "observed" in some not precisely defined sense) from other such statements. According to this view, for example, the kinetic theory of gases is not construed as an account of the composition of gases. It is taken to be a complex set of rules for predicting, among other things, what the pressure of a given volume of gas will be if its temperature is kept constant but its volume is diminished. However, the scope of application of a given law or theory may be markedly more limited than the scope of another. The claim that a theory T (e.g., the corpus of rules known as thermodynamics) is reduced to another theory T′ (e.g., the kinetic theory of gases) would therefore be interpreted as saying that all the observation statements which can be derived from given data with the help of T can also be derived with the help of T′, but not conversely. Accordingly, the question to which this account of inhomogeneous reduction is addressed is not the ostensibly asserted content of the theories involved in reduction, but the comparative ranges of observable phenomena to which two theories are applicable.

Although this proposed analysis calls attention to an important function of theories and provides a rationale for the reduction of theories, its adequacy depends on the plausibility of uniformly interpreting general statements in science as rules of inference. Many scientists certainly do not subscribe to such an interpretation, for they frequently talk of laws as true and as providing at least an approximately correct account of various relations of dependence among things. In particular, this interpretation precludes the explanation of macro-states of objects in terms of unobservable micro-processes postulated by a theory. Moreover, the proposal is incomplete in a number of ways: it has nothing to say about how theoretical terms in laws (e.g., "electron" or even "atom") may be used in connection with matters of observation, or just how theories employing such notions operate as rules of inference; and it ignores the question of how, if at all, the concepts of a reduced theory are related to those of the reducing one, or in what way statements about a variety of observable things may fall within the scope of both theories. In consequence, even if the proposed analysis is adequate for a limited class of reductive explanations, it does not do justice to important features characterizing many others.

The second proposed analysis of inhomogeneous reductions (hereafter to be referred to—perhaps misleadingly—as the "correspondence" proposal) is also based on several assumptions. One of them is that the terms occurring in the conclusion but not in the premises of a reduction have "meanings" (i.e., uses and applications) which are determined by the procedures and definitions of the discipline to which reduced laws initially belonged, and can be understood without reference to the ideas involved in the theories to which the laws have been reduced. For example, the term "entropy" as used in thermodynamics, is defined independently of the notions characterizing statistical mechanics. Furthermore, the assumption is made that many subject-matter terms common to both the reduced and reducing theories—in particular, the so-called observation terms employed by both of them to record the outcome of observation and experiment—are defined by procedures which can be specified independently of these theories and, in consequence, have "meanings" that are neutral with respect to the differences between the theories. For example, the terms "pressure" and "volume change" which occur in both thermodynamics and the kinetic theory of gases are used in the two theories in essentially the same sense. It is important to note,

however, that this assumption is compatible with the view that even observation terms are "theory impregnated," so that such terms are not
simply labels for "bare sense-data," but predicate characteristics that are
not immediately manifest and are defined on the basis of various theoretical commitments. For example, if the expression "having a diameter
of five inches" is counted as an observation predicate, its application to
a given object implicitly involves commitment to some theory of spatial
measurement as well as to some laws concerning the instrument used in
making the measurement. Accordingly, the point of the assumption is
not that there are subject-matter terms whose meanings or uses are independent of *all* theories, but rather that every such term has a meaning
which is fixed by *some* theory but independent of others. A third assumption underlying the correspondence analysis of inhomogeneous reductions, is, that like homogeneous reduction, and with similar qualifications referring to approximations, they embody the pattern of deductive explanations.

In view of these assumptions, it is clear that if a law (or theory) T
is to be reduced to a theory T′ not containing terms occurring in T, T′
must be supplemented by what have been called "rules of correspondence" or "bridge laws," which establish *connections* between the distinctive terms of T and certain terms (or combinations of terms) in T′. For
example, since the second law of thermodynamics talks of the transfer
of heat, this law cannot be deduced from classical mechanics which does
not contain the term "heat," unless the term is connected in some way
with some complex of terms in mechanics. The statement of such a connection is a correspondence rule. However, because of the first of the
above three assumptions, a correspondence rule cannot be construed as a
definition of a term distinctive of T, which would permit the elimination
of the term *on purely logical grounds* in favor of the terms in T′. Thus,
the notion of entropy as defined in thermodynamics can be understood
and used without any reference to notions employed in theories about
the microstructure of matter; and no amount of logical analysis of the
concept of entropy can show the concept to be constituted out of the
ideas employed in, say, statistical mechanics. If this is indeed the case
(as I believe it is), then the theory T is not derivable from (and hence
not reducible to) the theory T′, although T may be derivable from T′
when the latter is conjoined with an appropriate set of bridge laws.

What then is the status of the correspondence rules required for inhomogeneous reduction? Different articulations of the theories involved
in a reduction, as well as different stages in the development of inquiry
into the subject-matter of the theories, may require different answers;
but I will ignore these complications. In general, however, correspond-

ence rules formulate *empirical hypotheses*—hypotheses which state certain relations of dependence between things mentioned in the reduced and reducing theories. The hypotheses are, for the most part, not testable by confronting them with observed instances of the relations they postulate. They are nevertheless not arbitrary stipulations, and as with many other scientific laws their factual validity must be assessed by comparing various consequences entailed by the system of hypotheses to which they belong with the outcome of controlled observations. However, bridge laws have various forms; and while no exhaustive classification of their structure is available, two sorts of bridge laws must be briefly described.

a) A term in a reduced law may be a predicate which refers to some distinctive *attribute* or characteristic of things (such as the property of having a certain temperature or of being red) that is not signified by the predicates of the reducing theory. In this case the bridge law may specify the conditions, formulated in terms of the ideas and assumptions of the reducing theory, under which the attribute occurs. For example, the kinetic theory of gases formulates its laws in terms of such notions as molecule, mass, and velocity, but does not employ the thermodynamical notion of temperature. However, a familiar bridge law states that a gas has a certain temperature when the mean kinetic energy of its molecules has a certain magnitude. In some cases, bridge laws of the sort being considered may specify conditions for the occurrence of an attribute which are necessary as well as sufficient; In other cases the conditions specified may be sufficient without being necessary; and in still other cases, the conditions stated may only be necessary. In the latter case, however, any laws about the attribute will, in general, not be deducible from the proposed reducing theory. (Thus, though some of the necessary conditions for objects having colors can be stated in terms of ideas belonging to physical optics in its current form, the physiological equipment of organisms which must also be present for the occurrence of colors cannot be described in terms of those ideas. Accordingly, if there are any laws about color relations, they are not reducible to physical optics.)

In any case, such bridge laws are empirical hypotheses concerning the *extensions* of the predicates mentioned in these correspondence rules—that is, concerning the classes of individual things or processes designated by those predicates. An attribute of things connoted by a predicate in a reduced law may indeed be quite different from the attribute connoted by the predicates of the reducing theory; but the class of things possessing the former attribute may nevertheless coincide with (or be included in) the class of things which possess the property specified by a complex predicate in the reducing theory. For example, the statement that a liquid is viscous is not equivalent in meaning to the statement that there are certain frictional forces between the layers of molecules making up the liquid. But if the bridge laws connecting the macro-properties and the microstructure of liquids is correct, the extension of the predicate "viscous" coincides with (or is included in) the class of individual systems with that microstructure.

b) Let me now say something about a second sort of correspondence rule. Although much scientific inquiry is directed toward discovering the determining conditions under which various traits of things occur, some of its important achievements consist in showing that things and processes initially assumed to be distinct are in fact the same. A familiar example of such an achievement is the discovery that the Morning Star and the Evening Star are not different celestial objects but are identical. Similarly, although the term "molecule" designates one class of particles and the term "atom" designates another class, molecules are structures of atoms, and in particular a water molecule is an organization of hydrogen and oxygen atoms described by the formula "H_2O"; and accordingly, the extension of the predicate "water molecule" is the same as the class of things designated by the formula. Correspondence rules of the second sort establish analogous identifications between classes of individuals or "entities" (such as spatiotemporal objects, processes, and forces) designated by different predicates. An oft cited example of such rules is a bridge law involved in the reduction of physical optics to electromagnetic theory. Thus, prior to Maxwell, physicists postulated the existence of certain physical propagations designated as "light waves," while electromagnetic theory was developed on the assumption that there are electromagnetic waves. An essential step in the reduction of optics to electrodynamics was the introduction of Maxwell's hypothesis (or bridge law) that these are not two *different* processes but a *single* one, even though electromagnetic waves are not always manifested as visible light. Analogous bridge laws are assumed when a flash of lightning is said to be a surge of electrically charged particles or the evaporation of a liquid is explained as the escape of molecules from its surface; and while the full details for formulating a similar bridge law are not yet available, the hope of discovering them underlies the claim that a biological cell is a complex organization of physicochemical particles.

Correspondence rules of the second kind thus differ from rules of the first, in that unlike the latter (which state conditions, often in terms of the ideas of a micro-theory, for the occurrence of traits characterizing various things, often macroscopic ones), they assert that certain logically nonequivalent expressions describe identical entities. Although both sorts of rules have a common function in reduction and both are in general empirical assumptions, failure to distinguish between them is perhaps one reason for the persistence of the mistaken belief that reductive explanations establish the "unreality" of those distinctive traits of things mentioned in reduced laws.

3) This account of inhomogeneous reduction has been challenged by a number of recent writers who have advanced an alternate theory which rejects the main assumptions of both the instrumentalist and the correspondence analyses, and which I will call the "replacement" view. Since I believe the correspondence account to be essentially correct, I shall examine the fundamental contention of the replacement thesis, as presented by Professor Paul Feyerabend, one of its most vigorous proponents.

Feyerabend's views on reduction rest upon the central (and on the face of it, sound) assumption that "the meaning of every term we use depends upon the theoretical context in which it occurs." [1] This claim is made not only for "theoretical" terms like "neutrino" or "entropy" in explicitly formulated scientific theories, but also for expressions like "red" or "table" used to describe matters of common observation (i.e., for observation terms). Indeed, Feyerabend uses the word "theory" in a broad sense, to include such things as myths and political ideas.[2] He says explicitly that "even everyday languages, like languages of highly theoretical systems, have been introduced in order to give expression to some theory or point of view, and they therefore contain a well-developed and sometimes very abstract ontology." [3] "The description of every single fact," he declares, is "dependent on *some* theory." [4] He further maintains that "theories are meaningful independent of observations; observational statements are not meaningful unless they have been connected with theories." [5] There is, therefore, no "observation core," even in statements of perception, that is independent of theoretical interpretation,[6] so that strictly speaking each theory determines its own distinctive set of observation statements. And while he allows that two "low level" theories which fall within the conceptual framework of a comprehensive "background theory" may have a common interpretation for their observation statements, two "high level" theories concerning the nature of the basic elements of the universe "may not share a single observational statement." [7] It is therefore an error to suppose that the empirical adequacy of a theory can be tested by appeal to observation statements whose meanings are independent of the theory and which are neutral as between that theory and some alternative competing theory. "The methodological unit to which we must refer when discussing questions of test and empirical context, is constituted by a *whole set of partly overlapping, factually adequate, but mutually inconsistent theories*." [8]

Moreover, a change in a theory is accompanied by a change in the meanings of all its terms, so that theories constructed on "mutually inconsistent principles" are in fact "incommensurable." [9] Thus, if T is classical celestial mechanics, and T' is the general theory of relativity, "the meanings of all descriptive terms of the two theories, primitive as well as defined terms, will be different," the theories are incommensurable, and "not a single descriptive term of T can be incorporated into T'." [10] In consequence, Feyerabend believes the correspondence account of inhomogeneous reduction is basically mistaken in supposing that allegedly reduced laws or theories can be derived from the reducing theory with the help of appropriate bridge laws:

What happens . . . when transition is made from a theory T' to a wider theory T (which, we shall assume, is capable of covering all the phenomena that have been covered by T') is something much more radical than incorporation of the *unchanged* theory T' (unchanged, that is with respect to the meanings of its main descriptive terms as well as to the meanings of the terms of its observation language) into the context of T. What does happen is, rather, a *complete replacement* of the ontology (and perhaps even of the formalism) of T' by the ontology (and the formalism) of T and a corresponding change of the meanings of the descriptive elements of the formalism of T' (provided these elements and this formalism are still used). This replacement affects not only the theoretical terms of T' but also at least some of the observational terms which occurred in its test statements. . . . In short: introducing a new theory involves changes of outlook both with respect to the observable and with respect to the unobservable features of the world, and corresponding changes in the meanings of even the most "fundamental" terms of the language employed.[11]

Accordingly, if these various claims are warranted, there is not and cannot be any such thing as the reduction of laws or theories; and the examples often cited as instances of reduction are in fact instances of something else: the exclusion of previously accepted hypotheses from the corpus of alleged scientific knowledge, and the substitution for them of incommensurably different ones.

But are these claims warranted? I do not believe they are. Feyerabend is patently sound in maintaining that no single statement or any of its constituent terms has a meaning in isolation, or independently of various rules or conventions governing its use. He is no less sound in noting that the meaning of a word may change when its range of application is altered. However, these familiar truisms do not support the major conclusion he draws from them. The presentation of his thesis suffers from a number of unclarities (such as what is to count as a change in a theory, or what are the criteria for changes in meaning), which cloud the precise import of some of his assertions. I shall however, ignore these unclarities here [12] and will comment briefly only on two difficulties in Feyerabend's argument.

a) It is a major task of scientific inquiry to assess the adequacy of proposed laws to the "facts" of a subject matter as established by observation or experiment, and to ascertain whether the conclusions reached are consistent with one another. However, if two proposed theories for some given range of phenomena share no term with the same meaning in each of them, so that the theories have completely different meanings (as Feyerabend believes is commonly the case), it is not evident in what sense two such theories can be said to be either compatible or inconsistent with one another: For relations of logical opposition obtain only between statements whose terms have common meanings. Moreover, it is also difficult to understand how, if the content of observation statements is determined by the theory which is being tested (as Feyerabend maintains), those statements can serve as a basis for deciding between the theory and some alternative to it. For according to his analysis those observation statements will automatically corroborate the theory that happens to be used to interpret observational data, but will be simply irrelevant in assessing the empirical validity of an alternative theory. Theories thus appear to be self-certifying, and to be beyond the reach of criticism based on considerations that do not presuppose them. This outcome is reminiscent of Karl Mannheim's claim that truth in social matters is "historically relative": There are no universally valid analyses of social phenomena, since every such analysis is made within some distinctive social perspective which determines the meaning as well as the validity of what is said to be observed, so that those who do not share the same perspective can neither reach common conclusions about human affairs, nor significantly criticize each others' findings.

Feyerabend attempts to escape from such skeptical relativism by involving what he calls the "pragmatic theory of observation." In this theory, it is still the case that the meaning of an observation statement varies with the theory used to interpret observations. However, it is possible to describe the observational and predictive statements an investigator utters as *responses* to the situations which "prompt" the utterances, and to compare the order of these responses with the order of the physical situations that prompt them, so as to ascertain the agreements or disagreements between the two orders.[13] But if this account of the role of observation statements in testing theories is to outflank the relativism Feyerabend wants to avoid, the *secondary* statements (they are clearly observation statements) about the responses (or primary observation statements) of investigators cannot have meanings dependent on the theory being tested, and must be invariant to alternative theories. However, if secondary statements have this sort of neutrality, it is not evident why only such observation statements can have this privileged status.

b) Feyerabend's difficulties in providing a firm observational basis for objectively evaluating the empirical worth of proposed hypotheses, stems from what I believe is his exaggerated view that the meaning of every term occurring in a theory or in its observation statements is wholly and uniquely determined by that theory, so that its meaning is radically changed when the theory is modified. For theories are not quite the monolithic structures he takes them to be—their component assumptions are, in general, logically independent of one another, and their terms have varying degrees of dependence on the theories into which they enter. Some terms may indeed be so deeply embedded in the totality of assumptions constituting a particular theory that they can be understood only within the framework of the theory: e.g., the meaning of "electron spin" appears to be inextricably intertwined with the characteristic ideas of quantum theory. On the other hand, there are also terms whose meanings seem to be invariant in a number of different theories: e.g., the term "electric charge" is used in currently accepted theories of atomic structure in the same sense as in the earlier theories of Rutherford and Bohr. Similar comments apply to observation terms, however these may be specified. Accordingly, although both "theoretical" and "observational" terms may be "theory laden," it does not follow that there can be no term in a theory which retains its meaning when it is transplanted into some other theory.

More generally, it is not clear how, on the replacement view of reduction, a theory T can be at the same time more inclusive than, and also have a meaning totally different from, the theory T' it allegedly replaces—especially since according to Feyerabend the replacing theory will entail "that all the concepts of the preceding theory have extension zero, or . . . it introduces rules which cannot be interpreted as attributing specific properties to objects within already existing classes, but which change the system of classes itself." [14] Admittedly, some of the laws and concepts of the "wider theory" often differ from their opposite numbers in the earlier theory. But even in this case, the contrasted items may not be "incommensurable." Thus, the periodic table classifies chemical elements on the basis of certain patterns of similarity between the properties of the elements. The description (or theoretical explanation) of those properties has undergone important changes since the periodic table was first introduced by Mendeleev. Nevertheless, though the descriptions differ, the classification of the elements has remained fairly stable, so that fluorine, chlorine, bromine, and iodine, for example, continue to be included in the same class. The new theories used in formulating the classification certainly do not entail that the concepts of the preceding ones have zero extension. But it would be difficult to understand why this is so if, because of differences between the descriptions, the descriptions were totally disparate.

Consider, for example, the argument that thermodynamics is not reducible to statistical mechanics, on the ground that (among other reasons) entropy is a statistical notion in the latter theory but not in the former one: Since the meaning of the word "entropy" differs in the two theories, entropy laws in statistical mechanics are not derivable from entropy laws in thermodynamics (and in fact are said to be incompatible). Admittedly, the connotation of the word "entropy" in each of the two theories is not identical; and if the correspondence account of reduction were to claim that they are the same, it would be patently mistaken. But the fact remains that the two theories deal with many phenomena common to both their ranges; and the question is, How is this possible? In brief, the answer seems to be as follows. The word "entropy" in thermodynamics is so defined that its legitimate application is limited to physical systems satisfying certain specified conditions (e.g., to systems such as gases, whose internal motions are not too "tumultuous"—the word is Planck's—, a condition which is not satisfied in the case of Brownian motions). These conditions are relaxed in the definition of "entropy" in statistical mechanics, so that the extension of the Boltzmann notion of entropy includes the extension of the Clausius notion. In consequence, despite differences in the connotations of the two definitions, the theories within which they are formulated have a domain of application in common, even though the class of systems for which thermodynamical laws are approximately valid is more restricted than is the class for the laws of statistical mechanics. But it is surely not the case that the latter theory implies that the Clausius definition of entropy has a zero extension or that the laws of thermodynamics are valid for no physical systems whatsoever.

This difficulty in the replacement view in explaining how the "wider" theory, which allegedly replaces a "narrower" one, may nevertheless have a domain of common application, does not arise in the correspondence account of reduction. For the bridge laws upon which the latter sets great store are empirical hypotheses, not logically true statements in virtue of the connotations of the terms contained in them. Bridge laws state what relations presumably obtain between the *exten-*

sions of their terms, so that in favorable cases laws of the "narrower" theory (with suitable qualifications about their approximative character) can be deduced from the "wider" theory, and thereby make intelligible why the two theories may have a common field of application. Accordingly, although I will not pretend that the correspondence account of reduction is free from difficulties or that I have resolved them, on the whole it is a more adequate analysis than any available alternative to it.

IV

Let me now turn to the current controversy over the reducibility of biological laws to physical ones, in the hope that the above considerations may throw some light on the issues of the debate. Despite the remarkable advances of the preceding decades in discovering physicochemical mechanisms involved in living processes, no one disputes the fact that at present, physicochemical explanations for all biological laws are not available. However, while some outstanding biologists believe that such explanations will eventually be forthcoming, others (who also reject vitalistic doctrines) deny that the reduction of all biological laws to physical ones is possible. Various reasons for this denial have been given by a number of recent writers (i.e. Professors Barry Commoner, Walter Elsasser, Bentley Glass, and Michael Polanyi, among others), and all of these reasons deserve careful attention. However I must restrict myself here to examining only the important double-pronged argument presented by Bentley Glass.[15]

a) Glass begins the first part of his argument by observing that "random" behavior (behavior which eventuates in an ordered distribution of properties exhibiting statistical rather than uniform regularities that are formulated by statistical laws) is found at all levels of organized matter. For example, the Mendelian laws express statistical regularities resulting from the equal probability of an egg's fertilization by one of several kinds of sperm; and the Hardy-Weinberg law states the statistical regularities arising from the random mating of individuals in a population containing different genotypes. However, while both laws express regularities in the transmission of genes from one generation to another, the former is at the cell level of organization while the latter is at the level of interbreeding populations. But Glass also believes that the randomness of the units at one level of organization "does not necessarily depend" on the randomness of the units at lower levels.[16] On this important assumption, he therefore maintains that neither law is derivable from the other.[17] More generally, he concludes, "[S]tatistical laws of one level of organization are not reducible to the statistical laws of another." [18] In consequence, although physical laws which are established for nonliving systems also hold in living ones, they cannot explain all the laws of the latter.

It is clear, however, that the cogency of the argument depends on the validity for a *given set* of levels of organization of what I called Glass's "important assumption." But let me first note that the argument would have the same force if, instead of supposing that the laws at different levels are statistical, the laws were supposed to be strictly universal or "deterministic"; e.g., if it were supposed that eggs are fertilized by sperms in accordance with a deterministic law L, and individuals mated in accordance with a deterministic law L'. For even on this hypothesis, L' would not be derived from L, *unless* some bridge law were available which stated sufficient conditions for the mating of individuals in terms of the fertilization of eggs. However, it is not *logically impossible* that such connections exist, and the question of whether they do or not, falls into the province of empirical inquiry rather than of apriori reasoning.

Similarly, Glass is certainly correct in declaring that randomness at one level of organization does not necessarily depend on randomness at a lower level, so that his "important assumption" denies, in effect, the *availability* of certain bridge laws needed for reduction, not their *possibility*. Accordingly, his argument for the underivability of biological from physical laws is based on the present state of scientific knowledge, and does not show that physical laws cannot "be expected ultimately to explain *all* the laws of living systems." [19] However unlikely the establishment of the required bridge laws may seem at present, the argument does not altogether rule out the reduction of biological to physical laws. After all, the macroscopic (or "higher level") regularities found in chemical interactions are reducible to the microscopic statistical regularities formulated by quantum theory.

b) The second argument Glass offers for doubting the reducibility of biological to physical laws rests on the "uniqueness" of living organisms and the "indeterminacy" of the evolutionary process. One reason he mentions for the uniqueness of organisms is that in a sexually reproducing but not strictly inbred population, the genotype of each individual is not likely to recur throughout history. Accordingly, even statistical prediction is possible only if certain common characteristics are abstracted from "the infinitely varied individuals," [20] and only if the populations and samples are sufficiently large (a condition infrequently realized in biological study). On the other hand, the major reason he gives for the indeterminacy of the evolutionary process is that evolution takes place because of genetic mutations, whose possible kinds may recur with certain relative frequencies, but whose actual occurrences are unpredictable. In consequence, the evolutionary history of a population is determined by the generally unpredictable occurrences of random events, so that biological explanations "can in some respects not be reduced to the laws of physical science." [21]

This argument, like the first one Glass presents, calls attention to features of biological laws that are often neglected in discussions of their reducibility to physics. Nevertheless, I do not think it is quite as "unanswerable" as he believes it to be. i) In the first place, there appears to be a conflation of two questions that need to be distinguished: a) whether evolutionary developments or other biological phenomena can be *predicted*, and b) whether biological laws can be *reduced* to physical ones. An event is commonly said to be predictable (whether or not with maximum probability) if, and only if, two conditions are satisfied: a law (or set of laws) must be available which states the conditions for the occurrence of the event; and the initial and boundary conditions for the application of the law to a given instance must be known. Accordingly, one reason for our inability to predict an event may be that the requisite initial and boundary conditions are not fully known prior to the occurrence of the event, even though they may be ascertained subsequent to its occurrence and the event explained in retrospect. In this case, the possibility of reducing the law to another is obviously not excluded. A quite different reason for such inability may be that there are no known laws either for the event's occurrence, or for the occurrence of those of its properties in which we are especially interested. In this case, however, the unpredictability of the event is not relevant to the issue of reduction, since there is no candidate for reduction to some other laws. In either case, therefore, the indeterminacy of the evolutionary process and the limited value of evolutionary theory as an instrument for prediction do not count against the possibility of reducing the theory to physical laws.

ii) In the second place, though living organisms may be unique, so may many actually existing physical systems, especially if they are constituted out of numerous components. No two stars, or two specimens of quartz, or even two watches manufactured by some standardized process, are precisely alike in their properties or behaviors; and while we may often regard them as "essentially" alike, we are in fact ignoring differences of which we may be unaware, or which for one reason or another we think are unimportant. But in any case, science, like discursive thought in general, cannot deal with things insofar as they are unique; and as Dr. Glass makes clear, laws can be formulated for biological organisms only by prescinding from the combinations of characteristics unique to each of them, certain traits they have in common. In this respect, however, all branches of science are in the same boat, and nothing seems to follow from the special uniqueness of living organisms that bears on the reducibility of biological laws.

But Glass also notes that in biology, in contrast to what is generally the case in the physical sciences, the populations of individuals selected for study—that is, the unique organisms grouped together because they possess various characteristics in common which are believed to have theoretical significance—are frequently far too small to exhibit statistical regularities, or to permit the use of statistical laws for highly accurate predictions. This is indeed a difficulty. But it is an obstacle to the *establishment* of biological laws and the *forecasting* of evolutionary developments; it is not an objection to the possibility of *reducing* whatever biological laws may be available to physical ones.

Accordingly, I do not think that Glass has demonstrated the irreducibility of biology to physics—indeed, I do not believe that such a demonstration can be given, in part because physics is still a developing science. He has nevertheless given ample reasons for suspended judgment on the claim now fashionable with many microbiologists that the laws of physics *as currently constituted* comprehend all the laws of biology. For he has pointed out that bridge laws to connect biological with physical characteristics at different levels of biological organization are still lacking and are indispensable for the reduction of biology. He has also noted some of the serious difficulties that must be overcome if such bridge laws are to be established. Moreover, he has made clear—and I regard this as especially salutary at a time such as ours when reductive tendencies threaten to obliterate important distinctions—that although physicochemical analyses of biological processes have made, and will doubtless continue to make, enormous contributions to our understanding of biological phenomena, the reduction of biology to physics is not a necessary condition for the advancement of biological knowledge.

NOTES

1. Paul Feyerabend, "Problems of Empiricism," in R. G. Colodny, ed., *Beyond the Edge of Certainty* (Englewood Cliffs, Prentice-Hall, Inc., 1965), p. 180.
2. Paul Feyerabend, "Reply to Criticism," *Boston Studies in the Philosophy of Science*, vol. 2 (1962), p. 252.
3. Paul Feyerabend, "Explanation, Reduction and Empiricism," *Minnesota Studies in the Philosophy of Science*, vol. 3 (1962), p. 76.
4. Feyerabend, "Problems of Empiricism," p. 175.
5. *Ibid.*, p. 213.

6. *Ibid.*, p. 216.

7. *Ibid.*

8. *Ibid.*, p. 175.

9. *Ibid.*, p. 227.

10. *Boston Studies in the Philosophy of Science*, Vol. 2, p. 231; *cf.* also Feyerabend, "On the 'Meaning' of Scientific Terms," *Journal of Philosophy*, Vol. 62 (1965), p. 271.

11. Feyerabend, "Explanation, Reduction and Empiricism", pp. 28–9, 59.

12. Many of them are noted by Dudley Shapere in his "Meaning and Scientific Change", in R. G. Colodny, ed., *Mind and Cosmos*, Pittsburgh, 1966.

13. Feyerabend, "Problems of Empiricism", p. 21; and Feyerabend, "Explanation, Reduction and Empiricism", p. 24.

14. Feyerabend, "On 'the Meaning' of Scientific Terms", *Journal of Philosophy*, Vol. 62 (1965), p. 268.

15. "The Relation of the Physical Sciences to Biology", in Bernard H. Baumrin, ed., *Delaware Seminar in the Philosophy of Science*, New York, 1963.

16. *Ibid.*, p. 241.

17. *Ibid.*, p. 242.

18. *Ibid.*, p. 243.

19. *Ibid.*, p. 243.

20. *Ibid.*, p. 246.

21. *Ibid.*, p. 247.

THEORY MEETS EXPERIENCE

Mario Bunge

INTRODUCTION

This paper is concerned with scientific theories proper—that is, hypo-thetico-deductive systems—not with single statements or with amorphous doctrines. A scientific theory can make contact with experience in three ways: it can be tested for factual truth by means of scientific experience (observation, measurement, or experiment); it can be used to design and interpret observations or experiments, or it can be employed to practical ends. Thus a learning theory can be subjected to experimental verification, but it can also be used to set up experiments on the chemical basis of memory, and it can be applied to cure phobias. We shall deal here with the first kind of contact, namely the empirical test of scientific theories.

According to the dominant philosophies of science, scientific theories are graded chiefly on the basis of their performance in empirical tests. In turn, these tests would consist in the confrontation of the consequences of the theories with the relevant empirical evidence. Such evidence would be gathered rather directly, without the help of further theories, for the sense impressions must have the last word. This view has the appeal of simplicity but its naiveté is such that I am unable to subscribe to it. The following anecdote may explain why, or at least intimate my own view on the matter, which I feel is but a codification of the actual practice of confronting theories with empirical information.

Thirty years ago, at the start of my training as a physicist, I was assigned the task of weighing a tiny body with a precision scale. I had learned the rules of operation in a famous German manual, but wanted to know why those rules should be efficient: after all, I had come to physics through an interest in philosophy. In answering my question, my experimental physics professor referred me to a paper by his brother, a theoretical physics professor. I began to read the paper but very soon had to abandon it: The theory of the scale was but an application of rational mechanics, a subject that lay two years ahead in our curriculum. Consequently I was forced to postpone my study, returning to the laboratory rather crestfallen, bound to operate almost blindly—with little more than Archimedes' law of the lever—just like our laboratory technicians, who had some know-how but lacked the "know-why" that theory alone can give us. I learned to operate the scale but did not understand the ritual thoroughly, was unable to improve on it, and was incapable of understanding why one kind of scale should be preferable to another—for in science preference is grounded, and the basis of our preference often happens to be a theory.

This episode impressed me with the importance of theory in experimental physics as soon as one wishes to go beyond the received routine. The same impression was considerably reinforced a few years later, when I was confronted with some elementary spectroscopic work. This time the task was to perform a spectral analysis of the blood of a man suspected of having been poisoned. Here the very wording of the experimental results involved theoretical terms such as "spectral line," "spectral width," "wave-length," "absorption intensity," and "quantum numbers," with no counterpart in ordinary experience, and which made sense only in a theoretical context. As a result I lost even more of my faith in the official philosophy of science, according to which experience is the basis of theory: I realized that in science there is no experience without some underlying theory, for the very planning and interpretation of empirical operations are conducted in the light of theories rather than in conceptual darkness. I began to realize that experimental physics —as distinguished from gadgeteering—is a very complex undertaking, not only because it requires ingenuity, resourcefulness and dexterity, but also because it involves no end of fragments of variegated theories, which the experimentalist must master if only intuitively. This encouraged me in my resolution to become a theoretical physicist.

1. NONEMPIRICAL TESTS

1.1. *Agreement With Fact Not Decisive*

According to the official philosophy of science, agreement with fact is not only necessary but also sufficient for the acceptance of a scientific theory, because scientific theories are just data summaries or, at worst, codifications of data and slight extrapolations from them. In accordance with this view, if a theoretical prediction conflicts with an empirical datum it is the former, not the latter which has to go—and, indeed, without any appeal, for experience is the highest court of appeal. This view is methodologically, philosophically and historically untenable: first, because it is standard scientific practice to reject data when they conflict with established theories; second, because data are anything but given: they are produced and interpreted with the help of theories; third, because most theories do not concern observations and measurements, let alone acts of perception, but things—or rather idealized models of them; fourth, because—as we shall see—testable propositions seldom if ever follow from the assumptions of a single theory but, rather, are usually entailed by the theory in conjunction with additional assumptions and with bits of information other than those serving to check the theory (just as the generalization "All men are mortal" is insufficient to conclude that Socrates is mortal).

The received view is also refuted by the history of science. Indeed, the history of science abounds in examples of theories that have been upheld in the face of adverse empirical evidence—and rightly so, for the data proved wrong in the end. This was the case with the "anomalies" in all of the planetary motions except Mercury's: they were not interpreted as refuting Newton's celestial mechanics but as pointing to the incompleteness of the available empirical information or to the difficulty of effecting accurate calculations with his theory. It was also the case for certain delicate measurements, performed by competent experimentalists, that seemed to refute the constancy of the velocity of light and thereby both classical electrodynamics and special relativity. And it is the case with every new theory accounting for a sizable subset of the set of available data even though it conflicts with some of them, provided no better theory is in sight: the discordant evidence is then declared to be an insignificant residue, or at worst a sad fact of life—when not simply false. Such was the case with Einstein's theory of Brownian movement, which was decisive in establishing the atomic theory of matter. Indeed, the theory had been confirmed by the measurements of J. Perrin but it had been refuted by the equally delicate (but, as it turned out, ill-interpreted) measurements of V. Henri.[1] It was accepted, among other reasons, because it explained Brownian movement (even though it was doubtful that it predicted it accurately) and because it squared with other theories, such as the kinetic theory of gases and the chemical atomic theory. In any event, agreement (disagreement) with fact is seldom sufficient to accept (reject) a scientific theory.

1.2. Four Batteries of Tests

Whether we like it or not, every organic body of scientific ideas is evaluated in the light of the results of four batteries of tests: metatheoretical, intertheoretical, philosophical, and empirical. The first three constitute the nonempirical tests and all four together can give us a hint as to the viability or degree of truth of a theory.[2]

A *metatheoretical* examination is one bearing on the form and content of a theory: it will seek, in particular, to establish whether the theory is internally consistent (no petty task), whether it has a fairly unambiguous factual meaning as formulated, and whether it is empirically testable with the help of further constructs, especially hypotheses relating unobservables (e.g., causes) to observables (e.g., symptoms). An *intertheoretical* examination will try to find out whether the given theory is compatible with other previously accepted theories—in particular those logically presupposed by the theory concerned. This compatiblility is often attained in some correspondence limit, e.g., for large (or small) values of some characteristic parameter such as the mass or the relative speed. A *philosophical* test is an examination of the metaphysical and epistemological respectability of the key concepts and assumptions of the theory, in the light of some philosophy. Thus if positivism is adopted, phenomenological theories—such as thermodynamics, S-matrix theory and behavioristic learning theory—will be favored, while theories concerning the composition and structure of the system concerned will be neglected or even fought without regard to empirical evidence and to the thirst for deeper explanation. I am not advocating philosophical censorship but recalling that, as a matter of historical record, this kind of consideration is always made—sometimes for better, often for worse.[3]

If a theory is believed to comply with the accepted metatheoretical, intertheoretical and philosophical requirements, it may get ready for some empirical tests. (Whether it does in fact conform to the canons is another matter. And whether it will succeed in provoking the curiosity of a competent experimentalist, is yet another matter.) An *empirical* test is, of course, a confrontation of some of the infinitely many logical consequences of the initial assumptions of the theory, enriched with subsidiary hypotheses and with data, with some information obtained with the help of observations, measurements or experiments designed and read with the help of the given theory and of further theories. Thus in order to test a gravitational theory one will focus on some of its theorems and will build, with some of the concepts of the theory, a model of the physical system concerned that will incorporate only the relevant features of the real thing. The next step will be to design and execute certain measurements bearing on that model and based on theories such as optics and mechanics.

1.3. *The Priority of Nonempirical Tests*

No theory is given an empirical examination unless it is believed to have passed all three batteries of nonempirical tests. Most often some of these tests are not actually performed, either because they are exceedingly difficult (as is the case with consistency tests) or because it is intuitively felt that the theory satisfies the nonempirical requirements—an impression that very often proves to be wrong. The incompleteness of such tests does not diminish their value and it does not refute our contention that the nonempirical tests precede the empirical ones. In any event, demonstrably inconsistent theories can be written off with hardly any qualms, and completely off the track theories are seldom, if ever, considered for empirical tests. No matter how original it is, a scientific theory must be "reasonable" and "likely": it must be well built, it must not go against the grain of justified scientific beliefs, and it must not postulate items that are either metaphysically objectionable (such as an electron's ability to make decisions) or epistemologically opaque (such as a hidden variable with no possible overt manifestation).

In all three nonempirical tests consistency is involved: internal consistency, the consistency with other pieces of scientific knowledge, and the consistency with philosophical principles. Consistency is not only a logical virtue but also a methodological one. Indeed, an internally inconsistent theory may predict anything and may therefore be confirmed by mutually conflicting pieces of evidence. And a theory that fails to cohere with other theories will not be able to enjoy their support and suffer their control—as is the case with many pseudoscientific ideas. The worst that can happen to a scientific theory is not that it be refuted by experiments it has induced itself, but that it remain hanging in mid-air with neither friends nor foes.

As to the consistency of our scientific theories with the dominant philosophy and even the whole of our world view, we care for it because philosophy is indeed relevant to scientific research and in particular to the selection of research problems, to the formation of hypotheses, and to the evaluation of ideas and procedures. It goes without saying that subservience to a wrong philosophy can be harmful to research; thus intuitionist philosophy has blocked the advance of psychology in some countries. But it is a fact that consistency with the dominant philosophy is always sought or appreciated—and even believed to obtain when in fact it does not, as was the case of the relativistic and atomic theories in relation to positivism.[4] This makes a critical examination of philosophical principles even more necessary. But the adjustment between science and philosophy should be mutual rather than one-sided. The fact that a happy and fruitful marriage of philosophy and science is needed, makes it even more desirable. At any rate, although there are nonscientific philosophies, scientific research is permeated with a number of philosophical ideas.[5]

2. THEORY IS MADE READY FOR CONFRONTATION WITH DATA

2.1. *Theories Are Untestable in Isolation*

One century ago the great Maxwell [6] remarked that, when setting out to test candidates for law statements, one does not rush to the laboratory but starts by doing some further theoretical work: "the verification of the laws is effected by a theoretical investigation of the conditions under which certain quantities can be most accurately measured, followed by an experimental realization of these conditions, and actual measurement of the quantities." Note the three stages: experimental design (a piece of theoretical work), construction of the set-up, and performance of the empirical operations.[7] The experimental design will involve further hypotheses concerning the links of a given magnitude (e.g., gas pressure) with one that can be measured (e.g., the length of a liquid column), as well as a theoretical representation of the whole set-up. The same applies, *a fortiori*, to the process of verification of systems of hypotheses, i.e., theories.

It is impossible to subject a scientific theory to empirical tests without roping in other theories. For one thing, while every theory covers some aspects of its referents (e.g., its magnetic properties), any empirical operation involves real objects that refuse to abstract from all those aspects which every theory deliberately neglects. Secondly, a theory may be untestable by itself for failing to concern observable facts: it may restrict itself to making assertions about what happens or can happen, whether or not the events are observable. (But it may still have a factual content even though it may have no empirical content.) Thus a theory of electric circuits is about electric currents but it does not state the conditions of its own test: the latter requires a further theory, namely electrodynamics, which will bridge unobservables such as the current intensity to observables such as the deflection angle of a meter. In most cases we do not need a full theory but merely segments of various theories.

To put it another way: scientific theories are *untestable by themselves* both because they are partial and because they involve transobservational concepts that are not linked, within the theories, to any empirical concepts. These links, indispensable to test a theory, must be borrowed from some other area of knowledge. Thus a psychological theory will become testable to the extent to which objectifiers (behavioral, physiological, neurological, etc.) can be adjoined to it. In sum, if we wish to see how our theories fare empirically, we must call in additional ideas instead of eliminating every theoretical element by way of "operational definitions."

2.2. Adding a Theoretical Model of the Referent

The adjunction of fragments of other theories is necessary but insufficient to obtain results comparable with data: since in experience we handle individual things (a given liquid body rather than the body genus, this human subject rather than mankind, and so forth), we must add *subsidiary assumptions* concerning the relevant details of the system concerned. Thus in the case of a test of a theorem in electromagnetic theory we must add special hypotheses and data concerning the shape, charge distribution and magnetization of the field sources.

A general theory does not contain such subsidiary assumptions precisely because it is general. It is a comprehensive framework compatible with a whole family of sets of subsidiary assumptions. Every such set sketches a *theoretical model* of the thing concerned. Any such model is cast in the language of the theory although it is not dictated by the latter. Clearly a theoretical model may, but need not, be visualizable: being constructed with the concepts of a theory, it will be as abstract (epistemologically speaking) as the theory itself. Thus classical mechanics is consistent with a large variety of models of planetary systems; likewise, it is consistent with many models of liquids: the continuous medium model, the gas-like model, the crystal-like model (Ising's), and so on. A general theory cannot be tested apart from some model or other as long as the model is regarded as a theoretical image of the thing concerned rather than as a heuristic metaphor.[8]

2.3. The Importance of Specific Hypotheses

A subsidiary hypothesis concerning some trait of the object of study may mask the truth value of a general theory, particularly if few data are available, as is often the case in a new area of research. For example, suppose there are two rival theories concerning the Q-ness of matter—an imaginary physical property. Each theory hypothesizes its own functional relation between this peculiar property Q and the area A of the thing concerned. The first theory assumes that (in appropriate units) $Q = \frac{1}{2} A^{\frac{1}{2}}$, while the second postulates that $Q = (2/A)^{\frac{1}{2}}$. Suppose further that measurement yields the following bits of information: (a) $e =$ The linear dimensions D of the experimental object are of the order of unity; (*b*) e^* = The value of Q as measured on the experimental object is 1.0 ± 0.2. Unfortunately the shape of the thing is not observable: it must be guessed. This is where a subsidiary assumption must be adjoined: in order to set the theory in motion we must hypothesize a model of the thing—in this case a visualizable model of an unseen thing. Suppose the following situation occurs:

$$e: D = 1$$

$H_1 : Q = \frac{1}{2}A^{\frac{1}{2}}$	$H_2 : Q = (2/A)^{\frac{1}{2}}$
S_1 : the thing is a disk.	S_2 : the thing is a sphere.
$H_1, S_1, e \vdash Q_1 = \pi^{\frac{1}{2}}/4 \cong \cdot 4$	$H_2, S_2, e \vdash Q_2 = (2/\pi)^{\frac{1}{2}} \cong \cdot 8$

Clearly, the right-hand result is consistent—within experimental error—with the measured value of Q, i.e. 1 ± 0.2. But it would be folly to write off H_1 on this ground for, by replacing S_1 by S_2, we would come up with $Q = \pi^{\frac{1}{2}}/2 \cong .9$, which is an even better value of Q than Q_2. This case is imaginary of course but by no means artificial. Moral: Watch the model, for a good model can save (temporarily) a poor general theory, just as an inadequate model can ruin (permanently) a good general theory.

2.4. Assuming Models and Seeking Them

Theoretical scientists can be found to state, in prefaces and in concluding remarks, that every scientific theory is "based on" experimental data. But on reading the work sandwiched between empiricist covers, one finds that it does not fit this philosophy: unless it consists in a new theory it either (*a*) computes quantities that may (sometimes) be subsequently confronted with empirical results, or (*b*) combines given experimental data with a general framework in order to infer some specific feature of the system concerned. In either case work starts from some general framework rather than from scratch, if only because that general framework will suggest the kind of information to be sought in the laboratory or in the field. Thus energies and scattering cross sections, rather than precise positions—or, for that matter, entropies and stresses—will be computed or measured in the case of the scattering of atomic beams, because the general theory says that the former quantities are relevant.

More precisely, in theoretical science there are direct problems and inverse problems. A *direct problem* looks like this: Given both a general framework and a specific theoretical model of the system concerned, find either a general formula of a certain kind or an instance thereof.

Examples may be taken from physics: (*a*) given classical mechanics (general framework) and a definite fluid model (determined, say, by a certain distribution of masses, stresses and forces), compute the trajectory of an arbitrary particle in the fluid (i.e., a streamline); (*b*) given quantum mechanics (general framework) and the standard model of the helium atom (a three-body system kept together by Coulomb forces), deduce the energy spectrum; (*c*) given the same general theory as in (*b*) and the usual model of target as a central field of force, compute the scattering cross section for a beam of given characteristics.

The corresponding *inverse problems* would be as follows: (*a*) given classical mechanics and a set of streamlines, infer the mass and force densities as well as the stress tensor; (*b*) given quantum mechanics and a sample of an energy spectrum, guess the constituents of the system and the forces among them; (*c*) given quantum mechanics and a cross section vs. energy curve, infer the interparticle forces. In every case the inverse problem is, given a general theoretical body and certain empirical data, find the model which best fits both.

To put it symbolically, the general theory supplies a function f that relates the hypothesized model m to a testable consequence t, i.e. $t = f(m)$. Thus in the case of the direct scattering problem, t may be a phase shift and m the assumed hamiltonian (equivalently, the interaction force). An inverse problem, on the other hand, boils down to finding the inverse f^{-1} of f, so as to obtain: $m = f^{-1}(t)$. The effective inversion of f calls for the determination of the suitable information t, as well as applying or inventing a suitable mathematical technique. In no case is empirical information alone given, let alone sought: The very kind of information the experimentalist runs after is more or less suggested by the general framework. As a well-known specialist [9] in scattering problems remarks, "The most easily accessible [experimental scattering] information helps us not at all if we are not astute enough to find a procedure for obtaining that hamiltonian from it."

If the general theory is consistent and the direct problem is properly formulated and at all solvable, it will have a unique solution.[10] Not so with most inverse problems, which are characteristically indeterminate.[11] This holds particularly for the problem of finding a model on the basis of a general framework and a set of data: jointly, the two usually determine a whole class of models (e.g., hamiltonians) rather than a single model. To realize the indeterminateness peculiar to inverse problems (e.g., finding a model) we need not go into the ambiguities encountered in elementary particle physics.[12] We already find it in elementary problems such as the one of determining the intensity and the voltage of an alternating current from measurements which give only average values.

2.5. General Schema

Call T_1 the theory to be tested and S_1 the set of subsidiary assumptions added in order to derive some statements T_1', specific enough to come close to experience. S_1 will include a theoretical model of the system(s) under consideration and it may include simplifying assumptions such as linearizations. The theory T_1—an infinite set of statements—will be judged on the performance of the theorems T_1', which are not only finite in number but also partly alien to T_1 even though they are cast in the language of T_1. (One more reason for refusing to identify "theory" and "language.") Notice that the real situation, in which T_1 and S_1 jointly entail T_1', is a far cry from the standard view according to which T_1 single handed yields T_1', which would in turn be directly comparable to the empirical evidence.

As a rule not even the T_1' will be directly testable, for they will involve theoretical concepts such as the one of stress (whether mechanical or psychological) that have no empirical counterpart. In order to connect T_1' with experience we must adjoin a further batch of hypotheses, namely the objectifiers or indices of the unobservable entities and properties in question. Thus gravity is objectified by motion and appetite by amount of food consumed. Call I_1 the set of indices or objectifiers employed in bridging the gap between the theory T_1 and experience. These indices are not "operational definitions" but full blown hypotheses that should be checked independently even though they may go unquestioned in the process of testing T_1. They are hypotheses devised on the basis of the available knowledge A as well as of T_1 itself—for the theory under consideration must decide which kind of evidence will be relevant to it. At any rate, once the inventive process is over it must be possible to show that the objectifier hypotheses are well founded: that A and T_1 jointly entail I_1.

We still need some particular empirical statements if we are to derive specific predictions. Call E_1 the set of data fed into the theory. In order to introduce them into T_1 we must translate them into the language of T_1. For example, astronomical data, originally expressed in geocentric coordinates, will have to be translated into heliocentric coordinates. This data translation is done with the help of T_1 itself and of some fragments of the antecedent knowledge A. Let us call E_1^* the set of data couched in the language of T_1 and ready to be fed to it. In a careful logical reconstruction, A, T_1, I_1 and E_1 will entail E_1^*.

Finally, from the particular theorems T_1 and the translated data E_1^* we will obtain a set T^* of testable consequences—not just of the theory T_1 under examination but of T_1 in conjunction with all the remaining assumptions and data. T^* will face the fresh empirical evidence produced in order to test T_1.

In brief, the preparation of the theory T_1 for empirical testing is as follows:

Construction of a model of the referent	S_1
Deduction of particular theorems	$T_1, S_1 \vdash T_1'$
Construction of indices	$A, T_1 \vdash I_1$
Translation of data	$A, T_1, E_1, I_1 \vdash E_1^*$
Drawing testable consequences	$T_1', E_1^* \vdash T^*$

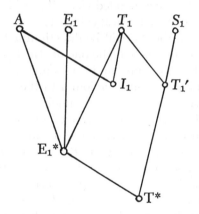

Figure 1. The derivation of testable consequences involves the antecedent knowledge A, some data E_1, a model S_1, and bridge hypotheses I_1.

3. NEW EXPERIENCE PRODUCED AND PROCESSED

3.1. *Interpreting What We See*

The next task is to produce a set E^* of data relevant to the theoretical predictions T^*. The performance of this task often calls for theoretical work, comparable in volume with that conducted for the previous stage.

Consider X-ray diffraction pictures, the main empirical tool of analysis for molecular biologists. These pictures make no sense except in a theoretical context: what one actually sees are dark spots and rings around a center. Such patterns bear no obvious relation to the spatial configuration of the atoms in the crystal; theory alone tells us the meaning of these (natural) signs. What one does in order to "read" such pictures is to hypothesize a given atomic configuration (call it T_1) with the help of several fragments of physical and chemical theories. Further, one admits that electromagnetic theory (call it T_2) accounts for the nature and behavior of X-rays. From T_1 and T_2 one computes (with the help of Fourier analysis) the theoretical diffraction pattern, i.e., the one that should result if both T_1 and T_2 were true. But this pattern is invisible: we need, in addition, some bridge to the observed picture. Diffraction patterns may be rendered visible by means of sensitive photographic plates. The mechanism of this process is explained by a third theory, namely photochemistry, which will be called T_3. An X-ray diffraction picture (a blind *datum*) becomes *evidence* for or against a molecular structure theory T_1 when it can be deduced from it with the help of auxiliary theories (electromagnetic optics and photochemistry), one of which explains the diffraction mechanism while the other explains the blackening mechanism. In short, T_1, T_2 and T_3 jointly entail E (see figure 2).

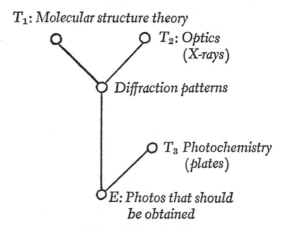

T_1: Molecular structure theory

T_2: Optics (X-rays)

Diffraction patterns

T_3 Photochemistry (plates)

E: Photos that should be obtained

Figure 2. An X-ray diffraction picture makes sense if it can be predicted on the basis of a model of the crystal and with the help of two auxiliary theories: one accounting for the nature of X-rays, the other for the blackening process.

The experimenter will, of course, start at the other end: He will produce E and will proceed to try to guess T_1 with the help of the theories T_2 and T_3, which he will take for granted in this particular context. His is an inverse problem (see section 2.4). When the crystal is very complex, as is the case of a protein which contains thousands of atoms, his guesswork is very intricate—so much so that only a small fraction of X-ray diffraction pictures have so far been deciphered; although he can always find some assistance in checking similarities to previous studies. Moreover, he may deliberately discard much empirical information and begin with a low resolution instrument, just as the astronomer often starts with a low power telescope. Unless he institutes the proper simplifications, he may get no pattern at all—and a pattern is of course what he is after. Just as a rough theoretical model is better than no model at all, so, digestible data are preferable to data indigestion.

The crystallographer's task would be greatly simplified if theoretical chemistry were more advanced: if it were possible to deduce all possible configurations that any given set of atoms could fit. Such a detailed calculation of possible molecular configurations requires a fourth theory, quantum chemistry, which has been around for four decades but is still not quite sufficient for such a formidable task. If and when a breakthrough is accomplished, the logical tree in Figure 2 will have to be supplemented with a branch descending from quantum chemistry to T_1. The unraveling of the "meaning" of many presently mysterious X-ray pictures depends on further theoretical development rather than on finer observation and measurement techniques.

3.2. Knowing What We Measure

Instructions concerning laboratory operations are sometimes worded in a pragmatic language that disguises their theoretical foundation, as may be illustrated with an example from classical physics. Every precision measurement involves electric measurements and every such measurement involves the comparison of electric resistances. One of the standard techniques for comparing electric resistances uses Wheatstone's

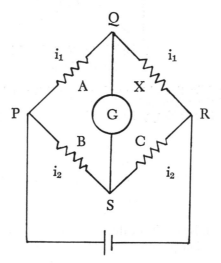

Figure 3. The Wheatstone bridge, in combination with elementary network theory, allows us to infer X from A, B and C.

bridge, a pons asinorum of modern instrumentation. The design and operation of the Wheatstone bridge are based on the elementary theory of electric networks, the central laws of which are Kirchhoff's and Ohm's. Figure 3 represents, in a fairly direct way, a theoretical model of the Wheatstone bridge in the equilibrium state, i.e., when no electricity flows through the galvanometer G. Under these conditions,

Kirchhoff's second law yields

$$V_{PQ} - V_{PS} = 0$$

for the left fork and

$$V_{QR} - V_{SR} = 0$$

for the right one. In turn, every one of these potential differences is, by Ohm's law,

$$V_{PQ} = A\,i_1\,,\ V_{PS} = B\,i_2$$

$$V_{QR} = X\,i_1\,,\ V_{SR} = C\,i_2$$

whence the final formula

$$X = AC/B$$

(The galvanometer G bridging the points Q and S of the circuit does not occur explicitly as a referent in these formulas, because it registers zero current.)

The preceding formulae may be summarized in the following *physical statement*:

P: In one of the branches of the Wheatstone bridge there exists a point S at which the electric potential has the same value as the potential at a given point Q in the other branch.

The technician will employ the following *operational statement* that translates the preceding proposition into the language of human action:

O: If one of the terminals of the galvanometer in a Wheatstone bridge *is connected* to a point Q *chosen arbitrarily* on one of the branches of the bridge, and if the other terminal *is displaced* along the other branch, a point S will be *found* for which the pointer of the galvanometer will be *seen* to come to rest at the zero of the scale.

(The italicized words are of course the pragmatic terms in the sentence.) Although the technician may be satisfied with this operational statement, O, the only justification for O is the preceding physical (and theoretical) statement P. Moreover, it is P which led Sir Charles to invent his bridge. (The mere observation that no current passes through G could otherwise be interpreted as indicating that the meter is out of order.) In general, however theory-free ordinary experience may be, no precision experience is possible in science without some theory, even though the description of the experience may not exhibit this dependence upon theory. An analysis of two typical measurements in modern physics will bear out this claim.

3.3. *Measuring Probabilities in Atomic Physics*

In the simplest case—the one studied by philosophers—probabilities are measured by counting relative frequencies. But indirect probability measurements, i.e., measurements via theoretical formulas, are about as frequent. A good example is the measurement of the intensity of a spectrum line as an index or objectifier of a transition probability. (For the concept of index or bridge hypothesis, see Section 2.5.) The link between the two is roughly this: The more probable a transition between two energy levels, the more intense the corresponding spectrum line. If the transition is highly probable, a bright line is seen, if the transition probability is low, a dim one, and if the probability is nil, no line at all. (If, notwithstanding the theory, a line is seen where it should be absent, then the corresponding transition is called forbidden and the suitable correction is made in the theory.)

Since many spectrum lines are visible with the naked eye, the claim could be made that when looking at any of them, what is actually being observed is a transition probability. This could do, on condition that it is realized that such an observation is heavily loaded with theory, to the point that without it what would be seen would be just a bright colored stripe. After all, the transitions in question are quantum jumps from one atomic energy level to another, and the probabilities are calculated with the help of theoretical formulas. Moreover, the experimentalist must design the equipment (light source, diffraction grating, photographic plates, wavelength measuring instrument, etc.) in accordance with several theories (notably optics). The latter requires not only the effective realization of the conditions assumed by the theories involved (e.g., the equal spacing of the grating lines) but also certain assumptions that cannot be controlled exhaustively. Among the latter assumptions the following occur: the arc temperature does not change from one photograph to the next; the atoms under study enter the arc stream at a constant rate; they do not appreciably absorb the light emitted by their kin. Once the empirical data have been collected and sifted (criticized and processed), theory comes in to compute the transition probabilities in terms of the measured quantities. The formula employed to infer such probabilities from the measurement outcome, is the Einstein-Boltzmann equation. The measurable magnitudes occurring in this formula are the temperature and the light intensity. While the former can be measured with high accuracy, the standard deviation of the measured intensity values is, even today, no less than about 30%. The whole procedure is so complicated and involves so many uncertainties that the first comprehensive and reliable table of "experimental" atomic transition probabilities [13] was published only in 1961 after 30 years of teamwork.

3.4. Measuring Probabilities in Nuclear Physics

In nuclear physics the probability of an event (e.g., a nuclear reaction) is usually given by the total cross section for that event: again, because the corresponding theory (quantum mechanics) says so (see Figure 4).

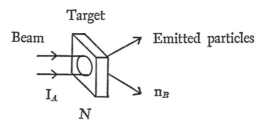

Target

Beam   Emitted particles

I_A n_B

N

Figure 4. Nuclear reaction A→B. The number n_B of particles emitted is related to the incident flux I_A by the theoretical formula: $n_B = I_A \, \sigma_{AB} N$, where σ_{AB} is the total cross section for that reaction and N the number of target particles presented to the beam.

In the total cross section the scattering angle is obliterated. Since the scattered intensity depends upon the angle, it is necessary to consider the differential cross section or cross section per unit angle and unit energy interval (a higher level concept serving to define the total cross section). Of course in the laboratory one measures the differential cross section referred to the laboratory frame of reference. If this value is to be compared with a theoretical prediction, it must be converted into a center of mass value. Thus translated, a measurement outcome may look like this (an actual figure accepted at the time of writing): At an angle of 20°8 and an energy of 156 Mev, the proton-proton cross

section in the center of mass frame equals 3.66 ± 0.11. (Different teams
of physicists will obtain values differing by as much as 15%.) In general,
for a scattering of A particles by B particles at the energy E and the
angle $\theta_{c.m.}$, one will have a statement of the form

$$\sigma(A\text{-}B, E, \theta_{c.m.}) = n \pm \varepsilon,$$

where n is a (fractionary) number and ε the total error. Note how far
from sense experience such a laboratory outcome is: A and B name
particle species, the members of which are imperceptible: they are objectified by means of instruments embodying several theories. The
energy E is measured indirectly and the scattering angle $\theta_{c.m.}$ is calculated from the measured angle. Finally the error ε is arrived at with
the help of statistics. In sum, the whole experimental procedure is permeated by theoretical ideas, and the very idea of a scattering cross
section (as distinct from a geometrical cross section) makes no sense
outside microphysics.

3.5. Empirical Evidence Neither Purely Empirical Nor Conclusive

Contrary to popular superstition, science has little use for pure (un-
interpreted, theory-free) data, and no evidence is definitive one way or
another. Even the data gathered with the naked eye are meaningless unless they can be integrated in a body of knowledge, and they are all subject to uncertainty. One of the archaeologists taking part in the excava-
tions (1967) of what may have been King Arthur's legendary Camelot,
declared at one point that *he thought he could see up to six or seven*
different layers of ruins—evidence that would not have been looked for
in the absence of the legend. During the 19th century all astronomers
saw that the nebulae (our present galaxies) were continuous (gaseous)
bodies rather than the clusters of stars which the late 18th century astronomers *saw*. And they failed to see what everyone can now *see* by
himself, namely the black dust clouds (e.g., in the rings of the spiral galaxies). We do not report what we see with mindless eyes but report,
rather, what we think we see: Scientific observation, unlike the observation of babies and empiricist philosophy, is permeated by hypotheses.[14]

Measurement does not eliminate observational uncertainty, although an analysis of measurement in the light of mathematical statistics can render the uncertainty precise. This, indeed, is the aim of calculating the standard deviation of the random errors of observation. But in
addition to these errors and to the mistakes in the design or operation
of laboratory equipment, one has to reckon with possible errors in the
theoretical part of any indirect measurement. Thus, before the 1920's

the size of the galaxies had been found to be roughly ten times smaller than their actual size. Similarly, in the early 1950's all intergalactic distances had to be multiplied by two overnight, when a mistake was found in the previous calculations. Contrarily, sometimes one knows there is something wrong with the data and cannot ascertain what it is. Thus at the time of writing the measured values of the rotation period of Venus go from 5 days (optical method) to 244 days (radar method).[15]

In sum, there are no hard and fast data: there are only hard skulls sheltering the belief in the ultimate character of data. Every experimental technique is based on assumptions that ought to be subjected to independent checks, and the practical implementation of any such technique is subject to conceptual mistakes and perceptual errors, as well as to objective random variations in both the object and the instrument involved. Empirical data are no more certain than the theories relevant to them; but both data and theories, though uncertain, are corrigible.

3.6. General Schema

Any empirical operation presupposes a body A of antecedent knowledge. A includes, in particular, a set E_2 of data and a heap T_2 of scraps of theories. Although E_2 and T_2 are criticizable on other occasions, they go unquestioned in the given empirical investigation: they will be taken as authoritative, however far from authoritarianism we may be. On the strength of A, and particularly of T_2, bridge hypotheses I_2 will be devised which will enable the experimenter to objectify unobservables and, conversely, to interpret his readings in theoretical terms. In short, A and T_2 entail I_2.

The next step is to design an observation or experiment, involving I_2, the outcome of which can be relevant to the theory T_1 under test. (There certainly is much poorly designed experimentation, but precisely for this reason it is of little worth and, even if aimless, it cannot be totally cut off from all theory.) The experimental design will involve a number of specific subsidiary hypotheses S_2 sketching a theoretical model of the equipment. From S_2 and T_2 certain consequences T_2' concerning the functioning of the equipment during the empirical operations will follow. In short, T_2 and S_2 jointly entail T_2'.

Finally the empirical operations proper will be performed. Call E_2 their outcome, or rather the empirical reports, once cleansed and condensed with the help of the theory of errors. To make sense, the E_2 must be read in terms of both the theory T_1 under test and the auxiliary theory T_2. That is, from T_1, T_2 (or rather T_2'), I_2 and E_2, we shall derive a set E^* of data relevant to T_1.

In sum, we have the following tree:

Constructing a theoretical model of the

    equipment $\qquad\qquad\qquad\qquad\qquad S_2$

  Deducing particular theorems $\qquad\quad T_2, S_2 \vdash T_2'$

  Constructing indices $\qquad\qquad\qquad A, T_2 \vdash I_2$

  Translating data $\qquad\qquad\qquad\quad E_2, I_2, T_1, T_2' \vdash E^*.$

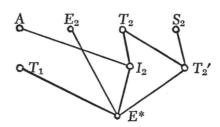

Figure 5. The raw data E_2 are dressed and cooked in theoretical terms with the help of antecedent knowledge A, the theory T_2 and the model S_2 of the experimental equipment, bridge hypotheses I_2, and even T_1 itself.

4. THEORY MEETS EXPERIENCE

4.1. *Statements: Theoretical and Empirical*

We are now in the possession of two sets of comparable statements: the theoretical predictions T^* and the empirical evidence E^*. Our present task is to confront them in order to draw some plausible "conclusion" concerning the worth of the substantive theory T_1, partly responsible for T^*. But before setting out to do this we must realize that T^* and E^*, though comparable, cannot be expected to coincide, for they are of different kinds. This point must be stressed in consideration of the standard view according to which the T^* are just consequences of T_1 alone, while the E^* might also be contained in T_1, the ideal being the equality of these two sets. (In fairness, the current theories of inductive logic [16] do not concern a scientific theory but an isolated hypothesis h and pure empirical evidence e, and they attempt to compute the degree of confirmation of h and the probability of the conditional "$e{\rightarrow}h$" given both the empirical evidence e and the conditional "$h{\rightarrow}e$". No actual examples—scientific examples, that is—of either conditional are ever mentioned, and the empirical evidence is regarded as sacrosanct.)

Let us insist that T^*, far from being a sample of T_1, is derived from T_1 jointly with a definite theoretical model (S_1), some data (E_1) and some bridge hypotheses (I_2). Likewise E^*, far from being a set of bare empirical statements, is a sample of interpreted outcomes of scientific experiences: otherwise it would not be comparable with T^*. Even so, E^* and T^* are not on the same level for, far from concerning the object in itself, any member of E^* refers to a couple object-empirical arrangement. (The Copenhagen interpretation of quantum mechanics pretends that this holds for every theoretical statement of this theory as well, but this is false: (a) the theory may concern free systems, i.e. things that are coupled to no measurement device, and (b) no general theory can account for the idiosyncrasies of every conceivable apparatus.) Change the apparatus or, preferably, the whole experimental arrangement, and a new set E^* of data is likely to result. If it does not, something may have gone wrong. At any rate, T^* and E^* are not quite on the same footing. The following analysis will make their differences apparent.

A quantitative prediction is a theoretical statement about the value of some "quantity" (magnitude) Q of some real system in a certain state. Actually the system described by the theory is not the real thing σ of the kind Σ the theory intends to account for, but an idealized sketch or theoretical model m of it. (Really, m is a theoretical model of the referent in a given state.) In a typical case, Q will be a certain real function, so that a prediction of a value of Q will take the form

$$Q_s(m) = r \qquad [1]$$

where the subscript s indicates the scale that has been adopted, while the value r of the function is some real number. (Still better, Q is a real valued function on the Cartesian product of the set M of models by the set S of scales.)

The experimenter handles the real thing σ with a certain experimental technique t which he implements with a certain sequence a of acts. (In microphysics an ensemble of similar systems, rather than a single system, will usually be available. But this is not always the case: thus individual nuclear reactions are "observable".) His results will depend not only on the thing σ but also on his technique t and its implementation a. More precisely, a single measurement result concerning the magnitude Q will take the form

$$Q_s'(\sigma, t, a) = r_a' \qquad [2]$$

where r_a' is again a number (rarely identical with the theoretical value r). (Better still: Q' is a real valued function on the set of ordered quadruples $\Sigma \times S \times T \times A$.) The point to note is that the measured Q' and the theoretical Q are altogether *different functions*. No wonder they seldom have the same values.

The individual measured values [2] are then processed with the help of mathematical statistics. The two most important outcomes are the standard deviation (a measure of the total error) and the average value, which is taken to be an estimate of the true value. A statement about the average Q' is of the form

$$\text{AV}_{a\epsilon A} Q_s'(\sigma, t, a) = r' \qquad [3]$$

where the subscript '$a\epsilon A$' means that the average is taken over a sample A of measurements. (Ideally A is infinite. Actually it is not, whence it is not stable. But its fluctuations decrease with the increasing size of the sample.) In general the average r' will differ from any of the individual values [2].

Once the average and the error have been computed, the experimenter may wish to go over his raw data [2] once again, to weed out or else justify any anomalous data that may have crept in. These black sheep will be those values lying beyond the limits agreed upon in advance (usually the 3 standard deviations limit). But if too many black sheep are found it will be necessary to proceed to a critical examination of the experimental procedure itself. The experimenter may then find that some of the assumptions have not been satisfied—for example that, contrary to hypothesis, every measurement act has influenced the subsequent act, i.e., that the condition of statistical independence has not been fulfilled. At any rate the experimenter does not accept his own results uncritically: he examines them in the light of both methodological theory (mathematical statistics) and substantive theory (e.g., mechanics). And the theoretician should not claim (as the Copenhagen school people do) that his own predictions concern measured values, for in general he does not know what experimental technique nor which steps to implement it will be adopted.

4.2. The Confrontation

Having emphasized that T^* and E^* are separated by a chasm, let us now bridge it. Let E^* be relevant to T^*—for otherwise we may come up against one of the paradoxes of confirmation.[17] Under this assumption there are only two possibilities: either E^* agrees with T^* or it does not. 'Agreement' here means less than identity and more than compatibility. A qualitative prediction such as "The scattered beam will be polarized" may be regarded as confirmed if, in fact, the beam proves even partially polarized. But if the prediction is quantitative, as in the case of "The degree of polarization of the scattered beam will be p [a definite number between 0 and 1]," then we need a different truth condition. The one tacitly adopted in physics seems to be the following: Let

$$p : P(m) = x \qquad [4]$$

be a theoretical prediction concerning a model m of the thing σ in a certain state, and let

$$e : P'(\sigma,\ t) = y \pm \varepsilon \qquad [5]$$

be the outcome of a run of measurements of P, on σ, with the technique t. The theoretical value is x, the average of the measured values is y, and the statistical scatter of these values is ε. The theoretical prediction p and the empirical datum e may be said to be *empirically equivalent* just in case the theoretical value x and the experimental (average) value y differ (in absolute value) by less than the experimental error ε- a tolerance agreed on beforehand. In short,[18]

$$Eq\ (p, e) =_{df} |x - y| < \varepsilon \qquad [6]$$

The precise meaning of the inequality relation will depend on the state of the experimental techniques. A theoretical statement and an empirical statement will be said to *agree* with one another if and only if they are empirically equivalent. Clearly, identity is a particular case of agreement.

If the "overwhelming majority" of the data E^* agree with the theoretical predictions T^*, then we declare T_1 to be *confirmed* by that particular set of data. Note, first, that we do not require every datum to agree with the corresponding prediction, and this because outlying data are bound to occur which can usually be discarded. But of course we must keep our mind open to the possibility that some such black sheep may actually be white. Note also that the theory under test is declared to be confirmed by a certain set of data and not just confirmed: this is a reminder that empirical tests, however prolix, are never exhaustive. Thirdly, note that we have not specified how strongly E^* confirms T^*. In actual science no degrees of confirmation are computed: the usual concept of confirmation is a comparative and not a quantitative one.

What if, on the other hand, E^* disagrees with T^*, i.e. if there is a sizable subset $E'^* \subset E^*$ of data that fail to match the theoretical predictions T^* ? According to both inductivists and refutationists we should then reject T^* and also T_1: Disagreement with experience refutes a theory and therefore forces us to give it up. However, this is not in keeping with actual scientific practice. In actual science one does not accept unfavorable evidence without further ado but subjects it to critical scrutiny, for any datum can be distorted by a number of factors. It often happens that the unfavorable evidence E'^* is rejected either because it is inconsistent with veteran theories or because it stems from poor design.

If E'^* is discarded, then there are two possibilities for the theory T_1 under test. If T_1 is a veteran theory, then we shall continue to use it while keeping in mind the anomalous E'^*—for, after all, they might prove not to be calumnies after all. If on the other hand T_1 has not yet proved its worth, while the unfavorable evidence is uncertain, then we should suspend judgment on the truth value of T_1 and wait for a new crop of more reliable evidence.

The negative outcome E'^* should be accepted if the auxiliary theory T_2 has been independently confirmed, if the experimental design passes a critical examination, and if the data are not mostly isolated values that can be discarded by the rules of thumb of mathematical statistics. But the acceptance of the unfavorable evidence E'^*, while committing us to reject the predictions T^*, does not entail the refutation of the substantive theory T_1. Indeed, a number of premises have been used, in addition to T_1, to derive the predictions T^* : the subsidiary hypotheses S_1 (including those sketching a model of the object concerned), the bridge hypotheses I_1, and the data E_1. We are faced with what may be called *Duhem's problem:* Given a set of premises entailing a set of consequences refuted (substantially if not totally) by experience, find the subset of premises responsible for the failure, with a view to replacing them by more adequate ones. This problem seems to be much more important than the problem of devising and computing degrees of confirmation.

In Duhem's view [19], when a theory disagrees with data, two equally legitimate procedures can be applied. One is to save the central hypotheses of the theory by eventually adding some auxiliary assumptions regarding either the referent of the theory or the experimental arrangement. The second way out is to correct some or all of the basic hypotheses, without having the slightest suspicion as to what to correct in the first place nor in what sense. Clearly, rationalists and conventionalists will recommend the first move while empiricists will recommend the second one. But in either case the prospects seem rather bleak.

Our previous analysis of the way T^* is derived (Section 2) confirms the complexity of Duhem's problem but at the same time it shows that a solution may be possible in every case provided care is taken to list the relevant premises. For, if the adverse empirical evidence is reliable, there are again two possibilities: either T_1 has stood up to tests in the past, or it is a newcomer. In the former case we should keep T_1 temporarily and subject the remaining premises responsible for T^* to a searching criticism. Of all these premises, usually the data E_1 and the bridge hypotheses I_1, though fallible, have been checked previously and in any case they are not usually questioned at the time T_1 is being questioned. Hence the most likely culprits are to be found among the subsidiary assumptions S_1, whether it be the theoretical model or the simplifying assumptions. We should then start by relaxing the latter and/or modifying (usually in the sense of further complication) the theoretical model. It is only after unsuccessfully trying many and widely different models that we must cast serious doubts on the theory T_1. Thus in the case of the current classical theories of liquids, what theoreticians do is to continually try more complex models of the liquid structure while retaining the laws of motion and, in general, the whole framework of classical mechanics.

On the other hand, if the theory T_1 under test is new or nearly so, then we shall subject both T_1 and S_1 to an exacting examination. Yet the suspect premises are not on the same footing: the more specific ones are the most likely to be false, for they take more chances and are less likely to have been tested. One should therefore start by questioning the subsidiary premises S_1—in particular the theoretical model—and the more specific axioms of T_1. The more generic postulates of T_1, those which T_1 shares with several other theories, are the least likely to be in need of reform, at least with regard to the domain in which they have been confirmed in the past. (When such extremely general and deep assumptions are shown to be wanting, then whole bunches of theories are likely to suffer reform.) In any case, this search for error need not be haphazard: it should proceed from the newer and narrower to the older and wider. An axiomatization of the theory under scrutiny should be extremely helpful in this search, for then all the presuppositions and the assumptions of the theory will be on display for all to see. Such an axiomatic organization of the theoretical material will be particularly useful if the three kinds of premises (the presuppositions, the generic postulates, and the specific ones) are clearly separated.[20] One will then begin by replacing the various specific assumptions one by one, and watching the effect of every such change on the testable consequences T^*.

Eventually one will come up with a new body T'^* of theoretical predictions, one which will agree with the total empirical evidence E^* or at least with a sizable part of it. Anything can come out of this readjustment work: a new theoretical model, and/or a slightly different theory, or else a radically new theory, or even a wholly different approach to theory construction. Criticizing theories in a constructive spirit, i.e. trying to build better ones, is one of the most rewarding experiences—one that dogmatists and carpers alike are spared.

In summary, when E^* is relevant to T^*, the confrontation process looks like this:

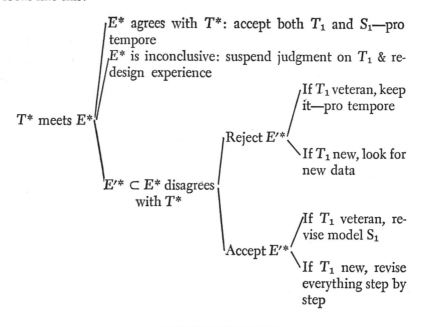

T^* meets E^*

- E^* agrees with T^*: accept both T_1 and S_1—pro tempore
- E^* is inconclusive: suspend judgment on T_1 & redesign experience
- $E'^* \subset E^*$ disagrees with T^*
  - Reject E'^*
    - If T_1 veteran, keep it—pro tempore
    - If T_1 new, look for new data
  - Accept E'^*
    - If T_1 veteran, revise model S_1
    - If T_1 new, revise everything step by step

5. CONSEQUENCES

If the preceding analysis is substantially correct, we must abandon the widespread belief that every theory *single-handedly* faces its empirical jury. First, because, in order to describe specific observable facts, a theory must be adjoined to some information, a definite model, and a bunch of hypotheses linking unobservables to observables; second, because the empirical jury is itself supported by a body of theory, a further model (of the empirical set-up), and some bridge hypotheses. In short, the theory under test calls for additional hypotheses and past experience, just as the new data intended to check it require some antecedent theory and further special hypotheses: Theory lives not on fact alone, and data are not self-sufficient either. This renders them both comparable and mutually controllable.

Consequently it is false that, as the inductivists claim, any theory should in principle *entail* the very same data from which it was induced. Not only are scientific theories not concocted out of pure data, but by themselves they entail none. Therefore theories cannot have any empirical content. Only single hypotheses, such as Snell's law of refraction and Galileo's law of falling bodies might be said to yield, by mere specification, any number of data—provided at least one item of empirical information is adjoined to them and provided the deep difference between theoretical and empirical statements is overlooked. But the theories to which these two hypotheses belong (wave optics and classical gravitation theory) are not testable just by instantiation. In other words, the conditional "h & $e_1 \rightarrow e_2$", which makes some sense for low-level hypotheses, cannot be exported to the domain of theories. As to the conditional "$e \rightarrow h$", it makes no sense for scientific hypotheses, much less for scientific theories, since no set of data implies a hypothesis, if only because the latter may contain predicates that fail to occur in the former. Yet it is the declared aim of most systems of inductive logic to evaluate the degree of confirmation (or logical probability) of conditionals of this kind (which explains why such theories are irrelevant to science). We might add that so far inductive logic has not faced the problem of devising reasonable measures of the degree of confirmation of quantitative theories: it has focused on stray hypotheses, and even here it has met with disaster.[21] This does not prove, of course, that this aim is chimerical, but just that the construction of systems of inductive logic relevant to science is a task before us.

A second consequence is that there can hardly be any *conclusive* evidence for or against a scientific theory. A set of data can, on occasion, confirm or refute a single hypothesis in an unambiguous way, but it is considerably less powerful in regard to a theory. While agreement between theory and experience (agreement over a given domain, that is) confirms the former, it does not point with certainty to the truth of the theory. It may indicate that both theory and data are sloppy, e.g., that compensating errors have crept into both. And disagreement between theory and experience cannot always be interpreted as a clean refutation of the former either. Confrontation and refutation, clear-cut though they can be in the case of single qualitative hypotheses—the case considered by both the inductivists and their critics—lose much of their edge in the case of quantitative theoretical predictions. This is not to say that scientific theories are impregnable to experience but rather that the process of their empirical test is complex and roundabout. (This renders the cogent and explicit, i.e. axiomatic, formulation of theories the more valuable, for it facilitates the control of the assumptions.) The complex and often inconclusive character of empirical testing enhances the value of the nonempirical tests, which are ultimately tests for the global consistency of the whole body of scientific knowledge.

Inductivism and refutationism are then inadequate, for both restrict themselves to single hypotheses, both neglect the theoretical model that must be adjoined to a general theory in order to deduce testable consequences, and both accept the tenets that (*a*) only empirical tests matter and (*b*) the outcome of such tests is always clear-cut. The failure of the currently dominant philosophies of science should not thrust us into the arms of conventionalism or any other philosophical expression of cynicism. We are entitled to hope that some of our theories are internally and externally consistent and that they have at least a grain of truth even though we may not be able to prove either property beyond doubt. For this hope is not blind faith: it is founded on the performance of our theories—on their tested ability to get along with other theories, to solve old and new problems, to make novel predictions, and to render new experiences intelligible and even possible.[22]

To summarize, theory and experience never meet head-on. They meet on an intermediate level once further theoretical and empirical elements—in particular theoretical models of both the thing concerned and the empirical arrangement—have been added. Even so, empirical tests are not always conclusive and they do not enable us to dispense with the nonempirical ones. To the extent to which all this is true, the dominant philosophies of science are inadequate. We must start afresh, keeping closer to actual scientific research than to the philosophical traditions.[23]

NOTES

1. S. Brush, "A History of Random Processes. I. Brownian Movement from Brown to Perrin," *Archive for the History of the Exact Sciences*, vol. 5 (1968) p. 5.

2. M. Bunge, "The Weight of Simplicity in the Construction and Assaying of Scientific Theories," *Philosophy of Science*, vol. 28 (1961) p. 120; also, *The Myth of Simplicity* (Englewood Cliffs, Prentice-Hall, 1963), Ch. 7; and *Scientific Research* (New York, Springer-Verlag, 1967), vol. II, Ch. 15. (Henceforth to be referred to as SR.)

3. See references in footnote 2 for case studies. The first scientist to explicitly demand that scientific constructs satisfy certain metaphysical requirements seems to have been H. Margenau, in *The Nature of Physical Reality* (New York, McGraw-

Hill, 1950), Ch. 5. For the importance of the prevailing conceptual framework and philosophical ideas in the conception and evaluation of scientific theories, see T. Kuhn, *The Structure of Scientific Revolutions* (Chicago, University of Chicago Press, 1962) and J. Agassi, "The Nature of Scientific Problems and Their Roots in Metaphysics," in M. Bunge, Ed., *The Critical Approach* (New York, Free Press, 1964).

4. M. Bunge, *Foundations of Physics* (New York, Springer-Verlag, 1967), Chs. 4 and 5, and "The Turn of the Tide," in M. Bunge, Ed., *Quantum Theory and Reality* (New York, Springer-Verlag, 1967).

5. M. Bunge, SR, vol. I, Ch. 5, Sec. 5.9.

6. J. C. Maxwell, "Remarks on the Mathematical Classification of Physical Quantities," *Proceedings of the London Mathematical Society*, vol. 3 (1871), p. 224.

7. For a detailed analysis of measurement and experiment see M. Bunge, SR, vol. II, Chs. 13 and 14.

8. For the concept of theoretical models see M. Bunge, "Physics and Reality," *Dialectica* vol. 19, (1965), p. 195, reference 5, Ch. 8, Sec. 8.4, and "Analogy in Quantum Mechanics: From Insight to Nonsense," *British Journal for the Philosophy of Science*, vol. 18 (1968), p. 265 and "Models in Theoretical Science," *Proceedings of the XIVth International Congress of Philosophy* (Wien, Herder, 1969), Vol. III.

9. R. G. Newton, *Scattering Theory of Waves and Particles* (New York, McGraw-Hill, 1966), p. 611.

10. For the conditions to be met by a well-formulated problem, see M. Bunge, SR vol. I, Ch. 4, Sec. 4.2.

11. For the analysis of a characteristic case, see M. Bunge, "A General Black Box Theory," *Philosophy of Science*, vol. 30 (1963), p. 346.

12. See reference 9, sec. 20.2.

13. W. F. Meggers, C. H. Corliss, and B. F. Scribner, *Tables of Spectral-Line Intensities* (Washington, D.C., National Bureau of Standards Monograph 32, 1961).

14. See N. R. Hanson, *Patterns of Scientific Discovery* (Cambridge, Cambridge University Press, 1958), Chs. I and II, and M. Bunge SR, vol. II, Ch. 12.

15. B. A. Smith, "Rotation of Venus: Continuing Contradictions," *Science*, vol. 158 (1967), p. 114.

16. See R. Carnap, *Logical Foundations of Probability* (Chicago, University of Chicago Press, 1950) and G. H. Von Wright, *The Logical Problem of Induction*, 2nd ed. (Oxford, Basil Blackwell, 1957).

17. For irrelevance as a source of the main paradox of confirmation, see Bunge, SR, vol. II, Ch. 15, Sec. 15.4, and "Problems and Games in the Current Philosophy of Natural Science," *Proceedings of the XIVth International Congress of Philosophy* (Wien, Herder, 1968), Vol. I.

18. M. Bunge, SR, vol. II, Ch. 15, Sec. 15.2.

19. P. Duhem, *La théorie physique*, 2nd ed. (Paris, Rivière, 1914), pp. 329 ff.

20. As an example see the axiomatization of quantum mechanics in M. Bunge, *Foundations of Physics* (New York, Springer-Verlag, 1967), Ch. 5.

21. A. J. Ayer, "Induction and the Calculus of Probabilities," *Démonstration, vérification, justification: Entretiens de l'Institut International de Philosophie*, Liège 1967 (Louvain, NauWelaerts, 1968).

22. For quantitative concepts of predictive performance, accuracy, and originality, see M. Bunge SR, vol. II, Ch. 10, Sec. 10.4.

23. I am grateful to Stephen Brush (Harvard) for his critical remarks.

MODELS FOR
SCIENTIFIC PRACTICE
(A RESPONSE)

Peter Caws

I accept Professor Bunge's analysis as an account of what might well be produced if a theory of a certain level of specificity and complexity were called on to show its empirical credentials. As an account keeping close to scientific research, it seems to me that it has much to recommend it. One can readily recognize the various stages and substages indicated, although I would question some of the points of detail: to insist, for example, that one needs a theory of photochemistry in order to use X-ray diffraction pictures seems to me extravagant. On the other hand some aspects of the account are extremely useful—for example, the attention drawn to the intermediate role of a model of the physical system compatible with, but not derived from, the theory under test, and the distinction made between direct and inverse problems in theoretical science.

What I wish mainly to discuss, however, is the setting of the paper in contemporary philosophy of science, taking my cue more from the negative things Bunge has said than from the positive. His use of such expressions as "the dominant philosophy of science" seems to suggest that there is a recognizable group of philosophers who take an extraordinarily simple-minded view of scientific theory, in contrast to which he offers a more adequate account. I hope that I shall not be defending a position he did not attack, but he was clearly attacking something, and if it was not that position then I don't know what it was.

When a thesis B is offered as a replacement for a thesis A (a replacement in a philosophical rather than a scientific sense) there are two strategies which the proponent of A may adopt. First, he may claim that nobody maintains A in the form criticized anyway; and second, he may claim that they do, but that they are justified in doing so. I shall adopt both strategies. I will not pretend not to know what is meant by "the dominant philosophy of science"; it is represented in its simplest form in Figure 1, where H, which is generally hypothetical (usually a set of hypotheses), and A, standing for ancillary information of some kind or other (bridge laws, antecedent data, boundary conditions etc.), lead deductively to O, which is an observation sentence. The general outlines

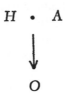

Figure 1.

of this model are accepted by very many contemporary philosophers of science, including Hempel, Nagel and a number of others. It can of course be complicated, but this is the basic version.

A very simple illustration of the model, which has caused a great deal of amusement on the part of critics, and which does not even involve theoretical terms, is: All ravens are black, therefore the bird we are about to see, being a raven, will be black. Note, however, that this is a heuristic paradigm, suitable for making elementary logical points in elementary classes in the philosophy of science. It is not intended to represent the conversation of scientists, but to indicate a basic feature of the logical structure of science. Strictly speaking the sentence 'This raven is black,' deduced from the generalization 'All ravens are black', is a different sentence from the sentence 'This raven is black', reported directly. We have, in fact, the situation of Figure 2, in which O and O' confront one another.

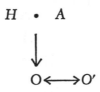

Figure 2.

This is, I think, the sense of Bunge's confrontation between I^* and E^*. It is precisely the formal identifiability of these sentences that constitutes the link between theory and experiment. Bunge, in discussing measurement, says that "the measured Q' and the theoretical Q are altogether different functions," and I agree: this corresponds in the simple case to the fact that O and O' are different sentences, in that they arise from different origins. But Bunge goes on at that point to remark that it is no wonder these functions seldom have the same values, and this seems to me seriously misleading.

This is a matter of degree, but it is crucial. Of course the predicted and observed values are almost never *exactly the same*, but if they are ever *sufficiently similar*, the condition for the empirical relevance of science is fulfilled. And there have, needless to say, been striking successes in producing essentially similar values. When, for example, it occurred to Newton in 1666 that the force of gravity might extend as far as the orbit of the moon, and he computed what the orbit of the moon would be if this were the case, he found the observed orbit and the predicted orbit to "answer pretty nearly." As a matter of fact they did not answer quite nearly enough, and he put those computations away. But it was in finding them to answer pretty nearly that the empirical and the theoretical began to come into contact.

Of course O has to be in the language of the theory, otherwise it couldn't be deduced from the theory. O', on the other hand, need not be in the language of the theory; the confrontation may involve a translation. And O' itself may take a good deal of preparation, so that the model could be made symmetrical by adding experimental conditions E plus another set of ancillary assumptions A', which together would yield the measurement or the observation which confronts what is deduced from the theory (Figure 3).

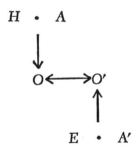

Figure 3

But of course the people who have maintained the so-called "orthodox" view know perfectly well that these complications are possible. The "all ravens are black" model isn't supposed to represent scientific theory in all its ramifications or scientific practice in all its detail, and to suggest even implicitly that it claims to do so is to misunderstand its role in the philosophy of science.

There is in fact a serious point (and here I switch to my second strategy) to the elimination of details; and I wish now to explain why, even when schemata as elegant as Bunge's are at our disposal, some of us might prefer to stick to the simpler model and refuse to see his as all that much of an improvement. There are two points of view from which a model of theory may be judged, the first having to do with its logical adequacy and the second having to do with its fidelity to the practice of science. Bunge's case rests, by his own avowal, on the latter, his final recommendation being that we must now start afresh, "this time keeping closer to actual scientific practice." But it seems to me that his schematization is still immeasurably far from actual scientific practice. It is as if I were to think it desirable to live in London, and were to move from New York to Boston in order to approach that ideal more nearly. The question is relative: you can be more or less schematic, and how schematic you are depends on what you want to do.

If the question arises as to what the scientist actually does, I say what he does is to test theories by confronting their consequences with evidence. Bunge says that is too schematic and oversimplified, and offers his analysis. I may, justifiably, reply that that also is too schematic. For if I *actually look* at what the scientist is *actually doing* I find that he is scratching his head, rummaging under his papers for a note made yesterday, mopping up the coffee spilled in the process. This is Bunge's theoretical teacher: the experimental teacher is cursing the laboratory assistant, telephoning to ask why the liquid nitrogen has not arrived, tapping his foot in time with the vacuum pump. There is perhaps not all that much to choose between a slightly more complex schema and a slightly more simple one; the degree of schematization is relative to the purpose at hand, and the purpose of the philosophy of science is often not at all to describe the activity of scientists, it is to clarify the nature and logical structure of science, which is a very different matter.

Let me make one final remark, which has to do with the relation of physics to the philosophy of science and is relevant, I think, to some recent difficulties with the simple model I have described. It used to be the case that examples in the philosophy of science were drawn largely from physics because they were simple and people could be expected to know them—the law of falling bodies, for example, or Boyle's law. I have the impression now that examples are sometimes drawn from physics because they are very complicated and people can be expected *not* to know them. Clearly the philosophy of science must reckon with quantum mechanics and other difficult aspects of recent physics, which is a rich source of complex philosophical problems and thus provides a welcome challenge to philosophers, a challenge which Bunge is unusually well equipped to meet. But I am not convinced that we have to change the basic conception of what science is and how it confronts experience in order to accommodate that complexity.

DO WE KNOW THE WORLD THROUGH SCIENCE?

Richard Schlegel

1. Introduction

The correctness of a scientific statement about the natural world is a problem to be decided by scientists. But the further question, of what an assertion that is obtained by the procedures of science tells us about the world, is a philosophical question. In a way, the question may seem to be foolish. Most assuredly, a scientific truth does give us information about nature: that the earth is a large oblate spheroid which revolves about the sun, for example, or that fresh fruits contain ascorbic acid, which is necessary for human well-being. But we might still ask, to what extent we have grasped the universe when we know what science tells us about it. If the multiplicity of potential facts about nature were all made available to us by science, and further, found to be organized into a coherent theoretical scheme, could we then say that we understood the universe? I want to discuss this question chiefly from the point of view of contemporary physics, although also using some considerations that obviously apply to natural science generally.[1]

2. Selectivity in Description.

There has actually often occurred among physicists and commentators on physics the vanity that now we have achieved a science which essentially tells us what the universe is: that although countless details remain to be worked out in this or that special field, we in principle understand how nature operates. A more cautious sentiment would be that physics has today achieved knowledge in a wide domain of nature, so that, although it would be foolish to speak of having encompassed the universe, we can say that the field has been secured for much of the natural world that we experience. An impressive listing can readily be made: the everyday terrestrial phenomena that are understood and controlled through mechanics, optics, electromagnetic theory, thermodynamics, and statistical mechanics; the extension of our knowledge of the universe in astronomy, even to the extent where, with the guidance of the relativity theory of gravitation, models of the entire cosmos are considered; the penetration of the atomic level of nature, with the intrepid development of the quantum theory that both comprehends a great array of phenomena and brings us intrinsically to the very limit of the space-time world that we know macroscopically; and, even biology and medical science seem to be succumbing to the firmness of analyses that explore structure and physicochemical process.

Yet even considering only those aspects of nature which are well within the purview of present-day science, there are serious limitations on the knowledge which we have of the natural world. To begin with, there is the great narrowing of the possible description of nature that comes with the selection that is made of aspects to be described. Each science selects in terms of the kinds of properties or processes which are the concern of that science: Hence, a chemist, a geologist, a physicist, and an engineer will generally attend to quite different aspects of a mineral sample. The physicist, to be sure, will usually be interested in just those aspects which are of wide generality in the study of nature, but nonetheless—or perhaps even therefore—much that is of importance in scientific description, in the light of other interests, will be omitted.

Any natural entity that we consider—in contrast to a conceptually isolated entity—does in fact have so many properties, and relations to other natural entities, that we cannot hope to achieve anything like complete description. There is, indeed, an inherent factor of defeat in the general descriptive process, applied to everything in the world, for, in time, the very descriptions could become material which must itself be described, if we were to attain a complete descriptive science for the natural world. And that descriptive material must also be described, and so on. We see an infinite regress in the descriptive process that aims for completion. I might point out that the accumulation of archives and books, which begins to embarrass some librarians, indicates that the very problem of keeping and describing description is not necessarily a trivial one.

3. Inadequacy of Description.

Descriptive scientific knowledge is not only partial, in the sense of referring only to selected aspects of the natural domain towards which it is directed, but also it is inadequate because of its symbolic, cognitive nature. This inadequacy is inherent in the nature of science, which is made up of communicable words, equations, graphs, photographs, and the like. In contrast, what I will term direct descriptive knowledge is the sensed, experienced knowledge of a part of nature. The sight, feel, and taste of an apple can be a basis for close description of the color, texture, shape, and mass of an apple, and, with the use of appropriate scientific procedures, the sensed qualities can be related to chemical and physical characteristics of various parts of an apple. But, a complete treatise on the apple gives information that is qualitatively different from the sense information that comes with direct contact.

Science, then, gives us cognitive knowledge of selected aspects of the world but should never be regarded as equivalent to the living experience of the natural world. Something inevitably is lost in the transition from direct experience to formulation in scientific description, because of i) the selection that is involved in such description and, ii) the difference between scientific description, which is essentially verbal, and direct experience, which is not. With respect to knowledge and understanding there is an advantage in going to scientific description, for we gain precision, generality, and perhaps explanation. But, obviously, there is a loss too. In the direct experience of a natural entity, there are potentially all of the properties and relations that belong to the entity as a part of nature, even though we give, or can give, our attention only to some of those properties and relations.

Can we say, then, that we come closer to complete natural knowledge—even though we lose the advantages of scientific knowledge—when we have the direct descriptive knowledge of sense experience? I think our discussion has indicated that in a large measure the answer is, Yes. But even with such direct experience, is it correct to say that we then truly know the object that is experienced? Surely not, for our sensed experience is hardly the basis for a statement of what an object is; rather, it is a basis for stating what we learn of the object in our relation to it. Scientific description attempts to winnow out the personal elements of that description, and to state only properties that are invariant, or, intrasubjectively verifiable. Direct experience is made up of elements that are personal to the observer, as well as elements that can serve as a basis for scientific description. Still, to return to our example, for a truly complete description of an apple, with the immediacy of direct knowledge rather than the cognitive, symbolic character of scientific description, it would seem that one cannot just be a person looking or feeling or tasting the apple. To know of the growth of an apple, of its hanging in a tree, of the effects of sun and wind, of the threats of insects—to know these matters in the directness of their occurrence in nature—it would seem that one must, in fact, be an apple. And so on throughout nature. How can even our direct experiences of any aspect of the natural world be anything other than knowledge of that aspect in relation to ourselves? It would seem that only by being the object, the natural entity, can we have truly correct knowledge of what it is and what are its relations to the rest of nature.

4. Awareness of Existence: Immediate Knowledge.

Perhaps we should stop here, by simply pointing out that knowledge is a property of human beings, and, since apples and stones and stars do not have knowledge about themselves we must rest content with the limited kind of direct knowledge of natural entities that we can have. Granted, we might say, that such knowledge is no more than that which comes from our relations to other entities, rather than from being other entities; still, it is the best we can do by way of direct knowledge, and, making use of it, we can formulate our highly successful scientific descriptive knowledge.

However, rather than give up, we can consider the circumstance that there is at least part of nature for which we do have the immediate experience that comes with actually being that which we describe: Namely, each of us directly knows what it is to be his or her own self. So, although we cannot know what actually it is to be other things, we have, through our own selves, one avenue of natural knowledge that is immediate and without the limitation of coming from a particular kind of external relationship.

Still, the knowledge that we gain of nature, by virtue of our being a part of it, is of course conditioned by what kind of part we are. Thus, as human beings we directly know what it is to have the hungers and fears and joys that biological organisms of many kinds do have. Also, we surely have some kinds of knowledge that are unique to human beings, especially with respect to our unusual cerebral endowments. In a general way, we have immediate knowledge of what it is to be, of what existence is in our natural world. In specific ways we learn of what we can and cannot do, of what is possible and what is probable in natural behavior. Such knowledge for human beings is, I would judge, always interwoven with verbalized, cognitive knowledge, but we can see in an animal the evidence of a large store of knowledge directly gained from experience, without intermediate verbalization.

There is a theme among our human traditions, to the effect that direct, immediate awareness is a key to much more than knowledge about ourselves and surroundings: rather, that it can be the key to the comprehension of the entire universe. We usually refer to this as a tradition of mysticism. Its followers assert that with appropriate preparation one attains a direct sense of unity with the ultimate being of the universe; a concomitant sense of satisfaction with one's comprehension of the cosmos, or of accord with it, is also reported. I shall not enter into a discussion of the merits and demerits of the claims of mystical experiences, about which I know very little, except to say that even in our empirical Western thought there is an at least partial dependence on direct intuition for some of our basic ideas, as, for example, the desirability of compassion among people, or the belief that we can reasonably achieve understanding. Such religious convictions as we may have are, of course, to a high degree often supported by directly intuited, nonverbal convictions.

5. *The Epistemological Continuum.*

Using a much oversimplified representation, we can see the mystical attempt toward gaining knowledge of the universe as one limit of an epistemological, one-dimensional continuum: That is, it is the limit in the direction of immediate, nonverbal, nonscientific knowledge, not even directed to any part of nature but rather arising within one's own self simply from one's own participation in the universe. The middle region of the epistemological continuum may be thought of as comprising the direct knowledge that we have of the various specific parts of the natural world, by virtue of our relations and interactions with those parts. The other direction of the continuum, away from the limit of mysticism, is toward the symbolic, analytical knowledge of science, rooted in sense experiences but developed, by deduction, postulation, and imagination, far beyond those experiences.

6. *Effects of Incompleteness of Science.*

I shall presently say more about the particular kind of knowledge that science does give us, but at this point I want somewhat parenthetically to point out that the highly partial nature of scientific description appears to be a factor in the problems that the application of science has brought to mankind. Our physical sciences have given us methods for control of our surroundings in many ways, but inevitably the partial, selective nature of scientific knowledge leads to such methods for only a few aspects of a natural domain rather than for its totality. We might well say that just as science abstracts certain determinable qualities for its description, likewise the technology that is based on science is concerned only with selected structures or processes of nature. Thus, it is obvious that a machine, as a steam engine, or a radio transmitter, is different from a naturally formed organism; it is simpler in its number of essential parts, and in the fact that it operates in accordance with a relatively small number of scientific principles that have guided its design. Also, obviously, man's technological artifices lack the richness of natural development that gives the stability of self-regeneration and self-mainte-nance to biological organisms.

Without the focusing on selected aspects of nature that is charac-teristic of the natural sciences, we could not have the specialized knowl-edge that has led to the locomotive, the automobile, the electronic com-puter, the nuclear reactor, or the medicinal antibiotic. The natural sci-ence of Greek antiquity, for example, or of pre-twentieth-century China, did not concern itself with specialized features, abstracted from experi-ence, to anything like the extent characteristic of Western science. As a consequence, in other than Western science there has not been the po-tentiality for development of a single process or structure far beyond that which is found in nature. In Western science, this abstraction of certain determinables seems particularly to be favored by the use of mathematics in science. The relations of a few selected and defined as-pects of nature—for example, electric charge, electric current, and mag-netic field—can be explored and understood with immense scientific fruitfulness, once an association is set up that permits all the deductive power of mathematical reasoning to be directed to the relationship. The resulting technological achievments are a mixed blessing, as we well know today. The harshness of living in an industrial city, the common despoliation of nature, and the threat of nuclear war are readily cited as unhappy concomitants of the desirable amelioration of circumstances of life that has come with applied science.

It might be expected that since in biological science we are consid-ering more complex aspects of nature than in physical science, less likeli-hood exists of bringing about developments that are strongly at variance with the natural order. More of the checks and balances of nature are inherent in biological knowledge because we are treating larger pieces of nature than are analyzed in the relatively high abstractions of physics. Still, for example, the instances of dangers in using modern drugs, or the unexpected undesirable effects of some insecticides, clearly show that in biology too we create problems as a consequence of the scien-tist's restriction of his studies to certain selected facets of nature. In a future time when science is far more complete than it is today, with all significant physical, biological, and social aspects brought into a coher-ent totality, we can think that science will have its own correctives and restraints, just as does nature, and man will be able to see clearly the net harm that may come from exploiting some single natural process. Until the day of unified science comes, if it ever does, increased caution in applying science is surely a precept that should rank high in guiding the affairs of man.

7. *Quantum Theory Limitation.*

Returning to the inherent lack of completeness in science, I want next to discuss a limitation that has become apparent in physics in this century. The new limitation, which is quite different from the incompleteness that comes with the abstraction of only certain features of nature for description and theoretical discussion, has made itself known with the exploration of the atomic level in the natural world. In prequantum physics, it was assumed that nature could be observed and reported by the scientist, with no accompanying interaction effects on nature. Man was regarded as being outside of the nature he studied, at least with respect to the very act of studying having any influence on nature. But in the quantum physics that is appropriate for the atomic aspects of nature, the information we obtain is in significant part determined by the way we arrange our observation procedure: not in the trivial sense, that we might observe a property A or a property B, and then elect to observe A rather than B, but in the sense that B is physically unknown and indeterminate if we observe A, and likewise for A if we choose to observe B. A further feature of our quantum physics is that we do not have any knowledge of how the natural processes operate which bring about the restriction to property A or to property B. That is, the structure of quantum theory does not give us—and indeed even forbids our having—any detailed description of what it is that occurs in nature to make one property indeterminate when we choose to observe its conjugate property. For the physicist, it is a concomitant of this aspect of quantum theory that there is in nature the indeterminism that is such a well-known feature of modern physics.

We can see the limit on descriptive knowledge that we have reached as associated with the fact that in quantum physics we are studying elementary particles of nature which must themselves bring us the information that we want to obtain about them. That is, we gain knowledge through a process of interaction between that which is being studied and our measuring apparatus (in everyday living, usually simply our own sense organs). Some physical entity must constitute the interaction —must be the carrier between object and apparatus. When we are studying atomic-sized particles, the carriers must be other atomic-size particles. The properties these particles have are not the same as the localizable and describable space-time properties of macroscopic nature, and this fact is an essential element in the limitation. But, also, because we have no smaller particles for studying novel properties of atomic-size entities, there is no way open to us for further investigation of those properties. We have reached a point where nature presents itself with qualities that are irrational and indeterminate, in the terms of our older macroscopic physics; and attempts towards futher elucidation are blocked by the fact that there is nothing smaller, no finer mesh, for studying the characteristic quantum behavior of atomic entities when they interact with each other or with our measuring apparatus. So, for the older kind of exact description we are left with no further appeal: Our study of *individual* atomic events in nature has become a study of ourselves interacting with nature, with the road ending there. For some, who do not like to give up the classical concepts of indefinitely extended spatial-temporal description, the situation is not a pleasing one. For most contemporary physicists there is no discomfort, and we might even find some satisfaction in having reached a micro-ground of being, where we and the nature of which we are a part simply *are*. We no longer need face indefinite divisibility of matter and continued articulation of microstructure, a prospect that came with the pre-quantum notions of a space and a time that may be physically described as closely as might be the variables in a corresponding mathematical continuum.

Of course, we should not say that our quantum physics is absolute and certain. The discovery of a finer mesh is possible, particularly at very high energies where our present quantum physics has not yet been abundantly tested. I think physicists would for the most part agree that the discovery of the new mesh is highly improbable in the common domains of nature where quantum theory has been so well confirmed.

It is further to be noted that the quantum theory also carries with it a suggestion of subjectivism with respect to the atomic processes of nature. I shall only briefly discuss this possibility, utilizing a simple hypothetical situation. Suppose five men are in a darkened room, into which the opening of a shutter will introduce a burst of photons. It is possible for the dark-adapted eye to perceive a group of just several photons—and indeed, perhaps even a single photon. We will assume a geometric arrangement such that with each opening of the shutter the number of photons admitted gives a possibility for only one of the five men to sense a flash of light. Further, we arrange the men so that the probability of receiving a light flash is the same for each man.

Now, we have a subjectivism in the hypothetical observing situation, in that only one man of the five can say when the shutter was opened. In pre-quantum physics, however, we would expect that with sufficient information about the physical situation we could predict to which man the light would go, with a given shutter opening. But quantum theory requires that the photon wave-functions be of equal magnitude with respect to all five men (assuming that the probability is the same for each man's observing the flash). Only with the actual observation by one man is there that change in the exact quantum-theory description that implies a concentration of sufficient light at one man's eyes to give the observation of a flash. The objective reality that quantum theory gives us, then, is that of the photon wave being at each of the positions of the five men. Only by virtue of one man's observation of the photons is there the reality of the photons at his position. This situation is not changed in principle if we substitute photographic film for the five men. For then, only with someone's examining the film— only with that person's awareness—can we learn that a burst of light was at a given location. The quantum-mechanical principle of superposition of states requires that we regard the physical process of development of the light spot on a film as being equally distributed over the five films, until we learn of the spot's being on one given film. Most of us probably will insist on believing that one film, and only one, has actually been exposed to light between the time of opening the shutter and the time of examination of the five films (even though, strictly, an extension of present quantum mechanics to the macroscopic domain would not justify this belief). But, in any case, no justification can be made for considering a photon to be approaching one and only one film. There is, we see, in quantum theory a constitutive subjectivism not present in the older physics; for, now we do not have man observing a reality presumably already in existence, but rather, man's observation —extended through instruments if you like—as an element in the coming into being of the reality.

8. Physical Theory and the Natural World.

The partiality that comes with limitation to selected aspects of any natural object, the relational rather than being-knowing-itself quality of most experience that is used in science, and the discovery that there is a natural limit on our description of the microscopic processes of nature —these are all factors of inadequacy in our knowledge of the physical world. In spite of these limitations, we do achieve satisfying and useful descriptive knowledge of nature.

We well know that to some extent in all science, and particularly in physics, the achievment of descriptive knowledge is closely associated with the growth of theoretical science. It is here, in the development of structural and logical relations between the elements that form the descriptive aspects of a give domain of natural being, that physical science has had an unprecedented success. The limitations on science seem to be transcended in its theoretical structure, where we do not claim to give any description of *this* particular entity or process, but rather, where we state conditions on nature's structures and processes generally. The limitation of selection becomes less important, because we are discussing properties of nature everywhere, perhaps in all or at least in many and varied manifestations. We might think, for example, of the hosts of physical and biological entities for which the laws of energy transformation are relevant. And, the limitation to relational knowledge is no longer so much to the point when we discuss, as we do in theory, correlations between properties that are themselves abstractions: It is the structure of the theory itself, rather than the experienced properties of nature, that becomes an essential element in our understanding of nature.

To what extent does physical theory give us valid knowledge of the way the world is? Certainly, in its abstraction, its universality, its precision, and in its breathtaking reach from elementary particle to cosmos, theoretical physics has gone far along the epistemological continuum, away from one's own feelings or intuition, or even from the experienced knowledge of our natural selves and surroundings.

The terms in which we formulate a physical theory are, we know, suggested by experience, but commonly do not at all denote a directly sensed aspect of nature. I spoke, a few sentences back, of theory as correlating properties that are themselves abstract. But it is perhaps not correct to speak of properties, abstracted from a richer manifold, as constituting the elements of a theory. Rather, theory is frequently formed of terms that are devised or invented. (Albert Einstein stressed this point in his writings about the construction of physical theory.) Even in what now seems to us a fairly concrete theory, that of Newtonian mechanics, such basic terms as acceleration, mass, and force are sophisticated ones that require abstract concepts for their definition, and, as the history of mechanics plainly shows, they are not terms which are simply suggested by experience. The conceptually devised character of elements in a theory is, of course, all the more pronounced for many of the terms introduced since Newton's time: potential energy, electrical field, entropy, angular momentum, to name just a few.

9. Mathematics and Theory.

There is, then, an ethereal quality about a physical theory: it is not built up by induction from the solid ground of observation, but is formed of inventions and imaginings. And yet, if properly established, it has been subjected to comparison with observation at all feasible opportunities, and further, in most cases, the terms of the theory are held, one to the other, in an iron-tight web of mathematical relationships. These have a bare emptiness, in contrast to the immediacy of experience, and yet often they will allow the theory to be extended in a manner such that it will describe properties of nature far removed from sense perception and reaching to the ends of the universe. Should we therefore conclude that secrets are disclosed in the mathematical framework, and that we learn in mathematical physics what is the essence of the natural world? Or, is mathematics a way of expressing complex logical relations among terms suitably chosen so as to give an orderly account of nature, but with no ultimate significance for what nature is? The question we ask may be phrased in the familiar terms of Pythagoreanism and of the Platonism of the analogy of the cave. Does number give the central truth about the universe; or, equivalently, is the mathematically formed physical theory the true idea, the true form, of which the matter and energy of experience are transient manifestations, as shadows on the wall?

It is to be emphasized that what is involved in the question we ask is not whether a physical theory gives a correct general description of the phenomena of interest. Rather, something more is sought. The limitations that we have discussed for descriptive science tell us that we cannot expect to have in that science other than a partial, relational account of the described objects. But we are now asking if in the mathematical form of physical theory we find a truth about nature that is not adventitious: that is not dependent on the aspects chosen for description or on the delineation of objects that arises from our relations to them, but does give a firm, invariant insight into what nature is. If, for the moment, we accept an affirmative answer, we might hopefully see an approach to final understanding of our world. As theory becomes increasingly inclusive in its description of nature, its formal content would, presumably, be closer to the elemental general structure of the natural world.

Let me give the simplest kind of example. We are able mathematically to describe the orbit of a planet, Mars, for example, around the Sun. The resulting geometric curve, approximately an ellipse and subject to time-dependent modifications because of the motions of other bodies in the solar system, is a mathematical description that escapes the relational dependence of much descriptive knowledge. No matter in what kind of coordinate system or with what variables the description is formulated we should expect to find an equivalence between the descriptions, with all of them denoting one and the same orbital curve.

Of course, the objection of selectivity is now very much to the point, for we have described only one of the multitude of aspects of Mars. We can point out, however, that the mathematical description of the orbit was achieved by applying to a given set of initial conditions the general laws of mechanics and the law of gravitational attraction between masses. Our mathematical formulation of *those* laws is, therefore, a statement of a very general property of the world, and, again, if the laws are correct, this property or its equivalent would be described with any approach to a description of general properties of nature. Mechanical interactions are, of course, again only a part of the processes of nature. But, as already indicated, we might look forward to a mathematical statement of an increasingly comprehensive theory.

10. *Logic, Mathematics, and Nature.*

The essential point at issue seems to be whether or not mathematical structure is in any way constitutive in nature. The general trend in our day has been to argue that it is not. The thesis that mathematics is reducible to logic, although far from established, has had sufficient success to give encouragement to a view that the physical content in physics is in the explicitly physical terms and axioms of a theory. Mathematics then has the role of complex rules of inference that enable the theoretical physicist to draw out what is implicit in his physical assumptions. There is also, however, a counter-opinion among practising theoretical physicists with respect to the thesis of a separation of physics and mathematics. The statement recently made by E. P. Wigner, that ". . . The miracle of the appropriateness of the language of mathematics for the formulation of the laws of physics is a wonderful gift which we neither understand nor deserve," [2] is illustrative of a lack of complete acceptance of the thesis.

In an effort towards clarification of the role of mathematics in physics I am going to discuss two historic instances in which physical theory has been signally advanced by mathematical guidance. The first is the prediction of the existence of electromagnetic waves by James Clerk Maxwell. The first of two salient steps in his coming to that prediction was the introduction of a term for the so-called electrical displacement current, such that a change of electrical field with time, $\partial E/\partial t$, gives rise to a magnetic field expressed by a non-vanishing curl H. This term had not previously been present in electromagnetic theory; Maxwell introduced it in analogy with the term that described the known existence of an electrical field in association with a time-changing magnetic field, that is, in analogy with the electromagnetic induction of Michael Faraday and Joseph Henry. The second step was a purely mathematical one; with the presence of the new term in the equations for electromagnetism, Maxwell found that he could derive a wave equation. The waves described by this equation had just the polarization and propagation properties of light waves, and the equation is the basis of the assertion of the electromagnetic nature of light.

Now, it is only with the new physical contribution supplied by Maxwell that electromagnetic theory could yield the inference of electromagnetic waves. In this sense, the view that we get no more physical content from a theory than we put in is supported. But the second step, the derivation of the wave equation, requires the use of mathematical reasoning that is algebraic and geometric, with no other physical content. Specifically, use is made of a rather complex vector identity, curl curl $a =$ grad div $a - \Delta a$. This equation tells us of relations between various derivatives of the components of a vector in Euclidean space. Since the use of the equation for the components of electrical and magnetic fields does lead us to the well-confirmed electromagnetic wave equation, we conclude that the field quantities do in fact have the behavior properties of mathematically defined vectors.

One might at this point wish to say, "The electrical and magnetic field quantities have been defined as vectors, hence it is hardly surprising that they behave in accordance with a vector equation." I think, though, that it is notable that physical quantities are found to be describable by a formalism precisely identical to that used for a mathematically defined quantity. On a simple arithmetical level we are able to find congruences between physical and mathematical magnitudes. That is, we can identify sets of two physical objects as being describable with respect to multiplicity by the number 2; we can do likewise for the number 3, for the number 4, and so on. Further, the inferences about multiplicity of physical objects that we draw, using the rules of arithmetic, are found to be valid among physical objects. The simple correspondence between mathematics and nature that we find for arithmetic clearly obtains for far more subtle kinds of mathematical thinking. In the instance of Maxwell's derivation, operationally defined quantities of experience are shown to have the same properties that are found, within a complex web of arithmetic, algebra, calculus, and geometry, for mathematically defined vectors. It would be easy, of course, to give many, many similar examples from the physical sciences.

It might be argued that the apparent mathematical properties of the natural world are illusory, in that in physics we have chosen quantities which are amenable to mathematical formulation. This argument is sound in its implication, which is certainly correct, that we could attempt to develop our physics in terms of properties that are not mathematically defined. But the fact that a mathematically formulated physics has been so strikingly successful in giving description, prediction, and understanding would seem to constitute abundant evidence that an inherent mathematical structure exists in our natural world.

I do not wish to claim any finality for the mathematical relationships of currently established physical theory, nor do I want to suggest any unique reality status for mathematical entities. And, I would hope that what I have said earlier in this paper amply indicates the defects of physics as a complete account of nature. Nonetheless, I see no valid reason for dismissing an irreducible mathematical aspect of nature: The concordance between appropriate mathematical inference and physical behavior immediately tells us that the natural world has at least in part a mathematical structure.

Further, I would like to submit that the assertion of inherent mathematical properties of nature is independent of whether or not the thesis of the reduction of mathematics to logic is correct. To the extent that this thesis is established, certain kinds of mathematics are subject to it. When such mathematics is used in physics, we should perhaps properly say that we find nature to be in accord with the relationships of logic, rather than those of mathematics. But in any event, we find that nature is not simply a haphazard assortment of events, but has a coherence among delineated entities which is the same as the coherence among the terms of logic and of mathematics. Hence, the assertion of the Pythagoreans, that "everything is number," was, I believe, not without validity, even though too vaguely and too inclusively stated. Likewise, the rationalist claim, that we may by reasoning gain understanding, has partial support in the success of physics: We do attain new knowledge of nature by use of logic and mathematics (assuming, of course, the appropriately formulated basic theory.) The Pythagoreanism and rationalism that we find in physics need not necessarily carry us away from a generally empirical outlook, for logic and mathematics may be regarded as having been developed in response to the properties of the natural world. Such a view, I believe, gains support in the difficulties that philosophers find in drawing a clear distinction between analytical and synthetic statements.

As a second example of the role of mathematics in physics I will cite the use in cosmological studies of the equation for the Doppler shift in light waves. The equation is very simple; neglecting relativistic corrections, its form is just that the wavelength of light from a receding source is increased by an amount proportional to the velocity of recession. In symbols, the increment $\Delta\lambda = v\lambda/c$, where λ is the unperturbed wavelength, v the recessional velocity, and c the speed of light. Now, as is well known, the interpretation of the observed shift in the spectral lines of radiation from galaxies, using the Doppler equation, provides the basis for our believing our universe to be in a state of expansion. The greater the distance of the galaxy, the greater the recessional speed; to date, observation has borne out this relationship with remarkable linearity.

The Doppler equation itself is firmly founded in physical theory; it is required both by classical concepts of wave behavior, and it appears as a direct consequence of the Lorentz transformations of the special theory of relativity. Many proposals have been made for an interpretation of the observed wavelength shifts from distant galaxies as being something *other* than the recessional motion required by the Doppler shift. However, none of these proposals has met the experimental or theoretical tests put to them; and, further, the kinetic interpretation of wavelength shifts is directly confirmed for nearby astronomical bodies whose motion is independently known, by methods which in no way require the Doppler-equation relationship. It may be pointed out, too, that there are supporting theoretical reasons for the expanding universe concept; we would, in fact, be in severe difficulties in our cosmological thinking if it should be shown that the galactic expansion is illusory.

The Doppler equation gives us, then, a mathematical relationship that will translate spectral line measurements into one of the basic empirical facts of our cosmology. In practice, the evidence seems minuscule in amount: a relatively few measurements of bright lines that have appeared on photographic plates which have been attached to telescopic spectrometers is all that we have. And yet, the application of the simple Doppler relation carries us to a conviction that our galactic universe is in a state of what in human terms could properly be called violent expansion.

The power of mathematics not only gives us the universality of induction generally, but also allows us to extrapolate a relation immensely far beyond the magnitudes of immediate experience. With the Doppler equation, we calculate recessional velocities of the order of two-thirds of the speed of light, for very distant galaxies. It would be easy to find other instances of how mathematics enables us to learn of spatial magnitudes, velocities, and so on, that are far beyond ordinary human direct experience—both in the direction of the very large and the very small. I do not believe that we would be able to gain this kind of information about our universe without mathematical reasoning; and in using such reasoning in physics we are, of course, utilizing the existence of mathematical properties of nature, as discussed in connection with our earlier example.

11. *Incompleteness of Mathematical Knowledge.*

The point I have now tried to emphasize is that it is largely because of its mathematical properties that we can grasp so much of the universe with our science. Since the time of Galileo it has been explicitly apparent that mathematics gives natural philosophy a method for discerning structures and relationships in nature. What we learn is surprisingly different from what we obtain by verbal discussion using language that is descriptive of sense impressions.

But we must not be led by the success of mathematical physics into an illusion of its completeness as knowledge of the world. Consider again the observed Doppler shift for the distant galaxies: Only one feature of the universe emerges, namely, its expansion. For a given galaxy, the enormous complexity of physical and chemical structure, the possible richness of life in some of the billions of stellar systems, perhaps even levels of awareness and culture far beyond our own—all this is omitted in the statement of galactic recessional motion. We probably understand even less completely the universe of galaxies, with the description of its expansion, than we understand, say, a human being with the statement that his weight is 150 pounds.

The rejoinder can be made that as physics is elaborated with respect to a given topic, more and more detail does come within its ken. Thus, in molecular physics we in principle now have a mathematical description of complex systems on the basis of a few very general atomic and quantum theory principles. It is indeed, just by virtue of their application to more restricted situations—to specific instances—that the general equations of physics have their explanatory and predictive power. However, when a general equation is being considered for a specific situation, we are considering that situation, not the general equation for its imputation to nature of a universal mathematical property.

The fact that quantum physics has brought us to an end point in the detailed space-time description of nature is now also of key importance: *The existence of specific atomic events, in a manner such that an individual event may be described independently of awareness of the event, is not supported by present quantum theory; hence, the possibility of an extension of general mathematical theory to a complete description of nature is not warranted by physical theory.* For the *individual atomic event* theory is helpless, and only with the *being* of the event in interaction-observation do we gain knowledge of it.

12. *Physics and the Epistemological Continuum.*

I want, now, to summarize and conclude by returning to a discussion of the epistemological continuum to which I earlier referred. At one extreme there is the way of gaining knowledge of the universe that comes with direct intuition. Some people claim by this method to comprehend, or even feel, the inner meaning and totality of existence. Without attempting to judge the validity of such claims, we can assert that each of us gains much knowledge of the natural world from his own intuition and feeling. Generalized in the manner of each individual person, this knowledge is a kind of non-scientific apprehension of the universe. The relations of a human being to the various facets of the universe determine the observations that can arise from these relations, and it is these observations, carefully symbolized and reported, that are basic in empirical science. But the knowledge that is thus obtained is no longer direct and intuitive knowledge, but is partial and relational. The abstractive processes of science result in knowledge of greater generality, as we go further along the epistemological continuum, away from direct, nonverbal intuitions, toward the quantitative, mathematical form of science that is at the other extreme of the continuum.

With a mathematical form of science, we found that nature has properties that correspond to the generality and structure of logic-mathematics. It is an attractive conception that with appropriate mathematics we also have a way of penetrating to the ultimate being of the universe. This Pythagorean concept is the scientist's parallel to the mystic's assertion that with no use of symbolic or linguistic devices whatever he is able to grasp the universe.

The pragmatic criteria of control in the external natural world, and the criteria of reproducibility and communicability, all strongly support the scientist as having true knowledge of nature. And, we do not want to forget that science gives us standards of verifiability and objectivity for knowledge which can lift mankind from the bogs of spurious ego- and ethno- centric convictions. But the abstract, partial quality of scientific knowledge does entail that the information and feeling that come with direct individual intuition be lost. Epistemologically, it is the knowledge at the feeling-intuition end of the continuum which is prior, and which forms a substratum out of which scientific knowledge can be developed. Mathematical scientific knowledge, in contrast, gives transcendent power and generality, and must, I think, be regarded as the great achievement of mankind during the past few centuries. To use a statement by Bertrand Russell, it is with such knowledge that man can be as ". . . a God; in action and desire we are the slaves of circumstance." [3]

And yet, both life and nature as individual instances are constituted by events of circumstance. Here—and this is a surprising development —our most powerful mathematical-physical theory has told us that individual atomic events cannot be comprehended by mathematical science. This result is a nicely satisfying one, in that it emphasizes that all of the epistemological continuum is necessary for knowledge. The vividness of direct intuition is not *mere* fact, in contrast to the power of a complete theory; nor, I have suggested, is the theory merely a useful logical ordering of an assortment of unalterable observations. Rather, events form a pattern similar to those that can be achieved in mathematics; but individually they have an assertion and potentiality that is independent of cognitive pattern.

We see, then, that in our day there has indeed been a change in the expectations from physical knowledge. Until a few decades ago, men had come to speak of physics as being on a path that would lead to a complete account of the natural world. But an analysis of the epistemology of science, *without regard for the explicit content of science*, readily shows us that much of our experience of the world is not caught within the web of science. And now, the content of physics itself has come to a comparable result, in the quantum-theory limitations on the description and/or prediction of atomic events, and even on the intra-subjective verifiability of such events.

Do we then, through physics, learn what nature is? The answer we have come to is, as we have seen, both Yes, in view of the formulation and discernment in physics of mathematical properties, and No, in view of the irreplaceable role of observation and feeling. There is, I hope, no contradiction between that which comes to us as cognitive science and that which comes simply as given and not within a rational scheme. To reconcile these two aspects of human experience is to succeed in an effort toward basic synthesis—a goal imperfectly achieved in the medieval reconciliation of faith and reason, and now again before us in conflicts between the uses of science and the demands of life, and also even, it would seem, in the presence both of mathematical pattern and irrational given in quantum physics. We are today certainly far short of that synthesis, but philosophy can do a service in bringing to us the truth, in a new context, that reliance on one part alone of the epistemological continuum is not adequate for mankind.

NOTES

1. I want to acknowledge that I owe much, in what I shall say, to discuscussions held in July 1967 at the University of Minnesota Center for the Philosophy of Science. I am grateful to Professor Herbert Feigl, for the cordial hospitality of the Center to me during that month. Also, I want to express my thanks to Professor Harold T. Walsh, of the Philosophy Department at Michigan State University, for the assistance and encouragement that he gave me with a critical reading of an earlier draft of this paper.

2. In the essay, "The Unreasonable Effectiveness of Mathematics in the Natural Sciences," *Symmetries and Reflections: Scientific Essays of Eugene P. Wigner*, p. 237. (Indiana University Press, Bloomington and London, 1967).

3. *The Autobiography of Bertrand Russell: 1872–1914* (Allen and Unwin, London, 1967), p. 168.

ON SOME ALLEGED LIMITATIONS
OF SCIENTIFIC KNOWLEDGE

(A RESPONSE)

Ernest Nagel

I believe myself to be largely in agreement with Professor Schlegel. I have been impressed and pleased by his moderate claims concerning the knowledge achieved in science in general and in physics in particular. His thought shows no trace of the boastfulness that characterizes many contemporary physicists, who appear to believe that at least in principle they know the answers to all the important questions about the world. In consequence, Professor Schlegel's account of what he thinks are the limitations of science seem to me timely and to merit attention.

On the other hand, his paper exhibits a not untypical bias of members of his profession in his unquestioned identification of science with physics, and in particular with mathematical physics. Whether he really thinks that all other branches of scientific inquiry are marked by the same features that are found in the highly abstract theories of physics, I'm not quite sure. But I'm fairly confident that some of the things he does say about the dominant role of mathematics, about the importance of finding invariants, about the general absence of descriptive terms which refer to the immediate qualities of objects, would not be so commonly believed if, instead of focusing on mathematical physics, one were to examine other branches of inquiry, such as chemistry, biology, and geology, even if one leaves out the so-called social sciences and human history. However, even if this point is waived, and even though I agree on the whole with Dr. Schlegel's view that our knowledge of various aspects of the world is, I find myself at odds with what I suspect are for him important parts of his argument; and I will devote the remainder of my remarks to the expected task of a commentator: indicating where, despite my agreements with his over-all conclusion, his account of our knowledge of nature seems to me in several ways unsatisfactory and requires modification.

There are three comments I wish to make, and shall make them in the order in which the corresponding points are presented in Dr. Schlegel's paper. He begins, with a discussion of the alleged limitations of knowledge. In the early part of his paper he refers to two such limitations, and subsequently he mentions a third one generated by developments in modern physics, and in particular quantum mechanics. The first of these consists of the selective character of knowledge, the second of its symbolic character. But I find it strange to characterize these features of knowledge as limitations. For to call them limitations suggests that it would be desirable to eliminate them and, perhaps, to substitute something else in their place. And they seem to me, not to be limitations or defects on knowledge, but, on the contrary, to be among its indispensable attributes. What would it be like to have knowledge of anything, if our knowledge of that thing were not selective? What would it be to have knowledge of anything, if the knowledge were not identifiably symbolic? For in the sense of the word that is relevant to scientific inquiry as well as to much common sense discourse, knowledge is propositional in form and can be given a linguistic or other symbolic formulation. But no statement can assert everything sayable about a subject matter, nor can it be identical with subjects about which it asserts something.

The notion that the selective and symbolic character of discursive thought is a limitation of knowledge, was expressed in Goethe's *Faust* when Mephistopheles declared that "Grey, my friend, is all theory; green is the golden tree of life." These famous lines suggest a contrast like the one Professor Schlegel makes between scientific knowledge (which is allegedly defective because of its selective and symbolic character) and what he calls immediate knowledge (which is ostensibly free from these limitations). But it is well to remind ourselves that those lines were uttered by the Devil: they express a romantic disparagement of discursive or theoretical thought, and the barely intelligible ideal of a knowledge that is identical with its own subject matter.

It is pertinent to raise the question whether our understanding of the world (however one construes the phrase "understanding the world") would be increased if scientific knowledge were not in fact selective. The answer seems to me clearly in the negative. For to understand any subject matter we cannot literally identify ourselves with it, but must in a sense rise above it in order to formulate various relations between selected features manifested in it. Dr. Schlegel in effect denies this, and claims that in at least one case we have knowledge that is neither selective nor symbolic—namely, the immediate knowledge, or direct awareness each one of us has of his own existence, the knowledge each of us possesses of what it is to be his own self. However, this is a misleading claim, and its plausibility depends on the ambiguity of the word "knowledge." In that sense of the word which is relevant to the present context, to say that one knows something is to assert something which is either right or wrong, true or false, probable or improbable. On the other hand, it is entirely unclear just how the immediate experience or direct knowledge Dr. Schlegel believes each of us has of his own self, could be right or wrong, true or false, probable or improbable. For example, if I never tasted a pineapple and then come to taste one, I would certainly have an immediate experience of a novel taste; and I could then make the valid cognitive claim that other pineapples have a certain taste under specified conditions. This claim is expressed as a proposition, which is either true or false, and so the claim is a claim to knowledge. But the immediate experience of tasting a pineapple is neither true nor false; accordingly, the immediate experience is not a case of knowledge at all, in the sense of the word "knowledge" that is relevant here.

The point I am trying to make is that in directing our attention to an alleged sort of knowledge which is neither selective nor symbolic, Dr. Schlegel is confounding two radically distinct senses of the word "know"—two senses that, in my judgment, are not species of a common genus, so that what he calls "immediate knowledge" cannot be regarded as free of the limitations he ascribes to discursive or scientific knowledge. Accordingly, I think he is wrong in maintaining that the selective and symbolic character of scientific knowledge constitutes limitations that are absent in direct experience (or immediate knowledge). On the contrary, those features of scientific knowledge which he regards as limitations ought to be counted among its virtues. For only by selective and symbolic representation is it possible to transcend the immediacy of what is directly experienced and to acquire some intellectual mastery of the relational structures in which things and events occur.

I turn now to my second set of comments, which bear on the limitations Dr. Schlegel believes are imposed on scientific knowledge by developments in modern physics, and especially by quantum theory. It would be silly for me to dispute with Professor Schlegel on technical matters of quantum theory, and I do not propose to do so. But one thing can be said without risk of contradiction—that while the interpretation of quantum theory to which he subscribes is currently the orthodox one among physicists, it is not the only possible interpretation. Indeed, a number of distinguished physicists have advanced other interpretations with strong reservations about the so-called Copenhagen interpretation accepted by Professor Schlegel.

In any event, basing himself on this interpretation Professor Schlegel maintains, in effect, that in studying the behaviors of individual atoms in nature the physicist is really studying his own interactions with nature. This claim could be construed as making a rather trivial point: that in conducting his experiments, there is an interaction between the instruments a physicist uses (which may include his own body) and the subject matter he is exploring with those instruments. However, this undoubtedly sound point surely does not depend on the special findings of quantum mechanics, and I do not believe this is all that Dr. Schlegel means to affirm by it. What he does wish to maintain is the far more radical thesis that it is, in principle, impossible to distinguish between the instruments (perhaps our own bodies) used to explore the objective realities in the world, and the realities themselves, and that in consequence there is an ineradicable element of subjectivity in quantum mechanics so that what the physicist observes is not an already existing reality, but rather the things he creates by his observations.

As I have already mentioned this is not the only reading that can be given to quantum mechanics, but I shall ignore the alternatives and assume that the interpretation Dr. Schlegel espouses is alone sound. What I find really puzzling is that Dr. Schlegel should find in the indeterminacy of the ultimate particles of physics to which he refers, a limitation placed on our knowledge of the way things are. For it seems to me a remarkable achievement of scientific inquiry to have discovered this fact, assuming it is a fact, about the fundamental particles of physical reality. Just why is it a limitation of our knowledge to have ascertained that the behavior of those particles is in certain respects not predictable because of certain allegedly inherent traits of the particles? And just why is such unpredictability equated with a lack of objectivity in our knowledge of basic physical processes? To be able to predict may indeed be desirable. But our inability to do so invariably, does not necessarily signify limitations or defects in human knowledge, but rather (as in the present instance) our success in discovering a basic feature of the things under study. In short, if there is indeed a radical indeterminism in the nature of things, it is surely one of the great triumphs of discursive thought and modern science to have found this out. It is not an achievement that can be intelligibly construed as testifying to limitations or inadequacies in scientific knowledge.

My final set of comments deals with the role that Professor Schlegel assigns to mathematics in modern science. Let me say at once that I agree completely with his insistence on the indispensable role that mathematics plays in modern physics. What I find unclear and doubtful is his apparent claim that nature itself has an inherent mathematical structure.

It will hardly be disputed that in talking about various aspects of the world we have frequent occasions to draw deductive conclusions from assumed premises. To take a simple case, we may argue that since all men are mortal and so-and-so is a man, so-and-so is mortal. But though we may often syllogize in exploring sectors of nature, must we regard the syllogism (as Dr. Schlegel apparently does) as expressing a fundamental structure of nature? The view that we must, seems to rest on the assumption that the language used in talking about a subject matter must have the same structure as (or be isomorphic with) that subject matter. But although in one form or another this assumption has been frequently made, no good case has been really made for it. It seems to me, at any rate, that languages having different structures can be used in codifying a fixed structure embodied in a given subject matter. And what holds for languages in general holds for those specialized languages we call mathematics. Accordingly, one would like to have from Dr. Schlegel a clearer statement of his grounds for supposing that the structures embodied in mathematics are to be regarded as being constitutive of nature itself.

But I must state more clearly my specific difficulties with Dr. Schlegel's contention. In the first place, the term "mathematical proposition" is ambiguous. Thus, in one sense of the term, the axioms of Euclidean geometry, for example, when suitably interpreted (so that by "point" one understands, say, the intersection of two light rays, and so on), are sometimes said to be mathematical statements. In this case, however, the axioms assert something about a specified sector of the natural world, and can be established as true or false not by the pure mathematician but by factual inquiry only. The mathematician is not competent to certify the axioms so interpreted as either true or false. Accordingly, the axioms do not count as mathematical statements in another sense of this expression. In this second sense of 'mathematical,' it is neither the Euclidean axioms nor the theorems derived from them that are said to be mathematical statements, but rather the statement that asserts the implicative relation between the axioms and theorems. In this second sense of "mathematical proposition," true mathematical propositions are necessary truths, but in this case empirical inquiry is not required to establish them as such.

In which of these two senses of "mathematical proposition" does Dr. Schlegel hold that the structures formulated in mathematical statements are constitutive of nature itself? He appears to be maintaining the thesis for "mathematical statement" as understood in the second sense—that is, for necessarily true statements whose denial would involve a contradiction. Thus he holds that the necessarily true statement that two plus two equals four formulates structural relations embodied in nature, and offers as partial evidence for this claim the example of two groups with two members each (as in the case of a set of two arms and another set of two legs), with the totality of elements in either the first or the second group being four. But there is a confusion here. The proposition of pure mathematics that two plus two equals four is indeed a necessary truth. However, the statement that when a collection of two arms is combined with a collection of two legs the resulting collection will contain four members is not at all necessary, but is at best a contingent truth about the way certain special kinds of objects behave. This will be evident if we notice the word "plus" is being used in the purely mathematical statement in a manner that is different from the use made of it in the statement about arms and legs. In the former statement, "plus" signifies a logical operation; in the latter statement it stands for a physical operation. It is not a necessary but only a contingent truth that two physical objects (e.g. limbs or balls or pieces of paper) when placed in some container that already contains two other physical objects will give four objects—it is not self-contradictory to suppose that the result of this operation is, say, five objects, even though in point of empirical fact the outcome is four things. But it is only when by "mathematical statement" one understands a contingently true one that the structures formulated in such statements can be plausibly said to be part of nature's constitution. Dr. Schlegel's view that the structures formulated by necessarily true mathematical statements are constitutive of nature seems to me entirely unwarranted, and to obtain whatever plausibility it has from confounding two quite different senses of "mathematical proposition."

In conclusion, I have some brief remarks on another aspect of Professor Schlegel's conception of mathematics. He has pointed out very clearly that mathematics is an admirable instrument for discovering and formulating invariant properties of nature. But he also suggests that knowledge of nature is to be equated with knowledge of the invariant properties of nature. I fail to see, however, why only what is invariant should be counted as part of nature, and why in consequence that which is variable should be regarded as lacking objective reality. Thus, consider the following simple example. If the path of an object dropped from an airplane is viewed from the ground, the path of the falling body has approximately the shape of a parabola; but if the path is viewed from the airplane itself, its shape is approximately that of a straight line. Accordingly, the shape of the trajectory varies with the perspective from which it is viewed, and is therefore not invariant to different frames of references. However, this is not the way the falling object is described in Newtonian physics, for its behavior is so stated that its formulation (by way of Newton's second law of motion) is invariant for a large class of reference frames. The advantages of such a formulation are impressive and well known. But while it is sometimes said that only what is invariant constitutes an "objective" part of nature as reality, it seems to me quite arbitrary (and indeed misleading) to take this position. For in the first place, no formulation of laws of nature is invariant to all possible frames of reference, so that even in the position under discussion what counts as objective or real is relative to some limited class of reference frames. And in the second place, although the description of the path of a falling body as that of a parabola is not invariant in the specified sense, it is nevertheless true (or an "objective" fact) that in a certain frame of reference the orbit of the body is a parabolic one—that is, the statement that the trajectory is parabolic in that perspective asserts something which is a genuine part of reality.

Accordingly, I agree with Dr. Schlegel when, in reply to his question whether physics tells us what nature is like, he answers in the affirmative. But I must dissent when he restricts the information he believes physics supplies about nature, to the mathematical (and invariant) properties of things. For despite his claim that physics omits all reference to the traits of things that are matters of sensory observation, this does not seem to me to be so—for example, he overlooks the fact that in making its various measurements physics must recognize and distinguish between different qualitative continua, such as differences in colors, sounds, and positions that are directly apprehended qualities. Moreover, while I also agree with Dr. Schlegel that there is much that physics does not tell us about the world, I must add that physics is not the whole of science and does not preempt the entire field of knowledge of nature.

A PRACTITIONER'S VIEW OF
THE BIOLOGICAL SCIENCES

Bentley Glass

I shall speak as a practitioner of one of the biological sciences—the science of genetics—and as one who has had a peripheral interest for some years in the history and philosophy of science. I will no doubt succeed in making my prejudices sufficiently apparent before my time is up and afford opportunity for my distinguished audience to thrust their rapiers into me.

Let me say, first, that in considering the current state of the study of the philosophy of science in this country and elsewhere, I am impressed by the fact that almost all of the individuals in the field have a background in physics or mathematics, and few indeed approach the subject from the side of the biological sciences. I think this is a distinct detriment to the development of the field.

At the present time, the biological sciences are clearly a spearhead in the advancing front of scientific knowledge. The techniques used in the biological sciences are rather different from those in the physical sciences. The presuppositions of the biologist are also often quite different. One may therefore expect that the viewpoint of the philosophy of science which would be assumed by a person with training in the study of biological processes and phenomena would be rather different than the viewpoints of persons who are concerned primarily with atoms and elementary particles or quantum mechanics. What I point out is really not a very new phenomenon in the development of the philosophy of science. Perhaps it has always been so, and the trouble has been that those biologists or persons with some biological training who have moved into the philosophy of science in past centuries have not always done credit to their understanding. Vitalism, for example, was for a long time the principal point of view introduced into the philosophy of science by biologists, and we can only regard the results as deplorable.

It has always impressed me, however, that if we go back all the way to the fourth century B.C. and start with the man who might be said to be the father of the philosophy of science, that is, with Aristotle, he was clearly primarily a biologist, and he approached the philosophy of science from the standpoint of his studies in biology. I used to enjoy arguing with my late friend Ludwig Edelstein, a great classical scholar, about the probability that Aristotle developed his philosophical views on the basis of his biological knowledge rather than the other way around. Since there is a great dearth of information about the actual facts in the early part of Aristotle's life, one can argue either side with confidence that one will not be disproved. Nevertheless, it seems clear to me that Aristotle's biology, undertaken at least as early as the period when he was a tutor to the young Alexander, materially influenced his philosophical views. In particular, the weighty doctrine of the Four Causes seems almost certainly to have grown out of his studies of the development of the chick embryo. I cannot conceive that this doctrine could very well have grown out of his studies of mechanics or other aspects of science, but it certainly was related to his studies of embryology. The way in which the embryo takes form and develops into a chicken as though it had foresight—a preview of its goal in life—clearly was one of the material reasons for his assumption of a Final Cause.

Through all the centuries that followed, when Aristotle was so great an authority in Western learning that any doctoral candidate, in order to ensure that his degree would be conferred, needed only to demonstrate, first, that he knew what Aristotle had said on his chosen subject and could quote it accurately, and second, that he was in accord with Aristotle's view, we find Aristotle's views of the nature of the world and of science generally prevailing.

Aristotle also was responsible for the early genesis of another idea that flowered in the seventeenth and eighteenth centuries into the concept of the Great Chain of Being, which Arthur O. Lovejoy, a man who had a very profound influence upon the development of my own thinking, has treated so definitively in his philosophical studies. The Great Chain of Being grew out of Aristotle's conception of a ladder of nature—a *Scala Naturae*. He recognized the existence of different levels of organization ascending from the plants through the creatures that were so subtly organized that it was very difficult for him, and even for biologists today, to be quite sure whether they are plants or animals; on up through the animals with blood that is not red, and then vertebrate animals with red blood, to reach Man, sitting at the top on the most precarious rung of the ladder of nature. This view, which fitted in so well with early Christian theology and became a dominant force in

Western thinking about man and nature, was not actually an evolutionary point of view, although it is sometimes thought to be such. So far as I can make out from what reading of Aristotle I have undertaken, no real implication can be found anywhere in his works of an actual movement from one rung of the ladder to another. All might have been brought into existence simultaneously or successively, yet not necessarily one from the other.

The great modification which came about in the biologist's view of the nature of science came from the introduction—primarily through the work of Darwin in the nineteenth century—of the theory of organic evolution and of natural selection, the mechanism whereby evolution takes place. I therefore claim that you really cannot develop a profound philosophy of science without taking into account the evolutionary nature of the scientist himself as a representative of the species *Homo sapiens*.

Science is a way of testing our knowledge about the world in which we live, the universe in which we have our being. Our ways of reacting to this universe are ways that have developed along evolutionary patterns in which every advance or change has resulted from the reproductive superiority in a certain environment of members of a species with certain hereditary characteristics, as compared with competitors with different hereditary characteristics.

We have bilateral symmetry. We have a particular kind of nervous system. We have a particular constellation of senses. All of these profoundly condition the nature of the reactions we can make to the external world, whatever its reality may be. Consequently we must admit that our science, and in particular (here I find myself strongly in agreement with Professor Schlegel) our ways of reasoning, result today from the evolutionary progress of the past, which proved that a certain kind of ability to reason logically was superior to other possible ways of reasoning. I thus do not claim—as no evolutionist would claim—that human logic is the best of all possible logics, or the only possible logic. I claim only that it manages to get us along satisfactorily in the particular kind of world in which we have evolved. Just so, our senses do not include all possible kinds of senses: we cannot detect with our senses either X-rays or infra-red; we cannot detect sounds above or below certain frequencies; we do not taste many kinds of chemicals, though it might be better for us if we could do so in the radically altered kind of environment we are creating for ourselves.

To pursue an example just a bit further, let me mention that there is a taste difference in the human species with respect to a particular kind of chemical substance known as phenylthiourea, or phenylthiocarbamide, commonly abbreviated PTC. This organic compound tastes intensely bitter to most persons, but about sixteen to twenty per cent of the human population—the frequency differs in different parts of the world—are unable to taste PTC at all. You might think this was simply a very peculiar circumstance without any great significance, but the existence of hereditary differences in a population always starts the geneticist on the trail of the reason. Why is it that the ability to taste PTC is more abundant in the population that the inability to taste PTC? For whenever hereditary differences arise in a population, they at once become subject to the action of natural selection. Although by chance alone some slight random increase might occur in the frequency of a fresh mutation that had never occurred in the species before, it is extremely unlikely that any new hereditary characteristics would ever reach the frequency of even one per cent in the population, let alone sixty or seventy per cent, without a profound action of natural selection in increasing the reproductive success of the possessors, that is, their viability up to the age of reproduction and their relative fertility. Hence we can be quite sure, on theoretical grounds, that the ability to taste PTC has some profound biological significance, even though we might not know just what it is. In recent years, it has been discovered just what this selective advantage actually is. It was first pointed out by the famous biochemist Richard Kühn in Germany, in 1949. Phenylthiourea is analogous to a considerable number of chemical substances which occur in ordinary plants, and which can paralyze the production by the thyroid glands of the hormone that regulates the rate of metabolism, the rate of energy output in the body. Consequently, individuals who can taste this substance as bitter are able to reject dangerous foods which might be eaten with relish by other individuals who do not possess this hereditary taste capacity and who might therefore become quite sick or die, or at least become rather lethargic as a consequence.

This well-established example illustrates the way in which our senses—our chemical senses, our sense of hearing, our sense of sight— and also our processes of reasoning must have evolved in response to the challenges of the environment over the millions of years it has taken for the human species to reach its present condition. Hence to me, as a biologist and student of evolution, it is really inconceivable to suppose that human logic does not have roots in the ability of man to function satisfactorily in his actual past terrestrial environment.[1]

I therefore agree with Professor Schlegel, even to the extent that probably mathematics also depends to some degree upon what you might call the grain of nature. Recent experiments carried out since World War Two show that a number of different animals—some mammals, some birds—possess a certain ability to count. A pigeon, in ingeniously designed experiments, has been shown to be able to count up to five—to distinguish, in other words, between one and two, or two and three, or three and four, or four and five—but above five it fails. It then reacts only as though all higher numbers were "many." Insofar as our own ability to enumerate lies at the basis of the capacity of the human mind to deal mathematically with various kinds of problems, we might say that the development of scientific logic and the development of mathematics are outgrowths, or perhaps to a large extent by-products, of the necessary evolutionary development of man in the particular world —the particular environment—that conditioned our evolution.

If therefore, we could conceivably have evolved in a quite different kind of world, in a very different set of circumstances, without doubt our mathematics, our physics, and our logic of science would be different than they are. At least I raise this matter as a problem worthy of very serious consideration by philosophers of science.

Another thing that this line of thought leads to is the inherent subjectivity of the scientist and of his primary data. Being the kinds of animals we are, having evolved with the particular senses and nervous systems and methods of reasoning we do possess, we cannot react quite other than we do because the processes of scientific reasoning are conditioned by the kind of neurobiological machinery with which we must carry out our reasoning. We are, therefore, always inherently looking *out* on the world, and the primary data of science are simply the sensory impressions which are received by the human body as changes take place in the external enviornment.

I was impressed as a young man by Eddington's discussion of the table, that famous discussion which raises the question: "Is the real table the constellation of atoms that are moving rapidly to and fro in almost empty space, or is the real table this thing of wood that I see and feel in front of me?" I have been even more impressed, I think, by a discussion directed by Erwin Schrödinger to this issue in the last book he wrote before he died, *Mind and Matter*. I should like to read a passage from a previous book in which I have discussed this subject:

From the description of science, as itself an evolutionary product in a human organ produced by natural selection, it may be guessed that I do not adhere to the view that either the processes or the concepts of science are strictly objective. They are as objective as man knows how to make them, that is true, but man is a creature of evolution and science is only his way of looking at nature. As long as science is a human activity carried on by individual men and by groups of men, it must at bottom remain inescapably subjective.

In a penetrating essay entitled "The Mystery of the Sensual Qualities," [2]

Erwin Schrödinger dealt with certain of these subjective aspects of science. It is a truism to say that science is based on sense perceptions, the primary observations the scientist makes of his instruments or directly of natural phenomena; but scientific knowledge ". . . fails to reveal the relations of the sense perceptions to the outside world," says Schrödinger. In our picture or model of the outside world as it is formulated and guided by our scientific discoveries, all sensory qualities are absent. To illustrate this point, which may not be readily admitted by everyone, Schrödinger discusses the relation between the wavelengths of light and the sensation of color. Take yellow, for instance. The wavelengths we sense as yellow are those of about 590 millimicrons, but there is nothing in the frequency to explain the yellowness of yellow. The yellowness is in the mind of the observer, and there seems to be no physical reason why a yellow sensation of color should be experienced when wavelengths of 590 mμ enter the eye, rather than a red or blue or any other sensation. In fact [here I depart from Schrödinger's discussion to interject a bit of reasoning of my own based on my knowledge of the genetic character of color-blindness] in a color-blind man the sensation evoked by wavelengths of 590 mμ is something quite different. A totally color-blind scientist may do refined experiments with instruments that measure wavelengths of light, refract them, focus them, do all sorts of things with them. But the totally color-blind scientist can never conceive what anyone else means by "yellow," and indeed, we have no real assurance that anyone else experiences what we ourselves do when we see yellow. All we know, in daily life and in science, is that persons whom we agree are competent observers agree to call some sensation which they experience when stimulated by light of 590 mμ "yellow."

Schrödinger pointed out, too, that radiation in the neighborhood of 590 mμ is not the only stimulus that will evoke the sensation of yellow. One can take waves of 760 mμ, which alone are pure "red," and mix them in a certain proportion with wavelengths of 535 mμ, by themselves "green," and the "competent observer" simply cannot distinguish the mixture from the color of pure 590 mμ waves. "Two adjacent fields illuminated, one by the mixture, the other by the single spectral light, look exactly alike, you cannot tell which is which." Moreover, states Schrödinger, this effect cannot be foretold from the wavelengths. Note that the midpoint between 760 mμ and 535 mμ is not 590 mμ. There is no numerical connection between the physical wavelengths and the mixture. The mixture that makes yellow has been determined empirically. There is no general rule that a mixture of two spectral lines of light matches one lying between them. Thus a mixture of "red" and "blue" wavelengths from the ends of the spectrum produces "purple" color, but there is no single spectral wavelength that evokes purple at all.

The same truth holds for each and every kind of primary sensation whether it be taste or odor, sound vibrations, or touch. A simple prick with a pin on the skin evokes different sensations—warmth, cold, pain, pressure —depending upon the site of the prick and the connections to the central nervous system of the particular receptors which have been stimulated. It is a well-known law of physiology that the nature of the sensation is not primarily a matter of the nature of the stimulus, but of the receptor. Either a receptor does not respond at all, or it responds by evoking the same particular sensation in every instance. Mild pressure on the eye makes one *see* colors, a severe blow makes one *see* stars. The eye can only see, and within it the individual receptors respond only to light, irrespective of wavelength if they are rods, or to light of specific wavelengths if they are cones.

To extend Schrödinger's analysis we may well recognize that our sensory apparatus and the structure of our nervous systems, within which arise our sensations, grow and develop as they do from the first beginnings in the human embryo because of the particular genetic constitutions we inherit from our parents. First and foremost we are *human* scientists, not insect scientists, nor even monkey scientists. The long past of our evolutionary history, with its countless selections and rejections of various kinds of genes and combinations of genes, has made us what we are. Try as we will, we cannot break the bounds of our subjective interpretations of the physical events of nature. We are born blind to many realities, and at best can apprehend them only by translating them by means of our instruments into something we can sense with our eyes or ears, into something we can then begin to reason about by developing abstract mental concepts about them, by making predictions on the basis of our hypotheses, and by testing our theories to see whether reality conforms to our notions.

Within recent years many psychological experiments have shown beyond any doubt that even the simplest concepts, developed in the mind on the basis of sensory experiments, are profoundly and inescapably subjective. They are related to past experience and to the capacity to learn from experience. A very young kitten learns from its experiences how to interpret visual cues of distance and directions in space, and shows alarm when placed on a so-called "visual cliff." [3] Yet it must learn this. It must first build into its mental structure some idea of how simple space relations are related to visual cues. Only thereafter can it function effectively in the real world it lives in. But a kitten, birdling, or human infant deprived of the opportunity to learn such things and to learn them at the appropriate age may be forever afterwards crippled in its mental constructs, just as literally as an animal that has lost a limb is forever mutilated.

This line of reasoning leads us to the conclusion that the objectivity of science depends wholly upon the ability of different observers to agree about their data and their processes of thought. About quantitative measurements and deductive reasoning there is usually little dispute. Qualitative experiences like color, or inductive and theoretical types of reasoning, leave great room for disagreement. Usually they can be reduced to scientific treatment only if the subjective color can by agreement be translated into some quantitative measurement such as a wavelength, only if the reasoning can be rendered quantitative by use of a calculus of probability. It nevertheless remains a basic fact of human existence that the subjectivity of the individual personality cannot be escaped. We differ in our genes, each of us possessing a genotype unique throughout all past and all future human history (unless we happen to possess an identical twin who came from the same fertilized egg we did). To the extent that our genes endow us with similar though not identical sensory capacities and nervous systems, we may make similar scientific observations, and we may agree to ignore the existence of the variables in our nature that prevent us from even making exactly the same measurements as someone else or arriving at exactly the same conclusions. But it is perilous to forget our genetic individuality and our own uniqueness of experience. These form the basis of the ineradicable subjectivity of science. In the last analysis science is the common fund of agreement between individual interpretations of nature. What science has done is to refine and extend the methods of attaining agreement. It has not banished the place of the individual observer, experimenter, or theoretician whose work is perhaps subjective quite as much as objective.[4]

This line of reasoning leads us to consider many interesting things that have happened in the history of science that the philosopher of science should ponder. One of the most interesting of these situations relates to the famous experiments of Gregor Mendel. R. A. Fisher, who was himself a notable mathematician, pointed out in 1936 that Mendel's results, as published in his two papers, are simply too good. The deviations from expectation on the basis of his own theory are too small to be expected by chance alone in experiments of such limited size. Ever since Fisher's paper was published we have been pondering the question: "Why are Mendel's experimental results too good?" Did Mendel or some assistant, as Fisher suggested, actually falsify the data? Was he really dishonest in reporting this greatest of biological experimental discoveries in the nineteenth century? Or did he throw out those particular cases, or the particular experiments which did not sufficiently fit the theoretical expectations that he had derived? In a recent collection of documents relating to Mendel's original discovery and the reactions toward it of scientists of the nineteenth and twentieth centuries, Curt Stern and Eva M. Sherwood [5] have collected and printed Fisher's critique which flatly holds that Mendel (or some assistant) was a dishonest scientist. Sewall Wright, himself a distinguished mathematical geneticist, has added a brief note to this book which is well worth the inspection and thought of every philosopher of science. He agrees with Fisher that the data are too good. There seems to be no question about that. The real question is how to account for it. The explanation that Wright prefers, and which I too regard as a better explanation than to believe that Mendel consciously practiced deceit, is that he made subconscious errors in favor of his expectations, and also excluded various progenies in which the results were extremely deviant or in which he used other criteria to determine that the progenies were not segregating.

The inherent subjectivity with which each scientist, no matter how honest he tries to be, necessarily approaches his experiment may well supply the explanation. If, on the basis of certain preliminary experiments, he has formed an expectation of what will occur, he naturally expects the same thing to happen again. He is then far more likely to make mistakes in the direction favoring confirmation of his hypotheses than to make mistakes discounting his hypotheses. This bias has now been well established as a psychological reality. Only since Pavlov's work and after gaining the understanding we now have of the importance of conditioning have we become sufficiently aware of the possibility of errors of this kind.

This is a danger with which I have had to grapple considerably in my own work. Some years ago I began a study of the effects of very low doses of ionizing radiations on the mutation of genes. It could be calculated by extrapolation from known relations of dose to mutation frequency that a five roentgen dose would increase the mutation rate by only about five per cent of the spontaneous mutation rate. Here was an experimental situation in which you had to demonstrate either the existence or non-existence of an increase of five per cent in a mutation rate—that is, in the rate over "background noise," as the physicist would say. To do this required the examination of many millions of fruit flies that were offspring of male and female fruit flies which had been subjected to the radiation. It was such a huge experiment that it could not be done all at once. The protocol that I designed was therefore one in which the experiment was repeated many times. In each replication of the experiment there were exactly matched controls and irradiated cultures—the same number of bottle cultures, same number of parent flies in each culture, same length of time, same age of parents at times of irradiation, same location randomized in the laboratory during the course of development—everything made as identical in the two series as possible. Nevertheless, as should be expected, variation of a random sort occurred. I used only two trained individuals to examine this enormous number of fruit flies. We called it our megafly experiment, because we had to go far beyond a million flies to get a meaningful result. Every fly had to be examined individually and then every suspected mutation tested and retested in order to determine whether a mutation had in fact occurred. I knew that if the observers knew which series had been irradiated, there would be an inevitable bias toward confirming the hypothesis that mutations are produced by X-rays, because everybody knows that mutations are produced by X-rays, and even at very low doses one would expect some to occur. It was therefore necessary to code these series so that only I, who performed the radiations, knew which series had been irradiated and which ones had not, while the observers who scored the flies had no knowledge of it until the experiment was over.

That is the kind of subjective bias that enters into a scientific experiment. Quite often it makes little difference because one is not working with differences that have to be established statistically by means of a very large body of data. When your experiment is of an all-or-none type, you can be quite confident of the results, whichever way it turns out. In present times, however, the scientist must deal more and more with situations in which his own subjective bias is a great danger in the correct interpretation of the results.

Another element I want to emphasize as being very important in the biological sciences is the necessity of relying upon operational definitions. I shall talk about it very briefly because the idea of operationalism is in most minds connected with Percy Bridgman's philosophy and is thought to be something with which only physical scientists have much concern. The theory of the gene—the unit of heredity—grew out of Mendel's experiments and, subsequently, from the work done with the fruit fly Drosophila at Columbia University in the second and third decades of this century, and later and elsewhere on a wider scale.

During the nineteen-twenties and 'thirties the gene was thought to resemble a sort of billiard ball, like a spherical Bohr atom—a little bead on a microscopically visible structure—a chromosome within the nucleus of each cell. The gene was concerned in some mysterious way with the determination of a particular hereditary characteristic or multiple characteristics. It was only in the late nineteen-thirties that geneticists began to question the validity of this concept of the gene. Until then, everyone had thought of the gene as a well-defined kind of particle that had certain properties and produced certain effects. Then, largely through a remarkable paper in which Louis Stadler [6] applied operational definitions to the concept of the gene, and some very heretical discussions of the subject by Richard Goldschmidt,[7] geneticists suddenly woke up to the fact that they really didn't know what they were talking about when they talked about "the gene."

In fact, three quite distinct operations are used in the study of the gene. One of these operations is that of the occurrence of mutations— the study of mutations occurring either spontaneously or by induction. The gene was in this sense the unit that was changed by mutation. Another operation is the recombination of the genes between the paired chromosomes that exist in each cell and are derived, respectively, from the maternal and paternal sides of the family. Crossing over is the name of this process, which occurs in all sexually reproducing species and even in some asexually reproducing species. This process is quite different from the process which defines the unit of mutation. The third operation is, of course, that whereby the gene produces some change in the characteristics of the individual as the individual develops—the gene functions in some way; that is, it controls the synthesis of some specific protein in the developing organism.

Stadler pointed out that it was very probable that these units were not identical. There was evidence to suppose that the unit of recombination in the chromosome was a larger and different sort of a unit, dependent upon entirely different biological processes than the process of mutation. Mutations might be either smaller than the unit of recombination, or larger, depending upon what kind of accidental alteration was brought about in the chromosome. The unit of function is not comparable to either of the other two, but, as studies in the nineteen-forties showed, was something generally much greater than either. Some geneticists have proposed that we should actually introduce several different terms to describe these different sorts of "genes"—the muton, or unit of mutation; the recon, or unit of recombination; and the cistron, or unit of function—but most of us go on talking about the gene. It is such a convenient term! Only, we must now recognize that what we refer to in any particular context depends upon the operation that has been used to derive that information.

In conclusion I shall make some remarks about the ethical aspects of science and the relation of the development of science, of evolution, and of man to ethics. I have pointed out in *Science and Ethical Values* that ethics, a human construct, definitely has an evolutionary basis, and a great deal of conflict is inevitable because values that promote survival in the evolutionary scheme of things at one level of organization are not necessarily those that promote survival at another level of organization. Thus we can say, for example, that in terms of the individual gene (in the cistron sense now, the unit of function or what a gene does), the gene that will survive the longest in the population after it has arisen, other things being equal, is the one that is most stable, that mutates least often, and that has effects which will promote the survival and reproduction of the possessor of the gene, rather than the converse.

Yet a gene may be very stable and nevertheless quite disadvantageous to the population in which it arises. In other words, the characteristics that determine the survival of the individual human being during life up to the age of reproduction and the particular characteristics that enable a gene to survive in a population may be in conflict with one another. Similarly, the survival of the individual may very well be adverse to the survival of the population to which it belongs. Consequently our ideas of what is wise and good to do for the continuation of a species or a population may come into gross conflict with what might be thought advisable to do at some other level of organization.

Man himself, as an individual, has only arbitrary limits. We think of ourselves as pretty well bounded by our skins, but each of us is constantly emitting molecules which can be detected by chemical means, or by a dog's sensory mechanisms, at a considerable distance. We carry an aura about us wherever we go, and our auras overlap with those of other individuals so that the boundaries of our personalities are really quite indefinite, perhaps extending out limitlessly into the terrestrial environment. A female moth gives off odorous particles that can be picked up by a male of that same species, but apparently not by males of any other species, as far as two miles in perfectly still air. The sensitivity of such detection passes our bounds of understanding at the present time, for the concentration of the molecules of odorous particles two miles away after simple diffusion would seem to be so dilute that no scientific instrument could possibly respond to it. The male moth is perhaps responding to only one molecule of the effective substance at any single instant, but that is enough to excite him and start him off in an appropriate direction.

We are not only limited physically to our own skins so as to overlap with other beings in a material way, but we have influences upon our environment and our environment has influences upon us that are intricate and important beyond gainsaying.

The moose on Isle Royale in Lake Superior [8] cannot live effectively as a moose population without the presence of about twenty wolves on that island; and the wolves cannot live without the moose. In the absence of the wolves, as demonstrated several times over, the moose will multiply until they strip all the bark off the young trees and have nothing more to eat during the winter time. They then starve to death in large numbers. The population has been almost exterminated several times. The first effort made to modify this situation was to bring some wolves over from the Cleveland Zoo, but these zoo-bred wolves preferred to stay around the camps of the forest rangers on the island and eat garbage. They would not chase the moose. They had to be trapped and shipped back to the Cleveland Zoo. Eventually some wild wolves came over from the mainland when the lake froze over. Wolves form a part of the ecosystem that is necessary to the survival of moose. Even the predator, in other words, is necessary for the well-being of the prey. We human beings are a part of a vast ecosystem, every part of which influences our own well-being. Until we begin to recognize in our human ethics that what we do in terms of polluting our water and polluting our air and modifying our genes with extraneous radiation, and so forth, has influences of an adverse kind upon the total system, such that man's continuation as a species becomes imperiled if we fail to heed these relationships, we will never attain a really valid system of human ethics. I do not say that all ethical values arise out of the evolutionary process. I have been charged with that view, and I emphatically deny it. I do say that you cannot really understand ethics without taking into account the evolutionary history of man.

Similarly, I maintain that science itself has an ethical basis. Science, as a way of learning about nature, cannot exist in the shape and form of a single isolated individual, because the very essence of science is that the sensory data obtained by one individual must be confirmed by comparison with those of at least one other competent observer. It takes at least two scientists in the world to produce science, and without this interaction between them, which of course involves honesty and integrity in reporting what is observed, one would have no basis for knowing whether any kind of sensory impressions, any primary data, were real or hallucinatory. One would not be able to develop a scientific logic.

I think that the gravest ethical problems of our present day arise from the advances which are being made in science at the present time, not in the nuclear sciences only, but especially in the biological sciences. I lack time to discuss that subject, but I insist that philosophers of science would do well to think a great deal more in the future about ethical problems than about logical problems.

I have been interested and delighted lately in reading a book published by my friend Theodosius Dobzhansky, of the Rockefeller University, a man who is one of the greatest evolutionary biologists of our day. Certainly not every biologist, nor every scientist, is going to receive this book with open arms. It will perhaps not be greeted by very many of them with cordial feelings, and yet it says certain things that I believe every scientist should ponder. In *The Biology of Ultimate Concern*,[9] Dobzhansky is suggesting that the ultimate concern of every man, whether scientist or not, is about the meaning of life—the meaning of his own life—its short endurance, its significance in the cosmos. Furthermore, he suggests that without an understanding of evolutionary biology one really cannot even begin to understand man's ultimate concern.

Dobzhansky traces, for instance, the development of self-awareness in animals, the evolution of a sense of individuality, as you can see it manifested in a dog. The development of consciousness is something that perhaps exists below the human level on the ladder of beings conceived by Aristotle, although we cannot be sure because we cannot get out of ourselves and into the minds of other animals to know. The dawn of conscience, which we can also observe below the human level, grows out of the awareness of the individual, because of the existence of others who form a social unit—a family, a herd, a population—that is greater than the individual and for which the individual's own life may need to be sacrificed. Dobzhansky speaks also of death-awareness, which is perhaps a strictly human concept, and out of which, in very great part, the ultimate concern of man must have developed.

Dobzhansky himself tends to lean toward a mystical view, similar to that of Teilhard de Chardin, about man's ultimate concern. It grows out of an evolutionary, biological consideration of the nature and meaning of life—of one's own life, of all life—the evolution of the cosmos, the evolution of man, and finally the emergence of Mind that transcends anything that is to be found on the strictly animal level. Whether one agrees with all of these points of view, or not, is not of so much consequence as the thought-provoking quality of the book in stimulating one's own thinking. I recommend it strongly to you for that reason.

NOTES

1. Since making the above remarks, I find that Charles S. Peirce expressed himself as of the same opinion: "Logicality in regard to practical matters . . . is the most useful quality an animal might possess, and might, therefore, result from the action of natural selection. . . ." "The Fixation of Belief," originally published in *Popular Science Monthly*, V. 12 (1877) pp. 1–15. Quoted from C. S. Peirce, in V. Tomas, ed., *Essays in the Philosophy of Science* (Indianapolis, Bobbs-Merrill Company, 1957), p. 7.
2. E. Schrödinger, *Mind and Matter* (Cambridge, Cambridge University Press, 1958), pp. 88–104.
3. Eleanor J. Gibson and R. D. Walk, "Visual Cliff," *Scientific American*, V. 202 (1960), cover and pp. 64–71.
4. Bentley Glass, *Science and Ethical Values* (Chapel Hill, University of North Carolina Press, 1965), pp. 76–81.
5. Curt Stern and Eva R. Sherwood, *The Origin of Genetics: A Mendel Source Book* (San Francisco and London, W. H. Freeman and Company, 1966), pp. 139–175.
6. L. J. Stadler, "The gene," *Science*, 120, (1954), 811–19.
7. R. Goldschmidt, *The Material Basis of Evolution*. (New Haven, Yale University Press, 1940).
8. Durward L. Allen and L. David Mech, "Wolves versus Moose on the Isle Royale," *Natl. Geographic*, 123 (1963) 200–219.
9. Theodosius Dobzhansky, *The Biology of Ultimate Concern* (New York, New American Library, 1967).

PHILOSOPHY OF HISTORY

HISTORICAL EXPLANATION

P. H. Nowell-Smith

I

Historians, I have found, often betray a quite peculiar mistrust of philosophers and a quite peculiar unwillingness to ask such philosophical questions as: "What am I doing?," "Why am I doing it?," "What are the criteria for acceptability for a historical description or explanation?" In part this attitude is a hangover from the days when philosophers would construct ambitious "theories of history" and would tell the historians *de haut en bas* what they ought to do and why they ought to do it. The historians' reaction to this pontifical posture was a proper blend of irritation, resentment, and ridicule. But this cannot be the whole story, since philosophers no longer adopt the pontifical posture. The phrase "philosophy of history" today means something quite different from what it meant for Hegel. Modern philosophers do not dictate; they try to find out. They assume that "we"—collectively—do know a great deal about the past and that it is the historians who have discovered what we know and are in a position to tell us; we do not try to tell them.

Though historians often disagree, historiography is not a free-for-all, a chaos in which one man is as entitled to his opinion as another. Some historical accounts—for example, Belloc's account of the Reformation in England or Tolstoi's account of Napoleon's invasion of Russia—are too incompetent or too perverse to be taken seriously. For the study of history is a *discipline*, a social and public enterprise carried on in accordance with accepted rules and methods and implicitly accepted criteria of acceptability. The historian knows that he must justify himself before a jury of his peers and that his view may not be accepted, or that it may be accepted for a time and rejected later.[1] But it is one thing for a man to fail to convince his peers that his view is true and quite another for him to convince them that he is not a historian at all but a charlatan.

213

From time to time, no doubt, a genius will revolutionize historiography, applying new methods, setting new and higher standards. But though the impact of genius may show that whole generations of historians have accepted inadequate or misguided standards, historians are surely right in rejecting novel and idiosyncratic explanations and theories that do not conform to the standards that they, here and now, as a corporate body, accept. Our interest, as philosophers, is logical and epistemological. Our first task is to discover what the accepted standards and methods used by historians actually are. Though we may later want to challenge them, our challenge will be justly dismissed by historians as an impertinence if they have reason to believe that we do not know what they actually are. The current hostility of many historians to philosophy of history may be due to the fact that some of the accounts which philosophers give of historical methods, and especially of historical explanation, extract from the historian only blank incredulity. "No, no," he wants to say, "*that* is not what I am doing *at all*."

Since Hempel published his essay, *The Function of General Laws in History* in 1942,[2] there has been much discussion of what has come to be known as the "covering-law model" of explanation. Hempel's theory runs as follows:

To give a causal explanation of an event is to derive deductively a statement to the effect that the event took place from premises which consist of some universal laws and statements of the initial or boundary conditions before the event took place. [To illustrate his thesis he gives the following example:] Let the event to be explained consist in the cracking of an automobile radiator during a cold night. The car was left in the street all night. Its radiator which consists of iron was completely filled with water and the lid was screwed on tightly. The temperature dropped during the night from 39°F in the evening to 15°F in the morning.

These are the initial conditions and Hempel then cites a number of generalizations (which he rather oddly calls laws) such as that water freezes at 32°F at normal atmospheric pressure, and that below 39.2°F its pressure increases with decreasing temperature and so on. It is easy to see that given a suitable set of initial conditions and laws, all of which are empirically verifiable, the statement "the radiator cracked" follows deductively from the premises. We could, indeed, predict that the radiator will crack if we had all this information in advance, and it is a cardinal feature of the covering-law theory of explanation that the information which is sufficient to explain an event which has occurred is also sufficient to predict that it will occur.

Hempel devotes much of his article to rebutting criticisms of this theory, but he nowhere explains why it should be accepted in the first place. The reason must, I think, be something like this: We have not explained why something happened until we have explained why just *that* thing happened rather than *something else*. The covering-law model fulfills this requirement admirably, since the premises *entail* the conclusion and thereby show that, if they are true, nothing else *could have happened*. The idea that I want to challenge is that a historical explanation must meet this requirement of acceptability.

II

History, I said, is a discipline, and the minimum conditions for something's being a discipline are (*a*) that something must count, if not as establishing or refuting a thesis, at least as being in favor of the thesis or against it; (*b*) that there should be agreement among those who practice the discipline as to the criteria for deciding what does and what does not so count; and (*c*) that these criteria must be agreed upon in advance. This last condition is necessary to rule out such bogus "sciences" as astrology; for, while astrologers do have an elaborate jargon in which they propound general principles, their predictions are protected against falsification by permitting the use of *ad hoc* hypotheses invented to save the principles after a prediction has been falsified. This is a very loose and generous way of formulating the necessary conditions of being a discipline, but it is important not to impose more stringent conditions at the start, for the following reason.

It happens from time to time that men are spectacularly successful in some particular field of intellectual endeavor; while others are still floundering in neighbouring fields, they hit on a method by means of which they manifestly succeed in doing what they set out to do. Since their success is due to their method, there is a strong temptation to believe that this wonderful method must be applicable elsewhere with equally happy results. This happened in the case of mathematics in the fourth and fifth centuries B.C., and in spite of the warnings of Aristotle it came to be believed that every respectable science must, somehow, be like mathematics. Descartes believed this at a time when other men were showing in practice that scientific investigation, though it makes great use of mathematics, cannot actually *be* mathematics, though it was left for Hume to tell us why this is so. Today, because of the spectacular success of the natural sciences, there is a tendency to suppose that historiography, if it is to be respectable at all, must employ methods and standards which are the methods and standards of natural science. If the covering-law theory of explanation is the correct account of explanation in the natural sciences, it must apply to historical explanation as well. But to accept this view uncritically is to be a victim of the same blindness that afflicted mathematizing philosophers from Plato to Descartes.

Consider the concept of an "argument." We have in formal logic and mathematics paradigms of good, knock-down arguments; the premises entail the conclusions; and if, armed with this criterion, we proceed to examine arguments in other fields, we find that none of them stand up to the test. But what does this show? Not, as we fondly think, that all arguments outside logic and mathematics are bad arguments, but only that if an argument is to be of the kind known as "deductively valid" it must *be* deductively valid! What then of arguments in a court of law? The standard of proof required here is not deductive validity. However strong the evidence that John Doe killed Richard Roe, it is always possible that he didn't; the law requires only that a proposition be proved *beyond reasonable doubt*. Just what this phrase amounts to is not easy to spell out, but it certainly does not amount to deductive validity. Long ago Aristotle remarked that only an ignorant man requires deductive rigor of a lawyer or puts up with probable reasoning from a mathematician.[3] So I suggest that we now take a fresh look at historical explanation without assuming that an explanation can only be respectable if its explanans entails its explanandum.

Entailment is certainly not required of all explanations. We explain why the Union Jack is the national flag of Great Britain and Northern Ireland by telling a story about the Acts of Union and the crosses of St Patrick, St Andrew, and St George. This explanation (provided that our story is true) is entirely satisfactory; but of course those who composed this flag might have concocted something quite different—a different arrangement of the three crosses, or a flag composed of roses, thistles, and shamrocks. So at least in this case a satisfactory explanation of what happened does not have to show why that happened rather than something else.

The standard reply to this argument is that the covering-law model is not supposed to be a model for all explanations, but only for all *causal* explanations. But why should we accept this either? Collingwood pointed out that there is a sense of "cause" in which it means to provide someone with a motive for doing something.[4] This is the oldest sense of "cause" in English and still one of the commonest. I can cause someone to slip by pushing him and I can cause him to slip by offering him a bribe. In the first case the explanation is only satisfactory if general laws about the movements of bodies can be invoked to back it, but we are not entitled to assume without argument that this must be true of the second case also. The fact is that Hume outlined, and his modern successors have elaborated and refined, an account of what it is to explain a natural phenomenon, which has two very attractive features: first, it meets the requirement of deductive rigor and thereby explains why this happened and not that; and, second, when we proceed according to it we are highly successful in predicting natural phenomena. So we may, if we like, say, This is what an explanation of a natural phenomenon ought to be; this is the standard we shall accept in this field. But to say, This is what a *causal* explanation ought to be, simply begs the question. We have not shown that all causal explanations must confom to this model; we have shown only that if we first decide to restrict the phrase "causal explanation" to explanations of this type, nothing that fails to conform to this type is a causal explanation.

Philosophers who espouse the covering-law model seem to suffer from a certain confusion of aim. They purport to be giving us a rational reconstruction of historical explanation which lays bare the underlying logic of what a historian does when he explains something. But there are signs that this is not what these philosophers are actually doing at all. Hempel uses only one example from the field of history: explaining why the Dust Bowl farmers migrated to California. But his treatment of this question shows that he is really concerned, not with the *historical* question, Why did these farmers migrate?, but with the *sociological* question, Why do people migrate? Historians explain why certain particular people did what they did at certain particular times, but Hempel offers an explanation of a general phenomenon—migration. The conclusion is irresistible; it is nothing but the unwritten academic law, Thou shalt not disparage the work of thy colleagues in other fields, that prevents Hempel's coming out openly on the side of Henry Ford. He is not so much giving us the underlying logic of what historians do as telling us to stop studying the past historically and take to scientific sociology instead.

As formally set out in connection with the cracked radiator example, Hempel's model employs a number of different generalizations (or laws); but of the Dust Bowl example he gives the following account. They migrated, he says, because continual drought and sandstorms rendered their existence increasingly precarious and because California seemed to offer so much better living conditions. He goes on to say that "this explanation rests on some such universal hypothesis as that populations will tend to migrate to regions which offer better living conditions." Notice that what was previously a handful of laws is now reduced to one law and that this law is nothing but the general hypothetical connecting the initial conditions with the event to be explained.[5]

Suppose, however, that we treat the cracked radiator example in the same way. The form of the explanation will no longer be the form in which Hempel originally gave it; for there will now be only one law, and that law is the general hypothetical, Whenever a car is left standing in the street and the radiator is filled with water and the temperature drops, etc., the radiator will crack. I have no doubt that this generalization is *true*; but it is totally nonexplanatory, for the set of laws which gave the original version its explanatory power has disappeared. That power was derived from the application to the particular case of cracking radiators of general theories about the expansion of water, the breaking point of iron under pressure, and so on. These theoretical statements have all disappeared, and what we are left with, even in a case of *scientific* explanation, is nothing but Hume's thesis that to say that A caused B is to say that A and B are members of classes, α and β, such that whenever an α occurs a β occurs.

The difference between the two models can be make plain by setting them out schematically, using L for laws, C for statements of initial conditions, and E for the statement of the event to be explained:

Model I   If $L_1 \ldots L_n$ and $C_1 \ldots C_n$, then E
               $L_1 \ldots L_n$ and $C_1 \ldots C_n$
               Therefore E

Model II   If $C_1 \ldots C_n$, then E
               $C_1 \ldots C_n$
               Therefore E

Both these are valid *modus ponens* arguments (whether or not they are explanations); there are laws in the first model but none in the second.

To return to the Dust Bowl case, the alleged law that people migrate to regions which offer better living conditions is no law at all, for very often they don't. So at this point Hempel introduces the notion of an "explanation-sketch." Historians, he says, do not give us full-fledged satisfactory explanations; they give us explanation-sketches. The generalizations on which they rely are of a loose probabilistic form: People in these conditions usually migrate, or tend to migrate, or *ceteris paribus* migrate. Hempel's motive for introducing this notion of an explanation-sketch is entirely laudable; he wants to say that explanation-sketches, lacking in rigor though they are, can be distinguished to their advantage form *pseudo*-explanations in terms of such concepts as the Hand of God, the Historical Role of the Proletariat, or the Manifest Destiny of the United States. Such pseudo-explanations are disreputable for two reasons. First, they make no concrete predictions and cannot be falsified: we do not know what the manifest destiny of the United States will bring forth tomorrow until tomorrow comes. Secondly, these pseudo-explanations do not, as genuine explanation-sketches do, point the way to further research. The law of migration in its strict form is false, and in its tendency form it is unsatisfactory. But we may hope, by taking a wide survey of cases of migration, to discover a more restricted law of the form: All people who believe that living conditions will be better elsewhere and who satisfy a certain condition, X, migrate, which is true. And this, indeed, is just how a scientist might well proceed. Given that most but not all A's are B's, he tries to discover a factor, C such that all AC's are B's; and if he succeeds he has discovered a law and turned an explanation-sketch into an explanation.

But historians do not in fact proceed in this way, a fact of which philosophers should take note, and the reason they do not is that their subject matter does not lend itself to this treatment. Any historical generalization to which no exception could be found would have to be one in which the initial conditions were specified with such a wealth of detail that it is most unlikely that it would cover any cases other than the particular case which the historian is trying to explain, and such a law would explain nothing at all.

It is a cardinal feature of the covering-law model that to give an explanation is to give a set of sufficient conditions, so that the information that is required to explain something that we know did occur would be sufficient to predict its occurrence. At this point a covering-law theorist might argue that if a historian gave a very detailed description of the initial conditions it would be difficult to deny that, given those conditions, the event could have been predicted. Professor Dray cites as an example, "Louis XIV died unpopular because he pursued policies detrimental to his subjects' interests." There is certainly no law to the effect that all monarchs who pursue such policies die unpopular. But if we gave a very detailed account of Louis's policies at the end of his reign, the persecution of the Huguenots, the attacks on the Jansenists, his treatment of the aristocracy, the lawyers, and the merchants, the last disastrous wars, and so on, certainly a time would come when we should have to say: Well, if *that's* how Louis carried on, *no wonder* he was unpopular. We should have to admit that a satisfactory explanation had been given and that the explanation is satisfactory because the event could have been predicted from the information used to explain it.[6]

But in the end this reply does not help the covering-law theorist for two reasons. First, the long and detailed story cannot function as an antecedent in a causal law; for it could not be tested in other cases because no other cases exist. Secondly, suppose we were to tell a quite different story about Louis's last years, mentioning quite different facts, facts which seem to have nothing to do with his unpopularity at all. We should now have another statement of the form: Such and such events occurred and subsequently Louis became unpopular, which is just as true as the first statement and therefore has, according to the covering-law model, just as much right to be called an explanation. The model cannot discriminate between the relevant and the irrelevant, a plausible explanation and an utterly unplausible one.

The basic error of the covering-law model is to suppose that an explanation and a prediction are logically equivalent and that causal explanation, like prediction, requires a cause to be a *sufficient* condition of the event to be explained. Hume, in giving his account of cause, had his eye on classical mechanics—he is always thinking of billiard balls; and Hempel, as we saw, takes his example from the same field. In these cases we do discover and apply general laws and theories; but in history, though generalizations of a kind are involved, they do not have the character that the covering-law model ascribes to them. Very often the thing to be explained is an unusual or surprising event (which is why it needs to be explained), and in searching for its cause we are searching for something which *made the difference,* some factor *but for which* things would have gone smoothly as before. A cause in history is a necessary condition, though not just any necessary condition. It follows from this that what is required for a satisfactory explanation is very much less than what would be required to predict the same event. If we actually see the brick hit the window we know that it was the impact of the brick that shattered the glass; but there is clearly no law to the effect that any brick hitting any pane of glass will shatter the glass. I should have to know the momentum of the brick, the thickness of the glass, how firmly it was in place, and much else besides.

To this it might be replied that in saying the cause was the impact of the brick I have only given an explanation-sketch; to turn this into a full-fledged explanation, I should have to give the detailed information that would also make prediction possible. But, apart from the difficulty of turning historical explanation-sketches into explanations, there is no case for saying that all this extra information would increase the reliability of the explanation. That is entirely satisfactory as it stands. When a practical scientist researches into causes—for example, of road accidents or of cancer or of economic slumps—he is interested in the elimination or control of these evils. For this purpose it is necessary for him to find sets of initial conditions and universal laws. The practical scientist has to find out what he has to do to prevent these occurrences and, to do this, he must know in what general conditions they are certain or likely to occur. But the historian is not, on the whole, interested in the general conditions under which some general type of event occurs because he is not interested in prediction or control. (Genuine historians do not set out to be prophets.) He wants to find out just why *this* event occurred; he already knows *which* event occurred. For his purpose, therefore, The glass broke because the brick hit it, is not just an explanation-sketch; it is an entirely satisfactory explanation as it stands, and its status as an explanation is in no way weakened by the fact that many panes of glass have been hit by bricks and have not broken. Of course historians are sometimes interested in general phenomena, but when and to the extent that they are I call them sociologists. The distinction between "historian" and "sociologist" may be arbitrary, but it points to a real distinction in both aims and methods. The covering-law model is not so much a false analysis of the idea of cause in history as a misleading one: It mistakes the nature of the general statements that do, openly or covertly, play a part in the texture of historical writing; it incorrectly locates their role; and it has nothing to say about the real philosophical problems involved. It would, for example, be absurd to ask whether, in the cracked radiator example, the construction of the radiator or the fall in temperature was the more *important* cause-factor. But the relative importance of factors which everyone agrees to place among the necessary conditions of a historical event is often a major center of historical interest and controversy.

III

If we turn, as I think we should, to the dictionary, for a start, we find that "to explain" is literally "to smooth out or unfold," and this is a very natural physical image for the metaphorical or ordinary sense of "explain," which is "to make intelligible," "to clear of obscurity or difficulty." A satisfactory explanation of something is one that leads us to say, and to say truly, Yes, now I understand; what was muddled or confused or obscure to me before is now clear. So the problem of historical explanation is, initially, one of discovering just what patterns or schemata are used by historians which actually *do* have this effect. This, of course, is a problem for philosophers, not for lexicographers.

One of the functions of an explanation is to remove surprise, and one of the ways in which surprise is removed is to show that a phenomenon which seems at first odd or surprising is, when we look more closely, "only to be expected" and it is "only to be expected" because things usually happen that way. If a child is puzzled by the fact that his toy gun sinks in the bath while his toy duck floats, he may be told that this is because his gun is made of iron and his duck of celluloid, the unspoken implication being, of course, that iron things sink and celluloid things don't. Now he understands; he is no longer puzzled. In early life a great deal of coming to understand the world consists in just this acquisition of a number of independent general truths of this kind. But does the child *really* understand? Does he know *why* the gun sinks and the duck floats? Has anything really been *explained* to him? One is inclined to say not, but that the real work of explaining begins only when we start to talk about densities and specific gravities, when, in short, we move into the realm of *theory*. I don't think it matters very much whether we call bringing a particular case under a generalization "explaining" or not, as long as we remember that, if we do choose to call it explaining, this is a very lowly and primitive type of explanation.

Being familiar is neither a sufficient nor a necessary condition of being understood or explained. To a man who lives by the shore, nothing is more familiar than the regular ebb and flow of the tides; but this does not mean that he understands why they occur. (Incidentally, he is well able to predict these movements also, which shows that the ability to explain and the ability to predict are not as closely related as, on the Hempel model, they ought to be). But, equally, reducing the unfamiliar to the familiar is not a necessary condition of giving an explanation either. When Clerk Maxwell explains the patterns formed by iron filings in a magnetic field by means of a theory of magnetism, he is certainly not explaining unfamiliar phenomena by showing that they fall under a familiar generalization. Learning that some particular phenomenon is an instance of a generalization and is "only to be expected" because things often happen that way is only a sign that there is *something to be explained*, that the phenomenon is not a *mere coincidence*, such as the fact that John and his wife were both born on the same day. But when Clerk Maxwell explains why iron filings form the pattern they do, he *does* show that these patterns are "only to be expected" but in a rather different way. They are only to be expected *if his theory of magnetism* is true, since they follow deductively from the theory, together with particular premises about initial conditions.

I would, therefore, accept this much from Hempel: that all explanations can be represented schematically as deductions; but the premises of the deductions are not generalizations, but theoretical statements. What provides the explanation is *theory*, and, even within natural science, there are many different kinds of theory of which it is the business of philosophy of science to give an account. I am not concerned with the philosophy of science; but once we see this, we are in a position to take a fresh look at historical explanation without assuming that explanatory theories in history must be similar to those used in natural science.

There are many different kinds of historical writing, but at the heart of all history is *narrative* history, or an account of a number of events occurring in a time order. In a recent book Professor Gallie goes so far as to say that narratives are not explanations and that explanations are only introduced by historians at special points at which the story might be difficult to follow.[7] He calls these "intrusive explanations," and what he has in mind can be illustrated from a passage in Prescott's *Conquest of Mexico.* As part of his narrative, Prescott describes several battles in which the small band of Spaniards defeated much larger forces of Mexicans, which is a surprising fact. So Prescott tells us that the Mexicans were terrified by the Spanish horses, having never seen horses before, and that they were unfamiliar with a mode of fighting in which one tries to kill his enemy. Among the Mexicans, Prescott tells us, the primary objective of warfare was to obtain victims for human sacrifice. Consequently the object was not to kill the enemy but to take him alive; so the Spaniards were not fighting fair. Now this is a general statement about Mexican warfare; it is not itself part of the narrative, but is inserted to help the reader of the narrative over a difficulty.

But though intrusive explanations of this kind do occur in history, Professor Gallie seems to me quite wrong in refusing to allow that the narrative itself can be explanatory. We find a Spanish empire in Central America in the sixteenth century, and we want to know how in the world it got there. Prescott's book is partly a *description* (of the country, its inhabitants, their customs, beliefs and institutions) but mainly a *narrative* and the purpose of the narrative is *to explain.* Gallie's reason for distinguishing between narrative and explanation is that, for the most part, the narrative is *self-explanatory*; explanations are not given because none are needed. It does not follow from this that the narrative, *taken as a whole*, is never intended to be an explanation of something. Very often a historian's aim will be to explain why, for example, a certain war broke out. To do this he will set the scene by describing the state of affairs in the countries concerned, their conflicting ambitions and foreign policies, and so on. He then narrates the course of events, the diplomatic exchanges, the threatening gestures, and the military preparations which led to the outbreak of war. Explanation here is partly setting out in detail just *what happened*; but it is also causal, for the historian is explaining *why* things happened as they did. Our task as philosophers is to investigate the general conditions which make us say of some explanatory narratives that they are satisfactory explanations and of others that they are not. That bringing a particular case under a generalization has *some* part to play here I do not doubt; but enough has been said, I think, to show that the general pattern or schema of historical explanations is not what Hempel thinks it is.

IV

To illustrate the explanatory use of narrative I shall consider in detail an example which I used many years ago and which may, therefore, already be familiar.[8] It is taken from Pieter Geyl's essay, *The National State and the Writers of Netherlands History.*[9] This essay is certainly explanatory. Its purpose is to substitute what Geyl believes to be the correct explanation of a puzzling state of affairs for the explanation that previously held the field. The puzzling state of affairs which requires explanation is this: The Dutch state emerged towards the end of the sixteenth century with boundaries roughly the same as those of modern Holland; and this is puzzling because this particular area had never before been a cultural, linguistic, religious, or political unit. On the contrary, ever since the settlement of the Franks a thousand years earlier, a Dutch linguistic area had comprised both the modern Holland and the northern part of the modern Belgium. In the fifteenth century a political unit, comprising Holland and the whole of modern Belgium, grew up under the foreign domination, first of the Dukes of Burgundy and later of the Hapsburgs. The revolt of the Netherlands in 1576 was a revolt of all but one of the seventeen provinces into which this area was divided against foreign Hapsburg rule.

As we all know, some of these provinces won their independence and became modern Holland, others were reconquered by Spain and became first the Spanish, then the Austrian Netherlands, now the sovereign state of Belgium. But the puzzling fact is that the boundary between these two new political units was not the boundary between the Dutch-speaking and the French-speaking areas. It used to be thought that the Spaniards were able to reconquer just those provinces that they did because these provinces were predominantly Catholic and hence put up less resistance to Spain than did the Protestant provinces to the north. But this, according to Geyl, cannot be the correct explanation, since, prior to the revolt, the Protestants were a small minority everywhere, and no stronger in the north than in the south. That Holland became a Protestant country while Belgium remained Catholic was, according to Geyl, a consequence, not a cause of the partial success of the revolt.

One philosophical point about the role of generalizations in historical explanations already emerges. The earlier explanation, that the politi-

cal boundary at the end of the revolt was due to a previously existing religious boundary, certainly rests on some such generalization as that people fight harder for their independence if their religion is different from
that of their oppressors than if it is the same. The role of this generalization is to make the earlier explanation at least *a plausible one*. But the
explanation is not *the true* one because the assertion of particular fact
on which it relies, namely that the northern provinces were more Protestant than the southern, turns out to be untrue. Put schematically, the
argument is valid, being of the form, Whenever A, then B; in this case
A; so in this case B, and the major premise is true. But the minor premise is false, and a great deal of historical controversy is, in fact, devoted
to the establishing or refuting of minor premises.

Geyl's own explanation takes the form of a narrative which may be
summarized as follows:

1) In 1572, four years before the revolt broke out, a small group of Protestant exiles had established themselves in the extreme northwestern provinces. They were drawn from all the provinces, and they established themselves in the northwest, not because this area was already Protestant, but
because it was the most accessible by sea (where Philip was weak) and
furthest removed from the seat of Spanish military power.

2) When the general revolt began in 1576 it was naturally these Protestants
who took the lead everywhere because they were already armed and organized.

3) Parma's counter-attack was launched from Luxembourg in the southeast.
His farthest advance was bounded by the strong barriers of the Rhine and
the Maas, rivers which traverse the area from the east to west.

4) That Parma was unable to cross these rivers and reconquer the whole
area was due to the fact that Philip ordered him to intervene in the French
civil war.

This example is instructive in several ways. First, a puzzling phenomenon is explained, not by being brought under a generalization, but by
means of a narrative which, selected from the vast mass of available
"facts," seems to the historian to be relevant—to form not just a list of
events in a time order, but a *pattern* which has explanatory power.

Secondly, the example illustrates the role that generalizations *do*
play in historical explanation. For there *is* a generalization underlying
each of the steps in the narrative and each of the facts Geyl has selected
to form his explanatory pattern. Rebels tend to establish themselves in
areas remote from the seat of power; groups who are already armed and
organized tend to take the lead in revolts; large rivers are an obstacle to
invading armies; generals ordered to dispatch a large part of their forces
to another theatre of war cannot successfully press their counter-attacks.

Forgive me if these generalizations are trite, but their triteness is part of the point. None of them could be called a law, for each of them has counter-examples; but each is, for the most part, true. It will now be objected that, if the underlying generalizations are not universally true, they do not explain what happened, for at each step the particular fact or event cited as the cause might have occurred without the effect oc-curring. This is so; and it is partly for this reason that no one could have predicted the outcome of the revolt. But, as I have already suggested, for an explanation to be satisfactory, it is not necessary that we be able to predict the event from the statements of which the explanation is composed. All that is necessary is that each step in the explanation be supported by a generalization that at least makes the explanation plausi-ble. The original phenomenon to be explained was a surprising one; to eliminate or at least to reduce our surprise, all we need to be shown is that, in the light of the particular facts mentioned in the narrative, it is not really surprising at all. For this purpose it is necessary only that each step in the narrative rest on a generalization that is, for the most part, true. This generalization need not be a universal law.

The covering-law model, then, in a weak form, a form which per-mits its alleged laws to be loose and indeterminate in formulation and to be only for the most part, not universally, true, does turn out to have some truth in it. The necessary conditions of our accepting a historical explanation as at least a plausible one are (a) That all the steps are in-stances of generalizations that are, for the most part, true; and (b) that none of the steps conflict too grossly with such generalizations. The model, I suggest, is an account of one of the criteria for accepting a his-torical explanation as a possible or plausible one, not for accepting it as the true or correct explanation. Its great defect is that it is unenlighten-ing because it has nothing to say about the real work that historians do, which is to establish the facts. The historian has first of all to establish, by critical study of the evidence, that something which people have be-lieved, perhaps for a long time, to be the case really is the case. Very often, of course, he upsets the received account of some historical event by showing that what people believed is not so. For example, it used to be believed that, in the English Long Parliament of the sixteen-forties, most of the members who supported the King were landowners and most of those who supported the Parliament were merchants. Some cur-rent explanations of the struggle between King and Parliament made use of this alleged fact; the dispute was interpreted primarily as an in-stance of class struggle. Recent researches, however, have shown that the alleged fact is no fact at all.

To return to Geyl's account of the revolt in the Netherlands, the last step in his narrative illustrates another important aspect of historical explanation about which the Hempel model has nothing to say. While all the other steps refer to what was going on in the Netherlands, the last step introduces something from the outside. The order from Philip to Parma to intervene in the French civil war comes like a bolt from the blue—which is not to say that the order is itself inexplicable or uncaused, but that it was not causally connected with what had been going on before in the Netherlands and hence with what has so far been mentioned in the narrative.

I argued earlier that the impossibility of historical prediction rested on the absence of universal laws of the kind that prediction requires. But there is another reason: the role of *accident*. An accident is not an uncaused event; it is the coincidence of two independent causal chains that happens to be remarkable because it has important consequences.[10] If I am wandering round the streets of a strange city, I meet and pass by many people and nothing remarkable occurs. But I may happen to meet an old friend "by chance" as we say, and he might offer me a job that alters the whole course of my life—I become an oil tycoon. Looking back on this event years later I might say that my subsequent success was "due to an accident" or "due to pure chance." The causal phrase "due to" here means that if this meeting had not occurred I would not have become an oil tycoon, but would have remained an impoverished philosopher. The positivist might argue that, strictly speaking, this chance meeting was predictable, for if the presence of each of two people is predictable, their meeting is predictable by anyone who has the information for making both predictions. But we call such meetings "accidents" because we are *not* in a position to predict them. An observer in a helicopter may be able to predict a collision between two cars at a crossroad; but the two drivers, knowing nothing of each other's movements, cannot predict the collision and therefore cannot avoid it. (Indeed we have the paradoxical situation that if they could predict it, they would avoid it and thereby falsify their prediction.)

If we cannot predict these accidental collisions, we cannot predict their *consequences*; and accidental collisions of this kind are very common in history. The familiar distinction between history and "mere chronicle" tempts us to overlook this important fact. As usually formulated, this distinction is made between a mere chronicler who just lists events in a time-order and a historian who links these events by means of a causal explanation. But to think in this way is to think of there being just one causal chain: A happened because of B, B because of C, C because of D, and so on. This notion of a single causal chain is clearly wrong, for the system of events that the historian describes and explains is never a *closed* system. Thus we can understand, for example, a government's domestic policy as an intelligible whole, and as long as all goes well we can even predict what the government is likely to do next. But then, at any moment, this smooth and intelligible course of events may be upset by some event that is totally unconnected with it. A war or a financial crisis in a remote part of the world may force the government to abandon, postpone, or modify its plans. This is one reason for insisting on the importance of *narrative*, on the description of just *these particular* events.

V

To explain is to make intelligible, and it is a fact about the human mind that it finds intelligible only what is orderly. I shall not now raise the question whether this is just a brute empirical fact or an *a priori* fact about the concepts of mind, intelligibility, and orderliness. Instead, I shall offer a new account of one pattern of order which can be found in narrative history and which gives such history its title to being called "explanatory." The relation of particular facts to general explanation is not that of instances to general law, but that of illustrations to general theme. Stubborn facts that refuse to be accommodated into a historian's account refute or weaken his thesis as counter-examples refute a general law, but in a characteristically different way. The historian's over-all theme is like a jigsaw puzzle, a pattern of facts that can be seen to fit together in a certain way. The main difference is that a jigsaw puzzle has a finite and known number of pieces that fit together in only one way, while in history this is not so. The historian can select from an infinite number of facts and can organize them in more than one way.

I shall give one more example to illustrate both the nature of historical disagreement and the role of generalizations in history. My example is again taken from Pieter Geyl, this time from *Napoleon: For and Against.*[11] The question I am going to discuss is: Why did a war break out between Napoleon and his enemies in 1803?

This question has been much discussed by historians and by biographers of Napoleon. It is an interesting question because declaring war on England is a puzzling thing for Napoleon to have done, a thing which requires explaining. It is an important question because the war was a watershed in Napoleon's career and, indeed, in the history of Europe. Up to this point the First Consul can be seen (and was seen by many of his contemporaries) as the consolidator of the Revolutionary settlement. The "natural frontiers" of France, the Rhine and the Alps, had been reached by the Revolutionary armies in 1794 and finally accepted by the hostile powers in treaties signed in 1801 and 1802. Now, if ever, there was an opportunity for a lasting peace—an opportunity that did not come again until Napoleon's final defeat twelve years later. Why, then, did the war break out?

Part of every historian's explanation will consist of a detailed tracing of the actual course of events, of a *narrative*. But this story can be told in many different ways. The idea of a "complete" account of *all* the events that occurred in these twenty months is clearly chimerical. The historian selects what to put in and what to leave out and how much weight to give to each item. The general point I want to make is that his overall theme controls his selection of facts and is also controlled by it. Very broadly, there are two rival versions of what happened.

According to the first, which, needless to say, is the view taken by Napoleon himself both at the time and when he wrote his *Mémoires*, the British never intended the Peace of Amiens to be final. Their foreign policy had been dominated for centuries by the principle of not allowing any great power to control the low countries, and they had no reason to change that policy now. Napoleon himself had no desire whatever to renew the war; this was forced on him by British intransigence and hypocrisy. His celebrated public outburst of anger against Lord Whitworth, the British Ambassador, was wholly genuine and wholly justified. Given *this* view of this particular incident, can we understand the rest of Napoleon's career? We can. According to Sorel, all Napoleon's subsequent campaigns, even the final Moscow adventure, can be seen as purely defensive. Britain, alone among his enemies, will not accept the treaty settlement; so Britain must be crushed. After Trafalgar, the policy of crushing Britain by invasion has to be given up; Britain must be starved into submission. To this end, Napoleon must control the entire coastline from the Baltic to Gibraltar, and all his continental campaigns can be explained as necessary consequences of this policy.

Now let us turn to a totally different account of these same events. It was Napoleon's own ambition that renewed the war, combined with his appreciation of the age-old maxim: "No war; no dictator." He had no intention of keeping the peace, and his outburst of indignation against Lord Whitworth was a brilliant piece of acting which, given the diplomatic conventions of the time, could not fail to lead to war. From this point on, those who take this general line diverge. They agree that Napoleon's ambition re-opened the war; but just what *was* his ambition? According to Masson, he was dominated by family feeling: His aim was to set up petty kingdoms for his relatives (which he certainly did). According to Bourgeois, he had from the first dreamed of the conquest of India and the fabulous East: he was to be a second and greater Alexander. According to Driault, he was to be a second and greater Charlemagne. According to Lefebvre he had no permanent and consistent aim at all: He was always ambitious, always an opportunist, always with a new goal beyond every immediate horizon.

As a philosopher, I am not competent or concerned to adjudicate between these rival views. My concern is with their logical structure, the ways in which they can be supported or weakened or, perhaps, if this should turn out to be possible, conclusively established or refuted. The logical "units" or "items" with which we have to deal are (1) descriptions of particular events, for example Napoleon's treatment of Lord Whitworth; and (2) statements of a general kind, for example about traditional British foreign policy or Napoleon's character and ambition. What I am going to suggest is that particular descriptions and general statements support each other in a complicated way.

A historian's general account of the career of Napoleon gets its *support,* not from consideration of parallel cases—Caesar, Alexander or Ghengis Khan—but from its ability to accommodate all or at least most of the main units or items of which Napoleon's career was made up. Each event subsequent to the re-opening of the war (the murder of Enghien, the subjugation of Austria, the cat-and-mouse game with Alexander) can, with a little pushing and pulling here and there, be made to fit any of the general patterns I have mentioned in the sense that, given any of these patterns, we can say, about each of these items: Yes, that is what one would expect Napoleon to have done at that juncture, given the truth of the general scheme. And each view is *weakened* by the inability of the historian to fit some particular item into his general scheme. (Thus Sorel has a hard time explaining why, if Napoleon's over-all aim was to put an end to British opposition, he struck camp at Boulogne two months before the battle of Trafalgar put the project of invading England out of the question.)

The structure of mutual support between particular items and general schemes or patterns is a complicated one which can best be introduced by means of a simplified model. So let us assume, although this is certainly *not* true, that all historians agree (*a*) as to which items are important and therefore have to be fitted into the scheme and (*b*) on the description of each item, that is the narrative account of each event. I shall refer to particular items as A, B, C, etc., and to general patterns of interpretation as P_1, P_2, P_3, etc. Each item supports a pattern, P_1, if, given that P_1 is true, the item is what one would expect to have occurred. In this way the more moves that Napoleon makes that can be seen as moves which, given the truth of P_1, one would expect him to have made, the more strongly is the interpretation, P_1, supported. Support becomes almost conclusive proof if two conditions are fulfilled:

(a) There are no, or at least only a very few moves that Napoleon makes which are moves that, given P_1, one would expect him *not* to make.

(b) There is no rival interpretation, P_2, which is as strongly supported as P_1.

Using arrows to represent the quasi-deductive relation between patterns and events, we can construct the following schemata.

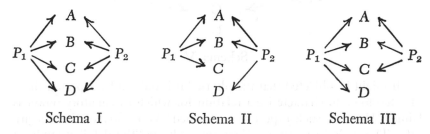

Schema I   Schema II   Schema III

In Schema I and Schema II, P_1 and P_2 have equal support, and neither is to be preferred to the other. In Schema III, P_1 has more support than P_2 and is therefore to be preferred. Interpretations fulfill the requirement of testability on this model, since it is always possible that new items, E, F, G, etc., will turn up whose presence will strengthen or weaken any of the currently accepted patterns.

But history is not as simple as this; we must now abandon our provisional false assumption that only one account of each item is generally accepted by historians. The renewal of war in 1803 is one item in Napoleon's career and, as we have seen, rival accounts can be given of that. Was his outburst of anger at Lord Whitworth genuine or was it a calculated sham? Which of these rival accounts are we to prefer? Here a historian's general account, P_1, may lead him to prefer the description A_1 because A_1 does follow quasi-deductively from P_1 while A_2 does not; A_2 may indeed positively conflict with it. But there may be a rival interpretation, P_2, in the field which stands in the same relation to A_2 as P_1 stands in relation to A_1. This can be represented by the following schema (IV) in which, because P_1 and P_2 are equally able to account for all the facts, we have no reason to choose between A_1, the account which P_1 requires, and A_2, the account required by P_2.

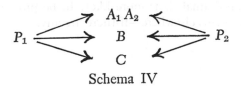

Schema IV

However, if it now occurs that an item, D, can be fitted into P_1 but not into P_2, we have a reason for preferring P_1 to P_2; and because P_1 requires A_1, we have a reason for preferring A_1 to A_2. In this way, as Schema V shows, a general interpretation of a whole stretch of history can support the historian's narrative account of some particular event.

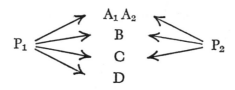

Schema V

It might be objected that the phrase "it is only to be expected that" is far too loose to characterize a relation for which explanatory power is claimed. How are such expectations formed? What makes them legitimate? The reply to these questions can only be "the detailed study of all the evidence bearing on the particular problem with which the historian is engaged." The very trite and very general generalizations which I mentioned in connection with the revolt of the Netherlands have some part of play; but the more important general statements which enter into the texture of history are not generalizations at all in the sense in which philosophers are accustomed to use that term. They are statements about the character, ambitions, or policies of particular individuals or about the characteristic ways of thought and action of particular groups or the political and economic life of a society. All of these are bounded in space and time. It is naive to suppose that men have always acted more or less as they act now; so general statements about the behavior of medieval monks or renaissance courtiers or Tory squires are not subject to confirmation or disconfirmation by twentieth-century experiment. But it does not follow that these statements are subject to no control at all; the control lies in the evidence, and, where this is copious, history can be written. If the understanding of a historical event must be likened to anything at all, it is not to the understanding of a natural phenomenon, but to the understanding of a literature. To a man puzzled as to how to interpret a passage in one of Shakespeare's plays, a wide and deep study of his other plays and those of other Elizabethan dramatists is more likely to be profitable than a survey of similar problems elsewhere—if there are any.

NOTES

1. Cf. J. H. Hexter, *Reappraisals in History*, (Longmans, Green & Co, 1961).

2. *Journal of Philosophy*, 1942. Reprinted in *Theories of History* (Ed. Patrick Gardiner) (Glencoe, Free Press, 1959)

3. *Nicomachean Ethics*. I.3.

4. *Metaphysics*, (London, Oxford University Press, 1940). Part IIIc.

5. Cf. Maurice Mandelbaum in *History and Theory*, V. 1, (1961), no. 3.

6. *Laws and Explanations in History*, (London, Oxford University Press, 1957), p. 35.

7. *Philosophy and the Historical Understanding*, (London, Chatto & Windus Ltd., 1964), p. 22.

8. *Proceedings of the Aristotelian Society*, 1956.

9. *Debates with Historians*, (London, B. B. Batsford Ltd., 1955). Chapter 9.

10. Cf. J. B. Bury, *Selected Essays*, (Cambridge University Press, 1930). Chapter 4.

11. Jonathan Cape, 1949.

CAN PHILOSOPHERS LEARN
FROM HISTORIANS?

Alan Donagan

In describing history as a science and aligning ourselves with the school of Ranke and J. B. Bury, we are doing no more than stating an ideal, to which we may cling, however unattainable in practice. . . . History is the science of men in time.—V. H. Galbraith.

In offering a paper with the title of this one, I am being impertinent, although I hope excusably. The bridge between philosophy and history must be built from both ends. To the present, philosophers have shown more zeal than historians for building it. The burden of my argument is that, in their zeal, they have been too impatient. Historians have had lessons to teach them which they have not waited to learn. Yet who am I, not a historian, to argue this? A philosopher who thinks he has learned some things from historians that most of his philosophical colleagues either reject or do not know about is in all probability deluding himself. To adapt an apology offered by Collingwood in a related connection: Not being a professional historian, I know that I am likely to make a fool of myself; but the work of bridge-building must go on.[1]

I

The last forty years have seen a reaction from the great tradition of philosophy of history begun by Dilthey and Windelband, and continued in Germany by Rickert, in Italy by Croce and Gentile, and in England by Collingwood. Philosophers nowadays tend to seek grist for their mills in sociology and psychology rather than in history, and to justify their doing so by invoking Sir Karl Popper's division of the sciences into those that are theoretical or generalizing, in which the primary interest is to establish universal laws, and those that are historical, in which the primary interest is to discover what individual events occurred and why they occurred. Since, in addition to this distinction, most philosophers

234

also accept Popper's principle that causal explanation consists at bottom in deriving a statement of the event to be explained from a statement of the occurrence of other events (the initial conditions) by means of universal laws, they inevitably conclude that in offering causal explanations truly scientific historians must draw upon the results of one or more theoretical sciences. Nor should it surprise us that, approaching history in this way, philosophers tend to identify philosophy of history with the theory of causal explanation in history.

Since it is not disputed that the results historians present and defend rarely if ever accord with the received philosophical conception, those results are presumably less than scientific. What, then, is their status? The most celebrated answer has been given by Professor Hempel:

What the explanatory analyses of historical events offer is, then, in most cases not an explanation in one of the senses indicated above, but something that might be called an *explanation sketch*. Such a sketch consists of a more or less vague indication of the laws and initial conditions considered as relevant, and it needs 'filling out' in order to turn into a full-fledged explanation.[2]

The greater part of this filling-out must be left to the theoretical social sciences; for it is obviously impossible to be precise about initial conditions unless one has precise statements of the laws by means of which the event to be explained may be derived from them. Hempel's view, then, implies that historiography will be able to provide few genuinely scientific analyses of past events until the theoretical social sciences are more highly developed.

An alternative to Hempel's austere censure has been proposed by Professor Nagel. It has become very popular, and since, prima facie, it accepts historical explanations as they are, I hope to be forgiven for dwelling on it.

According to Nagel,

[H]istorians are rarely if ever in a position to state *sufficient* conditions for the occurrence of the events they investigate. Most if not all historical explanations, like explanations of human conduct in general . . . mention only some of the *indispensable* (or, as is commonly also said *necessary*) conditions for those occurrences.[3]

In order to make palatable the fact that historians do not state initial conditions that are, according to relevant theoretical laws, sufficient conditions of the occurrences they claim to explain, Hempel declared that they offer no more than explanation sketches. Yet he did not doubt that the explanations sketched were attempts to indicate sufficient conditions. Nagel's concession that, in general, historical explanations are full-fledged and not sketches is, in fact, more radical than Hempel's denial of it; for it requires us to reinterpret most of the causal explanations that historians give.

Nagel's own illustrative example was F. W. Maitland's explanation of why, to the royal title she inherited from her sister Queen Mary I, Queen Elizabeth I of England added the curious appendage "&c." but not the style, "Supreme Head on Earth of the Church of England," which her father, King Henry VIII, had claimed, and which her sister had renounced. Maitland's explanation may be given in Nagel's words:

> [I]n order to avoid committing herself to either alternative for the moment, [both being in her judgement fraught with grave perils,] Elizabeth employed an ambiguous formulation in the proclamation of her title—a formulation which could be made compatible with any decision she might eventually make.[4]

Prima facie, this explanation has three parts. In the first, the Queen's adoption of "&c." in her title is derived from her intention to leave that title ambiguous. In the second, her intention to leave her title ambiguous is derived from her more ultimate intention to put off deciding what title she would finally adopt. And in the third, her intention to put off that decision is derived from a yet more ultimate decision not to confront, at that time, the perils with which either decision would have been fraught.

The natural interpretation of Maitland's explanation is that it purports to state why the Queen acted as she did, and not in some other way, that is, to state the *sufficient* conditions of her action. Needless to say, Maitland did not state his explanation in deductive form. A description in a school chemistry manual of how to make sulphur dioxide also purports to state the sufficient conditions for doing so; if you follow its instructions, you will make sulphur dioxide and not something else or nothing. Yet the description is not in deductive form, and it does not mention all the conditions necessary, *e.g.*, that you must set up your apparatus in an atmosphere like that of the earth. It could, however, be thrown into deductive form, provided that mention could be made of circumstances passed over in the manual as too obvious to need formal statement. If a similar concession is made for Maitland's explanation, there seems to be as little difficulty in throwing it, too, into deductive form.[5]

Why does Nagel deny this? Why can he not acknowledge the innumerable explanations of this kind that are found in the writings of historians to be statements of sufficient conditions, no less and no more deductive than the informal statements of sufficient conditions to be found in the writings of natural scientists? The answer is not far to seek: It is because he cannot bring himself to question Popper's principle that causal explanations involve universal laws. Prima facie, and I should maintain in fact, Maitland's explanation neither contains nor presupposes any universal hypothesis: the logical function of such hypotheses is discharged by statements about the Queen's intentions. But if one were utterly convinced, as Nagel is, that Maitland's explanation must presuppose a universal hypothesis, one would be constrained to agree that it is something like the one he gives, namely:

Whenever an individual is compelled to announce publicly which one of several alternative policies he is ostensibly adopting, the circumstances under which the announcement is made being such that he believes that the proclamation of a definitive commitment to one of those policies at that time to be fraught with grave perils to himself, the individual will formulate that policy in ambiguous language.[6]

Having foisted this monstrous hypothesis upon Maitland, Nagel is led into a veritable Serbonian bog. As Maitland's alleged hypothesis stands, it is false.[7] But it may be interpreted as a rough statistical generalization, although that is not its form.[8] In that case, since such a generalization will not permit the deduction of the *explanandum*, the initial conditions mentioned in the explanation cannot be sufficient conditions. At best, they are *necessary*.[9] Yet merely to state certain necessary conditions of an event is not causally to explain it. So the necessary conditions that are all historians offer as causes must be shown to be, in some respectable sense, "the most important, main, primary, chief, or principal factors." [10]

Not only antimethodological historians will have felt qualms at this. Do these problems arise from the nature of causal explanation in history? Or do they arise because the assumption I have called Popper's principle has been gratuitously invoked?

II

An important, and perfectly sound, logical point has been wrongly taken to set at rest doubts of the kinds I have been considering. As far as I know, it was first clearly stated by Professor Maurice Mandelbaum, in the first volume of the journal, *History and Theory*.[11] Independently, it has been more fully developed by Professor Morton White in his *Foundations of Historical Knowledge*.[12]

Those who hold that a causal explanation in history, fully stated, will consist of a statement of initial conditions (C) and a statement of pertinent laws (L), from which a statement of the event to be explained (E) is exhibited as following deductively, need not suppose that the laws in question will consist of the single generalization: *Whenever C then E*. Mandelbaum has reminded us that when a natural scientist explains a natural phenomenon—for example, that a fire left burning in a certain room went out in two hours, even though it did not lack fuel —by pointing out that the room was airtight, the laws he invokes are not about fire or air as such, but about the rate of oxidation of certain fuels at certain temperatures in certain kinds of atmosphere, and about the composition of ordinary air, and especially about the amount of oxygen in it.[13] By analogy, Mandelbaum argued, when a historian maintains that initial conditions described as being of the kind C are sufficient conditions for the occurrence of an event of the kind E, it would be simple-minded to infer that his explanation rests on a law that merely generalizes the explanation itself, namely, *Whenever an event of the kind C occurs, an event of the kind E will occur.* The laws for which historians look to social scientists are as little likely to be generalizations from historical explanations as those for which we all look to natural scientists are generalizations from everyday explanations of natural phenomena.

There is, however, a difference between the two kinds of explanation. In the example of the fire left burning in an airtight room, provided that the room is empty but for the burning fire and air, the generalization that can be constructed from the everyday explanation is true; namely, that if a room is airtight, a fire left burning in it will go out sooner or later, even if there is no lack of fuel. Not only is it true, but it can be deduced from the laws of chemistry. The generalizations that can be extracted from historical explanations, however, are in general false. We have already remarked Nagel's admission that the generalization he constructed from Maitland's explanation of Queen Elizabeth's use of "&c." in her title, which he acknowledged to be false as it stands, is in this respect characteristic of historical explanations generally.

White has proposed an ingenious variation on the kind of consideration advanced by Mandelbaum. Maitland's explanation of Queen Elizabeth's use of "&c." in her title may be interpreted, conformably with Nagel's analysis, as what Professor White would call a statement of a contributory cause. It is of the form:

(1)　*a* was *P*,

Therefore,
(2)　*a* was *Q*;

but, since "*a* was *P*" is only a contributory cause, the generalization:

Whatever is *P* is *Q*,

which is presupposed if the explanation as given is to be deductive, is false. Yet it is possible to suppose that Maitland, in advancing his explanation, thought that there were other contributory causes, to the totality of which we may refer as "*a* was *K*," such that the following would be a valid explanatory argument with true premises:

(1) Whatever is *K* and *P*, is *Q*.

(2) *a* was *K*.

(3) *a* was *P*.

Therefore,
(4) *a* was *Q*.

Even though only (3) and (4) are known by the historian to be true, and even though he cannot even formulate (1) or (2), he may have good reason to believe that (1) and (2) can be found. As stated, (1) is a mere generalization from the explanation and is therefore unlikely to be a law in any of the theoretical social sciences; but it may be deducible from laws the social sciences may one day establish. White's contention is that a historian may be able to give good reasons for concluding that his statement about a contributory cause of an event is part of a deductive explanatory argument, some of which, including the relevant laws, is unknown to him.[14]

I shall not go thoroughly into Professor White's discussion of what such reasons are. The chief one he mentions is this. A historical event (say, Queen Elizabeth I's addition of "&c." to the title she inherited from her sister) is explained as having a certain contributory cause (that by using "&c." the Queen left uncertain whether or not she would claim a title used by her father, which her sister had renounced). It is quite clear that any generalization by means of which a statement of the event to be explained can be deduced from this statement of a contributory cause, is false. A further contributory cause must therefore be sought; one mentioned by Maitland is that it would have been politically dangerous for the Queen either to have claimed or to have renounced her father's title. This addition is an advance, for the probability that somebody in a situation like the Queen's in respect of *both* putative contributory causes will act as she did is considerably higher than the probability that somebody will so act in a situation like the Queen's in respect of the first putative contributory cause alone.

Professor White contends that, the more contributory causes a historian can find, the more reason he has to infer that an explanatory deductive argument incorporates premises stating them. His reasoning is straightforward. Of a given set of contributory causes of an event of a certain kind, the generalization connecting all the members of that set with an event of that kind is necessarily of a higher probability than a generalization connecting the event with only a subset of those causes. When historians add to their explanations more and more premises about contributory causes, if they find that the probability of the generalization connecting *explanans* with *explanandum* becomes higher and higher, they are entitled to conclude that the limit of this process is a generalization with a probability of one, that is, a generalization that is true in all cases.

Two objections to Professor White's position call for consideration. The first arises from the interpretation already given of Nagel's example from Maitland. If that interpretation is sound, Professor White has confounded parts of a complex explanation in terms of intentions and situational judgements with statements of contributory causes in the manner of a natural science. It is, of course, true that as you give more and more of an explanation in terms of intentions and situational judgments, you make it possible to construct from your explanation generalizations of higher and higher probability. But the limit of this process is not, like the limit of the process of adding more and more statements of contributory causes, an explanation from which a true universal hypothesis can be constructed. Rather, it is an explanation in which the full statement of intentions and relevant judgments entails a statement of the event to be explained without the mediation of any generalization at all.

Let me briefly illustrate by a slightly simplified version of Maitland's explanation. Suppose it had been formulable as follows:

> (1) In November 1558 (henceforth, "at t"), being determined to be proclaimed Queen, Elizabeth knew that she must then decide under what title she should be proclaimed.

> (2) At t, Elizabeth was aware that she would at that time offend the Protestants by not adopting her father's title, "Supreme Head on Earth of the Church of England," and the Catholics, by adopting it.

> (3) At t, she resolved to postpone offending either, if that were both possible and consistent with more important considerations. (This itself requires explanation, which Maitland gave.)

> (4) At t, she judged that it would be possible to postpone offending either, but only by substituting an ambiguous phrase like "&c." in place of her father's contentious title.

(5) At *t*, she judged that such a solution would at that time be consistent with any other considerations that were more important. (Maitland went further into this.)

Therefore

(6) At *t*, Queen Elizabeth decided, in the title under which she would be proclaimed, to substitute an ambiguous phrase like "&c." in place of "Supreme Head on Earth of the Church of England."

I can discern no deductive chasm between the premise set (1), (2), (3), (4) and (5), and the conclusion (6), that must be bridged by a general law. I have no objection to adding that Elizabeth was a princess in sound health, but I think it superfluous: By introducing a given individual without a warning to the contrary, a historian gives his readers to understand that that individual functions normally for an individual of that kind (in this case, a woman), just as a natural scientist, in mentioning a piece of apparatus without a warning to the contrary, gives his readers to understand that it functions normally. Although it is true that between (6) and any subset of the premise set (1), (2), (3), (4), and (5), there is a logical gap, and also that any generalization by which that gap is bridged would be at best probabilistic, when the premise set is complete there is *no* logical gap. Hence any generalization constructed in order to bridge the nonexistent gap would be, not a law, but a superfluous tautology.[15]

III

The second difficulty in Professor White's position that ought to be mentioned does not presuppose my own interpretation of historical explanations like Nagel's example from Maitland. It has to do with the conception of man from which White's theory springs. That conception has been eloquently stated by Professor May Brodbeck in the General Introduction to her valuable anthology, *Readings in the Philosophy of the Social Sciences*.

Two centuries have passed since the vision of a science of man first fired the imaginations of the great social critics of the Enlightenment. Seeing man as part of the natural order, they envisaged a science of man and society, modeled on Newton's explanation of heaven and earth, by whose application the potentialities of man could be realized to form a more just and humane social order . . . . [I]n essence the vision has withstood all challenges.[16]

What challenges has it withstood? For an answer, we must look into the conception of man that "the great social critics of the Enlightenment" assailed.

Seeing man as part of the natural order, as the Enlightenment critics did, is at bottom seeing what men do as natural processes explicable
according to natural laws. It is, in Professor Richard Taylor's words, to
apply to the causal explanation of human action the principle of the uniformity of causation, "that the causal relations between changes or
states can be expressed in the form of general laws."[17] The pre-Enlightenment view of man, like the pre-Enlightenment view of causation, rejected the principle of uniformity. A cause (i.e., an efficient cause) was
conceived as something that had the power to produce a particular effect, and exercised it.[18] In this earlier, "metaphysical" sense of cause,
causes are not uniform: the cause of a statue's coming into existence
from a stone block is that a sculptor equipped with appropriate tools exercised his power to carve that block; but it is not implied that whenever a sculptor, his tools, and suitable material are brought together, a
statue is produced. Some causes necessarily exercise their power; thus,
fire cannot but heat cooler things to which it is applied. Other causes, in
particular human beings, angels, and God, choose whether or not to exercise their powers.

The pre-Enlightenment, nonuniformitarian conception of causation
has proved tenacious; it has never been extirpated from the speech and
thought of ordinary folk; and, powerfully advocated by philosophers like
Taylor, it is reappearing in philosophical discourse. The implications of
this for White's theory are plain.

The Enlightenment conception of the nature of man incorporates
the doctrine that, for every human action, there is an explanatory deductive argument involving laws, whether it is known or not. Hence, if the
Enlightenment conception be true, White's case for interpreting existing historical explanations as approximations to such explanatory deductive arguments is very strong. On the other hand, if the pre-Enlightenment conception of the nature of man is acknowledged to be a serious
possibility, his case is comparatively weak. Why interpret explanations
that contain no laws as approximations to explanations that do, if it is
possible that explanations of the kind in question do not accord with the
principle of uniformity? [19]

What could establish the existence, for all human acts, of explanatory deductive arguments involving laws? Or, in other words, what could
establish the Enlightenment conception of a science of man, and with
it, Popper's principle? I can think of nothing that would do it, except
the kind of thing that established the Newtonian conception of a science of nature: namely, in some department of human studies, to *discover* laws, and to construct explanatory deductive arguments that rest
on them. In face of such a discovery, the pre-Enlightenment conception

of how to study man would collapse, as Cartesian physics collapsed in face of "Newton's explanation of heaven and earth."

In the absence of such discoveries, which neither Professor White nor Professor Brodbeck nor any other serious philosopher claims have been made, how can Professor Brodbeck declare that "in essence the [Enlightenment] vision has withstood all challenges?" Far from withstanding all challenges, I submit that it has not withstood any serious challenge at all: its supporters imagine it to have done so, because they have failed to notice that they would consider nothing a challenge to it, except a proof of inconsistency. Apart from the implausible charge of inconsistency, what challenges could be offered to the Enlightenment ideal except the two that have been: that history, and successful research into human affairs generally, does not accord with it; and that no example of a complete explanation according to the Enlightenment ideal exists? Yet these are both simply denied to be challenges. Research that does not accord with the Enlightenment ideal is dismissed as unscientific:

There are clearly two factions within the social disciplines [Professor Brodbeck writes]. One of them exuberantly embraces the scientific ideal; the other exalts its own intuitive understanding as being superior in logic and in principle to scientific explanation of the ways of man.[20]

Passing over this description of "the other faction," we need only note that the Enlightenment ideal has ceased to be questionable; it has become "the scientific ideal." But philosophers like Dilthey, Rickert, Croce, and Collingwood did not repudiate the scientific ideal; they put forward anti-Enlightenment opinions about its nature. As for the objection that the Enlightenment ideal has not, in two centuries, led to successful research that satisfies its own conditions, that is dismissed by Professor Brodbeck as "irrelevant sniping at unfulfilled promise."[21] It is not denied that "as yet social science [in the Enlightenment manner] only barely deserves the name of science."[22] What matter? One day it will, and even if it does not, nothing else would be science.

Except for general philosophical arguments in support of a naturalist metaphysics, the Enlightenment vision of a science of man has at present little to commend it. Defenses of it that eschew such general arguments have an unmistakable air of *petitio principii*.[23] It need surprise nobody that historians tend to have what Professor Leonard Krieger has called "a visceral reaction against . . . 'the covering law theory' . . . which, rightly or wrongly [they] view as supra- or trans-historical, and consequently as a species of academic imperialism by the mother country of all the sciences."[24] If philosophers have provoked this hostility by

showing themselves to be, in Krieger's harsh but just words, "interested
. . . in the remains rather than the views of historians," [25] the remedy
is in their own hands.

IV

So far, I have discussed chiefly the views of my fellow philosophers,
and my theme has been that philosophical mistakes about history are
being made because philosophers have persisted in theorizing in terms
of preconceptions they have been unwilling to reconsider in view of
what historians say and do. The preconception that has been my example is Popper's principle about the nature of causal explanation. I propose now to turn to some other philosophical topics on which historians
have shed light.

History and Narrative.

That the principal aim of history is to produce true narratives of
what actually happened in the past has been accepted as a truism by
philosophers of widely divergent opinions: it is at the heart of W. B.
Gallie's and A. C. Danto's [26] recent books, and it is sympathetically
treated by Morton White.[27] It has been usefully questioned by Maurice
Mandelbaum, to whose work I am indebted.[28] The advocate of the conception of historiography as the writing of narrative whom I shall consider is, however, not a philosopher, but a historian, Professor J. H.
Hexter.

In a forcible paper, "The Rhetoric of History," Professor Hexter
laid down two rules for writing history:

> (1) Historians are concerned and committed to tell about the
> past the best and most likely story that can be sustained by the
> relevant extrinsic evidence (the Reality Rule).[29]

> (2) Historians should place in footnotes evidence and informa-
> tion which, if inserted in the text, diminish the impact of what
> they, as historians, aim to convey (the Maximum Impact
> Rule).[30]

I do not think that anybody will question that these are sound rules for
narrating past happenings, whether in books, or even in articles in the
American Historical Review. And if historiography in this sense were
what analytical philosophy of history is properly about, I think we
should be constrained to agree with Professor Hexter that a "paradigm-
shift" in our understanding of it is now due.[31]

Even among historians there is a view opposed to Hexter's, according to which the concern of a historian is to inquire into the past rather than to write the best and most likely story about it that can be sustained by the relevant evidence. The sacred text for this other view is Lord Acton's advice to his fellow students in his Inaugural Lecture, "Study problems in preference to periods." [32] It is, indeed, not accidental that the "great, mute" [33] Acton, who could not seriously begin, much less complete, his projected *History of Liberty*, should have exalted inquiry over narration, and should have declared that "John Hunter spoke for all of us [i.e., all historians] when he said: 'Never ask me what I have said or what I have written; but if you will ask me what my present opinions are, I will tell you.'" [34]

In any generation, there is a large and growing deposit of established historical fact; and every historian must know at least that part of it which bears on his inquiries. The deposit of established fact, however, seldom if ever suffices for the construction of a historical narrative of any complex event of major significance. Hence, in constructing a narrative, especially on a large scale, a historian must combine what has been established by others with his own discoveries, and also with much that he cannot show to be true or even probable. As common readers, we value large scale narratives by good historians, not because we delude ourselves into thinking of all they contain as true or probably true, but because what a good historian has concluded to be "the best and most likely story that can be sustained by the extrinsic evidence" is more likely to be true than the productions of his inferiors. Even after it has been superseded, other historians value the work of a great narrative historian (e.g., Ranke or Henry Adams or S. R. Gardiner), as a fertile source of ideas for further research.

In Acton's view, the proper fruit of historical research is not a narrative, but a study of a problem or complex of problems. A recent book by another distinguished historian, Professor V. H. Galbraith,[35] persuasively seconds Acton:

We can, with Bury, indignantly deny that history is a branch of literature, even while we are legitimately envious of our brother historians whose works run into several editions. . . . The study of history is a personal activity— it is an individual reading the sources of history for himself. . . . Its essential value lies in the shock and excitement aroused by the impact of the very ways and thought of the past upon the mind, and it is for this reason that actual original documents—themselves a physical survival of that past —exercise such fascination. . . . The purpose [of lectures and textbooks] is to lead the student himself to the sources, from the study of which whatever power our writing and talking have is derived. Where this object is not achieved, we have failed.[36]

The conception of history as discerning and solving problems by the use of "actual physical survivals" of the past, as research rather than its descendant at a second remove—the construction of narratives, may be caricatured as dry-as-dust pedantry. Yet accounts of research are embedded in most classical narratives, from that of Herodotus to the present. Sir Winston Churchill's *Marlborough, His Life and Times* is absorbingly readable throughout its great length. I think I am not alone in finding it most absorbing, except for three great battle pieces, when (in Chapters 21, 22, and 25 in the first volume) Churchill abandons narrative for a study of the nature of the Carte Collection of Jacobite papers in the Bodleian library, and particularly of the misnamed "Camaret Bay Letter." In Chapters 21 and 22, Churchill demonstrates that the Jacobite papers in the Carte Collection are a set of secret service memoranda; that one of their functions was to further intrigues within the exiled Jacobite court, especially by supporting the claims of this or that Jacobite minister to influence in England; and that purported decodings of cipher communications containing the alleged texts of letters from English notables are not reliable evidence that such letters ever existed. In Chapter 25, Churchill adds a powerful argument, which he acknowledges to fall short of a legal proof, that one such text (allegedly of a French translation of a cipher letter from Marlborough betraying a military operation) was a deliberate fraud designed to raise the credit of one of the Jacobite ministers by demonstrating his influence with Marlborough.

I suggest it is not an accident that the books by historians that make the most difference to other historians are characteristically *not* narratives with footnote references in justification, but historical analyses of evidence that is described, if not quoted, in the text.

History and Epistemology.

Galbraith's view of the nature of history prompts a criticism different from Hexter's of the "precise, accurate, and logical jabbing" [37] of analytical philosophers at history. The topic in philosophy of history that has "exercise[d] a fateful fascination" [38] upon analytical philosophers has been historical explanation. Historians do indeed give explanations, and causal explanations. Churchill's study of the papers in the Carte Collection is full of them. But they emerge from studies of problems arising from documents and other evidence (e.g., archaeological relics), almost as by-products. They are not, as a rule, what a historian *explicitly* offers to prove, or at least gives strong grounds for accepting. Hence it is not altogether implausible (although I think it mistaken) to put them down as incomplete until the results of the theoretical social sciences are in.

We find a considerable difference when we turn from the explanations embedded in historians' writings—out of which, as Professor Hexter complains, analytical philosophers "hack" them—to historians' claims to establish a certain past fact from evidence. There is no question of "hacking" Churchill's claims about the Camaret Bay Letter from a flow of narrative; it is left outside that flow by Churchill himself. The same is true of the illustrative specimen of historical research in Part III of Galbraith's *Introduction to the Study of History*, a lively piece with the unexciting title, "Who Wrote Asser's Life of Alfred?" To go no further: both Churchill and Galbraith claim to prove certain conclusions. To give some examples:

Here we have the fact established upon unimpeachable and responsible authority that King James's Memoirs ended at the Restoration in 1660 (Churchill).[39]

[I]t is certain that no such letter in Marlborough's handwriting ever reached Saint-Germains (Churchill).[40]

There can still be two opinions as to whether it was Leofric who wrote [Asser's] Life [of Alfred]. But the discussion of this narrower problem has at least shown that the author of the Life lived more than a century after Alfred's death (Galbraith).[41]

These are all claims to have *demonstrated* something: to have attained knowledge. There can be no question of treating them as incomplete, as awaiting the results of any other science. Yet for only the first is there a direct statement in a document, and both Churchill and Galbraith would laugh at the suggestion that all direct statements in documents are true. Where, in the writings of contemporary epistemology, is one to look for an analysis of these knowledge-claims?

I hope to be forgiven for stating, in the spirit of Newton's queries, three theses:

(1) All three of the above knowledge-claims are true.

(2) In demonstrating their truth, both Churchill and Galbraith employed or presupposed hypotheses about the intentions and judgements of those who wrote certain documents, or caused them to be written, and of others; without such hypotheses, it would be impossible to demonstrate their truth.

(3) In their demonstrations, neither Churchill nor Galbraith employed or presupposed any law of human behavior.

Were these three theses to be established, the solution of the problem of the nature of causal explanation in history would be a matter of routine.

Fact and Theory in History.

I have alluded to both Churchill's and Galbraith's claims to have established certain facts about the past; and I have pointed out that neither imagined that such claims could be made good simply by finding a document, official or otherwise, in which a sentence occurs which states the fact in question. The following remarks by Galbraith sufficiently refute the delusion that historians can simply accept as fact what they find in records:

Records, in fact, can no more be taken at their face value than chronicles. . . . Magna Carta, issued as the free grant of King John to his subjects, was in fact a treaty between the king and his barons, which the king at least never meant to observe. . . . The facts regarding the deposition of Richard II in 1399 were obscured by a too simple reliance on the official *Rolls of Parliament,* which at this moment are a partisan compilation intended to justify his successor, Henry IV.[42]

How then, is it possible for historians to extract truth even out of public records? Again, I go to Galbraith for an answer:

in using records as evidence, we have to subject them to a sensitive criticism which seeks to discover the materials behind them, *and the impression they were intended to produce.* Indeed, speaking very roughly, it will be found that most records—from Acts of Parliament to balance sheets of public companies and diplomatic notes—have some sort of bias of their own, and seek to conceal the truth or part of it. The result of the vast extension of research by the use of official documents has thus been to make the writing of history more difficult but very much more exciting.[43]

Historians can extract the truth from documents by forming hypotheses about "the materials behind them, and the impression they were intended to produce" that fit *all* the available evidence better than any alternative. Both constructing such hypotheses, and relating them to the evidence available, are difficult and delicate operations. Sometimes the results of such operations are quite certain; more often, they are highly probable.

To those who find it hard to believe that anything as purely intellectual as the "sensitive criticism" of which Galbraith speaks could ever extract hard fact from subtly falsified documents, the best answer I know is found at the close of Dashiell Hammett's great detective novel, *The Thin Man.* Hearing of the solution of the crime, reached by elaborate theorizing, the detective's wife responds, "Then you're not sure;"

he replies, *inter alia,* "Now don't say we're not sure. It doesn't make any sense otherwise." When a historian is in a position to say that, his work is done.

NOTES

1. Cf., R. G. Collingwood, *The Idea of Nature* (Oxford, Clarendon Press, 1945), p. 3. Collingwood was speaking of the philosophy of science, and his remark began, "Not being a professional scientist. . . ."

2. Carl G. Hempel, *Aspects of Scientific Explanation* (New York and London, The Free Press 1965), p. 238. For a valuable comment, see Morton White, *The Foundations of Historical Knowledge* (New York and London, Harper and Row, 1965), pp. 89–90.

3. Ernest Nagel, *The Structure of Science* (New York and Burlingame, Harcourt, Brace and World, 1961), p. 559.

4. Nagel, *op. cit.,* p. 552. Maitland's explanation was accepted by J. B. Black, *The Reign of Elizabeth,* (Oxford, 1936). Black furnishes this note: "The '&c.' had indeed been used by Mary until Wyatt's rebellion; but with the opposite intention, i.e. as a "means of dropping the supreme headship" (*ibid.,* 8n).

5. See section II of this paper. I have argued for a similar conclusion about an artificial example, in "Historical Explanation: the Popper-Hempel Theory Reconsidered," (*History and Theory,* 4 (1964–5), 1–26; reprinted with slight alterations in W. H. Dray (ed.) *Philosophical Analysis and History* (New York, 1966), 127–59). I go into the matter more thoroughly, and in connexion with historical examples, in "Alternative Historical Explanations and Their Verification," *The Monist,* 53 (1969), pp. 58–89. A different, but related and suggestive, analysis of Nagel's example is given by Michael Scriven in W. H. Dray (ed.), *Philosophical Analysis and History,* 246–50, 255.

6. Nagel, *op. cit.,* p. 556.
7. *Ibid.*
8. Nagel, *op. cit.,* p. 557.
9. Nagel, *op. cit.,* p. 559.
10. Nagel, *op. cit.,* p. 582.
11. Maurice Mandelbaum, "Historical Explanation: the Problem of Covering Laws," *History and Theory,* V. I (1961).
12. Morton White, *The Foundations of Historical Knowledge* (New York and London, Harper and Row, 1965).
13. This is, strictly speaking, not a law; but it makes no difference.
14. White, *op. cit.,* pp. 84–91.
15. For further discussion of this point, see Charles Taylor, *The Explanation of Behaviour* (London, 1964), p. 33.
16. May Brodbeck, *Readings in the Philosophy of the Social Sciences* (New York and London, Macmillan, 1968), p. 1.
17. Richard Taylor, "Causation," in Paul Edwards, ed., *The Encyclopedia of Philosophy* (New York and London, Macmillan and the Free Press, 1967), V. II, p. 57b. Cf. Richard Taylor, "Causation," *The Monist,* No. 47 (1963–64), pp. 287–8, 292–6.
18. *Encyclopedia of Philosophy,* V. II, p. 58; *Monist,* No. 47 (1963–64), pp. 287–91.
19. Richard Taylor explores these matters in *Action and Purpose* (Englewood

Cliffs, Prentice-Hall, 1966), esp. Ch. 7, Sect. entitled "How an Important Question is Begged," pp. 95–6.

20. Brodbeck, *op. cit.*, p. 2.

21. Brodbeck, *op. cit.*, p. 2.

22. Brodbeck, *op. cit.*, p. 2.

23. A recent example is Leon J. Goldstein, "Theory and History," *Philosophy of Science*, V. 34 (1967), pp. 23–40. The following is characteristic: "If Mrs. Woodham Smith is right about what factors led to the climactic events at Balaclava, *it is clear enough* that there must be sociological and psychological regularities in terms of which it is these factors rather than others that are relevant" (*loc. cit.*, pp. 37–8, my italics). Professor Goldstein freely concedes that Mrs. Woodham Smith asserts no such regularities; but that they exist "*is clear enough*." Argument is superfluous.

24. Leonard Krieger, "Comments on Historical Explanation," in Sidney Hook, ed., *Philosophy and History* (New York, New York University Press 1963), pp. 136–7.

25. Krieger, *loc. cit.*, p. 136. The context makes plain that the "views of historians" that he has in mind are their views about what they do as historians.

26. W. B. Gallie, *Philosophy and the Historical Understanding* (New York, Shockens Books, 1964), and A. C. Danto, *Analytical Philosophy of History* (Cambridge, Cambridge University Press, 1965).

27. White, *op. cit.*, Ch. 6, esp., pp. 220–1.

28. Maurice Mandelbaum, "A Note on History as Narrative," in *History and Theory*, IV. 6, (1967), pp. 413–19. Mandelbaum employs a narrow conception of narrative as "linear," which restricts the scope of his conclusions.

29. J. H. Hexter, "The Rhetoric of History," *History and Theory*, V. 6 (1967), p. 5.

30. Hexter, *loc. cit.*, p. 6.

31. Hexter, *loc. cit.*, pp. 12–3.

32. John, Lord Acton, *Essays on Freedom and Power*, sel. and ed. Gertrude Himmelfarb (New York, Meridian Books, 1955), p. 48. Collingwood described this as "Lord Acton's great precept" in *The Idea of History* (Oxford, 1946), p. 281.

33. The gibe is by Sir Winston Churchill, *Marlborough, His Life and Times* (in two volumes, London, 1947), Vol. I, p. 874 (in Vol. II, Ch. 21, of the original edition).

34. Acton, *op. cit.*, p. 45.

35. Galbraith's only large scale book is *The Making of Domesday Book* (1961), although he has written many articles and lesser studies. His *Introduction to the Use of the Public Records* and *An Introduction to the Study of History* (London, 1964) offer much food for philosophical as well as historical thought.

36. V. H. Galbraith, *Introduction to the Study of History* (London, Hillary, 1964), pp. 60–2.

37. Hexter, *loc. cit.*, p. 12.

38. Hexter, *loc. cit.*

39. Churchill, *op. cit.*, V. I, p. 319.

40. Churchill, *op. cit.*, V. I, p. 379. This statement, it should be noted, is distinct from Churchill's further statement that Marlborough did not betray the Camaret Bay expedition, for which he claims only high probability.

41. *Introduction to the Study of History*, p. 128.

42. *Introduction*, 13.

43. *Ibid.*, pp. 13–14 (my italics).

ON IMPORTANCE IN HISTORY
W. H. Dray

I

In his already well-known book, *Foundations of Historical Knowledge*,[1] Morton White has given new life to an old philosophical question about history: what follows for our assessment of the "objectivity" of historical accounts, from the fact that, in writing the history of anything whatever, historians do, and must, *select* from what they know to be true about their chosen subjects. What I have to say in this paper has arisen from my response to part of his own answer to this question.

In approaching his chosen question, White distinguishes, usefully I think, between two orders of facts one might expect to find in any work that aims to narrate the history *of* something such as a nation or society.[2] The first he calls the "charter members" of the history, or of its underlying chronicle: those facts which are offered as somehow central or basic to the subject being treated. In a short history of the United States, White suggests, these might be such occurrences as the Revolution, the Civil War, the First World War, the Depression, and the Second World War. The second order of facts consists of those whose status is derivative from the first, notably those which are causes and effects of the basic facts, reference to which helps to round out a continuous and more significant historical narrative. The sorts of grounds which a historian might have for including the basic facts, White holds, would be different from those needed to justify the inclusion of the derivative ones; and he goes on to distinguish and label a number of possible views as to what these ought to be.[3]

Thus, on what he calls the principle of aestheticism, what should be preferred is what is most interesting or aesthetically pleasing; on the principle of abnormalism, what is most unusual or bizarre; on the principle of moralism, what is morally instructive; on the principle of pragma-

251

tism, what is useful in relation to present problems; on the principle of essentialism, what constitutes the "main tendencies" or "essential nature" of the subject; on the principle of encyclopaedism, what comes closest to expressing the whole truth about it; and on the principle of modified encyclopaedism, what best organizes all available evidence pertaining to the subject. With the possible exception of essentialism, because of the difficulty of giving a clear meaning to the notion of "main tendencies"—which he views as a hangover from a metaphysical view of the "essence" of the individual—White holds that historians use principles of all these diverse sorts. He himself is content simply to accept what he finds; and he confesses in the end, to "pluralism" about the basis on which facts are admissible into a historical account.

The analysis which White gives of the principles of selection to be found in historical work strikes me as being a fruitful one. And as the rest of this paper will show clearly enough, I am far from wanting to object to his conclusion that the historian's own value judgments may not only influence his results, but also have an indispensable structural role to play in determining them. Two aspects of what White says, however, I find both hard to accept and also a little surprising, in view of the direction of several of his own earlier attempts to treat the same fundamental question about history.

The first of these is his conceding that, although some of the principles reviewed, like encyclopaedism, have at least objectivist tendencies, by contrast, say, with overtly subjectivist ones like aestheticism, there is no basis for regarding one principle of selection as more appropriate or fundamental in historical work than another, or as coming closer to expressing what is involved in a piece of writing's counting as a history of its subject at all. This accords ill with his earlier and surely more acceptable doctrine that a history written, let us say, on a purely aesthetic principle of selection—where this means aiming at what White himself calls a "pleasing effect," or even a "genial summary"—would be open to a charge of trivality.[4] For it would fail to take seriously the historian's obligation to get as close as possible to saying what a past period of his subject was really like, or to construct, at any rate, something which could conscientiously be offered as a "representative" account of it.

It also seems odd to me that, in giving historians a carte blanche for their principles of selection as he does, White should give the appearance at least, of arguing that a historian's selecting his facts with a view, say, to teaching moral lessons, or to helping to solve problems of the present—other than the present problem of finding out what the past was like—could be the features of his work that make his constructions better *as works of history*. Surely no philosophical theory of the selective aspects of historical enquiry can afford thus to ignore the difference between history and *uses* of history, no matter how legitimate some of those uses may be held to be. On this point, it seems to me that philosophers like Michael Oakeshott, who insist on a distinction between the historical and the practical "pasts"—between viewing the past for its own sake and viewing it for the sake of the present—are on sounder ground, although it may be necessary to reject some of the strange conclusions they sometimes try to draw from this.[5]

The second surprising feature of White's account is the total absence from it of any consideration of what he had previously recommended as the objectivist criterion of selection par excellence: the so-called criterion of "causal fertility." The historian, he had then claimed, should select the facts which have the greatest "causal significance." [6] It is not entirely clear to me how White thought the employment of this principle of selection would ensure that a historian's account would, in some important way, be more "representative" of its subject, although he did claim this to be the case. Nor am I certain that I have correctly understood the construction he himself intended to place upon the metaphor of "causal fertility." His own brief explication suggests an analogy, but nothing more than this, with the way in which one set of axioms in mathematics might be more deductively fertile than another. But one very natural interpretation to place upon the notion would be that the significance of an event in history is to be judged with reference to its consequences. It is by selecting in this way, it may be said, that the historian will make sure that what he tells us is something *of consequence.*

Such a view of what should govern selection in history is, in fact, often expressed in philosophical writing. According to J. H. Randall, Jr., for example, "the 'meaning' of any historical fact is . . . what consequences follow from it." [7] According to Arthur Danto, "to ask for the significance of an event, in the *historical* sense of the term" is to ask "with what different sets of *later* events it may be connected." [8] Charles Frankel seems even more clearly to have had something like White's fertility principle in mind when he claimed that one of the chief reasons for choosing what he called "terminal consequences" for a history—perhaps the only facts to which *he* would have conceded the status of charter members—is that they are the "most pregnant in still further consequences." He goes on to elucidate this notion with the image of some events having more causal lines "radiating out" from them than others.[9] It should be noted that if something like this is what is envisaged by the "causal fertility" principle, White's not mentioning it in his more recent statement cannot simply be attributed to his having distinguished the derivative facts—which *are* said to owe their place to their causal roles—from the basic ones. For although we might want to say, for example that the Dred Scott decision is a derivative fact, since it belongs to a history of the United States only because it was one of the causes of the outbreak of the American Civil War, we could also plausibly insist that the Civil War itself has to be included among the basic facts because it was an event with such tremendous consequences.

There is an implication behind the latter sort of claim that I miss in White's more recent review of the principles of selection in history: the implication that a historical account, although it may do other things, ought at least to tell us what is important about its subject. We are doubtless grateful when a historian tells us something interesting; we may excuse him when he lapses occasionally into sermonizing; we may be wary, suspecting distortion, when he directs our attention almost exclusively to those elements of the past which bear directly on present problems. But we should simply not know what to make of it if, while still insisting that he was recounting the history of a nation or society, he made no attempt to contrast what was important in it with what was not, and to construct his narrative accordingly. It is true that White, later in his book, talks from time to time about historians making judgments of importance. But the only principle of selection on his list that at all suggests this commonplace about the historian's task is the very one he finds most dubious—the essentialist requirement that the historian should search out the main trends or essential features. I should therefore like to see what happens if we nudge the discussion of historical selection more directly towards the question of what the criterion of importance in historical thinking is. And in this connection, I should like especially to explore the claim that what should guide historians above all in the construction of their narratives is their judgments of what is *causally* important.

II

That historians can, and should employ some notion of causal importance as a basis of selection seems to me scarcely open to question. But can we go further, as the earlier White apparently did, and claim that this kind of importance is the only kind to be recognized in the construction of a history? Or could we say, at least, as Danto appears to do, that this is the only kind justifying our calling an event *historically* important?

In answer to the first of these questions, one obvious move would be to point out that causal importance, being a relational notion, makes the importance of the selected event, say, the Civil War, depend on the importance of something else, causally related to it—for example, the legacy of bitterness in the South. For it seems odd to suggest that an event could be important by virtue of its being related to things that were not themselves important. But if the importance-conferring consequences must also be important, either they, or some consequences of theirs, will presumably have to be so in some different, non-relational sense, which, following general practice, we might call *intrinsic*. It seems to be on the basis of reflection of this sort that Danto, for example, concedes that historical importance ultimately presupposes *non*historical importance. The argument here would not show, incidentally, that the later events and conditions whose importance gives an earlier event its historical importance must lie within the particular history into which the earlier event is to be selected. It would not show, therefore, that the historian's use of a relational notion of importance commits him logically to *selecting* any events for their nonrelational importance. Indeed, the events whose intrinsic importance is considered to confer historical importance *could* all lie within the historian's own present. However, we might well suspect the standard of value of any historian who wrote on such a myopic assumption.

It thus seems reasonable to expect that a historian's selection of charter members because of their causal importance would normally give him grounds for selecting other elements of his history because of their intrinsic importance—such as continuing Southern bitterness, perhaps, in the case of the Civil War. But I should want to claim, too, that what is taken to warrant the inclusion of a charter member of a narrative would often be the recognition that *it* was important, quite apart from such considerations. Thus, to use one of Danto's examples, the place of Vico in the history of European thought is secure in spite of the fact that his influence was meager. And even where events clearly *do* belong in a history because of the consequences they had—like the Civil War in a history of the United States—it is often not very plausible to maintain that their title rests on this consideration alone. A charter member of a historical narrative could have a mixed title. And perhaps most do.

It is not easy to say anything very illuminating, of a general sort, about the way judgments of intrinsic importance enter into historical selection. It may be useful to draw a distinction, however, between two levels at which such judgments may have to be made in constructing the sort of history White has in mind.

At the first level, what is involved is selection of *kinds of human activities and experiences* that are judged to be important in themselves. The shift in historical writing from a concern chiefly with the activities of governing classes to a concern with the way of life of ordinary men, which has been pointed to by W. H. Walsh in this connection, illustrates a change of judgment at this level.[10] So does the shift, from emphasis on political affairs to emphasis on economic ones. The latter shift *could*, of course, result not from changed judgments about the relative intrinsic importance of economic and political life, but rather from changes of explanatory theory on the historian's part. If he has become a convert to the economic interpretation, for example, his selection of economic materials into a history might reveal a change only in judgments of *causal* importance, which could affect his choice both of its derivative and of its charter members. The selection of predominantly economic materials could also simply reflect a historian's decision to write an economic rather than a political history of the nation or society he was concerned with, in which case we could not conclude from what he wrote—as we could if he had offered it as *the* history of the nation or society—that he regarded economic affairs as more important intrinsically. But the need to distinguish history written, say, with an economic view of what is intrinsically important both from history written on an economic interpretation, and from economic history, does not imply that the economic historian, in his turn, would have no judgment of intrinsic importance to make—in this case, about various aspects of economic affairs. Judgments of intrinsic importance, in other words, although not judgments of relational importance, are nevertheless properly made relative to the chosen scope of particular histories. In the case of White's basic historian of the United States, a general history appears to be the aim. If so, it seems fair to say that his choice of charter members indicates a strongly political conception of what is intrinsically important.

The second level at which historians may make judgments of intrinsic importance is in the selection of *particular actions, events or conditions* within the chosen areas of human experience: the selection, say, of Roman administration because it was efficient, or the court life of Louis XIV because it was elegant, or Victorian hymn-singing because it was devout, or the anti-Semitism of the Nazis because it was daemonic. White, of course, is quite aware that value judgments of this sort are made: he says himself that a historian may regard Kant's epistemology as important simply because it was profound.[11] But in that case, the *principles* of selection White formulated seem to me rather misleading. For if, in making such selections, the historian involves himself in moral considerations, it is not because, like White's moralist, he looks for moral instruction, either for himself or for others; it is because he recognizes the obligation, as a historian, to make clear the moral quality of what was done. If he involves himself in questions of utility, it is not because, like White's pragmatist, he is looking for what can be applied

to present problems; it is because he accepts the responsibility of showing how well or badly the men of the time coped with theirs. What we
expect from a historian, in other words, is an account that is at the same
time an *accounting* of the past: an *assessment* of what men have done
and suffered, within the limits of a chosen career. That is not to say that
historical selection is to be seen simply as a competition in which what
is judged to be most valuable on moral, aesthetic, pragmatic, intellectual, or other grounds attains the prize of entry into the historian's narrative. For whatever the full sense may be in which historical selection
ought to be guided by some principle of "representativeness"—and I
should agree with the earlier White that to explicate this notion is one
of the chief tasks of philosophy of history—at least part of what is involved is the historian's having to be guided by his judgments of *dis-
value* as well as *value*: we want to be shown the *range*. This, incidentally, is an aspect of history which makes it hard to understand what
could be meant by any suggestion that the time has come for the discipline to be superseded, or absorbed, rather than just aided, by the social
sciences. The latter could scarcely be expected to assume such a task.

But if judgments of intrinsic importance, in the sense indicated, are
an indispensable aspect of the construction of a history, this need not be
interpreted as bringing into question the centrality of causal importance
in historical thinking. There does seem to be an element of truth in
Danto's claim that if we were asked about the specifically *historical* importance of an event, we should almost automatically point to what it
led to. To do otherwise, as he suggests, would raise doubts about our
having understood the question. Thus Vico's work, although we may
judge it intrinsically important as a human achievement, may still be
said to lack historical importance because it was ignored. Similarly, the
shape of Cleopatra's nose, although we may judge it, ungallantly, to be
of little intrinsic importance, has been thought tremendously important
historically. That historians generally agree that Cleopatra's beauty has
been grossly overrated as a "factor" in history in no way undermines the
point. For the basis for the criticism is that very little can, after all, be
attributed to it. What has to be noticed here, however, is that if historical importance is a causal notion, then what is not a *historically important event* may still be an *important historical event*. And it may need
to be selected into a narrative because it is important, even though not
historically important.

I do want to object just a little, though, to Danto's exclusive appropriation of historical importance for causally potent events. I think that
considerations other than what an event led to, can justify our speaking
of it as historically important, and justify the historian's selection of it *as*
historically important, although what we have in mind in so regarding it

may still be its relations to other events. Perhaps none of these further relational considerations are of a kind which would be relevant to the selection of a narrative's charter members. But since the only reasons actually mentioned by White for selecting derivative members were their being causes or effects of charter members, it may be useful to note some other relevant relationships.

First, an event may sometimes be regarded as historically important, not because of what it caused, but because of what it *anticipated*. W. H. Walsh has recently cited the interest of historians of logic nowadays in certain developments of medieval logic because of the way they "foreshadow" more recent achievements.[12] Leonardo's drawing of flying machines may owe their place in a history of the Italian Renaissance to this sort of consideration, among others.[13] Most great historical events, ages, or movements—such as the Reformation or the rise of Marxian socialism—have set off a historical search for what foreshadowed them. It seems to be in this sense, for example, that Crane Brinton finds significance in the fact that in the opposition between Girondins and Montagnards during the French Revolution, we can see a later struggle between bourgeois and proletarian at least "dimly outlined." [14] Anticipations may be the more important, of course, if they are also *signs* of what is coming. But they needn't be. And even when they are, they need not themselves cause what they are signs of. To cite Crane Brinton again: the September Massacres of 1792 may be significant as a "foretaste of the Reign of Terror." [15]

An event may also be judged to be historically important, even though not very significant in itself, because of what it *revealed*. Thus an author of the *New Cambridge Modern History*, while discussing the "decline in the vogue of the longer essay" in the twentieth century, calls attention to "the deplorable cessation of the *Edinburgh Review*" to show just how unfavorable the new conditions were to this type of compositon.[16] In a similar way, it could be said that the charge of the Light Brigade was important because of what it revealed about the leadership of the British Army. It may perhaps be thought that what is at issue in such cases is only the historian's solution to what might broadly be called an aesthetic problem: the problem of how best to express what he is trying to convey to his readers—just *how badly* reform of the army was needed, for example. If so, it should be noted that the sense in which we would have to speak here of an aesthetic principle of selection is quite different from what White intended by his use of this term: that is, the selection of an item simply because it made a good story, whether or not it could be said to be "representative" of the way things really were.

Still another reason why an event may be judged historically important, in the context of narrative construction, is that it marked the *beginning or ending* of something which is itself judged to be significant. Modern historians, writes D. E. Lee, are drawn to the question of the causes of the First World War because "the event seemed to be of great significance as a turning point in world history." [17] In such a case, perhaps the kind of importance attributed could appropriately be called "epochal," although this should not be interpreted as excluding less striking cases, such as the historical importance of the first flight of the Wright brothers, deriving from its ushering in the air age. Clearly, whether something is a turning point or not depends on the relations it has to what comes after it. But once again, an event's being important for what it begins need not rest on what is begun being a consequence of it. Thus, when Raymond Aron writes that a turning point in history must be "the sufficient origin of a long or important evolution," I am suspicious of the word "sufficient" at least.[18] The importance of turning points for historical narrative would seem to have some connection with a characteristic way—it isn't usually called explanation—in which historians bring intelligibility into their subject matter: that is, through the use of concepts like periods, phases, or steps of a career. This is something which has not been much discussed by contemporary philosophers of history, although it is perhaps touched on by Walsh, when he speaks of the historian's "colligation" of events and conditions into connected wholes of various kinds,[19] or by Oakeshott, when he represents, the historian as constructing characteristically historical "individuals" through the recognition of discontinuities in the flux of events.[20]

III

Having now compared causal importance with some other kinds, both relational and non-relational, and having acknowledged the centrality of the causal kind in historiography, let me go on to look a little more closely at the notion of causal importance itself. According to Frankel and Randall, the causal importance of an event is to be determined with reference to its consequences. What would be involved in the comparative appraisal of two historical events with respect to their consequences? It would be natural to assume, as I implicitly did earlier, that what would be at issue is which of them had the *more important* consequences. But there is, of course, another possibility: that one event is causally more important than another if it has *more* consequences than the other. We might refer to these, respectively, as qualitative and quantitative interpretations of causal importance.

It may perhaps be thought that no one would seriously be tempted by the quantitative interpretation of the notion. Yet something resembling it does seem suggested by Frankel's image of more important events having more causal lines radiating out from them. A similar impression may be derived from the tendency of historians themselves to represent the consequences of important events as "far-reaching and long-term." [21] Even if it appears plain that it should be the *nature* and not just the *number* of an event's consequences that an appraisal of its importance should take into account, it might still be argued that a qualitative interpretation would at least presuppose the feasibility in principle of the quantitative one. For how could a historian claim to have noted the importance of an event's consequences unless he could also claim that he knew what those consequences were? To be bothered by this, it is not necessary to be ready actually to impose on the historian the procedure of checking off an event's consequences one by one. It is simply that if what a historian might call his "rough estimate" of causal importance is to be meaningful *as an estimate,* then it would seem that the idea of such a check ought at least to make sense.

However, theoretical objections may be raised to the whole idea of counting consequences.[22] As a route into the discussion of causal importance, let me briefly consider two likely ones. The first derives from the general difficulty of the idea of counting events, actions, or states of affairs at all, unless we restrict ourselves to units of a certain kind. Is a revolution or a war to count for one or for more than one? If a historical item of this sort appeared on the list of consequences attributable to one candidate for causal significance, could its case be improved by counting its components separately? I am not sure that an entirely satisfactory answer can be given to such a question. But it is, at any rate, the beginning of an answer to point out that our notion of what can be a consequence would not permit *indiscriminate* list-doctoring. The First World War, for example, may well be judged to be a consequence of the European alliance system of the preceding decade. But it is surely doubtful that the military collapse of Russia, or the tank's baptism of fire, could seriously be attributed to that system. Status as a consequence does not necessarily transfer from an event to its component events. Nor is it necessarily retained by the same event under every description we may apply to it. It was a consequence of a public outcry, it may be said, that the government suffered electoral defeat. But need it have been a consequence of that outcry that the election took place? Surely, it might simply have been time for it.

A second theoretical objection to the quantitative interpretation—a problem also sometimes raised for utilitarian theories of ethics—is that the consequences of everything that happens must surely accrue endlessly, destroying any basis for comparison. One answer to this, not available to the ethical theorists, would be that, so far as historical enquiry is concerned, chains of consequences clearly *do* come to an end; they end, if not sooner, then in the present, since the task of the historian is to study what *has* happened, together with the significance which it *has* attained. An object of present historical study may, of course, turn out to have further consequences as time goes by; and in that case we shall have to change what we say about its historical importance. This is a well-known reason for holding that all history must continually be rewritten—and for denying the possibility of more than embryonic contemporary history. Danto would say that, in such cases, the actual significance of historical events, and not just our judgment of it, changes with the increment of further consequences. And this seems to me the right conclusion to draw: doubly so for anyone making libertarian assumptions.

This answer, however, clearly does not take us very far towards representing comparison of consequences in history as a feasible enterprise. For a more radical answer, we need to look with some care at what sort of thing could be regarded as a *chain of consequences* in history. It is natural to think of this abstractly as a chain of conditions in which each link is a sufficient condition for the occurrence of a successor, which is called its consequence—perhaps on the model of the old tale of the kingdom that was lost for want of a nail. Three links of such a chain could be diagrammed thus (using a triple arrow to represent the sufficient condition relationship):

$$A \Longrightarrow B \Longrightarrow C$$

Here A is the lack of a nail, B is the lack of a shoe, and C is the lack of a horse. Each of these conditions is sufficient for its successor: this follows from the fact that it constitutes a failure to satisfy a condition judged to be necessary for the nonoccurence or avoidance of that successor. If we could assume that managerial flexibility was necessary for successful competition in world markets, a similar relationship would presumably underly our calling the competitive failure of British industry a consequence of managerial *inflexibility*. And we could perhaps find some further condition for which the failure of British industry was sufficient in the same way.

But the events which historians are most likely to raise consequence questions about are seldom points of origin for such chains of sufficient conditions. The more typical case of a chain of consequences in history is composed of conditions which are no more than necessary for their successors.[23] The hackneyed, but still instructive, example of the assassination of the Archduke Ferdinand in 1914 is a case in point. If we say that this had as its consequence the Austrian ultimatum to Serbia, we certainly do not mean that other conditions, like the determination of the Imperial government to stamp out nationalism in its domains, were not also relevant to the sending of the ultimatum. And if we say that a consequence of that ultimatum was the Russian mobilization, this would, once again, not be taken as denying the relevance of, say, Russian memories of previous defeats for Pan-Slavism. We might diagram the situation thus (using double arrows for the consequence relationship where it is at the same time a necessary but not sufficient condition relationship, and single arrows for the necessary condition relationship alone):

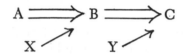

At every stage of the developing chain, in other words, further conditions like Austrian policy (X) and Russian memories (Y), together with perhaps still other conditions not shown on the diagram, are considered necessary for the completion of a sufficient set of conditions for the ultimatum (B) and the mobilization (C). It is important to note, however, that these additional conditions are *not literally within what is called the chain of consequences at all.*

Now it may perhaps be objected that, although the historian will in practice probably be content to call a succession of mere necessary conditions, a chain of consequences, the ideal would always be to expand what he reports into a sufficient condition chain—for example, by incorporating into it whatever additional conditions he considers to have been necessary at each stage. And it may be added that, on the assumption (which many would make) that every historical event, since it happened, must have *had* a sufficient condition, there would always be a sufficient condition chain for the historian to discover. In fact, the chances of finding a sufficient condition chain, originating in a historical event of the sort we have been considering, is extremely small—even if we limit our search to those having the minimum three links. And it is important to see that the difficulty of finding such chains owes nothing to any doubt which there may be about historical events always *having* sufficient conditions.[24]

To illustrate the difficulty, suppose, for the sake of argument, that in the case of the assassination of the Archduke, we took the assassination and the Imperial policy together as a jointly sufficient set of conditions for the sending of the ultimatum, and that we changed the specification of what counts as the first link of our chain accordingly. We should now have a sufficient condition relationship between the first and second links, between assassination in face of that policy and the ultimatum. But how should we continue this transmutation of a necessary condition chain into a sufficient condition one? What should we represent the ultimatum, in its turn, as a sufficient condition of? Certainly not the Russian mobilization, which originally constituted the third link. For that we also need Russian memories. But if, in response to this, we conjoin these memories with the ultimatum, in order to make the second link sufficient for the third, we shall at the same time destroy the sufficient condition relationship which we have just been at pains to ensure between the first and second links. For the assassination together with the Imperial policy are not sufficient for the *conjunction* of the Austrian ultimatum and the Russian memories, our revised second link. The price of incorporating the rest of an alleged sufficient set of conditions at each stage, in other words, would be the destruction of the *chain*, in the desired sense of a series in which at each stage we have something which is sufficient for the next.

My purpose in dwelling on this, however, is not just to defend the respectability of the more usual sort of consequence chains cited by historians. It is rather to facilitate calling attention to two ways in which consequence tracing along such chains, from a selected point of origin in history, may in fact come to an end long before reaching the present. The following example will serve to illustrate the first of these ways. It was a consequence of sectional strife in the Canadas of the 1860's, it is sometimes said, that the legislative union established in 1841 reached a state of political and constitutional deadlock. It was a consequence of this deadlock that a wider British North American federation was formed in 1867. In each case, what was merely a necessary condition of its successor takes it as its consequence, although various other conditions were also clearly necessary, notably the activities of certain politicians. But although we could extend the chain of necessary conditions further—say, to the expansion of the new Dominion to the Pacific Coast with the entry of British Columbia in 1871—the chain of *consequences* cannot similarly be extended, at any rate in that particular direction. The entry of British Columbia, we would naturally say, was a consequence, not of the federation, but of Sir John. A. Macdonald's political vision and vigorous negotiations. The extended situation could be diagrammed thus:

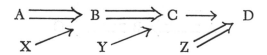

Here the contribution of Macdonald (Z), like the earlier activities of all the Fathers of Confederation (Y)—and like the Austrian policy and Russian memories of our previous example—is a necessary condition which lies outside the putative chain of consequences. Yet unlike them, it *usurps*, as it were, the consequence-appropriating role of a rival condition which is within the chain, namely, the existence of the federation of 1867 (C). The latter becomes just an opportunity for Macdonald's nationalist endeavors. In the terminology of Hart and Honoré's *Causation in the Law*, Macdonald "breaks" the chain of consequences originating in the deadlock of the 1860's (B): we can follow it no further.

There is a second and more subtle reason why it may be impossible to trace the consequences of a given event indefinitely along a chain of the more typical historical sort. This is the fact that, even when a chain itself remains "unbroken," in the special sense of "breaking" just exemplified, the consequence relation does not always remain transitive throughout.[25] That is, it cannot just be assumed that, in a given chain, if each link is a consequence of its predecessor, every link is a consequence of the originating one. The chain connecting the assassination of the Archduke with the outbreak of the First World War has usually been regarded as a transitive one. A common view of how the British army escaped from Dunkirk in 1940 offers perhaps an even more celebrated example of transitivity. The escape, it is said, was a consequence of the German failure to encircle the British; and that failure was a consequence of Hitler's impatience to capture Paris. At the same time, it can be said that the escape itself was a consequence of Hitler's impatience. The consequence relationships in these examples could be diagrammed thus:

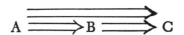

But not all consequence chains in history are interpretable in such a transitive sense. A variation on an example mentioned earlier yields a case that isn't. The First World War may be said to have been a consequence of the European alliance system; the political upheaval in Russia in 1917 may be said to have been a consequence of the war; but the upheaval is hardly a consequence of the alliance system. The intransitivity of the consequence relationship in such a case could be diagrammed thus:

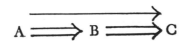

Now I must confess that I know of no convincing explanation of why consequence chains in some cases, at some points, become intransitive. But I do think that the account given by Hart and Honoré of what usually *breaks* a chain of consequences in legal thinking—namely, the contribution made at a certain stage by the voluntary interventions of human agents or by abnormal conjunctions of circumstances [26]—throws light on analogous historical cases. Thus, it is plausible, in the example from Canadian political history, to regard the chain-breaking contribution of Sir John A. Macdonald's initiatives to the country's westward expansion as a "voluntary act," in a sense in which the equally necessary contributions of Canadian politicians (including Macdonald) to the earlier federation movement were not. For the latter could be said to have been "forced" by the circumstances of political deadlock. A way *had* to be found out of it.

An example of the way abnormalities, rather than voluntary acts, may be regarded by historians as breaking a consequence chain is J. B. Bury's account of the intrusions of the barbarians into the Roman Empire in the West. These, Bury tells us, were due to a "conflux of coincidences"—premature deaths, unplanned skirmishes, congenital idiocy in high places, and the like—all of which he thinks makes it impossible to trace a continuous chain of consequences to any condition in the antecedent state of the Empire itself.[27] The refusal of Crane Brinton to trace a long chain of consequences through French history perhaps illustrates the roles of *both* voluntary actions and abnormalities as chain-breakers in historical thinking. "No sensible man, [he writes,] would now maintain with Taine that the Constituent Assembly was responsible for Sedan. Socialism, Utopian and Marxian, the unpredictable fact and legend of Napoleon, the almost equally unpredictable fact of Bismarck, and a hundred other novel elements, went to produce the France of 1870." [28] In both examples, it should be noted, it is the *nature* of the chain-breaking conditions that the historian calls to our attention. He is not simply reminding us that if we ignore these conditions no sufficient sets for what ensued can be discovered.

IV

In considering what seems to me a plausible interpretation of the causal fertility principle, I have concentrated on some ways in which consequence-tracing from a selected point of origin can be limited—in particular, the way chains of consequences either break down or become intransitive. These possibilities do not show that consequence chains never *do* continue endlessly to the present: but they suggest the unlikelihood of this, and the unlikelihood of very remote consequences in history generally. This is far from constituting a full account of what is involved in an evaluation of an event's importance by reference to its consequences. But it does, I think, indicate a direction in which philosophers of history might feel it worth while to direct further investigation.

In conclusion, I want to make just three remarks. First, I should draw attention to the fact that what I have said about consequence-tracing has taken the notion of having *consequences* very literally. Since what little discussion there is of the notion of causal importance is often quite specifically phrased in terms of this notion, this seems to me a legitimate thing to do. But before leaving the subject, I should make it clear that I do not think we would normally limit our estimate of the historical importance of an event to what is conferred on it by (let us call them) consequences *proper*. For as many philosophers have pointed out, there is a wide range of other causal expressions, and historians often use these, rather than the language of consequences, in indicating conditions which would clearly have to be taken into account in such an estimate. An event's importance may be found, for example, in what it led to, whom it influenced, what opportunities it provided, who was encouraged or discouraged by it, or took it as a model, as a warning, and so on. In some cases, furthermore, we could not naturally rephrase what the historian claims in the form, "B was the consequence of A." It may well be correct, for example, to deny that the debacle of the Second Empire was a consequence of the activities of the Constituent Assembly. But, without wanting to fall into the exaggeration feared by Brinton, namely, that the French Revolution is the "key" to French history, the connection between the two may still be relevant to an estimate of the place of that Revolution in that history.

The recognition of the relevance of other "causal" relationships obviously reduces what I have been referring to as the practical feasibility of any precise appraisal of an event's historical importance. Since such other relationships can be expected to have their own limiting criteria, however, we need not thereby be thrown back upon the doctrine that every successor for which an event is a necessary condition will be relevant. In this connection, Danto's formulation of what is historically important, which is sometimes simply in terms of an event's "connections" with later ones, is perhaps too broad. But—and this is my second remark—it could be misleading, too, to say without qualification that what is at issue is an event's *causal* connections with what came after it. For if merely "conditioning" is too weak a relationship here, "being the cause of" is certainly too strong—at any rate, if we take the term "cause" as it is actually used by historians. Indeed, what a thing caused may include even less than what we can call the consequences of it. Saying this, of course, commits one to allowing that some consequences were not caused by what they are consequences of. But it is easy enough to exemplify this apparent paradox. It was a consequence of John Kennedy's going to Dallas, it might be said, that he was shot. But his going there did not cause him to be shot, or cause anyone to shoot him.

My third remark brings me back to what was said at the beginning of this paper about historical relativism. It will be clear that, as I have interpreted it, the causal fertility principle is not, in White's sense, an objective one. For the judgment that an event was important because of its consequences, unless this is a merely quantitative appraisal, will require the historian's value judgement regarding the importance of the consequences. But such judgements may have a still further, and more covert, role to play if consequences are the sort of thing which can be cut off from an originating event by chain discontinuities (and possibly also intransitivities). For the conclusion that an action is sufficiently voluntary or an event is sufficiently abnormal to count as a chain-breaker is one which may require such judgments. A historian who did not think of political deadlock as an especially pressing problem, for example, might regard the activities of Macdonald and others in the crisis of the 1860's as no less voluntary than the political maneuverings of the post-Confederation years. He might deny that those earlier activities were in any sense "forced" by the circumstances, and conclude, therefore, that the federation movement was a consequence, not of the deadlock, but of the meddling of the politicians. And the more jaundiced a view he took of the federation itself—the more he was opposed, say, to strong central government—the more likely he would be to do this.

Clearly, if the decision as to whether a conditioned successor event is not just an *important* consequence but even *a consequence at all*, could vary in such a way with the value judgments of historians, then the latter are even more structurally grounded in historical thinking than any mere list of subjective, or quasi-subjective principles of selection would suggest. In one of their infrequent extrapolations of their analysis of causal concepts from legal to historical contexts, Hart and Honoré make a point of denying that historians need to become "moralists" in tracing the consequences of events.[29] Unless this just means that they can always stop using the concept of "consequence" they already have, I do not see that such a view can be defended.

NOTES

1. Morton White, *Foundations of Historical Knowledge* (New York, Harper & Row, 1965).

2. *Ibid*, pp. 230ff. White appears to be dealing exclusively with what I have elsewhere called descriptive, rather than explanatory, history, and the concern of the present paper is similarly limited. (*Cf* my *Philosophy of History*, New Jersey, Prentice-Hall, Inc., 1963, pp. 29ff.)

3. White, *op. cit.*, pp. 238–57.

4. *Cf* M. White, *Religion, Politics and the Higher Learning* (Cambridge, Harvard University Press, 1959), pp. 72–3. See also his "Can History be Objective?" reprinted in H. Meyerhoff (ed.), *The Philosophy of History in Our Time*, New York, 1959, pp. 195–6.

5. I have discussed some of these in "Michael Oakeshott's Theory of History" in B. C. Parekh and P. T. King, eds., *Politics and Experience* (Cambridge, Cambridge University Press, 1968), pp. 19–42.

6. "Toward an Analytic Philosophy of History" in M. Farber, ed., *Philosophic Thought in France and the United States* (Buffalo, State University of New York Press, 1950), pp. 718–20.

7. J. H. Randall, Jr., *Nature and Historical Experience* (New York, Columbia University Press, 1958), pp. 42–3.

8. Arthur Danto, *Analytical Philosophy of History* (Cambridge, Cambridge University Press, 1965), p. 11.

9. Charles Frankel, "Explanation and Interpretation in History" reprinted in P. Gardiner, ed., *Theories of History* (Glencoe, Free Press of Glencoe, Inc., 1959), p. 422.

10. W. H. Walsh, "The Limits of Scientific History," reprinted in W. H. Dray, ed., *Philosophical Analysis and History* (New York, Harper & Row, 1966), p. 65.

11. Walsh, *op. cit.*, p. 255.

12. Walsh, *op. cit.*, p. 66.

13. I owe this and another example to Mr. D. R. Newman.

14. Crane Brinton, *A Decade of Revolution: 1789–1799* (New York, Harper & Row, 1934), p. 289.

15. Brinton, *op. cit.*, p. 90.

16. *New Cambridge Modern History*, Vol. XII, *Era of Violence, 1898–1945* (Cambridge, Cambridge University Press, 1960), p. 126.

17. D. E. Lee, ed., *The Outbreak of the First World War: Who Was Responsible?* (Cambridge, Cambridge University Press, 1963), p. vii.

18. Raymond Aron, *Introduction to the Philosophy of History*, trans. by G. J. Irwin (London, D. C. Heath & Co., 1961), p. 162.

19. For his most recent discussion of this notion *cf* W. H. Walsh, "Colligatory Concepts in History" in W. H. Burston and D. Thompson, eds., *Studies in the Nature and Teaching of History* (London, Humanities Press, 1967), pp. 65–84.

20. M. Oakeshott, *Experience and Its Modes* (Cambridge, Cambridge University Press, 1933), p. 120ff.

21. *Cf* Burston and Thompson, *op. cit.*, p. 118.

22. For a good recent discussion see L. Bergstrom, *The Alternatives and Consequences of Actions*, Stockholm, 1966.

23. As it would seem best to focus attention on points more central to the concerns of this paper, I here deliberately avoid involvement in the question of the

sense in which a cause in history must be such a necessary condition, although this is admittedly a difficult and complicated one.

24. A metaphysical doubt which I, in fact, share, but which is irrelevant to the issue here.

25. This property of some causal series has been discussed by Hart and Honoré, although only in passing. *Cf Causation in the Law*, London, 1959, p. 40.

26. See especially Hart and Honoré, *op. cit.*, pp. 31ff.

27. J. B. Bury, *Selected Essays* (Amsterdam, Argonaut Press), editor's introduction, pp. xxvi–xxvii.

28. Bury, *op. cit.*, p. 289.

29. Bury, *op. cit.*, p. 59.

THE LOGIC OF THE SUCCESSION
OF CULTURES

David Braybrooke

No one I know spends much time nowadays denouncing the idea that
some sort of logical—or dialectical—process is at work in history. I take
this as a sign that the idea has been so thoroughly depreciated as to fall
beneath contempt. It is certainly not a sign of the idea's securely enjoy-
ing widespread acceptance. I think few respectable philosophers are
ready to give the idea any credit at all.

It is, one might say, an idea that Hegel blew up so big that it burst.
Even those faintly respectable philosophers who amuse themselves by
toying with the rehabilitation of Georg Wilhelm Friedrich Hegel seem
to have passed over the idea; it is one extravagance that they are content
to leave in the box.

Maybe in the overblown form that Marx or Engels ascribed it to
Hegel the idea never was in the box in the first place. I shall not try to
decide. I shall not try to rehabilitate Hegel by demonstrating the unwarranted extravagance of the Marxist interpretation of his work. I am
bound to say, however, that there is some truth in the idea of a historical dialectic, taken as Marx took Hegel to mean it; if Hegel meant it in
this form, my remarks will tend to rehabilitate him whether I wish to or
not.

Cultures succeed one another in history; and the succession works
out the way it does at least in part because of requirements of logic. Just
as Hegel said, or as Marx or Engels understood him to say, cultures are
liable to be beset by internal contradictions the resolution of which
leads to their being supplanted by other cultures likewise vulnerable.
Furthermore, just as Marx and Engels said, the chief source of these internal contradictions lies in technological change.

The idea of logic at work in history deserves another hearing. I
shall give it another rendition in this paper by performing, on an instru-

ment newly made available in the logic of norms, some variations on a theme by Engels.

In the third chapter of *Socialism: Utopian and Scientific*, Engels gives a brilliant précis of the Marxist view of the social transformations by which capitalism was brought about and the impending transformations by which it is supposed to be taken away. I want to fix upon one aspect of these transformations—upon changes in the rules for appropriating the products of industry—and to represent these changes by drawing upon von Wright's logic of norms.[1] I shall then discuss certain issues that I believe are raised and illuminated in a fresh way by this representation.

Engels says something like this: Before capitalism came in, production was carried on by *petty industry*. Then, every worker typically owned his own tools, which were "small, dwarfish, and circumscribed" in character. There was no doubt about his owning any product which he made with these tools; nor was there any question of conflict between claims to the product based on owning the tools on the one hand and on performing the labor on the other. The product "belonged wholly" to the individual producer, "as a matter of course;" and "his property in the product was . . . based *upon his own labors*" (Engels' italics).

Capitalism came in with a change in technology that upset these traditional arrangements; instead of kits of small tools owned by individual workers, technology now called for heavy machinery brought together in factories, that is, for "*social* means of production only workable by a collectivity of men." Now "no one person could say [of] the yarn, the cloth, the metal articles . . . that came out of the factory: 'I made that; this is *my* product'" (Engels' italics again). Nevertheless, "the old forms of appropriations" continued in the sense that as before the owners of the tools claimed ownership in the products. "The socialized producers and means of production and their products were still treated just as they had been before, i.e., as the means of production and the products of individuals. Hitherto, the owner of the instruments of labor had himself appropriated the product, because as a rule it was his own product and the assistance of others was the exception. Now the owner of the instruments of labor always appropriated to himself the product, although it was no longer *his* product but exclusively the product of the labour *of others*."

"The means of production, and production itself, had become in essence socialized. But they were subjected to a form of appropriation which presupposes the private production of individuals." This emergent contradiction is one of the chief contradictions inherent in the character of capitalism; and in it originate the social antagonisms with which capitalism is beset. "Socialised production" is incompatible with "capitalistic appropriation."

I do not think that Engels' account is entirely consistent; that fact perhaps excuses my treating it very freely. I have no doubt, either, that historians would now have all sorts of historical objections to the truth of the account at various points. It will still serve my purposes as a prime source for illustrating the conceptual issues raised by accounts of cultural change.

The concept of acquiring ownership—of obtaining property in a product of industry—plays a central role in Engels' account. What this concept involves may be explicated by drawing on von Wright's logic of norms to represent the general combination of norms that the concept of acquiring ownership in a product involves, namely, a combination of two norms addressed to N, the person acquiring the property,

$$(1) \quad P \; d(\sim pTp) \; \& \; P \; d(pT\sim p)$$

and two norms addressed to other people (all others),

$$(2) \quad O \; d(\sim pTp) \; \& \; O \; f(pT\sim p),$$

where $P \; d(\sim pTp) \; \& \; P \; d(pT\sim p)$ represented *permissions*, permission to "transform the world" from one in which a given product is not claimed $(\sim p)$ into one in which the product has been appropriated (p); or (given that it has been appropriated) permission to "transform the world" from one in which the product is claimed to one in which it no longer is (having been sold or given away). $O \; d(\sim pTp) \; \& \; O \; f(pT\sim p)$ represent, respectively, a prescription and a prohibition: a prescription addressed to others to give up a product not in N's possession so that N may have it, and a prohibition against changing things (without N's permission) so that N no longer has it.

A thing may be acquired by one person or by several persons jointly (since joint ownership is an acknowledged possibility). But acquiring something is normatively exclusive in this sense: For everything that is acquired there is at any given time a completely enumerable class of persons who acquire it; and it would be logically inconsistent for the same source of norms to lay down the combination of norms (1) both for people in that class and for people outside the class, in respect to the same thing c.

As a logic of "norm-kernels," von Wright's logic of norms does not afford the means of expressing all the features of norms that he himself notices; and there are further features. I shall add to his symbolism subscripts indicating, first, the members of the class of persons acquiring ownership, and, second, the thing in which ownership is acquired. It is to be understood in every case that the subscript completely enumerates the class of persons acquiring ownership and that different symbols for persons appearing in other subscripts refer to different persons. Thus

$$P \ d(\sim pTp)_{(N, \ c)} \ \& \ P \ d(pT\sim p)_{(N, \ c)}$$

and

$$P \ d(\sim pTp)_{(M, \ c)} \ \& \ P \ d(pT\sim p)_{(M, \ c)}$$

apply to different persons, who cannot both be the single members of the completely enumerated classes in question; the two combinations therefore contradict one another.

In the present case, we suppose that both the combinations of norms (1) and (2) are contingent on $\sim wTw$ & $\sim tTt$, that is to say, on the world having been changed from one in which N had not put his labor into the given product to one in which he had done so; and simultaneously from one in which N had not used his tools to make the given product to one in which he had. In a finer analysis, which made fuller use of von Wright's logic or norms than I shall have space or time for here, the full combination of formulas that I have written out here would be carried throughout and perhaps elaborated further. Instead of elaborating, I shall do the opposite; I shall *condense* these norms into the formula $O \ d(\sim rTr)$, a prescription addressed to everyone (including N) that N's right of ownership to the given product shall be recognized. This condensed norm, like the norms in the two combinations, holds if the conditions $\sim wTw$ and $\sim tTt$ are fulfilled. Hence we may write

$$(3) \ \sim wTw_{(N, \ c)} \ \& \ \sim tTt_{(N, \ c)} \rightarrow O \ d(\sim rTr)_{(N, \ c)} \ ^2$$

where the subscripts remind us that both the conditions and the norm have to do centrally with given persons N and particular products c.

$$(3) \ \sim wTw_{(N, \ c)} \ \& \ \sim tTt_{(N, \ c)} \rightarrow O \ d(\sim rTr)_{(N, \ c)}$$

is, of course, perfectly consistent with

$$(4) \sim wTw_{(N,\ c)} \rightarrow O\ d(\sim rTr)_{(N,\ c)}$$

and

$$(5) \sim tTt_{(N,\ c)} \rightarrow O\ d(\sim rTr)_{(N,\ c)}$$

though (3) by no means implies either of these statements. Now I wish to represent the stage of *petty industry* as one in which both (4) and (5) are accepted, without any conflict arising from them, because in fact for every N and every c,

$$(6) \sim wTw_{(N,\ c)} \longleftrightarrow \sim tTt_{(N,\ c)},$$

i.e., whenever a person N does put his labor into a product c he also uses his tools in working on it and vice versa. Of course (as we shall see again in a moment) (4), (5), and (6) represent only a small fraction of the norms that embody the culture or establish the social structure of society in the stage of petty industry; but we may, with Marx and Engels, regard them as a crucially important fraction—as the very place in which, to speak very metaphorically, history shifts gears for a change in culture.

Let us now suppose that (6) ceases to be true for every N and every c; let us suppose indeed that for every N and every c such that $\sim wTw_{(N,\ c)}$ it is now true that some other person M supplies the tools, and thus $\sim tTt_{(M,\ c)}$; and vice versa. A complete separation comes about between tool-owners (capitalists) and people performing labor. Now

$$(7) \sim tTt_{(M,\ c)}\ \&\ \sim wTw_{(N,\ c)} \rightarrow \sim (\sim tTt)_{(N,\ c)}\ \&\ \sim (\sim wTw)_{(M,\ c)}.$$

((6) and (7) are contraries: They cannot both hold, though they might both fail.)

What will now happen to (4) and (5)? With (6) no longer true, they now lead to a contradiction within the culture, a contradiction in the logic of norms. For consider any product, c, now produced. There will be at least one pair of persons, M and N—perhaps many more than one pair—so related to c that

$$\sim tTt_{(M,\ c)}\ \&\ \sim (\sim tTt_{(N,\ c)})$$

and

$$\sim wTw_{(N,\ c)}\ \&\ \sim (\sim wTw)_{(M,\ c)}.$$

By (5), M acquires c: for

$$\sim tTt_{(M,\,c)} \to O\,d(\sim rTr)_{(M,\,c)}$$

But by (4), N acquires c: for

$$\sim wTw_{(N,\,c)} \to O\,d(\sim rTr)_{(N,\,c)}.$$

If we look back at the more fully explicated combination of norms that $O\,d\,(\sim rTr)$ stands for, however, in the case of any N and any c, we see that

$$O\,d(\sim rTr)_{(N,\,c)} \to \sim O\,d(\sim rTr)_{(M,\,c)}.$$

$O\,d(\sim rTr)_{(N,\,c)}$ and $O\,d\,(\sim rTr)_{(M,\,c)}$ stand to each other as contraries (if one holds, the other fails). For the full combination of norms behind $O\,d(\sim rTr)_{(M,\,c)}$ is such as to give M the permissions $P\,d(\sim pTp)$ & $P\,d\,(pT\sim p)$ and to address *other* people, including N, with the prescription $O\,d\,(\sim pTp)$ and the prohibition $O\,f(pT\sim p)$; whereas the norms behind $O\,d(\sim rTr)_{(N,\,c)}$ reverse the situation, permitting N to do things that only M is permitted to do by the first combination, and laying down a prescription and a prohibition applying to M, which he would otherwise be free of, while removing them from N, to whom they would otherwise apply.

The contradiction $O\,d(\sim rTr)_{(M,\,c)}$ & $\sim O\,d\,(\sim rTr)_{(M,\,c)}$ leads to crisis. For, given the inconsistent instructions that now follow from (4) and (5), either people will hesitate to do anything; or they are liable, some to accept M's claim, and some to accept N's—which may be expected to lead to actual blows—to conflicts physical as well as logical.

One solution to the conflict would be to restore (6), the equivalence of $\sim tTt_{(N,\,c)}$ and $\sim wTw_{(N\,c)}$. Both capitalists and socialists rule this solution out. I shall not consider it here, though it would be interesting to inquire into the content of the normative barriers raised against this solution.

The capitalist solution, we might say as a first approximation, is to abandon (4) in favor of (5). Performing labor no longer entitles N to appropriate c, whereas claims based on owning the tools that have been used continue to be honored.

The socialist solution, which Marx and Engels expected to emerge only after an epoch of experience with the capitalist one, amounts (equally simply stated) to prohibiting anyone M from obtaining a position such that $\sim tTt_{(M,\,c)}$. (5) might be accepted still—it is otiose to cancel it—but it is never activated. The antecedent is never true, and the consequent $O\ d(\sim rTr)_{(M,\ c)}$ never holds in conflict with the consequent of (4).

We might ask, why was the capitalist solution adopted at all? Why was the move to the socialist solution not made at once? (There is a further question why passing through capitalism should make men ready to adopt the socialist solution.) These are very large questions and all that I can do, or want to do, with them here is to show that the logic of norms has some part to play in answering them.

One might be inclined to say that the capitalist solution came about simply because the capitalists were in a better bargaining position. Some workers had no choice but to work in the first new factories. The products which these factories put out were cheaper than those made by artisans in petty industry. These artisans were thus driven out of business and themselves thrown onto the labor market to seek work on the capitalists' terms. But this cannot be a complete explanation since it does not even touch on the question why this process was allowed to occur. Did anything in the prevailing norms give (5), the toolowners' claim, some advantage over (4)?

I think, following a suggestion of Engels' text, we may reasonably think there was. For was it not at least approximately the case that (4),

$$\sim wTw_{(N,\ c)} \rightarrow O\ d(\sim rTr)_{(N,\ c)}$$

was understood as applying mainly—paradigmatically—to workers who made the products c all by themselves, from beginning to end? But with the change in technology, the relevance of $\sim wTw_{(N,\ c)}$ became doubtful. Yet before the extensive use of the joint stock company—a development so late in capitalism that it remains peripheral even in Marx's analysis—no such doubt was attached to the relevance of $\sim tTt_{(M,\ c)}$. (5) applied in favor of the capitalist; it was still one individual man who owned the tools. Thus the situation was this: (4) and (5) conflicted, but (4) was of doubtful relevance, while the application of (5) remained clear. Surely this difference favored the acceptance of (5), in effect, in place of (4).

Another consideration may have favored dropping (4) in favor of (5) once they came into conflict: namely, the tendency (which can be logically explicated at least in part) to resolve such conflicts by analogy and the fact that analogy with the form of employment hitherto most common favored (5). For whatever was the case within petty industry itself, in the larger society surrounding it the predominant form of economic undertaking—especially in England, which led in industrialization—was a form of agriculture, in which the employer (the landowner or tenant farmer) who supplied the land and other means of work claimed everything beyond wages. The farm laborer, work as hard as he might or had to, had no claim to the crops produced on his employer's land with his employer's tools. Many of the recruits to the industrial labor force of capitalism either had worked as laborers under this system of agriculture or were perfectly familiar with it.

Logic and the logic of norms help us to specify the logical basis of the crisis raised by the transition from petty industry. How much the crisis amounted to would have depended in part—but in part essentially—on how unified and coherent the society was. Some societies might tolerate contradictions between norms and the concrete conflicts resulting more readily than others. Those societies with a sophisticated bureaucracy and a complex explicit code of laws, one conjectures, would not tolerate contradictions very easily at all. (von Wright has illuminating things to say in this connection about the necessity of presupposing that there is "one rational will" behind the norms considered if it is to be held they cannot coexist when contradictory.) [3]

There is a further (though connected) dimension of variations: The resolution of the crisis, if it is felt with some urgency that the crisis has to be resolved, may be logically self-conscious in various degrees. Among the possibilities in this range we might include

(I) turning to (5) rather than (4) without any public discuscussion or widespread awareness that (4) and (5) now led to an explicit contradiction

(II) perceiving the contradiction, and choosing (5) rather than (4) on the basis of (4)'s no longer having any clear application or on the basis of the analogy with agriculture, but without anyone's making either basis explicit as a rule for resolving the contradiction.

Toward the logically self-conscious end of the range of resolution, the favor for (5) might come from the explicit application of a rule. Such a rule would have to be a higher norm, above the system of the first instance, for no system can contain within itself the means of eliminating its *own* contradictions. One might, to be sure, not only have (4) and (5) contradicting one another; one might have a situation in which if $\sim[(4) \mathbin{\&} (5)]$ and (4) were assumed, there would follow the negation of some other norm S (or even possibly, the negation of some theorem T of the logic of norms). It would still be possible to choose the other side: One may choose (4) or (5), accepting it that

$\sim(5) \rightarrow \sim S$, maybe accepting it that $\sim(5) \rightarrow \sim T$. (Here one might draw encouragement from Quine: Just as we could always choose to revise the fundamental principles of logic we *could* in principle so revise our concept of norms as to accept $\sim T$.[4])

But higher norms might be found (and possibly truly ascribed to the society under study) from which resolution in favor of (5) would follow by explicit deductions. Such might be, for example, to formalize the two previously discussed informal routes to choosing (5) rather than (4), a higher norm prescribing that when two norms come into conflict and the application of one (or of the condition it embraces) becomes unclear, the other should be followed; or a higher norm prescribing that of the two norms (about, say, distribution of property or income) the one most favored by current analogies should be adopted. Either of these norms could be regarded as a special case of a norm about norms, which would have the form

$$\sim(C_1\, n_1 \,\&\, C_2\, n_2) \rightarrow O\, d(n_1\, T \sim n_1) \,\&\, O\, d(n_2\, T\, n_2)$$

which is to say, if two norms n_1 and n_2 have the characters C_1 and C_2, respectively, and (for some reason) it happens that both cannot hold, then n_1 is not to be recognized any longer, though n_2 is to be.

Higher norms with this form might embody, besides prescriptions about applicability or about analogies, fundamental ethical principles, whether formal (e.g., C_1 might mean "not universalizable" while C_2 meant "universalizable") or concrete (e.g., C_1 might mean "counter-utilitarian," while C_2 meant "in accordance with the principle of utility.") Or perhaps they would prescribe that the norm favored by a popular vote should be chosen.

Revision of norms (other than by simple suspension) may be treated along similar lines. The considerations operating in revision are perhaps more likely to be conscious, but even so they would vary in degree of explicitness. At the logically self-conscious end of the range, they might operate as higher norms. Revision of (5) to apply to corporations, for example, might conceivably have been guided by a higher norm to the effect that when an entity exercised any powers of a given set, then if there was no objection on grounds such as g_1, g_2, g_3, etc., it would be *permitted* to exercise other powers of the set. Corporations were acknowledged as entities with the power of *holding* property (of receiving property as gifts or by purchase). Applying the cited norm to them, and assuming $\sim(g_1 \vee g_2 \vee g_3 \ldots)$, one could conclude to permitting them to acquire property in the course of the productive process.

The higher norms that might have operated to bring about the revisions called for by socialism would be even more interesting. For example, there might have been a norm *within* the (object) system to the effect that *joint* efforts and uses of *jointly* owned tools are to be rewarded by *shares* in the claim to the product. (Indeed, there surely was such a norm, covering various sorts of cooperation.) Hence there would be cooperative parallels (4)′ and (5)′ to the norms of personal appropriation (4) and (5). These, too, might come into contradiction and the contradiction might be resolved in various ways; cooperative (5)′ would be one way of generating the capitalist solution. But it might be seen that preventing the contradiction from arising between (4)′ and (5)′ would not, as in the case of (4) and (5), require retrogression to petty industry. One might invoke (or adopt) a higher norm to the effect that plural N_4's (workers) are *not* to be separated from plural N_5's (tool-owners); and then supply whatever new social devices are necessary to bring about the sharing. In fact, a higher norm such as this one seems to represent the essence of socialism.

What do these illustrative findings about the working of logic in history signify as regards historical explanation?

I note first, that the illustration goes far enough to show that logical considerations may dominate the description of historical events, including events on the grand scale of the transition from petty industry to capitalism. In the illustration, logical considerations make it clear (I think) that something had to be done: (4) and (5) could not both be carried forward to the changed arrangements for production. Furthermore, logical considerations make clear *what* had to be done: some sort of revision of norms had to occur before the ambiguity and conflict created by the contradiction between (4) and (5)—which emerges when (6) ceases to hold—could be resolved. We may imagine a disjunctive array of alternative revisions, in which we could list the most likely possibilities among the first disjuncts. Logical (or metalogical) considerations may be drawn on to formulate and order this list of possible solutions to the problem.

On the basis of this account of the transition between petty industry and capitalism, several explanations, and perhaps explanations of different types, could be formulated. I shall consider two:

I

$$P_1: (N_4 \neq N_5) \rightarrow \sim[(4)(\sim wTw_{(N,\,c)} \rightarrow O\ d(\sim rTr_{(N,\,c)}) \&$$
$$(5)(\sim tTt_{(N,\,c)} \rightarrow O\ d(\sim rTr_{(N,\,c)})]$$

$$P_2: (N_4 \neq N_5)$$

P_3: $\underline{(\sim tTt_{\,(N,\,c)} \to O\, d(\sim rTr)_{\,(N,\,c)})}$

$\therefore \sim(4)\,(\sim wTw)_{\,(N,\,c)} \to O\, d(\sim rTr)_{\,(N,\,c)})$

II

P_1: $(N \neq M) \to \sim[O\, d(\sim rTr)_{\,(N,\,c)}\, \& \,O\, d(\sim rTr)_{\,(M,\,c)}]$

P_2: $(N \neq M)$

P_3: $(4)\, \sim wTw_{\,(N,\,c)} \to O\, d(\sim rTr)_{\,(N,\,c)}$

P_4: $(5)\, \sim tTt_{\,(M,\,c)} \to O\, d(\sim rTr)_{\,(M,\,c)}$

P_5: $\sim tTt_{\,(M,\,c)}$

$\therefore \sim(\sim wTw)_{\,(N,\,c)}$

The point of symbolizing these explanations is to make their logical features more visible; and thus to show in what ways they invite logical manipulation. I shall not be abdicating any claims for the virtues of logic if I provide English translations:

P_1: N_4's not being identical with N_5 implies that it is not the case both that $N(N_4)$'s putting his labor into making c implies that c becomes his property and that $N(N_5)$'s supplying his tools for making c implies that c becomes *his* property.

P_2: N_4 is not (in any case) identical with N_5.

P_3: If N (any N) supplies his tools for making c then c becomes his property.

Therefore, it is not the case that if $N(N_4)$ puts his labor into making c that c becomes his property.

(There is a certain awkwardness, both in the symbolized version and in the translated one, due to the presence of quantificational notions and the absence of quantificational symbols. No doubt such symbols will be available in future developments of the logic of norms. For the time being, perhaps we may make do by understanding "M" or "N" or "N_4" or "N_5" to stand for representative figures—workers or tool-owners so typical that what is true of them is true of every other member of the classes to which they belong.)

P_1: N's not being identical with M implies that it is not the case both that c becomes N's property and that c becomes M's property.

P_2: N is not identical with M.

P_3: N's putting his labor into making c implies that c becomes N's property.

P_4: $M's$ supplying his tools for making c implies c becomes $M's$ property.

P_5: M does supply his tools for making c.

Therefore, it is not the case that N put his labor into making c.

What shall we make of this conclusion? Very possibly N might have been observed to have been doing the work of making c; hence $(\sim wTw)_{(N,\ c)}$, which contradicts the conclusion just reached. But that is not surprising, if it is looked upon as one way in which the conflict between (4) and (5) manifests itself. The contradiction might be eliminated by eliminating (4), i.e., premise P_3. Or it might be eliminated by *reinterpreting* $(\sim wTw)$, so that this is now understood not to refer to any kind of observable labor, but only to specially designated kinds of property-entitling work. The conclusion of (II) would in that case amount to asserting that N had not performed *property-entitling* work on c.

As they stand these explanations have the form of valid arguments and turn chiefly on logical considerations. We might say, for instance, that the crucial first premise of each argument is a theorem of the logic of property, a special development of the logic of norms.

But do these explanations stand alone, without requiring the support of explanations of another sort? They stand alone logically; but I do not think they would be accepted if other sorts of explanations were not available to play supporting roles. Let us consider their relation to two types of explanations that may be distinguished (perhaps among many other kinds) in history and social science: action explanations, which explain what people do by formulating social rules or norms which their actions exemplify; and behavior explanations, which explain how people behave by describing the process of past conditioning by which given items have been installed in their behavioral repertoires.[5]

At first sight, the explanations that I have been discussing here do not seem to fall into either of these categories of explanation. They invoke norms rather than patterns of reinforcement, so they are evidently not behavior explanations. But they do not have the form of showing that a given action exemplifies a certain norm or norms; on the contrary, if they treat given actions at all, they show them to result from conflicts of norms; and in many cases (as the preponderance of my examples suggest) they do not seek to explain given actions, but rather the emergence of social consensus on certain formulas — norm-formulations or the formulation of conditions on which the existence of norms depends.

These differences may be important enough to warrant looking upon conflict-of-norms explanations — explanations that describe a conflict and invoke a principle according to which the conflict logically demands (and so will obtain) resolution—as a distinct kind of explanation. Where it is not possible to establish the existence of higher norms, which can be held to prescribe how the conflict is to be resolved, the case for recognizing conflict-of-norms explanations as a separate category will be particularly strong.

Yet the possibility of invoking these higher norms in the course of some conflict-of-norms explanations suggests a way of illuminating the whole class of these explanations by assimilating them to action explanations of the defined basic kind. When higher norms do figure in conflict-of-norms explanations, then we do (it may be held) have action explanations, for the resolution of the conflict amounts to an action (the act of recognizing one norm rather than another, the act of accepting one condition rather than another as being applicable) and this action is shown to exemplify a norm: a higher norm prescribing that whenever there is a conflict of norms of such and such a sort the conflict is to be resolved by adopting such a solution. Conflict-of-norms explanations in which higher norms are not introduced (because such higher norms cannot be ascribed to the people and societies involved) may be regarded as defective cases of action explanations of this higher kind, meaning by "defective" only that they would be regarded as more perfect if higher norms could be brought in.

If we assimilate such explanations to action explanations (on a higher level than ordinary action explanations, since we now deal with norms for dealing with norms; but still following the basic form), then the relationship of such explanations to behavior explanations can be quite simply and clearly summed up (though the summary will inevitably pass over a great variety of details). Wherever an action explanation is offered, a behavior explanation can be asked for, too. In the case of the present explanations, they would be asked for by raising questions about what sort of conditioning led to the people in question accepting certain analogies, or to their having as much (or as little) regard for consistency as they have shown, or to their adopting the higher norms that seem to have been invoked in order to resolve the conflict. All sorts of considerations, from toilet training in childhood to the general respect in which people are taught to hold logicians, might figure in the processes of conditioning (positive and negative reinforcement) which lead to the acceptance and maintenance of these behavioral patterns rather than others. Among the reinforcements, it should be noted, there will generally be a number of actions (actions of rewarding or failing to reward) that themselves are susceptible both of action explanations and of behavior explanations.

Are action explanations ever offered by historians? (I could actually raise my argument on a weaker foundation, by asking only that action explanations be relevant, whether or not historians or anyone else in fact cared to offer them.) I think they are in fact commonplace (which does not at all mean that the norms or rules invoked in them are mere truisms). I conjecture that they guide narratives more often than general laws do; or rather, let us say, the regularities that guide narratives are very often those that correspond to norms because of the acceptance of the latter. Whenever (however rarely in the course of certain narrations) the historian embarks on an explanation going beyond narration, he is likely to offer an action explanation. Sometimes, as the example of Engels shows, the action explanation in question is one of the peculiar sort that we have been dealing with here, an explanation turning on a conflict of norms.

There is, on occasion, something like a dialectic in history; and the dialectic is explanatory.

NOTES

1. G. H. von Wright, *Norm and Action* (London, Routledge, 1963).

2. (3) is an instance of what von Wright calls "a hypothetical norm-proposition." *Op cit.*, p. 169. We are supposing that the specifically subscripted norm O d($\sim$rTr) $_{(N, e)}$ comes into force when $\sim$wTw $_{(N, e)}$ and $\sim$tTt $_{(N, e)}$; the consequent of (3) says that such and such a norm is in force.

3. von Wright, *op. cit.*, pp. 147–52.

4. Cf. W. V. Quine, "Two Dogmas of Empiricism," in *From a Logical Point of View* (2nd ed., Cambridge, Mass., Harvard University Press, 1961).

5. Cf. the introduction to D. Braybrooke, ed., *Philosophical Problems of the Social Sciences* (New York, Macmillan, 1965).

SOCIAL DETERMINISM
AND FREEDOM

Mihailo Marković

Contemporary philosophical thinking has been split into two entirely different, incompatible modes of approach and methodologies of solving philosophical problems: on the one hand a scientific, value-free realism, which lays stress on positive knowledge and assumes methodological requirements of precision, empirical validity, and logical exactness; on the other hand, an antiscientific, value-laden romanticism, which is mainly concerned with the criticism of the present, either in the name of a utopian vision of the future or of a great, idealized tradition of the past. The discrepancy is not only the consequence of an excessive specialization and of the strong impact of specific national traditions, but it is also the expression of a sharp polarization within the intellectual world under the influence of certain powerful social factors.

The unprecedented growth of scientific knowledge and technology, which gave rise to a substantial increase of human power over nature and over at least some of the blind forces of history, supports the basically rationalistic idea (originated within eighteenth-century Philosophy of Enlightenment and implicit in all scientific trends of contemporary philosophy) that by using proper methods and techniques of inquiry man can reach reliable knowledge about the laws of nature, adjust to them, and thus become powerful, rich, and happy. The other aspect of this conception of scientific and technological rationality is obviously a philosophy of efficacy and success *within* a given framework of social and individual life. The very framework has not usually been challenged by this type of philosophy; it has been concerned, rather, with the validity of means for given ends; it does not question the rationality of the ends themselves. The problem of human freedom hardly enters the circle of really interesting and "meaningful" problems; if it does, it is usually reduced to a much narrower problem of *rational choice* within a given determined framework of alternatives. One can therefore venture to say that this philosophy has been strongly supported by a widespread attitude of conformism and utilitarianism. Its great power lies, however, in the fact that it is a theoretical expression and rationalization of a general drive toward the affluent society.

This basically cerebral, realistic, intellectualistic philosophy, today meets with a strong oppostion among all those lonely thinkers who prefer "the logic of the heart" to "the logic of reason," and who rebel against the prospects of an abundant but impersonal, inauthentic, unfree life in a mass society of the future. New experiences in political life, modern arts, social and psychological research, indicate the presence of unpredictable new forms of irrationality and sickness and strengthen the feeling that living in abundance and apparent external power does not make men happier, and that, after the successes of science and technology, man has created a basically unfree, unreasonable, and suicidal society. Thus a strong anti-Enlightenment attitude has gradually emerged: there is evil in men, human existence is basically meaningless, the role of reason and knowledge is negligible, no determinism and progress are apparent in history, all modern civilization is only the culmination of human estrangement and self-forgetfulness. This emphasis on human irrationality and lack of order in history usually goes together with a very hostile attitude toward science, scientific method, and logic. The revolt against the given present reality implies a refusal to admit that it has any roots in the past, or that (no matter how flexibly) it determines the frame of possibilities for the future. This is why the future is considered the primary dimension of time, and possibilities are construed as unlimited ranges of entirely open courses of action. The principles of absolute freedom and responsibility have been opposed to the principles of reality and determination.

However, this anti-Enlightenment philosophy (which has most consistently been expressed in philosophy of life and existentialism) is only a powerless, romantic expression of revolt against inhuman aspects of modern society. It is a supersession of the unsatisfactory concrete situation in abstract thoughts; i.e., it is an alienated form of disalienation.

In order to make any real step towards the solution of the essential anthropological problem of human freedom a philosophy is needed:

(a) which supersedes both the learned superficiality of common-sense reasoning based on fragmented descriptive data and the barren abstractness of speculative considerations with a unity of critical theoretical vision and concrete knowledge of the given historical situation, as a whole;

(b) which studies the determining factors of the given situation in order to find out which possibilities are *really* open and which human projects are *really* feasible, not just in order to conform to what is most probable;

(c) which considers human praxis as one of the essential detemining factors in history; such an activistic philosophy does not only ask what possibilities are *given* but also what new possibilities can be *created by* suitable action;

(d) finally, within the framework of such philosophy freedom is much more than the lack of external compulsion while choosing one among given possibilities; full freedom is the ability for self-determination and for changing the very conditions of a deterministic system.

The general principle of determinism can be formulated in the following way: *If a certain state of a dynamic system* S *is given in the moment* t_o, *then a unique set of states of* S *will occur in the moment* t'.

This formulation can be applied both to the future and the past. Also it allows ontological, epistemological, and axiological interpretation. In case the moment t' precedes the moment t_o, the principle of determinism expresses the possibility of reconstructing a past situation starting from the given present one. In case the moment t' follows t_o, the principle expresses the possibility of bringing about or predicting the future on the basis of the present.

When interpreted *ontologically*, the principle states that all events in nature and human society are necessary, in the sense of occurring according to certain objective laws which are independent of any particular subject.

Epistemological interpretation of the principle of determinism is constituted by the assertion that there is a method by which, whenever the state of a given dynamic system at a certain time is known, the state of that system in any other time can be described (predicted if in the future, retrodicted if in the past).

In connection with the social and historical sciences it is important that, as a special case, there should also be an *axiological* interpretation of the principle of determinism. According to this, the notion of the state of a system might, among other things, be definable in terms of a (conscious or unconscious) tendency to realize a certain goal. To "determine" would mean, then, to bring about the state of the system which corresponds to the given goal.

Another important characteristic of the general principle of determinism is that it embraces, as special cases, both classical rigid determinism and various weaker forms of determinism, which, being incompatible with the former, have often been labelled "indeterminism." The language in which that famous dispute used to be expressed was rather misleading. The real issue between classical determinism and indeterminism was not whether there were or were not any scientific laws by which events in nature and human society could be somehow determined (in a stronger or in a weaker way). The real difference between those two conceptions consists in the fact that they assumed different notions of the *state of a system* and different interpretations of the idea of a *class* of determined states.

The notion of the *state of a system* presupposes (a) a language with specified syntactical and semantical rules; (b) a logical method for drawing inferences; (c) a set of data as well as of confirmed empirical generalizations concerning the given field of objects; (d) a certain general body of knowledge and awareness of a goal (of inquiry and action) which allow us to distinguish between relevant (important, essential, etc.) and irrelevant (insignificant, accidental, etc.) features of the given field of objects; this ability to discriminate allows us to establish the boundary conditions of the dynamical system S under consideration; (e) finally, knowledge of the initial condition of S in t_o.

Now the specific interpretation of the notion of the state of a system from the point of view of classical determinism is the special case where: (a) the language at our disposal contains rules which allow us to speak meaningfully not only about classes but also about individual objects, (b) inferences can be drawn in a deductive way, (c) laws of the given field are provable within an axiomatic system, (d) full and precise knowledge of all boundary and initial conditions is, in principle, possible. The fulfillment of all these requirements allows us to reduce the class of possible future (or past) states to just one element. In all weaker forms of determinism this class contains several elements. This is the consequence of the fact that strong conditions which hold for rigid determinism cannot be fulfilled: Either we can speak meaningfully only about classes, but not about individual objects, or/and deductive inference is not always possible, or/and laws have the form of probability statements, or/and full description of boundary and initial conditions is not possible. What follows, then, from a given state of the system in t_o is a disjunction of alternative states in t' which could be expected with a greater or lesser degree of probability. Thus, nondetermination in one specified respect might still involve determination in some other respect. All scientific methods of dealing with dynamic processes, no matter how complex, could be ordered within the continuum of a single unifying concept, taking as the criterion of ordering the *degree of determinacy*, that is, the degree of sharpness with which we can make predictions about the states of the system S in t' when we know the state of S in t_0.

The essential difficulty in explicating the principle of determinism is the interpretation of the very notion of *determination*. What does it mean to say that *if* a state of a system in t_0 is given or known, then a class of states in t' occurs or can be predicted. What kind of necessity is here expressed by the implication *if . . . then?* The informative value of the principle obviously depends on what we wish to deny. The first thing we want to deny is that the class of determined states of the system is either empty or is a universal class. In other words we deny both (1) that a system can be without any history and be nonexistent in any future or past moment, and (2) that all *logical* possibilities are open. Therefore, the most flexible formulation of the principle of determinism would have a negative form: It is not the case that if a state of a system S is given in the moment t_0, then none or any state could follow at the moment t'. Paraphrasing Spinoza's dictum *Omnis determinatio negatio est* one might say that all determination is essentially exclusion of certain possibilities.

Each system S opens a field of possible states P and contains certain limiting conditions LC, and to say that a certain x is *necessary* with reference to S means that x is a nonempty subclass of the class of possible states P and that all other possibilities of the field P except x are excluded due to the given limiting conditions LC. Obviously by introducing new elements into the class of limiting conditions the degree of determination (the scope of elimination) increases until we get the special case where the subclass of allowed possibilities contains only one member: This is the special situation described by classical determinism.

The kind of necessity we have here (expressed by the connective *if . . . then* in the principle of determinism) is by no means *logical* necessity (as has sometimes been argued by rationalist philosophers). The class of limiting conditions contains both logical (syntactical and semantical) rules and empirical conditions, among which established empirical laws play the key part. We may therefore call this type of necessity *empirical* (or *factual*). Here, the term, "necessity" is not the name of some mystical glue which sticks events together; it can rather be construed as an abbreviation for the more complex expression, "that which resists all attempts of elimination." It should be noted that the concept of empirical necessity is relative to a whole set of assumptions, rules, and information constituting the given system S. Any change in the system, any discrepancy between the system and the real structure of corresponding objects, allow deviations ("chance events") from what has been considered "normal" and "necessary" within the system. Contrarily, chance events with respect to one system (S) may be reinterpreted as necessary events with respect to a richer and stronger system (S').

The applicability of the idea of determinism to the social sciences and history has often been challenged in our century. From what has been said earlier, it follows that the rejection of determinism often goes with a romantic anthropological revolt against positivistic conformism and indifference toward the problem of human freedom. When determinism is construed in a classical, rigid way and freedom is exalted to an absolute principle of authentic human practice, these two ideas are really incompatible.

The denial of determinism and causality in the social sciences often also has roots in the tendency to draw a too sharp demarcation line between the natural and social sciences, and between nature and history in general. The views of the Neo-Kantian Baden school are typical in this respect. As according to Windelband and Rickert, social sciences deal with unique, unrepeatable events; they cannot generalize and explain but only describe and understand. (They are *ideographische, verstehende* contrasted with *nomothätische, erklärende Wissenschaften.*) On the other hand, a number of idealistic philosophers, *e.g.* Dilthey, Croce, Collingwood, and others, have questioned the objectivity of historical facts and emphasized the role of value judgements in the process of interpretation. There is no need to reject all insights of these great philosophers, especially if these insights are taken as arguments for the thesis that very important differences exist between the natural and social sciences. Nevertheless they introduce a dualism which is by no means tenable. The only nature which is relevant to our lives and to scientific research is nature transformed by human (physical and mental) practice and viewed in the perspective of human language, experience, and practical needs. Thus, the subject of the natural (and technical) sciences is not nature "in itself" but nature that has already become part of human history. Accordingly, there is a tendency to overlook the fact that even in the most exact natural sciences value judgements play a certain role *e.g.*, in the controversies about the theory of relativity and quantum mechanics) and that the interaction between object and subject in the process of inquiry takes place throughout science.

If, however, we deny any dualism between the natural and social sciences and if we cannot see any really new or convincing reason for giving up a conceptual apparatus which is highly suitable and, in fact, indispensable for the explanation of social events, still it does not follow that the only alternative left to us is the unification of concepts and methods, characteristic of logical positivism. By the very fact that, after all, history is made by man and that even blind, impersonal social forces are ultimately the mean values of individual human actions (which are to a certain extent free and unpredictable), deterministic structures of social processes must be much more complicated, dynamic, and discontinuous.

The most important specific features of social determinism are the following:

(1) In the social sciences the notion of a *system*, to which the principle of determinism is relative, becomes rather vague. The range of phenomena on which a natural process depends is often very limited and can easily be identified and isolated. We are usually interested only in a small number of properties of the examined natural process. In order to explain them and predict their future change, it suffices to take into account a small number of other properties with which they usually stand in some relatively simple functional relationship. Even in the most complex systems of natural phenomena, where classical deterministic methods cannot, in principle, be applied (for example in quantum mechanics), the number of independent variables is small and specifiable, and their relations are rather simple. The main source of difficulties here is the impossibility of giving a full description of the initial conditions of the system. That the system of social phenomena must be much more complex follows already from the fact that social beings are also physical, chemical, biological, etc., beings. All features of the world are already contained in them; we can disregard most of them for methodological reasons, but the fact remains that in human society we deal with concrete totalities, not with quite abstract properties.

Another more complex aspect of the systems dealt with in the social sciences consists in the fact that human beings do not often respond immediately to external stimuli. They are capable of learning and of delayed reactions, and we hardly ever know where in the past the most important determining factors of a certain pattern of behavior are located. For a natural object the past is dead: There is nothing in the past which has not already been crystallized in the present form and which can play any important role in the future. For a social being a constant recurrence to the past is characteristic: The reinterpretation and reevaluation of past experiences and tradition play an important role in all subsequent life, and only in the future will there be realized some consequences of and reactions to past events. Thus the sense in which social phenomena have a history is entirely different from what is sometimes being called the "history" of a natural process.

The consequence of all this is that the notion of system in social sciences should embrace a great number of relevant variables from various spheres at various levels and in different times. As all these are hardly specifiable, the boundary conditions of the system are more or less vague. As the interaction among the variables is not fully controllable, the social scientist can hardly ever use simple deductive methods for projecting possibilities. Therefore statistical inference plays an even more important role than in the most complex disciplines of natural science.

(2) A system with reference to which we speak about the determination of a process is not just a collection of mutually related phenomena *in themselves*. The criteria of the relevance and importance of certain phenomena for some others depend on the nature of the problem, on the goal of research, and, eventually, on the general epistemological and value orientation of the person interested in determination. Therefore, a system is a *meaningful* structure. Even in the natural sciences practical needs, interest in rapid technological progress, philosophical assumptions, theological, ideological, and other prejudices may considerably influence the choice of problem, selections of data, conceptual apparatus used for the interpretation, classification and generalization of empirical material, and especially the final decision whether to accept a theory or to persist in challenging it. All history of natural sciences from Copernicus and Galileo to modern disputes on relativity, determinism, evolution, genetics, cybernetics, etc., shows convincingly that absolute objectivity of the results of natural sciences is only a matter of faith of a layman.

There is no doubt, however, that value considerations play a much greater role in the social sciences. Although science is a universal human product and the requirements of scientific method secure a considerable degree of impartiality and universal intersubjectivity, the very nature of social research is such that its results can be highly relevant to the particular interests of the social group (class, nation, race) to which a scientist belongs. Even if we disregard the cases of deliberate pragmatic behavior, the fact is that scientific methodology at best provides only necessary and *not* sufficient conditions of truth. If there is not always just one single road to truth in each situation, it is obviously possible to choose among the alternatives the one which best suits the interests and goals of the particular group. A scientist may not even be aware of certain deeply rooted values, norms, and preferences. When they influence and direct his work very strongly—when he presents half-truths as truths, favorable statistical frequencies as established scientific laws, useful correlations as casual relations, projects for the future as the already existing reality—he has clearly assumed the role of the partisan of a particular creed.

Between science and ideological or theological rationalization are many transitional cases. Particular values in question need not be restricted to one nation or class or race or religion, but may hold for a whole civilization. Thus the problem is how to be fully objective in dealing with the problem of Ancient Greece, the Renaissance, or the Enlightenment when we are not even sufficiently aware of how many fundamental value assumptions of modern Western philosophy and sciences stem from those cultures. On the other hand, it is very difficult to reach a really objective position toward, say, China, while instinctively rejecting the basic values of the Chinese cultural tradition, especially of Confucianism, Taoism, and Buddhism. What follows from all this is not that objective determination in social sciences is altogether impossible but only that it deserves a more careful analysis.

It would also be wrong to conclude that objective determination is possible only under conditions of a value-free social research. What is necessary is only to develop a self-awareness and self-criticism with respect to all kinds of *particular* value considerations (including these of a whole particular civilization). Universal human values which express the interests and needs of mankind as a whole are by no means incompatible with truth and scientific method. Without them science would be reduced to mere positive knowledge and devoid of true critical spirit.

(3) A third important specific characteristic of social determinism is that social laws cannot be very precisely formulated and quantified: The abstract concepts which they contain do not always have operational import. Consequently, the degree of their confirmation is usually not very high.

Because of these epistemological and methodological difficulties, social laws should be conceived as *tendencies* and not inevitabilities. There are also ontological reasons for construing them in this way. Social laws only exceptionally (*e.g.*, in economic science) express relations of functional dependence between simple, relatively invariant properties. In most cases they are expressions of statistical central tendencies of a mass of individual chance events. Many laws dealing with micro-phenomena, in the natural sciences also have this statistical or probabilistic form. Specific features of social laws, as contrasted with the statistical laws of natural sciences are, firstly, different reasons for which an event can be considered a chance event, and secondly, the limited validity of the law of great numbers.

In general, an event is considered *accidental* with reference to a system if it has not been fully determined by the properties of the system. In nature the reason for deviation is usually an unpredictable interaction of factors within the system or interference of factors which do not belong to the system. In society a chance event is the consequence of the fact that the individual agent is a conscious being who is able to choose among various possibilities of his action, and who is able to behave in a quite extraordinary, unpredictable way, overcoming the limits of his character and his habits, abandoning tradition, or rebelling against external social coercion.

Had people always acted consciously and freely, had society been just an aggregate of mutually isolated individuals, there would have been no order and determination in history. We would have to accept Bury's theory of Cleopatra's nose, according to which all history is just a series of accidents. However, human beings do not always behave as free agents, and they are not just isolated individuals. In a reified world man is reduced to a thing, to a fragment of a machine in the process of production, to an object of manipulation in political life.

A reified human being fails (out of inertia or fear) to make use of his ability to discriminate and choose; or his choice is not conscious and critical, thus unconscious psychic forces prevail; or again, being a split personality, he acts contrary to what has been chosen; or finally, many counter actions of various isolated individuals cancel each other out. This situation is rather similar to those in nature: Each individual action seems to be a chance event, and due to many unpredictable and uncontrollable collisions of individual wills, the outcome of an action differs considerably from what has been intended. When the number of agents and their actions increases, the deviations from a central statistical tendency become increasingly negligible. Thus the deterministic structure of the processes in "reified" social situations (for example in a market economy) are very similar to those in thermodynamics, microphysics, genetics, etc.

However historical processes have, at least temporarily, an entirely different, typically *social* deterministic structure in a really human world, in a genuine social community,

(a) where there is a considerable amount of solidarity and coordination of individual practical efforts;

(b) where there is a fairly adequate knowledge of the historical situation and a correct estimate of the realm of really open historical possibilities;

(c) finally, where there is a critical awareness of the existing social reality and its limitations.

Under these conditions the "law of great numbers" no longer holds. The historical process does not lead to the *most probable* state but to the one which is *optimal* from the point of view of human needs and goals, although it might be on the very margin of the range of real possibilities.

Thus a new quality of social determination emerges: highly creative, rational, and intense practice of sufficiently well organized social collectives makes possible departures from the middle roads of history to highly risky, but also much faster and radical paths, which open whole spectra of new possibilities that would otherwise remain hardly attainable. In such a case it is possible to speak about a discontinuity within social determinism. Man becomes free in a new, hitherto unknown sense. This is no longer freedom only with respect to certain laws which are completely independent of the human will. Man, of course, cannot abolish laws while he remains within the limitations of a given system. However, a human community which takes the risk and far exceeds the usual patterns of behavior, is able to transform the *conditions under which certain laws hold*. This is what happens in all times of great social change and creation of new economic and political system.

(4) A fourth important specific characteristic of social determinism is in connection with causality in social processes. Some social scientists regard causality as a concept of natural sciences and oppose its application to history and social sciences. They overlook, among other things, that the idea of cause has developed in connection with human practice and only afterwards was transferred, by analogy, to natural phenomena. Hume was right in saying that without our immediate experience of practically producing certain changes the ordinary classical idea of causality would lack ground. He was wrong, though, in denying that *we do have* an immediate experience of production. A great part of the explanation of historical events, certainly, consists in establishing the character of human actions that produced them.

The concept of cause in its application to physics and other natural sciences has been gradually modified and generalized, and the idea of *efficient cause* tends to disappear. After Galileo, the question "how" instead of the question "why" came into the center of attention of natural scientists. And still, the idea of cause as an active antecedent condition which is necessary and sufficient for a given change is an indispensable assumption in every experiment, in all laboratory work.

In society not only are there many more causes than in natural processes, but also the concepts of *necessity* and *sufficiency* of conditions acquire a different meaning. Only when we examine an already completed process *a posteriori* shall we be able to conclude that in the absence of certain events it would not have taken place, while their presence decisively influenced its course and outcome. Here we have included human practice as a *known* quantity, but we can never be sure about this variable *a priori*. Therefore we must often speak about "necessary" and "sufficient" conditions with certain qualifications: In the same objective conditions at a different moment people may behave differently, for they can acquire experience from their behavior in the past; they can assess differently the consequences of their actions; they can, for various rational or irrational reasons, act in an unusual, abnormal, entirely unexpected way; or, finally, they can change their objectives. The latter is especially interesting to us because it constitutes one of the essential characteristics of social determinism.

In nature causes are chiefly material phenomena. In society a cause can be *the awareness of a certain objective*. This dimension of causality has often been entirely neglected by all those historians and social scientists who believe that history is the result of blind impersonal forces, geographic, economic, political, and others. While they completely ignore the role of conscious human projects, others like Thucydides or, more recently, Collingwood, reduce it to a purely subjective, personal motivation of a free and responsible *individual*. This dilemma is surely false: An increasingly important role in history is being played by *the goals of large social groups*, which are both objective and in a double sense; they imply the change of *really existing states*, they are an expression of the interests and needs of a whole *social group* (class, nation, etc.).

While in the early phases of human history there prevailed relatively simple and crude forms of causality, which were constituted by external and impersonal factors and which were comparable to causality in nature, later, on a higher level of historical development with progressive extension of the range of human possibility, an increasingly important role in determining major social events is played by practical engagements of individuals and groups for freely chosen goals. This is one of the essential aspects of the process of the supersession of the "realm of necessity" by the "realm of freedom" to which Marx refers at the end of *Das Kapital*.

Speaking about necessity and freedom as two different realms or spheres or stages of history could be misleading and could strengthen a popular belief that one excludes the possibility of the other. The consequences of any conception which assumes the logical incompatibility of these two ideas are very serious. It seems unrealistic to hold that in our behavior there is no determination whatsoever, but if we accept the opposite view, then it seems to follow that there is no reason for holding people responsible for their actions. The only way to solve this old problem is to show the limitations in the initial opposite concepts and to remove the contradiction between them by making them more concrete and flexible by introducing necessary distinctions and qualifications.

That is what was attempted in preceding sections as far as the notion of social determinism is concerned. If we can speak meaningfully about the determination of the whole *class* of alternative future states, if practical activity of social groups is one of the most important determinant factors and if this activity depends, among other things, on freely chosen goals and values, it seems that both room for human freedom has been created within the very notion of social determinism and *vice versa*, for a determinism that has a *social* character and that presupposes a certain initial freedom of human action.

The problem of freedom, however, cannot be reduced to the question of the *possibility* of freedom within a generalized deterministic structure. The essential question here is: Under what conditions *is* a historical subject free? As freedom of social groups and communities implies freedom of individuals, we can concentrate on the latter. The main dilemma is, then, do we take freedom in a descriptive or in a predominantly critical and normative way? Or, in other words, is personal freedom a matter of immediate awareness of the given subject or a matter of critical evaluation of the whole situation?

In the former case a subject would be free in the sense of being confronted with several possibilities of choice and having the opportunity to choose the most favorable among them without any external coercion. However, this approach may immediately be challenged by asking the following questions and making the following remarks:

(1) Did the given subject *know* about *all* possibilities of the situation? People usually take less freedom than is available in a given situation. One of the reasons for this waste of opportunities is insufficient knowledge of constant forces (laws) operating in the given field. Old theories (of the Greeks, Spinoza, Hegel, Engels), according to which freedom is essentially knowledge of necessity, are no longer tenable as they stand because they reduce freedom to conformism and voluntary slavery. However, these theories had at least one merit: Without considerable relevant knowledge, freedom would degenerate into an arbitrary choice of imaginary states of affairs which have no chance of ever being realized. Thus, a choice may be considered free only if the chosen possibility is a *real* historical possibility, i.e., if it is compatible not only with logical rules, but also with all relevant empirical conditions and laws of the given system. It would be odd to say that a choice was free even though it was made on the basis of false assumptions. Ignorance is in-

compatible with freedom, although its negation, knowledge, is only its necessary (and not a sufficient) condition.

(2) A much more important reason for a widespread escape from freedom is the unwillingness to take the risk, to jeopardize an already established position in practical social life, to risk even one's very existence. Hegel in his famous analysis of the relationship between the master and the servant in *Phänomenologie des Geistes* shows how, in the conditions of social struggle, freedom can only be the result of the acceptance of possible death. Man ("self-consciousness" in Hegel's terminology), who depends too much on life and who fears death, becomes a slave, subordinated to the will of his master and, in the best case, experiences freedom only in his thought, *i.e.*, in an alienated way.

Even if we disregard particular historical conditions under which social relationships acquire the form of the merciless fight for the position of a master who satisfies his greed (*Begierde*) by appropriating the results of the work of a servant, the more general question is: Can one ever be at the maximum level of possible freedom in his time if he does not overcome his fear while taking the risk of exploring practically the limits of his possible being?

(3) A free choice presupposes the existence of a criterion of an assessment and selection among alternative possibilities. The question, then arises whether the subject is aware of his standards of evaluation, whether these have ever been critically examined, whether they eventually correspond to his needs.

(4) The next step in the critical analysis of freedom is an examination of the authenticity of the very needs that direct the whole process of free selection. Is it not the case that many of these needs are artificial, built in by the powerful influences of the social surroundings to which the individual belongs? And how are we to distinguish these from those needs that are true and authentic? Theoretically, this question can be answered only by developing a whole anthropological theory. A more concrete and descriptive answer would be the following: while we are satisfying our genuine and basic needs we have an immediate experience of the intensity and wealth of life, of our own power, of our self-fulfillment. On the other hand, it is characteristic of artificial needs that their satisfaction is often followed by the feelings of emptiness, satiety, boredom, uprootedness, powerlessness—in one word, nothingness. It is important to note that some of the basic needs of a developed personality who has become a true social being are a need for solidarity and social justice and a need for such kinds of activity, including material production, which will satisfy the needs and enrich the life of another person.

(5) The development of a critical self-consciousness opens up some new problems. First, is not even my self-consciousness (at least partly) a result of manipulation? Then, is my authentic self a simple totality or a dynamic field with considerable tensions among more or less egoistic and more or less altruistic social motives and impulses? Usually, my self can be fulfilled in more than one way. This implies that every realization of one possibility of my self is at the same time the negation of some other possibility of my authentic self. Is not, then, every freedom at the same time an act of the limitation of freedom, not only with respect to somebody else but also to myself? Social determinism and freedom presuppose each other; they are necessary moments of human praxis in a concrete historical situation.

To sum up, what has been overlooked by many philosophers who wrote on this subject is that both determinism and freedom make sense only with respect to a certain context or situation, or, more precisely, with respect to a certain *system*, constituted by the language and logic at our disposal, by the problem and goal of our inquiry, and by certain information which we consider relevant to our problem.

Determination, then, means elimination of all other logically possible states except one unique class of real possibilities, which in the special case of strict classical determinism contains only one element. The more laws and other limiting conditions there are, the more restrictive they are, the higher is the degree of determinacy of a system. Instead of just two ways of examining and describing this situation (determinism in the classical sense and indeterminism) we have, in fact, a continuum of deterministic methods varying in the degree of determinacy.

In society and the social sciences the very notion of the system, for various reasons which I mentioned, is rather vague—the number of variables is much greater, value considerations play a much more important role, and the behavior of each individual member of the system is not always and fully predictable.

When society or a privileged group in society succeeds in manipulating individuals to a great extent by coercion or by suitable education and propaganda, or when individuals are isolated, unorganized, and governed by blind social forces or by laws of great numbers,—*e.g.*, in the relatively free market—the degree of freedom of individuals is very low or the degree of determinacy of their behavior is very high. Of course, people may have illusions about their freedom: They can imagine that they are free whenever an external authority leaves them two or more possibilities among which to choose. This imaginary freedom is, in fact, determined by the criteria of choosing and by the character of our needs, which can be artificial ones, and also by our unwillingness to accept any risk.

However insofar as individuals live in a situation which allows them a choice, and also insofar as they have critically examined and accepted their criteria of choosing, and to the extent to which they are ready to risk their social status—their security and eventually even their lives—their behavior becomes increasingly free. Freedom here does not mean denial of any causality or determination, and by no means can we speak about absolute freedom.

There are various steps of this relative freedom. At the lowest level freedom is merely choice among given alternatives. The level of freedom depends on the extent to which we control various limiting conditions of the system, and according to how well we are able to realize those real possibilities which (no matter how probable they might be) best correspond to our needs.

The highest historically possible level of freedom is characterized by the fullfillment of fundamental human needs which have been developed during the preceding history and which constitute the necessary basis for future self-production of men. This level can be attained only when associated individuals by their coordinate efforts succeed in fully superseding the unsatisfactory existing system and create conditions for a new one, in which different laws and limiting conditions will hold and which opens a larger field for human praxis.

IS THERE A
"PHILOSOPHY OF HISTORY"?

Henry Steele Commager

The philosophy of history is a chewed up subject. How convenient if I could fall back on the disclaimer of James Ford Rhodes in his presidential address to the American Historical Association—that he had little new to say, but that "to a sympathetic audience, to people who love history, there is always the chance that a fresh treatment may present the commonplaces in some different combination, and augment, for the moment, an interest which is perennial." I lack even this consolation, for I very much doubt that this audience can be described as one that "loves" history; it is, rather, one that loves philosophy and is sternly determined to keep history in its place, though by no means certain just what that place is.

The initial, elementary, persuasive, ubiquitous difficulty in our discussion of history, or of the philosophy of history, is semantic. For there are, needless to say, two quite different meanings in the word *history*, and we here at this conference use the word in both senses. There is history as what happened, which is what most of you are concerned with; and there is history as the record of what happened, which is what I am concerned with. As most people use these meanings interchangeably, it is no wonder that we aggravate implicit confusion. How much better if we would speak of history as what happened, and use the word *historiography* for the record of what happened; how unfortunate that this is so dreadful a word.

It should be clear that history as *what happened*, over some thousands or tens of thousands of years, has no inherent philosophy. It is only in historiography that we can discover, or insinuate, some philosophy. History has no philosophy, but historians do. Whatever philosophy is found in history has first been put there by some historian—or perhaps by some philosopher. When the historian purports to discover some laws or principles of history, they are laws and principles of his own making or his own discovery and application; when the philosopher reads some purpose into history, it is his own reading.

Indeed the very concept of history is an artificial one. There is nothing that is in fact *history* as there are atoms, rocks, or chemicals. These things exist in Nature; they would be there if man passed away from the scene. But history does not exist in Nature, but merely in man's imagination, and it is not there unless man is there to imagine it and formulate it. It is a sophisticated concept whereby man organizes his collective memory and imposes order and meaning on an incoherent past. If it is not, as Napoleon said it was, an agreed-on lie, then it is an agreed-on story. What happened at any one moment—let us say Washington crossing the Delaware or the assassination of Lincoln—is not *merely* an agreed-on story; but to put together a thousand or a hundred thousand disparate events and call them the Battle of Trenton or the American Revolution, the biography of Lincoln or the history of the Civil War, is to agree on a story.

This, to be sure, does not get us very far, for it can be said about a great deal that makes it possible to carry on life and conversation and perhaps to create civilization. Thus the concepts of civilization, of culture, of a nation are all fictions, or, if you prefer, abstract concepts, to which we give what we pretend is concrete form.

History, Diderot is accused of saying, is the other world of the philosophers. Turn this around, and it is even more true. Philosophy is the other world of the historian. It is to history what theology is to morals, and philosophy has, too, much of the mystery, the complexity, the special vocabulary and the professionalism of theology.

Some historians yearn for the other world; they are, perhaps, the orthodox. Some reject the concept of another world; they are the atheists. Some toy with the possibility of its existence, but do not take it seriously; they are the agnostics. Some are materialists who do not believe in the other world or in anything not known to the sensations. Some are dilettanti who simply don't care, one way or the other; they are the entertainers.

What is most impressive is that so few of those who are in the habit of calling themselves historians have, in fact, concerned themselves, in any formal way, with the philosophy of history or, for that matter, with the methodology of history. The problems that agitated a Hegel, a Fichte, a Herder, or that concern a Toynbee, an Isaiah Berlin or a Karl Jaspers, do not concern them, not consciously in any event. Even the laborious techniques, the sophisticated and self-conscious methods, set forth in the shelf of handbooks that all graduate students are supposed to ponder, they brush aside or ignore. Macaulay, Green, Lecky, Tocqueville, Guizot, Taine, Von Sybel, Troels-Lund, Parkman, and Henry Adams take what is called methodology in their stride, confident that it is the common sense of the matter, as indeed it is. Mostly, they take the philosophy of history in their stride too, confident that if there is any such thing, it will emerge, in its own way, from what they write.

It is little wonder that almost all speculation about the philosophy of history comes from philosophers rather than from historians, and that such speculation as does come from historians, comes from those who do not write history, but only speculate about it. If we fasten our attention on the great historical writers (does this beg the whole question?) from Thucydides through Gibbon to Mommsen and to Churchill, we will, I think, be impressed with how little any of them have to say about historical philosophy. Doubtless all of them had a philosophy, and some of them may have had a philosophy of history, but how few ever formulated or even confessed one. The great creative historians of the past simply took philosophy for granted.

This is just what Professor Bernard Bailyn of Harvard said for himself and his generation in one of these symposia:

In so far as my concern has been with understanding, teaching and writing about what has happened in the past, I have never once felt it necessary to work out precise answers to such questions . . . questions of objectivity and subjectivity, the nature of fact, etc.—in order to advance my work in history. . . . Though I have discussed with other historians such matters [as the problems of the philosophy of history] I have never yet heard from them, either, a statement to the effect that their work in history has been affected one way or another by such considerations. (*Philosophy and History, A Symposium*, ed. Sidney Hook, New York University Press, New York 1963, p. 94.)

I know no major historian in American who would take exception to this observation. Most practicing historians are impatient with philosophies of history, or even with historical philosophy, and pay respect to them only on ceremonial occasions such as this, or, like Henry Adams, after they have ceased to write history.

I suspect the situation is much the same in other areas where philosophers seem to impose themselves on practitioners. I very much doubt that great composers, from Bach to Beethoven, paid much attention either to the philosophers of music or to musicologists. I doubt that practicing artists from Titian to the Impressionists paid much attention to what the philosophers of art had to say; there are few exceptions here—Reynolds with his annual discourses on Art, or Whistler, or Henri; but how superficial their observations when contrasted with the profundities of a Winckelmann or a Hauser! Poets and novelists, who are habituated to reading, doubtless read the critics and philosophers, but it may be doubted that they conform to them or are greatly influenced by them. Some of them, like Henry James, provide their own philosophy, to be sure, but it turns out, on examination, to be more methodology than philosophy. Thus, the separation between the philosopher and the practitioner, in the realm of history, is not surprising but familiar.

When I say that it is the philosophers, not the historians, who speculate about history, I am speaking of formal and overt philosophers. In a sense, all historians are philosophers, as all thoughtful and articulate men are philosophers. History, like religion, art, literature, is imbued with philosophy, because all who think about it or contribute to it confess a point of view, an attitude, a body of convictions or of prejudices. The trouble with talking about these is obvious enough, namely, that every thoughtful historian has his own philosophy, and we cannot talk about all of them. We can, however, put some of them in groups and talk about them collectively, and I shall try to do this. But let me be quite clear: I will be talking not about philosophies of history, which are nonexistent, but about philosophies held by historians, which are ubiquitous.

Perhaps the historian is closer to the lawyer than to any other professional interpreter. The lawyer and, of course, the judge reconstruct the past, whether of an automobile accident, a crime, a will, or a labor dispute. They cannot recover the whole of the past, nor can any jury or any court; all are confronted by gaps in the evidence, by witnesses who disagree or who are interested parties or who lie, by stupidity and blundering. The lawyer and the judge can never be really sure of their facts, and they can never be sure that they have all the relevant evidence. Like historians, they have to take a good deal on faith; they have to fill in the gaps with their own imaginations—or get along without them altogether. They have to make judgments about character; and they have to test evidence and arguments by precedents. What they finally arrive at is not, in fact, ultimate justice or ultimate truth; it is an approximation of both, or so they hope. But unless they are incompetent or corrupt, what they arrive at is usually acceptable and enables the court and society to get on with the job. The lawyer and the judge know that neither their findings nor their principles are final; that new evidence may crop up that will change things; that new points of view—philosophies if you will—will put a different face on many matters, invalidate old opinions and precedents, and create new ones.

We call the work of judges and jurisprudents the science of the law, and we talk about the philosophy of law just as we do about the philosophy of history. Needless to say, law is not a science, and not since the eighteenth-century faith in Natural Law have sensible jurisprudents talked about the philosophy of law as—to use Justice Holmes's apt phrase—"a brooding omniscience in the sky." Each generation works out its own philosophy of law, at one time clinging to concepts of Natural Law, at another imagining something called Historical Jurisprudence, later coming to what we call Sociological Jurisprudence, then on— if on is the *mot juste*—to Legal Realism. These are, of course, concepts and attitudes jurisprudents read into law and what is more, write into it. When they write it what they have is not something called LAW with capital letters, but particular laws, just as historians do not have something called HISTORY, in capital letters, but particular histories.

Doubtless the quickest way to get to the philosophy of history is to turn to the thing itself, that is, *history*. This, I note, is something that philosophers who write about the subject are very reluctant to do. It is only when historians such as Trevelyan, Nevins, Rowse, or Wedgwood turn their attention to historiography or historical philosophy that history gets into the picture. It may be argued, to be sure, that we cannot talk seriously about history, either as past or as record, until we know what it is, and that to discuss particular histories, those by Thucydides, for example, or Gibbon, or Namier, is to beg the question. This is worse than pedantry; it is a confession of bankruptcy, for on this principle we cannot talk about philosophy, or education, or politics or art, or anything very important. Indeed, carry this principle to its logical conclusion, and young men and poets will be debarred from talking about love until they can define it.

May we not say, without being thought Philistine, that history is what those we regard as great historians write, just as we say that higher education is what goes on at Harvard and Columbia, Oxford and Cambridge, Upsala and Leyden; or just as we agree to suspend the effort to define political parties or to discover any philosophy that controls them, and study them in terms of Democratic and Republican, of Whig and Tory, of Conservative and Labour parties?

If history is what historians write, historical philosophy is the philosophy which historians entertain when they write their histories, or which they are tempted to subscribe to when they study history, or which they impose on history, consciously or unconsciously. Strictly speaking, then, there are as many historical philosophies as there are historians; in other words, all history is subjective. This does not mean that history as *past* is not a reality; of course it is. It means that what the historian, or what a group or a school of historians, agree on as a particular past is a subjective matter. History itself has no pattern, but historians impose a pattern upon it; they call that pattern "history" and pretend that it was there all the time. But it was not; it was in their minds all the time. Take for example, a convenient term such as *The Enlightenment*, one we all use as if it were indeed a real thing. In fact, what happened in the Spain of Charles III, in Pombal's Portugal, in Leopold's Tuscany, in Sonnenfels' Austria, in Frederick's Berlin, in the Stockholm of Gustavus III and the France of the Encyclopaedists, did not at the time have continuity or sequence or order. But we have put these and a thousand other things together and called them, collectively, The Enlightenment. We go even further. We require that all other events of this era fit into The Enlightenment, one way or another; if they are not willing to fit into our pattern, we reject them as if they were damaged goods.

If general terms such as *Enlightenment, Renaissance, Ancient Times, the Church, militarism, democracy,* and *religious toleration,* which are the coinage of the historical realm, are in reality abstractions or, as Toynbee says, myths, what purpose do they serve? Perhaps the simplest answer is that we cannot get along without them. What are we to substitute for the terms *Reformation* or *Enlightenment* or *United States?* It is important, however, that we keep in mind their symbolical or mythological character. They are agreed-on fictions, as indeed the value of our dollar bill is an agreed-on fiction or as the sanctity (I speak now in secular terms) of a marriage ceremony is an agreed-on fiction. They differ from such ceremonial fictions as the dollar bill or the marriage ceremony in that they do not have a universally agreed upon character. Everyone knows just what a dollar bill stands for, and when prices are marked in dollars we know that the storekeeper's dollar and our own dollar are the same thing. But when we use the words *democracy* or *Renaissance* or *militarism,* we cannot be sure that any two people mean the same thing by them. How familiar this is even now, in our current crisis. President Johnson read very different meanings into such terms as *vital interest, commitment, the SEATO Treaty, Communism,* and so forth than did Mr. Walter Lippmann or Senator William J. Fulbright. The fact is that as every historical philosophy is the philosophy of an historian, so important historical terms are to be defined as terms used by particular historians. Not only is historical philosophy subjective, the historical vocabulary is subjective as well.

Yet our situation is not really desperate, though it is vexatious. The trouble with historical terms is the trouble with almost all terms. We can, and do, speak of the beauty of a sunset, the melody of a Beethoven sonata, the fragrance of a rose and the virtue of a saint without any scientific agreement on the meaning and sense of these terms. So when, over the generations, scholars have worked out an agreement on what is implied by such words as *Renaissance* or *Reformation,* and on those aspects of Renaissance and Reformation that especially deserve attention, we need not quarrel with them. We do, after all, study Italy in the fifteenth-century, not Turkey; we study art and letters and science and philosophy, not, let us say, electricity or carpet-weaving. We acquiesce in this vocabulary, in these fictions about what is interesting, what is important, because in fact they have proved themselves profitable. Over the generations and the centuries men have found that there was a lift to the spirit, an excitement in the mind, in studying fifteenth-century Florence or sixteenth-century Venice that was not, on the whole, to be found in studying Greenland during these centuries, or the history of the Algonquin Indians. These are not scientific findings, but personal and subjective conclusions.

When the historian reconstructs a chapter of the past he tries to be what he calls *scientific,* and sometimes he flatters himself that he is certainly objective, and is perhaps scientific. The will-o'-the-wisp of scientific history bemused Ranke and has bemused his disciples ever since. Surely it is unnecessary to point out that no historian is, or can be, truly impartial or truly scientific, in the sense that a chemist or a physicist or a biologist can be impartial and scientific. Every historian is not only conditioned by, but dominated by his own fate, and none has ever been abe to surmount that fate. I have in mind not ostentatious interests and prejudices, but basic and built-in conditions. Almost every historian with whom we are acquainted, past or present, is European rather than Asian or African; he is civilized rather than primitive; he is in all likelihood white (occasionally, in the United States, black) rather than yellow or red or brown; he is, with some exceptions, a product of the Judeo-Christian tradition. He was, until recently, male rather than female, and he is mature rather than adolescent. He is "modern" rather than ancient or medieval, for the overwhelming body of history has been written in the past two or three centuries. These basic factors condition our history so powerfully, that particular influences of nationality or party are relatively unimportant.

It is this elementary consideration that makes so many of the solemn philosophies of history of the past irrelevant. After all, those who formulated such universal explanations as the working out of the will of God, or of a Zeitgeist, or of the principle of Progress, or of cycles, were in every case western white men brought up in a particular tradition. They were, all of them, parochial. The God who guided the destinies of man turned out to be the Christian God, usually even the Catholic; the absolutes and universals of a Herder turned out to be not merely European but German. Theories of progress were not based on a study of the Inca and Aztec civilizations or of the societies of Polynesia or of Japan, but on that of the Europeans. Almost alone among modern philosophers of history—perhaps of all philosophers of history—Arnold Toynbee has sought to embrace all civilizations in his theory.

The philosophy of history, then, is the philosophy of historians who write it. Does this leave us with a thousand different philosophies of history? Indeed it does, and if we are a Feuter or a James Westfall Thompson we try valiantly to say something about most of them. Fortunately for us, historians, like critics, artists and jurists, tend to arrange themselves into more or less neat patterns; and we can, with some justification, deal with them as groups, ignoring the idiosyncrasies. Carlyle and Michelet were not really alike, but they are forever linked together in studies of romanticism, cultural nationalism, and historiography. So, too, with Prescott and Motley in the United States, or Von Sybel and Treischke in Germany. We know that all German historians of the nineteenth century were not followers of Ranke, and—as it is more nearly contemporary and subject to observation—that not all modern English historians are disciples of Sir Lewis Namier. Yet we speak of a Ranke school and a Namier school, and, what is more, we can rely on a general understanding of these terms.

If we reject the notion that laws or philosophies are inherent in the stuff of history and embrace instead the assumption that groups, or schools, of historians display a preference for one or another approach to history, and that we may therefore speak of Schools of historical philosophy, we can get on with the job. For now our inquiry is directed not to the hopeless task of discovering philosophies *in* history but to the more rewarding task of finding the pervasive attitudes towards history and the uses of history which any one school or age displays. Our interest now is both philosophical and historical: to discover how the prevalent use of history by any one generation illuminates the character and the philosophy of that generation.

This approach is familiar enough in other realms, in belles lettres, for example, or art or music. It has been applied to historiography by a few major scholars—Dilthey, Cassirer, Max Weber, Meinecke, Jaspers, Collingwood, Croce, among others. With most of these, however, it has been subordinate to something else—to literature or philosophy. I suggest quite simply the study of historiography, that is, of the uses of the past, as history.

In a broad way we can discern two persistent and overarching uses of history from the beginning of that study to our own time. The first, and incomparably the longest, the largest, the most distinguished, is that which we associate with Dionysius of Halicarnassus and with Bolingbroke: It is that history is philosophy teaching by examples. The second, which has had champions for some centuries and which is very much in the ascendancy in the past century, is history as the scientific and comprehensive reconstruction of the past.

I will mention but pass by two subsidiary concepts of history. The first of these held the field for centuries, and without opposition or challenge: that history is quite simply the unfolding of God's plan for man. I do not deal with this because I imagine none of you is prepared to entertain it in any but a symbolical sense; because even if it were true there would be very little to say about it except Amen; and because, it must be confessed, it did not produce very good history anyway. The second merits only a word, but an amiable word. It is history as entertainment—as indeed, to borrow Jacques Barzun's phrase for science— a Glorious Entertainment. Certainly, this is one of the things that keeps history going. It is why children read history, usually in the form of poems or hero stories; and why the majority of adults read history, usually in the form of historical novels like *Gone With the Wind* or plays like *Macbeth*. Scorn not the popular history, the historical novel, the historical drama! Winston Churchill, who has some claim to be considered the greatest English historian of our time, said that he learned all of his English history from Shakespeare's plays; that is of course a slight exaggeration, but the important thing is that he thought it was worth saying.

Let us then consider what has been the prevalent and persistent use of history: history as philosophy teaching by examples. This was the argument of Thucydides and of Tacitus, Plutarch and Livy. "What chiefly makes the study of history wholesome and profitable," says Livy, "is this, that you behold the reasons of every kind of experience set forth as on a conspicuous monument; from these you may choose for yourself and for your own state to imitate, from these mark for avoidance what is shameful in the conception and shameful in the result." So said Machiavelli, that "those who wish to learn the achievement of this end (virtue and triumph) need not take any more trouble than to put before their eyes the lives of good men . . . in whose lives they will see so much mutual confidence and satisfaction existing between the governing and the governed that they will desire to imitate the conduct of these men." So said Sir Walter Raleigh in his ambitious *History of the World*, that "the end and scope of all history is to teach us by examples of times past, such wisdom as may guide our desires and actions."

The purpose and end of history was to discover those grand moral laws that man should know, and knowing, obey. This was the search that sent the great eighteenth-century historians back to the Ancient World and persuaded them to reflect on the rise and decline of empires; this was what persuaded them to study the Orient, Europe, America, and even the islands of the Pacific. All particular histories were like tributaries, each one carrying its own sediment of truth, pouring it into the main stream of history, where the historians could dredge it up. "The course of things has always been the same [wrote Bolingbroke]. National virtue and national vice have always produced national happiness and national misery." And the great David Hume—now there is an authority philosophers will listen to—added: "Mankind are so much the same that History informs us of nothing new or strange in this particular. Its chief use is only to discover the constant and universal principles of human nature."

No use to elaborate on anything so familiar; it may be said that in the eighteenth century every historian and statesman in Europe and in America subscribed to this view of history, or every one except Vico and Justus Möser and nobody read them anyway. "One cannot remind oneself too often of crimes and disasters," wrote Voltaire, for "These, no matter what people say, can be forestalled." Clearly the Founding Fathers agreed with this principle. All of them were immersed in history, especially the history of the ancient world. Almost all of them wrote history, though not under that title; they called their histories *Notes on Virginia* or *The Federalist Papers* instead. They drew on history to justify independence, guide them along the paths of federalism, provide examples for every experiment in politics and warnings against every danger. Washington drew on history when he warned his countrymen against the baleful influence of factions and parties; Jefferson invoked history when he denounced the Alien and Sedition Acts; Madison and Hamilton called on history to justify the arguments of *The Federalist*.

Nor did the habit of looking to history for moral lessons and for sustenance end with the Enlightenment. Lincoln began his Gettysburg Address with a reminder of what had happened four score and seven years ago, and Winston Churchill tells us, in one of the moving passages of his *Second World War* that when he heard the news of the attack on Pearl Harbor he knew that Britain was saved: "I had studied the American Civil War fought out to the last desperate inch . . . I went to bed and slept the sleep of the saved."

I need not elaborate upon the second major school of scientific history, or, as it is now popular to call it, technical history. Most historians today count thenselves practitioners of scientific history, and the Xerox machine and the computer have bemused a good many into the realm of technical history: the study of a particular episode or problem so intensively that we can claim to have all the important facts about it, and to be able therefore to reconstruct it. It is a kind of cousin to the monkey-Shakespeare theory: that if an infinity of monkeys hit the keys of an infinity of typewriters for an infinity of time, they would write the works of Shakespeare.

Needless to say, even if we were to concede the most daring claims of the scientific or the technical historians, we would not be very far along the path of a true reconstruction of the past. Technical history may be able to tell us how many people actually voted in Kent County, Connecticut in 1770, and that is a useful item, not less useful because it tends to confirm the guesses of George Bancroft about democracy in eighteenth-century America. (It is a bit like the triumph of the computer investigation of authorship of *The Federalist Papers*, which confirmed the analyses of Douglass Adair.) But technical history cannot tell us why anyone voted, or failed to vote; or why he voted as he did; or what were the considerations in his mind, or the prejudices, that persuaded him to vote; or what were the results of *his* voting.

In theory, the moralistic historians and the scientific historians are far apart, for they confess to different philosophies of history. The first looks to history for what it teaches; the second is interested in the past for its own sake. In fact, however—and how often this is true—the two work out pretty much the same way. Both are narrative and both are analytical. Romantic historians sought to know the truth and to reconstruct the past; and some of them, such as Parkman in America and Lecky in England, did it so well that it has not been improved upon by their technical successors. Technical historians do not, in fact, eschew philosophy; they turn out, on closer examination, to be very much interested in what the past has to say about the present. The Namier who organized a scientific and technical research into members of Parliament in 1760 was also the Namier who wrote profound interpretative essays on the revolutions of 1848 and other matters. The Laslett who is on the way to explaining for us just how large families were in seventeenth-century English villages, just when girls got married, just how they lived within the family, is also the Laslett who studies the political theories of John Locke and has a good deal to say that none of his colleagues like about what Oxford and Cambridge Universities should be.

One thing that should be said, if only parenthetically, is that a great history, like a great novel or a great work of art, is an integral whole. Great philosophical historians—a Troels-Lund, a Lecky, a Parkman—are scientific. Great scientific historians—a Maitland, a Holdsworth, a Meinecke—are philosophical. A work of history is the product of a single mind brooding on historical material. It is not something that can be dressed up to meet all conceivable objections. It must have its own character and integrity, and to monkey around with it, adding a bit of demography here, a bit of psychiatry there, a bit of social anthropology or sociological theory elsewhere is to endanger both the integrity and the usefulness of the work.

When we read history, we may read it in three ways: first, for entertainment (and to disparage the importance of pleasure and entertainment in history is like underestimating the importance of the body in education); second, as those who wrote it (particularly in the long period before 1900) meant us to read it, that is, as a story illustrating, or proving, great moral truths; third, as an index to the mind of the individual and of the generation that produced it. Here we find a *philosophy* of history, namely, the philosophy of the school, or the age, that produced a particular body of historical literature.

We may not always be entertained by the history we read, though most of the history that has somehow survived does have the power to please, excite, and edify. We need not accept the great moral truths that former historians found as they contemplated the history of the past, though we do, in fact, accept many of them, and we do persist in finding "lessons" in history. It is the third activity that permits us to act a bit like philosophers, or like historians interested in philosophy. For here, as in literature and art and science we can read something of the *Weltanschauung* of a generation or an age. Some societies have cultivated history rather than literature or the arts—American society of the eighteenth century for example—and here a study of what uses the society made of history throws a flood of light on the philosophy cherished by the society.

It is for example, in history, better than elsewhere, that we can read what Americans of Jefferson's generation thought of the nature of man, and of the relation of man to society and government, and of morality to politics. It is in their historical and political writings that we read their theory of Progress, a theory which differed markedly from that entertained by the *philosophers* abroad; what they conceived to be the nature of the Enlightenment; to what extent they believed in the liberty of the mind; how they hoped to overcome the corruption and selfishness of man. We can read here why they went to Rome rather than Greece for their lessons, to the era of the Commonwealth rather than to the Restoration; why they thought that they were part of history for some purposes, but not for others; why they thought that America represented a new page in the book of history.

The subjective nature of history can be illustrated by the varied historical interpretations that rage about us today. We are witnessing, even now, convulsive efforts to formulate some philosophy of history. These are inspired, in part at least, by the deep crisis of our time: the crisis of American involvement in Vietnam. We note at once that a philosophy of history is not a product of calm reflection, in a vacuum, but of clamorous demands of realities. A score of theories emerge to explain our involvement. Some are immediate and, technically, superficial or false: that we "committed ourselves there" or that the Vietnamese fired at the *S. S. Maddox*. Some are broader and more general: that we are confronted by Communism, which is aggressive and dangerous, or that we have a "vital interest" in Vietnam. A few are more philosophical: that we are experiencing something called "the Agony of Power," or that we are responding to the "Wave of the Future."

All of these explanations and responses to particular events represent, in various forms, a philosophy of history. All attempt an explanation of a series of historical events important enough to seem to require an explanation and all are based, presumably, on the same available facts. All, too, reflect much the same larger experience with modern life, substantially the same education, the same body of moral presuppositions, the same standards of conduct, the same familiarity with history. All those who work out theories to explain the war in Vietnam have, or could have, the same knowledge of Communism, the same knowledge of American foreign policy, the same knowledge of Asia and China and Vietnam, the same knowledge of modern war and atomic weapons, and so forth.

There are variations here, but they are minor and are accounted for by human frailty. The differences in philosophy, that is, in interpretation of history, must spring from something else. And, of course, it does. It springs from different views of life, of nationalism, of war, of mankind. The explanations—*philosophies* if you will—*are all subjective*. They do not depend exclusively on logical response to a body of known facts, as they would if they were objective and scientific, but on subjective response to selected facts, on the attitudes inherent in the commentators and historians.

What is true of the interpretation of the war in Vietnam is true of almost all historical interpretation, or all those explanations we dignify by the term philosophy. Just as the explanations of our presence in Vietnam turn out to be intensely personal, so most explanations in history, in all ages, turn out to be fundamentally personal. In all cases—from Herodotus and Thucydides and Plutarch and Josephus to Voltaire and Gibbon, Michelet and Carlyle, Maitland and Holdsworth, Macaulay and Churchill, Croce and Toynbee—what we discover to be the philosophy of history turns out to be the philosophy of the particular historian.

The philosophy of history is not something inherent in history, as certain properties are inherent in chemicals or gases. Rather, it is something that is inherent in the historians. It is not a product of logic within history or even a product of logic in the historian; it is the product of the individual experience and personality of the observer.

If, with all the information at our disposal—more perhaps than previous generations had for comparable episodes of history—our best scholars cannot agree on where the war in Vietnam fits in or on any interpretation of the war, what reason is there to suppose that the conclusion and principles and laws worked out for the other hundreds or thousands of chapters of history stand on any sounder ground or provide any surer contributions to the formulation of laws or of philosophy? If we cannot even agree whether we are in Vietnam because we are required to be there by the mystique of power or because we succumbed to the arrogance of power, why should we suppose that there was, or could ever be, agreement in the infinite number of accepted chapters of history which furnish so many of us with our principles and our laws?

We come back, then, to history as individual, history as subjective, and history as contemporary. We come back to historical philosophy not as something inherent in history but as something inherent in the mind of the historian.

The romantic historians of the nineteenth century—Carlyle in England, Michelet in France, von Sybel in Germany, Motley and Parkman in America—were likewise moralists. They too studied history only to come away with their deepest convictions happily confirmed by the evidence of the past; they too studied the past to indulge these convictions. They turned to the same history that had attracted Gibbon and Voltaire, Raynal and Holberg, but unlike these they read from it the lesson that Providence had intended men to organize into national states. They studied the art, literature, philosophy and morals, that the philosophers had studied; but unlike them, they discovered that men were everywhere not the same, but very different, and that social institutions, far from being forever fixed, were controlled by laws of change and of evolution. Where their predecessors had been bemused by Man, by Society, by Humanity, they celebrated the Individual.

The scientific and technical historians, too, tell us as much about themselves and their societies as about the past. They do, to be sure, throw light on the past, but it is not a light that leads. They search out, or create, statistics, but they do not search out meaning. A Namier gives us all the relevant facts about every member of the Parliaments of the 1760's and '70's, but he cannot tell us as much as did Lecky or a George

Otto Trevelyan about why they failed to understand the greatest issue of their time or to solve it. The method of the Namier school is to pile up evidence which may eventually explain something—not big problems like why the American colonies revolted, but small problems like why the Commons voted the way it did on a certain measure. The method, and philosophy, of the Trevelyan school is quite different. It is frankly subjective. It says, come, let us contemplate this fascinating chapter of our history, let us exercise our judgment on it, and our imagination; let us try to understand why Americans were so stubborn and so impatient, why Englishmen were so stupid; let us see if we cannot draw from this chapter of our history valuable lessons about the triumph of freedom and constitutionalism over tyranny. The Namier method is to confine oneself to ascertainable data and let the data speak for itself, if it is willing to do so; the Trevelyan method is to bring to focus on the problem of the American Revolution not only all available data (and far less was available in the first decade of the century than in the third and the fourth), but all that we know, or think we know, or imagine about the period and about human nature—to try to understand through facts and through imagination what seems important.

The Namier school is interested in the record, and technical historians expect the facts to speak for themselves. It can, however, never assemble a complete record, or even a satisfactory record, for while it may record overt and public facts it cannot, in the nature of things, record covert and private facts. The facts never do, in fact, speak for themselves, not even in a statistical abstract, where somebody has had to arrange them first. The Namier and the technical schools assume that facts have some intrinsic importance, and I note that some of our philosophers cling to the notion that some facts are, intrinsically, more important than others —those that have more important consequences. But even such words as *importance*, *value*, or *consequences* are subjective; there are no cosmic values. What is important to Trevelyan is not important to Namier, and vice versa. A "value," we sometimes forget, is not something concrete, like a diamond; it is something a historian or a society has hit upon or conjured up. Such values—let us say progress, or freedom, or population increase, (which was a primary value in the 18th century, but is now a non-value) or rugged individualism, or beauty—are given substance and are imposed upon the quivering facts of the past. Surely it is elementary to note that not only each generation and each society, but each individual has different values, and that no two generations, societies, or individual historians agree on the value or on the "importance" of anything, whether it is the Inquisition, the Declaration of Independence, a Mozart sonata, or a professional football game. Cotton

Mather's views of Salem witchcraft were very different from those of James Truslow Adams; Pope Paul III's view of the Inquisition markedly different from that of Henry C. Lea; and George Fitzhugh and Theodore Parker, contemporaries and historians read different values into slavery. The notion that if we somehow had all the facts about witchcraft, the Inquisition, or slavery, we would be able to write an objective and scientific history of these institutions is, of course, a delusion.

There is a further and deeper difficulty with technical history: that it rests on a series of unfounded assumptions. It assumes, for example, that if only we can get all the facts about a subject, let us say, the population of Rochester, we will be in a position to explain something or say something meaningful about Rochester. But the only kind of facts you can get about the population of Rochester are statistical. We can, if we are assiduous, compile a directory of every inhabitant; that is, we can collect the kind of fact that permits itself to be recorded. But to suppose that when we have a list of every inhabitant of Rochester, we are in position to say anything meaningful about that city (except that at a particular moment its population reached a certain number) is absurd, especially when we consider the fact that the Census of 1960 "missed" about six per cent of the total population! The kind of facts we can get turn out to be quantitatively interesting but qualitatively insignificant.

We then come to a second misguided assumption: that when the historian has all the facts about population or housing, these will point to some inevitable and universally accepted conclusion, just as a collection of all the facts about a combination of chemicals, or about the pattern of genes, points to an inevitable conclusion. This is simply not true. We do know, thanks to the labors of careful historians, all the overt facts about Lincoln's relief of Fort Sumter and the attack on that fort. Yet, historians have quarreled over the whole story for a hundred years and still do and forever will. The point is that we do not and cannot know the really essential facts—those about Lincoln's mind and character, his hopes and fears, his motives, and his purposes, and his guesses—nor about those of all the others who made the fateful decisions. Here the historian supplies his own interpretations. He does it on the basis of the known facts, but more, on the basis of his own understanding of the situation, of the character of Lincoln, of the character of Beauregard, of the attitudes of members of Lincoln's Cabinet and of Major Anderson in the Fort, and so forth. That is, to make sense of this chapter of our history—a chapter fraught with "important" consequences—the historian, even the computerized historian, must use his imagination. In a good historian it is a well-disciplined imagination. If the historian is wise, judicious, learned, critical, profound, his explana-

tions carry weight (not necessarily conviction, for now the character of
the reader enters into the equation). If he is superficial, inaccurate,
narrow, and prejudiced, his explanations do not carry weight. Once
again, it all comes back to the historian—all, that is, that is really
important.

Technical history, then, like philosophical history, tells us a good
deal about the historian who professes it, and about the age that embraces it, or segments of it, and thus provides us with a philosophy of
that particular history. We can see, already, how naturally technical history fits into our own era. It rejects meaning, design, and purpose, as our
literature and art reject these things. It rejects the notion that history
can wrest moral lessons from the past, because it does not really believe
in moral lessons. It rejects the notion of progress, as our age has rejected
that notion, and perhaps that possibility. It confesses a passion for the
technical, the mathematical, the mechanical and thus reflects that passion of our whole generation for processes, statistics, and machines, and
for the compilation of miscellaneous data regardless of its relevance to
anything that we can agree upon. It is fascinated by impersonal processes,
abstractions, and concepts, rather than with actual events, or actual people. Indeed, it does not really believe in actual people—only people as
statistics—and it provides us with no biographies such as Freeman's
R. E. Lee or Churchill's *Marlborough* or G. M. Trevelyan's *Garibaldi*.
Technical history gives us instead studies of demography or of voting
patterns, or of the fluctuations of trade in corn. In this, too, it reflects
our current psychology: the passion of the arts for the abstract and
the non-representational; of literature for the non-novel, the non-hero,
the non-plot; of music for sounds that are miscellaneous and shocking
rather than harmonious; of critical studies that concentrate on grammar
or word sound rather than on philosophy. Technical history thus blends
in with technical fiction, technical poetry, technical art and music, even
—as with Kinsey and his school—technical love.

I suspect, if I may venture into the realm of prediction, that philosophers will continue to find some philosophy of history and to inquire,
even with the aid of mathematical symbols, into such problems as causation. I suspect that historians will continue to be fascinated by the glit-
tering promises of technical history but will find them disappointing;
that they will discover that technical history leads only to more and
more technical history, without throwing much light on fundamental
problems of historical interpretation. I suspect that methodology will
continue to be the common sense of the matter, learned instinctively by
practitioners who are experienced, honorable, and judicious. I have no
doubt that traditionalist historians, narrative or romantic or philosophi-

cal, will avail themselves, moderately, of the technique of technical history (if you do it immoderately, you will find yourself overwhelmed by the mechanisms and unable to get on with writing), but persist in their familiar habit of reconstructing the past imaginatively as well as scientifically and interpreting that past in individualistic and personal ways. For what is impressive, or sobering, as you chose, is that almost all of us—scientists as well as statesmen, teachers who know better as students who do not, technical historians as well as narrative—do in fact persist in turning to history for lessons.

Perhaps we should not, but that is another matter. Perhaps we are led astray more often than we are enlightened. Perhaps recourse to these lessons is a kind of escape from rigorous thinking about present facts. And clearly—no perhaps about it—we usually find the lessons we look for! Yet a habit so pervasive, an instinct so deep, must be rooted in our nature. When we reflect that for over two thousand years the most affluent minds of the Western world—not of the East we must recognize—have found wisdom, or stimulation or solace in the contemplation of the past, we may be allowed to suspect that there is something more here than mere self-indulgence.

The *moralistic* and *edifying principle* of history, barred from entrance to Clio's temple at the portals, sneaks in, nevertheless, through the windows. Repudiated, now, in the best of academic circles, in favor of science and techniques, it insinuates itself into every chapter and every page of our histories. It is there in the choice of subject, in the approach to the subject, in the language in which it is clothed, in the moral assumptions which permeate it—assumptions about what is reasonable, what is interesting, what is right and wrong. You and I may not be able to tell instantly whether a particular scientific historian dealing with the Commonwealth and Restoration era of British history is indeed Puritan or Royalist, but any Chinaman reading the book could tell at once that it was written by an Englishman or an American. You and I may not be able to tell instantly whether a particular history of the westward movement of the American pioneer was written by a New Englander or a Texan, but it is a fair guess that an Indian, or a Mexican, could tell that it was written by an American. Our character is there in all of our histories, our preoccupations, our assumptions, our beliefs, our prejudices. We cannot escape them, we cannot eradicate them. As long as they are there, our histories will not be objective or scientific, but subjective and philosophical.

Let us sum up what has not been, after all, very abstruse. I have rejected the notion of any philosophy of history inherent in the stuff of history itself, and submitted that the only philosophies of history are in the minds of historians or of those who read the historians. Such historians are legion, but in a very broad way they fall into two large groups or schools: the moral-philosophical school, which studies history for the lessons it has to teach us; and the scientific-technical school, which studies history in order to reconstruct the past as it actually was. Neither of these schools is truly philosophical nor wholly scientific, but philosophers and men of science can be found in both schools. We no longer read the philosophical school with any confidence in drawing clear moral lessons from history, nor can we study the technical school with the expectation of a recovery of the total past or a scientific recovery of the past. But we can read both, sometimes with pleasure, occasionally with profit, but confident that we can find out more about *them*—about the thinking and character of the particular era or school in which we are interested. We read history for historical reasons: to understand, through history, not so much the past itself as the notion of the past that historians entertain.

It is the philosophical school of history that is the oldest, the richest, and the most rewarding. This school, born with Herodotus and Thucydides, and flourishing with almost undiminished vigor for five or six centuries in the ancient world, and for the past two centuries, seems still to have an undiminished vitality, though more perhaps outside the Academy than within its walls. It has had, and still retains, remarkable assimilative powers: the ability to absorb culture and religion, to meet the interest in heroes and villains, the capacity to point morals and adorn tales, the readiness to satisfy now the demands of cosmopolitanism, now the requirements of nationalism, the readiness to take in and profit from sociology and psychology, economics and law, and to use new techniques and mechanisms. Over the centuries it has lent itself to use and abuse, and has provided—or been required to yield—material for a hundred different philosophies. It is the hospitality of philosophical history to the needs of various societies and cultures, its flexibility and adaptability, that explains much of its vitality. It is, too, its well-protected inscrutability. It is like a never-failing well; it invites every historian of every generation to dip into it at will, but remains always full, always fresh, always pure.

NOTES ON CONTRIBUTORS

BRAND BLANSHARD   Sterling Professor Emeritus at Yale University. Publications include: *The Nature of Thought, Reason and Goodness,* and *Reason and Analysis.*

RICHARD TAYLOR   Professor of Philosophy at the University of Rochester. Author of *Metaphysics,* and *Action and Purpose.*

GILBERT RYLE   Editor of *Mind;* Waynflete Professor of Metaphysical Philosophy at the University of Oxford. Author of *Concept of Mind, Dilemmas,* and *Plato's Progress.*

STUART HAMPSHIRE   Professor of Philosophy at Princeton University. Publications include: *Spinoza, Thought and Action,* and *Freedom of the Individual.*

WILLIAM P. ALSTON   Professor of Philosophy, The University of Michigan, Author of *Philosophy of Language.* Contributor to various philosophical periodicals.

KENNETH STERN   Associate Professor at Smith College. Contributor to various philosophical publications.

JOHN CATAN   Associate Professor of Philosophy, State University College, Brockport, New York.

ERNEST NAGEL   University Professor, Columbia University. Publications include: *Structure of Science, Logic Without Metaphysics,* and *Sovereign Reason.*

MARIO BUNGE   Professor of Philosophy, McGill University. Author of *Metascientific Inquiries; The Myth of Simplicity; Causality, the Place of Causal Principles in Modern Science; Scientific Research;* and *Foundations of Physics.*

PETER CAWS   Professor of Philosophy, Hunter College of the City University of New York. Author of *The Philosophy of Science, a Systematic Account.*

RICHARD SCHLEGEL   Professor of Physics at Michigan State University. Author of *Time and the Physical World,* and *Completeness in Science.*

BENTLEY GLASS   Distinguished Professor of Biology, and Academic Vice President, State University of New York at Stony Brook. Publications include: *Genes and the Man, Science and Liberal Education,* and *Science and Ethical Values.*

P. H. NOWELL–SMITH   Professor of Philosophy, York University. Author of *Ethics.* Contributor to various philosophical periodicals.

ALAN DONAGAN   Professor of Philosophy, University of Chicago. Author of *The Later Philosophy of R. G. Collingwood;* contributor to various philosophical periodicals.

W. H. DRAY   Professor of Philosophy at Trent University. Author of *Laws and Explanations in History,* and *Philosophy of History.*

DAVID BRAYBROOKE   Professor of Philosophy and Politics at Dalhousie University. Coauthor (with C. E. Lindblom) of *A Strategy of Decision: Policy Evaluation as a Social Process.* Editor of *Philosophical Problems of the Social Sciences.*

MIHAILO MARKOVIĆ   Professor of Philosophy, University of Belgrade. Author of *Formalism in Contemporary Logic,* and *The Dialectical Theory of Meaning.*

HENRY STEELE COMMAGER   Professor of History, Amherst Col-
lege. Publications include: *Majority Rule and Minority Rights; The
American Mind; Freedom, Loyalty, Dissent; The Nature and Study of
History; Freedom and Order; The Search for a Usable Past;* and *The
Commonwealth of Learning.*